Competing Catholicisms

RELIGION IN TRANSFORMING AFRICA
ISSN 2398-8673

Series Editors
Barbara Bompani, Joseph Hellweg, Ousmane Kane and **Emma Wild-Wood**

Editorial Reading Panel
Robert Baum (Dartmouth College)
Dianna Bell (University of Cape Town)
Ezra Chitando (University of Zimbabwe)
Martha Frederiks (Utrecht University)
Paul Gifford (SOAS)
David M. Gordon (Bowdoin College)
Jörg Haustein (University of Cambridge)
Paul Lubeck (Johns Hopkins University-SAIS)
Philomena Mwaura (Kenyatta University, Nairobi)
Hassan Ndzovu (Moi University)
Ebenezer Obadare (University of Kansas)
Abdulkader I. Tayob (University of Cape Town)
M. Sani Umar (Northwestern University)
Stephen Wooten (University of Oregon)

Series description
The series is open to submissions that examine local or regional realities on the complexities of religion and spirituality in Africa. Religion in Transforming Africa will showcase cutting-edge research into continent-wide issues on Christianity, Islam and other religions of Africa; Traditional beliefs and witchcraft; Religion, culture & society; History of religion, politics and power; Global networks and new missions; Religion in conflict and peace-building processes; Religion and development; Religious rituals and texts and their role in shaping religious ideologies and theologies. Innovative, and challenging current perspectives, the series provides an indispensable resource on this key area of African Studies for academics, students, international policy-makers and development practitioners.

Please contact the Series Editors with an outline or download the proposal form at www.jamescurrey.com.

Dr Barbara Bompani, Reader in Africa and International Development, University of Edinburgh: b.bompani@ed.ac.uk
Dr Joseph Hellweg, Associate Professor of Religion, Department of Religion, Florida State University: jhellweg@fsu.edu
Professor Ousmane Kane, Prince Alwaleed Bin Talal Professor of Contemporary Islamic Religion & Society, Harvard Divinity School: okane@hds.harvard.edu
Dr Emma Wild-Wood, Senior Lecturer, African Christianity and African Indigenous Religions, University of Edinburgh: emma.wildwood@ed.ac.uk

Previously published titles in the series are listed at the back of this volume.

Competing Catholicisms

The Jesuits, the Vatican and the Making of Postcolonial French Africa

Jean Luc Enyegue, SJ

James Currey
is an imprint of
Boydell & Brewer Ltd
PO Box 9, Woodbridge
Suffolk IP12 3DF (GB)
www.jamescurrey.com
and of
Boydell & Brewer Inc.
668 Mt Hope Avenue
Rochester, NY 14620–2731 (US)
www.boydellandbrewer.com

© Jean Luc Enyegue, SJ, 2022
First published in hardback 2022
Paperback edition 2024

The right of Jean Luc Enyegue, SJ
to be identified as the author of this work has been asserted in accordance with
sections 77 and 78 of the Copyright, Designs and Patents Act 1988

All Rights Reserved. Except as permitted under current legislation
no part of this work may be photocopied, stored in a retrieval system,
published, performed in public, adapted, broadcast, transmitted,
recorded or reproduced in any form or by any means, without the
prior permission of the copyright owner

The publisher has no responsibility for the continued existence or accuracy of URLs for external or third-party internet websites referred to in this book, and does not guarantee that any content on such websites is, or will remain, accurate or appropriate

British Library Cataloguing in Publication Data
A catalogue record for this book is available from the British Library

ISBN 978-1-84701-271-5 (James Currey hardback)
ISBN 978-1-84701-377-4 (James Currey paperback)

*For Georges Celestin Ngoa Mbida
and Salomé Pauline Afana*

Contents

List of Illustrations	ix
Acknowledgements	xi
List of Abbreviations	xiii
Glossary	xv
Chronology of Jesuit Missions in Chad and Cameroon	xvii

Introduction: The End of the Jesuit Mission in Africa?   1

Part I The Jesuit Project in West Africa: French Catholicism and Colonialism in Chad, 1935–58

Introduction   25

1. Era of Confusion: The Vatican's or France's Wider Agenda? 1935–46   30

2. Founding Era: The Conservatism of Frédéric de Bélinay, Jesuit Pioneer in Chad, 1946–58   57

3. Colonial Era: Joseph du Bouchet and the Building of the Jesuit Mission in Chad, 1947–58   75

Part II The Outward Mission: Education and Competing Catholicisms

Introduction   95

4. Era of Civilisation: Popular Education and Islamism   98

5. Era of Accommodation: Mission towards the Southern 'Ethno-Religionists'   124

6. Era of Revolution: Bishop Paul Dalmais and Chad's Cultural Revolution, 1958–75   141

Part III The Postcolonial Mission and Catholicity: From Chad to Cameroon, 1962–78

Introduction 175

7 Era of Consolidation: The Rebirth of Missionary Catholicism after Independence, 1962–73 177

8 Era of Experimentation: M.-P. Hebga, First Cameroonian Major Superior, 1968–73 194

9 Era of Dissent: Cameroonian Jesuits and Global Catholicism, 1974–78 226

Conclusion 255

Bibliography 273
Index 295

Illustrations

Map

1	VPAO missions in French West Africa	xx

Figures

1	F. de Bélinay's portrait, 1943	2
2	Joseph du Bouchet with a French colonial official, Archambault, 1954	61
3	Bishop Joseph du Bouchet visiting Archambault, 1951	76
4	André Meynier with Brother François Catt and Father Victor Waton	85
5	André Martin teaching the Catechism in Archambault, 1953	97
6	A child praying in front of a wall painting by Fr André Martin, Archambault, 1953	102
7	Ila, a young Chadian pupil, discovers his country on a globe, 1955	128
8	Felix, boy catechist and interpreter, behind Fr André Martin, Archambault, 1953	131
9	Dalmais during a visit to Kyabé, 1954	139
10	Bishop Dalmais' response to *La Croix*, 31 August 1973	149
11	Meinrad-Pierre Hebga, SJ, Yaoundé 2003	165
12	*L'Église du Cameroun: schéma historique, 1890–2000* by Nicolas Ossama (2011)	187
13	*Christianity Without Fetishes: An African Critique and Recapture of Christianity* by F. Eboussi Boulaga (1984)	196

14	Revd Mveng's artwork for the mosaic above the altar at the Cathedral of Notre-Dame-des-Victoires de Yaoundé, used for the book cover of *Faith, Power and Family: Christianity and Social Change in French Cameroon* by Charlotte Walker-Said (2018)	206
15	Charles Vandame celebrates mass in the Novitiate, Bafoussam, 2018	240
16	Éric de Rosny at a pan-African Assembly cultural event, Bonamoussadi Spiritual Center, Douala, 17 November 2011	250
17	Mveng, wall painting, Jesuit Community, Hekima University College, Nairobi	260
18	Pedro Arrupe, wall painting, Jesuit Community, Hekima University College, Nairobi	270

Full credit details are provided in the captions to the images in the text. The author and publisher are grateful to all the institutions and individuals for permission to reproduce the materials in which they hold copyright. Every effort has been made to trace the copyright holders; apologies are offered for any omission, and the publisher will be pleased to add any necessary acknowledgement in subsequent editions.

Acknowledgements

I express my heartfelt gratitude to Professor Dana L. Robert for her excellent mentorship. Her seminar on the history of Christian missions helped me elaborate the earliest version of this study. She has since guided it along until its completion. Professor John K. Thornton's ability to communicate his passion for the archives and for history to his students, and his mastery of languages, inspired me as I was doing my own research in different and multilingual archives.

I thank Professor Jeffrey P. von Arx for his generosity in agreeing to read the draft chapters of this work at an early stage. I am also indebted to the Revd Simon Smith and Dr Seth Meehan of Boston College's Institute for Advanced Jesuit Studies (A-IAJS) for proofreading this work with extreme generosity and diligence.

My deepest gratitude to my Jesuit superiors, especially Revd Eugène Goussikindey and Hyacinthe Loua, who, as provincials, encouraged me in my doctoral studies and gave me the time I needed to complete this work. The Jesuit Conference of Canada and the United States, the Jesuit Community of Boston College, and LaFarge House in Cambridge, Massachusetts, provided a community of Brothers, scholars, and friends who supported me during my research.

There is no good historical work without a good archive. I am indebted to Revd Jean-Yves Grenet, former provincial of France. He provided food and shelter in the Jesuit community of Rue de Grenelle for a month during my research in France. More importantly, he opened the private collections of the Jesuit Curia of France and granted me access to the archives of the Jesuit Province of Francophone Western Europe in Vanves, France. The professionalism and joyful service of the principal archivist, Barbara Baudry, and her assistant, Marina Kounkou-Kekolo, made my research in the archives more productive, and I especially thank Marina for bringing me numerous boxes and scanning pages without complaint.

My gratitude also to the Very Revd Arturo Sosa, SJ, superior general of the Society of Jesus, for allowing access to documents related to the Generalate of Revd Pedro Arrupe. Revd Brian Mac Cuarta, Academic

Director of the Archivum Romanum Societatis Iesu (ARSI), and the Jesuit Community of Saint Pietro Canisio provided food and shelter during my research in Rome. The Administrative Director of ARSI, Revd Raúl Gonzalez, and his team provided crucial assistance in the Roman archives.

Revd Festo Mkenda, former director of the Jesuit Historical Institute in Africa (JHIA), has been a friend and confidant, in addition to helping me with research opportunities at the Institute. His team at the JHIA, especially Sara Ndung'u, Philip Opiyo, and Denis Mũnyua, put at my disposal the documents, space, and friendly working environment required for successful research in Nairobi.

Revd Agbonkhianmeghe Orobator and the Jesuit community of Hekima University College in Nairobi helped me to articulate the concept of Africanisation. I thank Revd Yves Djofang, Director of CEFOD, and the Jesuit community of N'Djamena for their support during my research in Chad.

To my friends at the Center for Global Christianity and Mission, the faculty and students of Boston University School of Theology – especially Professors Claire Wolfteich, Nancy Ammerman, Christopher Evans, Peter Paris, Christopher Brown, Wesley Wildman, Shelly Rambo, Rady Roldán-Figueroa, David Decosimo, and Nimi Wariboko.

To the JESAM (Jesuit Conference of Africa and Madagascar) group in Boston, to the Boston College Jesuit Grad Students group, I express my gratitude for shared experiences, scholarship, and for their joy and friendship. I thank Norbert, Jean, Eric, Cris, Jim, Paul, Terry, Quang, and my fellows at LaFarge House in Cambridge, Massachusetts. They created an environment of scholarship and brotherhood.

Last but not least, I thank Elizabeth A. Foster and Charlotte Walker-Said for their encouragement and advice. Charlotte read the final draft of this book. I cannot thank her enough for her friendship and generosity.

My deepest gratitude to Jaqueline Mitchell, Commissioning Editor of the James Currey imprint at Boydell & Brewer, who has guided me during the process of publication with diligence and patience. Without her tireless effort, this book would not have been completed.

Abbreviations

AAS	*Acta Apostolicae Sedis*
A-CDOY	Archive – Centre Diocésain des Oeuvres de Yaoundé
A-ACE	Archives of the Jesuit Province of Central Africa
ACEEAC	Association des Conférences Episcopales d'Afrique Centrale (Association of Catholic Episcopal Conferences of Central Africa)
A-CEFOD	Archive – Centre d'Etudes et de Formation pour le Développement
AEF	Afrique Equatoriale Française (French Equatorial Africa)
AFD	Agence Française de Développement (French Development Agency)
A-Fr	Collection of the correspondence of the provincial of France, Jesuit archives, Vanves, France
A-IAJS	Institute for Advanced Jesuit Studies, Boston College, USA
AJ	Archives Jésuites, Vanves, France (Jesuit archives)
AOF	Afrique Occidentale Française (French Western Africa)
A-Pa	Collection of the Former Jesuit Province of Paris, Jesuit archives, Vanves, France
A-PAO	Central Archives of the Jesuit Province of West Africa, Douala, Cameroon
AR	*Journal of the Archivum Romanum Societatis Iesu*
ARSI	Archivum Romanum Societatis Iesu, Rome
ATR	African traditional religions
B-Af.C	Press reviews and news items, Jesuit archives, Vanves, France
Card.	Cardinal
CETA	Conférence des Églises de Toute l'Afrique (All African Council of Churches)
CFC	Centres for the Formation of Catechists

ABBREVIATIONS

COTONFRAN	La Compagnie Cotonnière Equatoriale Française
CYA	Catholic Youth Association
DRC	Democratic Republic of Congo
GC	General Congregation (of the Jesuits)
INADES	Institut Africain pour le Développement Économique et Social (The African Institute for Economic and Social Development)
JAC	Jeunesse Agricole Catholique (Catholic Agricultural Youth)
JAF	*Jésuites de l'Assistance de France* (Newsletter of the French Jesuit Assistancy)
JEC	Jeunesse Estudiantine Chrétienne (Catholic Student Youth)
JESAM	Jesuit Conference of Africa and Madagascar (also known as JECAM)
JHIA	Jesuit Historical Institute in Africa
JOC	Jeunesse Ouvrière Chrétienne (Christian Youth Workers)
M-Ly	Collection of the former Jesuit Province of Lyon, Jesuit archives, Vanves, France
NMCSR	National Movement for Cultural and Social Revolution
NPAO	*Nouvelles de la Province d'Afrique de l'Ouest* (Newsletter of the Jesuit Province of West Africa)
N-VPAO	*Nouvelles de la Vice-Province d'Afrique de l'Ouest* (Newsletter of the Vice-Province of West Africa)
PAO	Jesuit Province of West Africa, Douala, Cameroon (Francophone)
PUCAC	Presses de l'UCAC
RESRAT	Rencontre Sacerdotale et Religieuse des Africains au Tchad (Priestly and Religious Meeting of Africans in Chad)
SIM	Sudan Interior Mission
STU	Société d'Urbanisation du Tchad Urbanisation (Society of Chad)
UCAC	Université Catholique d'Afrique Centrale
UPC	Union of the Populations of Cameroon
VPAO	Jesuit Vice-Province of West Africa

Glossary

Apostolic Prefecture In Roman Catholicism, a mission territory under the leadership of an apostolic prefect which has not been established as a diocese.

Assistancy Group of Jesuit provinces, otherwise known as a Conference. There are currently nine assistancies: Africa, Latin America South, Latin America North, South Asia, Asia Pacific, Canada and the United States, Central and Eastern Europe, Southern Europe, and Western Europe.

Consultor Member of a consult, the advisory board of a provincial, regional, or mission superior, or the superior of a local community.

Dependent Region A Jesuit jurisdiction with a major superior (regional superior); part of a province.

General Congregation (GC) The highest Jesuit jurisdiction, a gathering of Jesuit representatives from all countries of Jesuit faith, held to elect the superior general or, exceptionally, to discuss urgent matters that cannot be discerned or decided by a single individual. In five centuries of Jesuit history, there have only been thirty-six GCs.

General Consult Presided over by the superior general and gathering on a daily basis, the general consult consists of general counsellors: 4 general assistants, the 9 Regional Assistants, and other Counsellors the superior general might appoint. The general consult constitutes the central government of the order.

General Assistants The four general assistants exercise 'a provident care for the physical health of the superior general, for external matters, and for other areas […] They ought also to be counselors of the superior general and should assist him in matters of doctrine and business.'[1]

---

[1] John W. Padberg, Martin D. O'Keefe, and John L. McCarthy, *For Matters of Greater Moment: The First Thirty Jesuit General Congregations* (Saint Louis, MO: The Institute of Jesuit Sources, 1994), CG1, Decree 80.

Province Geographical unit of the Jesuit Order. Although their number and boundaries are not static, there are around eighty worldwide, each headed by a provincial.

Province Congregation Gathering of elected representatives of a Jesuit Province, usually in preparation for a GC.

Province Assembly Gathering of members of a Jesuit Province to discuss matters of province-wide interest.

Provincial Head or major superior of a province. Appointed by the superior general, he is directly responsible for the training, care, and assignments of Jesuits under his jurisdiction.

Regional Assistants The nine regional assistants 'help and support the superior general in his decision-making'. They are responsible for communication with their respective assistancies. Each regional assistant has one or more secretaries, who help to develop specific areas of the apostolic mission of the Society.

Superior General Elected by a GC, the superior general is the highest authority of the Jesuit order, with powers over the appointment of Jesuits in governing positions, the creation of new communities, apostolates, and jurisdictions.

Vicariate According to Canon Law 371 §1: 'An apostolic vicariate or apostolic prefecture is a certain portion of the people of God which has not yet been established as a diocese due to special circumstances and which, to be shepherded, is entrusted to an apostolic vicar or apostolic prefect who governs it in the name of the Supreme Pontiff.'

Chronology of Jesuit Missions in Chad and Cameroon

1850 First Christian Missions in Cameroon
1875 Birth of Frédéric de Bélinay
1890 Arrival of the Pallottines in Cameroon
1898 'Pacification of Chad'
1918 President Woodrow Wilson's 'Fourteen Points' sets the framework for the Peace
1919 Pope Benedict XV's *Maximum Illud* advocates missionary work
1920 First Protestant Missions
1926 Pope Pius XI issues an encyclical, 'Rerum Ecclesiae', reinforcing the missionary vocation of the Catholic Church
1930 Birth of Engelbert Mveng
1931 Jesuit Father Frédéric de Bélinay meets Lt Mazodier, part of the colonial expedition, in Paris
1935 F. de Bélinay goes on an exploratory trip to Chad
Ordination of the first Cameroonian priests
1936 Superior general of the Jesuits, Vladimir Ledochowski, creates the Middle East Mission. Chad is initially part of it
1944 Brazzaville Conference is held to establish the future of the French colonial empire
1946 Apostolic Vicariate of Chad created, with de Bélinay as Vicar. Charles Margot is appointed the mission's vice-superior
1947 J. du Bouchet arrives in Chad. The vicariate is established as an apostolic prefecture with J. du Bouchet as prefect
Chad Mission receives official recognition

Lettres du Père Charles Margot provides regular updates on the life of the mission

Alioune Diop founds *Présence Africaine*

1949 First catechism translated into the Sara language

1951 Cameroonian Engelbert Mveng joins the Jesuits

1955 Paul Dalmais becomes head of the Chad Mission

1956 Publication of *Les prêtres noirs s'interrogent*, with a contribution by Meinrad-P. Hebga

Bishop Pierre Bonneau invites the Jesuits to Douala, Cameroon

1957 30th GC of the Jesuits

Dalmais is appointed Bishop of Fort-Lamy

The first Jesuits arrive in Douala

Dalmais assumes directorship of Libermann High School

1958 Death of de Bélinay. Dalmais is installed as Bishop of Fort-Lamy

1960 Independence of Eastern Cameroon, Chad, Côte d'Ivoire, Burkina Faso, Congo, Benin, Central African Republic, Senegal, Niger, Mauritania, Gabon, Togo, among other ex-colonial African states

1961 Independence of Western Cameroon

Jean Zoa becomes Archbishop of Yaoundé

First Jesuits arrive in Nigeria

1962 Opening of the Second Vatican Council. Bishop Zoa ordains Bishop Henri Véniat

The African Institute for Economic and Social Development (INADES) is founded in Abidjan, Côte d'Ivoire

1963 The Jesuits agree to take charge of the major seminary at Otélé

Mveng's *Histoire du Cameroun* is published

1965 Pedro Arrupe is elected superior general of the Jesuits

First session of the 31st GC of the Jesuits

End of the Second Vatican Council

1966 Arrupe visits Chad for the first time?

Arrupe holds an African Missions Conference in Rome with all African 'major superiors', i.e. heads of Jesuit missions, regions, and provinces

Second session of the 31st GC

Arrupe's conference on 'Church and Culture'

1968 Victor Mertens is appointed Arrupe's adviser for Africa

Creation of the Cameroon Dependent Region of the Jesuits. Hebga is appointed regional superior, and Philippe Durand-Viel, superior of Yaoundé, and personal delegate of the provincial in Cameroon

1969 Unification of the French provinces

1970 Arrupe orders a survey of the situation of the Jesuits worldwide

Arrupe takes part in the Symposium of African Catholic Bishops in Abidjan, Côte d'Ivoire. Discussions are held about the creation of an African assistancy

1971 Creation of the African assistancy. Mertens is appointed Regional Assistant for Africa

Card. Hyacinthe Thiandoum is informed about the arrival of Jesuit Pierre Souillac (France) in Dakar, Senegal

First contact between the Jesuits and Burkina Faso

1972 Arrupe addresses the major superiors of Africa and Madagascar in Douala, Cameroon

Arrupe appoints new consultors for the Chad Mission. Jesuit missionaries in Chad gather at Dunia

1973 Creation of the Vice-Province of West Africa (VPAO). Charles Vandame is appointed vice-provincial

Cameroon Region suppressed

Canadian Jesuits arrive in Senegal

1974 Publication of Eboussi's 'Dé-mission'

VPAO province assembly

32nd GC of the Society of Jesus

1976 Publication of Hebga's *Émancipation des Églises sous-tutelle* (Emancipation of the Churches Held by the Jesuits)

1978 Publication of Mveng's 'De la sous-mission à la succession' (From Submission to Succession)

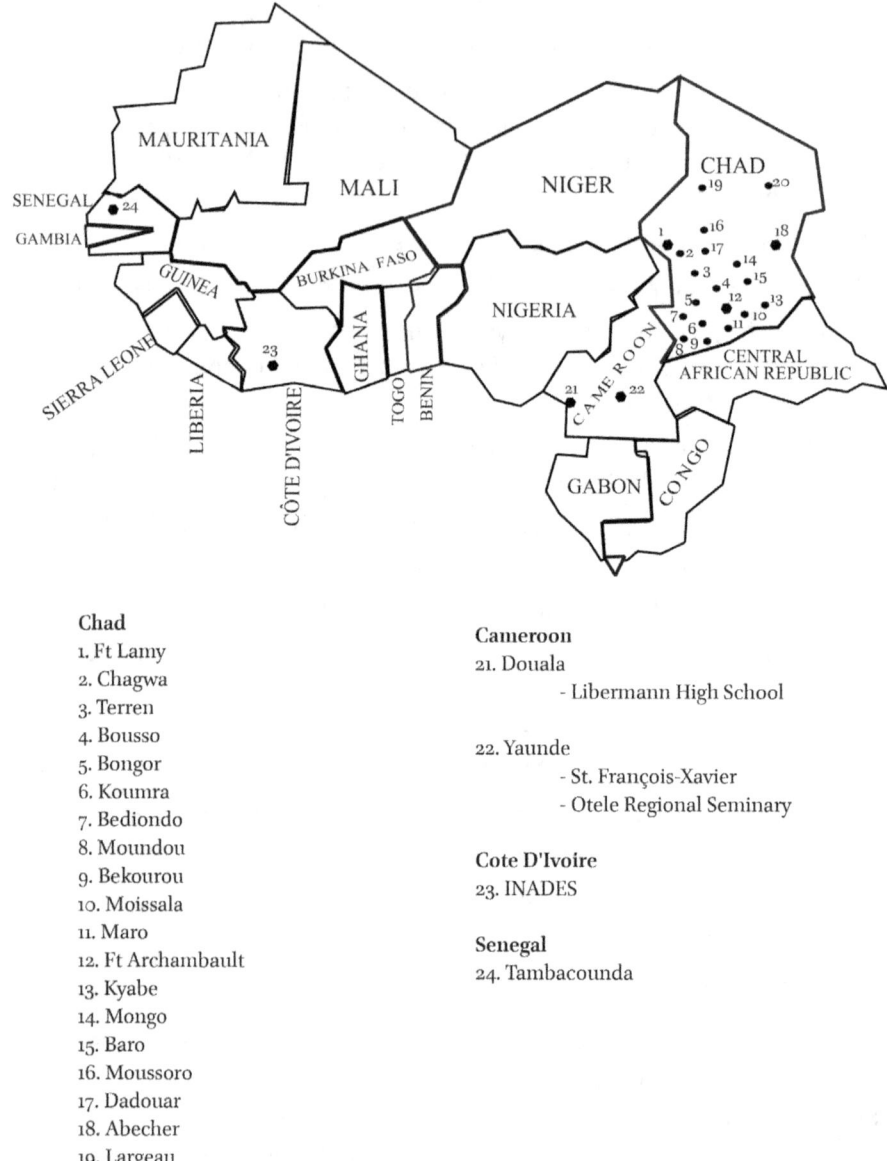

Chad
1. Ft Lamy
2. Chagwa
3. Terren
4. Bousso
5. Bongor
6. Koumra
7. Bediondo
8. Moundou
9. Bekourou
10. Moissala
11. Maro
12. Ft Archambault
13. Kyabe
14. Mongo
15. Baro
16. Moussoro
17. Dadouar
18. Abecher
19. Largeau
20. Fada

Cameroon
21. Douala
    - Libermann High School

22. Yaunde
    - St. François-Xavier
    - Otele Regional Seminary

Cote D'Ivoire
23. INADES

Senegal
24. Tambacounda

Map 1 The VPAO territory in French West Africa, showing the sites of important Jesuit missions in 1973 (Denis Munyua, Archives JHIA, Nairobi).

Introduction: The End of the Jesuit Mission in Africa?

Éric de Rosny was among the first European Jesuits to settle in Cameroon, in 1957, three years before Cameroon's independence or political Africanisation.[1] Now, in 1970, he faced a crisis second only to that of the Second World War, which he had witnessed as a child.[2] Could this be 'mission terminée', as de Rosny would later refer to it in his book *L'Afrique des guérisons*, the end of the French Jesuit mission in Africa, and the beginning of the transition from missionary Christianity to African Christianity?

'Mission terminée'. For lovers of African literature such as Jesuit missionary Éric de Rosny, *Mission terminée* was the title of a popular novel by Cameroonian novelist Mongo Beti.[3] For de Rosny, fiction had now turned into reality. An existential crisis was dividing his soul.[4] One can imagine him seated at a window in the Jesuit community of Rue de Grenelle, 7th arrondissement, looking up at the Paris night sky, and searching for a star that might give him direction, inspiration, or a word from above. Meinrad-Pierre Hebga, his Cameroonian religious superior, had not responded to de Rosny's last letter requesting guidance on what he should do in the light of the pope's declaration to the African people that they should rule themselves religiously as much as politically. This silence from his superior was doing nothing to calm de Rosny's nerves. Perhaps he understood

---

[1] In this book, I take this to mean the making of African independent states and religious organisations rooted in African cultures and realities, led by Africans and for Africans.
[2] Éric de Rosny, *L'Afrique des guérisons*, Collection Les Afriques (Paris: Karthala, 1992), 14.
[3] First published in 1957, re-edited: Mongo Beti, *Mission terminée* (Paris: Buchet-Chastel, 1975).
[4] Éric de Rosny, 'Mission terminée?' *Etudes* (May 1970): 737–46.

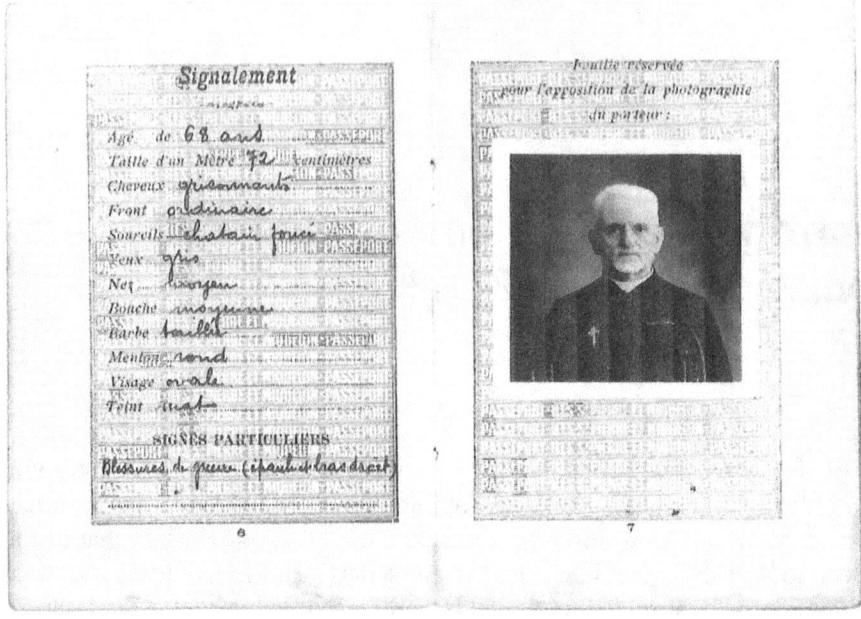

Figure 1 F. de Bélinay's portrait, from his passport, 1943 (Archives JHIA, Nairobi).

that Hebga wanted him to decide by himself the question he alone could answer before his God and his own conscience: whether or not to return to Cameroon as a missionary, and for what purpose, if the mission was over.

When De Rosny had arrived in Cameroon in 1957, the Jesuits of Lyon Province had just turned down the invitation to take over Libermann, one of Cameroon's most prestigious secondary schools in Douala. Lyon, in neighbouring Chad, where the Jesuits had been established since 1935, they told him, had greater and more urgent priority. The Jesuit mission in Chad was considered vitally 'strategic' for Roman Catholicism and stability in the entire region. It was also strategic for France as a nation.[5] Lyon Province had no intention of diverting resources elsewhere, not even to Cameroon.

In 1957, the superior general of the Jesuits, Father Jean-Baptiste Janssens (1889–1964), confirmed that Chad should remain a mission of the Jesuit Province of Lyon. He declared Cameroon a mission of the province of Paris. Janssens, it seems, was deploying two different *'francités'*, two modes of being French (Paris vs Lyon), in the different African territories.

---

[5] Paul Dalmais, 'Le Tchad, mission strategique', *Vivante Afrique* 203 (June–July 1959): 3–6.

While Chad and Cameroon had some sociological similarities, they had different religious histories. Christianity in Cameroon was mature, with its own Cameroonian clergy, many Cameroonian bishops and a dozen African Jesuits. Chad, on the other hand, was still a traditional mission, with just one diocesan priest, François Ngaïbi (1920–80).

Cameroon and Chad, however, are, to my mind, inseparable – geographically, linguistically, culturally, and economically – and since the 1950s they have shared a Jesuit destiny. The creation, in 1973, of the Jesuit Vice-Province of West Africa (henceforth, VPAO) further cemented this common destiny. Yet, a clash between their different historical dynamics of Africanisation was also perhaps inevitable.

Ten years after Cameroon's independence, de Rosny thought the storm had passed. The new nationalism and African independence of the 1960s had not destroyed the Christian missions as the Vatican and most scholars of Christianity had feared.[6] Yet, seated at his Paris window, he had never been more troubled. The words of Pope Paul VI in Kampala a few months earlier seared his soul.[7] Speaking to the Ugandan people in 1969, the pope had sealed de Rosny's fate: 'Africans should now become their own missionaries.'[8] Missionaries like de Rosny felt that their mission in Africa was, indeed, at an end. Following political Africanisation in the 1960s, the words of the pope had set the tone for the acceleration of ecclesiastical Africanisation.

Éric de Rosny was not one to run away from a battle, however. He was a veteran of the French War in Algeria in the 1950s, and his natural competitiveness had been reinforced by years of Jesuit training. He was taught that members of the Society of Jesus, founded by a man with a military background, Ignatius of Loyola (1491–1556), were always driven by the search for excellence, the *magis*. They strove for the Greater Glory of God (*Ad Maiorem Dei Gloriam*).

Looking up at the Eiffel Tower, with its beautiful sparkling lights, de Rosny turned from consideration of surrender to questioning the entire notion of this being the end of the Jesuit mission in Africa. While radical

---

[6] Not the least among these scholars were Kenneth Scott Latourette and R. Pierce Beaver. Cf. Kenneth Scott Latourette, 'Colonialism and Missions: Progressive Separation', *Journal of Church and State* 7, no. 3 (Autumn 1965): 330–49 – here, p. 341; R. Pierce Beaver, 'Missions and the New Nationalism', *Journal of Church and State* 3, no. 2 (November 1961): 149–71 – here, p. 151.

[7] Pope Paul VI, 'Excellentissimis Viris et Legatorum Coetu in Ugandensis Republica', *Acta Apostolicae Sedis* (henceforth *AAS*) 61 (1 August 1969): 580–86.

[8] Ibid.

African priests, emboldened by the new discourse on Africanisation, considered missionaries like him foreigners, de Rosny felt he could still count on the support of those African bishops determined, like the Vatican and the Roman Curia of the Jesuits, to keep Christianity universal, free from colonialism, nationalisms, and particularisms.[9] Even amid the shifting dynamics of ongoing Africanisation, the Church in Africa could remain somewhere both missionaries and Africans could feel at home.[10]

De Rosny resolved to return to Cameroon in 1970. Once there, he went through traditional initiation and became a Cameroonian by adoption. In 1972, he became an 'nganga' and later one of the leaders of a Douala traditional initiatory society.[11] Only in this way could his soul find peace again. As a fully professed Jesuit, de Rosny had obeyed the pope's command: he had become a missionary for what had become his own people, the Cameroonians who had adopted him.

Nevertheless, De Rosny was a careful reader of history. He knew what the pope declared in Uganda to be true. Ecclesial Africanisation was an irreversible reality. The numbers of European Jesuits were decreasing, affecting the supply of missionaries to Africa and elsewhere. In Cameroon he lived with prominent Cameroonian Jesuits who had become leaders of the Africanisation of Christianity, including his own superior, Hebga, one of the intellectual African leaders of the movement for ecclesial independence, who had contributed to the first manifesto of African theologians in 1956.[12] With de Rosny, they shared living quarters with prominent Cameroonian Jesuits such as Engelbert Mveng and Fabien Eboussi Boulaga, and lesser known ones such as Nicolas Ossama and Emmanuel Teguem.[13]

That Hebga was de Rosny's superior was a sign of an already radical shift in favour of Africanisation. Indeed, it marked an escalation of progress in the history of the Society of Jesus in Africa. Saint Ignatius of Loyola, founder of the Jesuits,[14] first sent missionaries to the African

---

[9] Pope John XXIII, 'Encyclical Letter "Princeps Pastorum"', *AAS* 51 (1959), paragraphs 24–26.

[10] de Rosny, 'Mission terminée?' 741.

[11] Éric de Rosny, *Les yeux de ma chèvre: Sur les pas des maîtres de la nuit en pays Douala* (Paris: Pocket, 1996).

[12] Meinrad-P. Hebga, 'Christianisme et négritude', in *Des prêtres noirs s'interrogent*, Rencontres 47, ed. A. Abble (Paris: Présence Africaine, 1956), 189–203.

[13] Teguem was a 'working-class' Jesuit Brother who, unlike the other early Cameroonian Jesuits, remains an obscure figure. He left the Jesuits in 1969.

[14] Ignatius of Loyola, 'Al P. Nunes Barreto, Roma, 24 Febrero 1555', in *Obras*

kingdoms of Kongo (Congo) and Ethiopia in 1554–55.[15] In the part that constitutes today's VPAO, Portuguese Jesuits had missionised in Cape Verde and Guinea Bisau in the sixteenth century[16] and the Spaniards were in Fernando Po in the nineteenth century.[17]

In French West Africa, Chad was the first and most important mission, with Frédéric de Bélinay (1875–1958) first exploring the country in 1935. By 1970, when de Rosny was writing, there were growing numbers of Jesuits in Francophone Cameroon, French Jesuits in Côte d'Ivoire, Canadians in Senegal, and one citizen of Congo Brazzaville, Ernest Kombo (1941–2008). There were also more than a dozen New Yorker Jesuits in Nigeria. Thousands of kilometres separated Brazzaville and Dakar – countless micro-cultures and historical realities, too. Yet, in the growing restructuring of the Society in this region, these missions and their Western personnel were to be united at exactly the time when the Vatican had made Africanisation a priority.

De Rosny believed that missionary Christianity might still survive if missionaries like him agreed to be 'born again' and become 'Africans'. This conviction was not shared with the same urgency by his fellow Western colleagues working in Chad. Yet, under the initiative of Pedro Arrupe (1907–91), freshly elected superior general of the Jesuits (r. 1965–83), Chad was in the process of shifting its jurisdictional status with the restructuring of African Jesuit missions.

Completas de Ignacio de Loyola (Madrid: BAC, 1982), 965–66; Ignatius of Loyola, 'Recuerdos que podrían ayudar para la reducción de los reinos del Preste Juan a la unión de la Iglesia y religión Católica, Enviados al P. Juan Nunes', in *Obras Completas de Ignacio de Loyola* (Madrid: BAC, 1982), 957–64.

[15] On these early missions, see: Fikru Negash Gebrekidan, 'Ethiopia and Congo: A Tale of Two Medieval Kingdoms', *Callaloo* 33, no. 1 (2010): 223–38; Léon de Saint Moulin, *Histoire des Jésuites en Afrique: Du XVIe siècle à nos jours* (Namur: Éd. Jésuites, 2016); Philip Caraman, *The Lost Empire: The Story of the Jesuits in Ethiopia* (Notre Dame, IN: University of Notre Dame Press, 1985); Festo Mkenda, *A Mission for Everyone: A Story of the Jesuits in Eastern Africa (1555–2012)* (Nairobi: Saint Paul, 2013).

[16] P. E. H. Hair, 'Jesuit Documents on the Guinea of Cape Verde and the Cape Verde Islands, 1585–1617 in English Translation', *History in Africa* 16 (1989): 375–81; Nuno da Silva Gonçalves and Philip Kiley donor, *Os Jesuitas e a Missão de Cabo Verde (1604–1642)* (Lisboa: Brotéria, 1996).

[17] José Irísarri, *Misión de Fernando Poo, 1859* (Barcelona: Ceibas, 1998); Jean Luc Enyegue, 'The Jesuits in Fernando Po, 1858–1872: An Incomplete Mission', in *Jesuit Survival and Restoration: A Global History, 1773–1900*, ed. Robert Maryks (Leiden: Brill, 2015), 466–86.

Competing Christianities

This book shows the coming together of a diverse West African world to form a single Jesuit jurisdiction with Westerners comprising the majority of its personnel. This transformation was taking place, as we have seen, at the same time that the Vatican was increasing pressure on the Church in Africa to Africanise, and when in some places, such as Cameroon, Uganda, Tanzania, or Zaïre, the implementation of the Vatican's policy had already become a reality. The book begins with the arrival of Frédéric de Bélinay in Chad in 1935 and ends a decade after the Second Vatican Council, when the African reaction to Africanisation had become sharper with the successive publications of Eboussi Boulaga's 'Dé-mission' (1974), Meinrad-Pierre Hebga's *Émancipation d'Églises sous tutelle* (1976), and Mveng's 'De la sous-mission à la succession' (1978).

The narrative of this book, and of de Rosny's mission in Africa, is shaped in terms of competition. This is an attempt to rescue a 'dangerous' word which religious organisations concerned with unity would often rather discard. Competition, however, is often the unnamed source of the numerical growth and success of the Christian churches. In this book I argue that if competition works for economics and markets,[18] for politics,[19] sport, and education,[20] it works, and has worked in the past, in the fields of religion and Christian missions.[21] Competition is not inherently antithetical to Christianity and its unity. On the contrary, the history of the Jesuits shows that competition is an integral part of their growth and expansion.

As I will show, the beginning of Jesuit missions in French Africa in the 1940s to the 1970s illustrates the competing nature of the Jesuit order and of Christianity. It demonstrates the impact of competition on the

---

[18] Rodney Stark and James C. McCann, 'Market Forces and Catholic Commitment: Exploring the New Paradigm', *Journal for the Scientific Study of Religion* 32, no. 2 (June 1993): 111–24; Fenggang Yang, 'The Red, Black, and Gray Markets of Religion in China', *The Sociological Quarterly* 47, no. 1 (Winter 2006): 93–122.

[19] Doris Kearns Goodwin, *Team of Rivals: The Political Genius of Abraham Lincoln* (London: Penguin, 2009).

[20] Paul F. Grendler, 'The Culture of the Jesuit Teacher 1548–1773', *Journal of Jesuit Studies* 3 (2016): 17–41.

[21] Robert D. Woodberry, 'Missionary Roots of Liberal Democracy', *American Political Science Review* 106, no. 2 (May 2012): 244–74; Roger Finke and Rodney Stark, 'Religious Economies and Sacred Canopies: Religious Mobilization in American Cities, 1906', *American Sociological Review* 53, no. 1 (February 1988): 41–49.

rapid expansion of Christianity in Central and Western French Africa during the second half of the twentieth century, and the tensions – sometimes bitter – inherent to it. The lines of this competition were drawn in French West Africa in the 1970s around the debate over the Africanisation of Christianity: was this a Christianisation of African cultures? Or an Africanisation of Christianity? Are the two stances even antithetical?

For the Vatican and French missionaries in Western Africa, the Africanisation movement was primarily a process by which African cultures were Christianised and stripped of all elements that seemed to contradict their Christian faith. To create a local African Church or a Jesuit jurisdiction in Africa was to transplant the Church universal on African soil. However, African Jesuits interpreted statements made in the 1970s by Pope Paul VI and Pedro Arrupe (then superior general of the Jesuits) differently. To these Africans, to Africanise Christianity was to make Christianity in Africa as African as it was French in France. This process consisted in creating an African Christian leadership and adapting the Christian faith to African beliefs and needs. As this book shows, taken radically, the Africanisation of Christianity could lead to a form of Gallicanism at best or, worse for Roman Catholicism, schismatic division similar to that of the Protestant Churches in Africa. By adopting the concept of 'inculturation' instead of Africanisation, Catholic Church authorities settled for a middle path. They not only encouraged African leadership, but pursued the Christianisation of African cultures. In that process, however, they ostracised African defenders of the Africanisation of Christianity.

As well as representing different, often competing perspectives of the Catholic agenda for the evangelisation of French Africa in the mission field, the Vatican, the French Jesuits, the rising Cameroonian indigenous clergy and leadership, and the first Cameroonian Jesuits also competed with different Protestant groups. Sharing the common aim of converting African traditional religionists and different groups of African Muslims to Christ, Catholic and Protestant missions also worked to contain the spread of anti-religious ideologies such as Communism.

This book examines three critical aspects of the Africanisation of the Jesuit Mission in Africa, its engagement with colonialism and postcolonialism, and increasing Pan-Africanism: (1) How did the Vatican and the Jesuit agenda(s) in Chad and Cameroon complement and compete with each other? (2) How did the global Catholic agenda, which both the Vatican and the Jesuits represented, interact with other religious groups in French Africa, especially Protestant missions, African traditional religions (ATR), and the different groups of Muslims? (3) What was the African reaction to this diverse and competing global agenda of Christianisation, especially after Chad and Cameroon had come together as part of a single Jesuit jurisdiction in 1973?

Competing Catholicisms tries to answer these questions by exploring the impact of Jesuit missions on the development of Christianity in French West Africa from the end of the First World War (1939–45) to 1978, a little more than a decade after the end of the Second Vatican Council (1962–65). It portrays the history of Christianity as a movement in which different Catholicities (the Vatican and different Jesuit missions) and different Christianities (Roman Catholicism and different Protestant missions) compete with each other for the evangelisation of Africans and against the perceived common threats of a diverse Islam and Communism. The Jesuits were simultaneously representatives of a Vatican 'Ultramontanism' in Africa, of French Gallicanism, and of Catholic Africanism. Their competing interpretations of Catholicity generated internal conflicts among their members, yet successfully secured the survival of Christianity as a missionary movement in which Western missionaries worked alongside a rising African clergy and leadership. Analysis of the rebirth and strengthening of missionary Christianity a decade after African independence is also intended to shed light on the role France played in shaping the politics of postcolonial Africa.

Catholicisms and Neocolonialism in French West Africa

Recent literature has contributed to a better understanding of French Catholicism at the end of the empire and African decolonisation or political Africanisation. In her most recent masterly book, historian Elizabeth A. Foster proposes four major developments that shaped Roman Catholicism in French Africa after the Second World War: the unravelling of the French colonial empire, the emergence of a Catholic left in France, the rise of an African Catholic and political elite, and the 'tensions' within Roman Catholicism itself.[22] Foster shows how, on the eve of African independence, movements like the 'Catholic Négritude', led by lay Catholics including Alioune Diop and other Catholic students in France,[23] demanded

---

[22] Elizabeth Foster, *African Catholic: Decolonization and the Transformation of the Church* (Cambridge, MA: Harvard University Press, 2019), 8–10.

[23] Elizabeth Foster, 'Entirely Christian and Entirely African: Catholic African Students in France in the Era of Independence', *The Journal of African History* 56, no. 2 (2015): 239–59.

the de-occidentalising of the Catholic Church so that the Church could abide by its claimed universal premise.[24]

French Catholic conservatives, in contrast, worried that the Church was betraying its French 'base' by supporting anti-colonial movements.[25] Anti-colonialism, French conservatives argued, would lead to the 'Africanisation of the church as a whole, which would debase its rites and chase French language from its African schools'.[26] For paternalistic and often racist reasons,[27] more than a few French missionaries in Africa also resisted this movement. Foster states that despite the Vatican's overt push for Africanisation, the Church had remained, itself, a 'European preserve'.[28]

As the title of this book suggests, *Competing Catholicisms* focuses on the tensions within Catholicism. It continues the work started by Foster in Francophone Africa as a recipient of global Catholicism in the first half of the twentieth century and immediately after the Second Vatican Council. It critically assesses how French Jesuits' progressiveness operated in Francophone Africa in light of what John McGreevy has called the Jesuits' 'New Global Ethos'.[29] In fact, that a Jesuit became pope in this critical time in global history, as Foster notes at the end of *African Catholic*, and the fact that Pope Francis is seen as progressive both reflect the trajectory of the history of the Jesuit order after the Second World War and its impact on Roman Catholicism more broadly. The roots of this Jesuit progressivism can be found in post-war France, and its first global manifestation was the election of Pedro Arrupe as superior general of the Jesuits (r. 1965–83).

Examining the work of the Jesuits in West Africa can help to bring nuance to the traditional cliché of a monolithic Vatican conservatism. In fact, as this book will show, there was an active Roman-led progressivism

---

[24] Foster, *African Catholic: Decolonization*, 59.
[25] Ibid., 84–85.
[26] Ibid., 153.
[27] Elizabeth Foster, 'A Mission in Transition: Monsignor Joseph Faye and the Decolonization of the Catholic Church in Senegal', in *In God's Empire: French Missionaries and the Modern World*, eds O. White and J. P. Daughton (New York: Oxford University Press, 2012), 257–77.
[28] Foster, *African Catholic: Decolonization*, 271.
[29] John T. McGreevy, 'Restored Jesuits: Notes towards a Global History', in *The Jesuits and Globalization. Historical Legacies and Contemporary Challenges* (Washington, DC: Georgetown University Press, 2016), 131–46; John T. McGreevy, *American Jesuits and the World: How an Embattled Religious Order Made Modern Catholicism Global* (Princeton, NJ: Princeton University Press, 2016).

aimed at the African Church in the twentieth century. The Vatican, through several papal encyclicals, religious leaders like Arrupe, and leading African Jesuits were champions of this Africanisation. However, the book also shows that French conservatism, including among the Jesuits, was exported to Francophone Africa at the same time that Jesuit progressivism was rising in France and among Africans. Discussions in this book emerge from this paradoxical context of the resilience of Western conservatism in Africa alongside Africans' resistance to it. African nations achieved their political and ecclesiastical self-determination in the 1960s. Yet, leaders trained during the colonial era helped to maintain policies and structures which were at odds with the new era.

Analysing those policies and structures in the Church helps to explain neocolonialism in Francophone Africa. While the Catholic Church was attempting to maintain its mission in some shape or form in Africa, the French powers during decolonisation were simultaneously preparing strategies to maintain France's interests in its African colonies. French missions and French colonialism shared the same vision and had common enemies during the decolonisation period. Colonial administrators favoured Francophone African statespersons who were loyal to France. Political neocolonialism ensued from the loyalty to France of early Francophone leaders.

This book shows that the same policy of favouring past loyalties applied to the Church in the selection of African ecclesiastics. Those chosen were primarily loyal to Rome and the Roman vision of the Church in Africa. Their experience of political neocolonialism would lead prominent African Jesuits to the conclusion that the enduring French leadership of their order on African soil as well as the geographical map of Jesuit provinces in Africa was a form of spiritual neocolonialism. Progressive initiatives led to discontent and dissent among Jesuits working in Francophone Africa. As stated elsewhere, Africans saw the implementation of Jesuit progressivism in their region as not bold enough. They described it as 'New Wine into Old Wineskins'.[30] Jesuit progressivism in Africa thus warrants more scrutiny.

The Jesuits' transformation in Western Africa is significant for several reasons. They were representatives of the rising Catholic left in Europe and Africa. They were a significant part of conservative Catholicism in French West Africa. Unlike the Holy Ghost Fathers and other French congregations discussed in Foster's work, the Jesuits were latecomers to the

---

[30] Jean Luc Enyegue, 'New Wine into Old Wineskins? African Reactions to Arrupe's Governing Vision (1965–1978)', *Archivum Historicum Societatis Iesu* 88, fasc. 176 (II 2019): 385–420.

region. They had no previous missionary commitment in French Central and Western Africa until their exploration of Chad in the 1930s and their institutional establishment in 1946. Their history in West Africa began with decolonisation and the making of postcolonial Francophone Africa.

Chad, where the first Jesuits landed, was for them a new missionary land. It received its first Catholic missions in only 1929. Yet, this book shows that the progressive-leaning Jesuitism of France in the 1940s did not quickly materialise there. The early Jesuits' approach to the Chad Mission focused on evangelism, and stayed away from the urgent leadership change that characterised most Christian churches and missions in the 1950s. They resisted ecclesiastical Africanisation.

In Cameroon, in contrast, European Jesuit Éric de Rosny successfully Africanised by fully adopting a Cameroonian culture. Philippe Durand-Viel, another defining character of the establishment of the Society in Cameroon, was a former provincial in France. His task in Cameroon was to restrain the radical progressivism of his Cameroonian colleagues as they rose to positions of power and became intellectual Church leaders in their country. De Rosny's form of Africanisation was celebrated, while the African leaders of Africanisation were increasingly ostracised.

This conflict between Europeans and Africans did not, however, prevent Rome from creating a regional Jesuit jurisdiction that covered all of Francophone Western and Central Africa. As historian Gregory Mann has demonstrated, non-governmental organisations (NGOs) created new networks of solidarity and aid in Sub-Saharan Africa after independence, beyond established nation-states. In his work, Mann underscores the fluctuating nature of African anti-colonialism[31] and accurately analyses the paradoxes of the Fourth Republic's dealings with the citizenry of Sub-Saharan tirailleurs.[32]

The novelty of Mann's 'non-governmentality', however, actually pre-dated the rise of humanitarian NGOs on African soil. The most effective regional organisation with a transnational humanitarian impact in French Africa was the Catholic Church under the leadership of the Papal Legate Marcel Lefèbvre. The map of the VPAO and the structure of its leadership followed the same transnational model of governance. The emerging Catholic episcopal regional conferences and those of religious jurisdictions such as the VPAO simply

---

[31] Gregory Mann, *From Empires to NGOs in the West African Sahel. The Road to Nongovernmentality* (New York: Cambridge University Press, 2015), 21.

[32] Gregory Mann, 'Immigrants and Arguments in France and West Africa', *Comparative Studies in Society and History* 45, no. 2 (April 2003): 362–85 – here, p. 380.

imitated what was already set up during the late colonial period. Unlike the NGOs, the principle of non-governmentality does not simply apply to the Catholic Church. The transnationality of its jurisdiction replicated the organisation of a global religious order on African soil.

Further, linking the work of the Catholic Church in Africa to NGOs helps address what Paul Gifford considers the NGO-isation of Roman Catholicism as opposed to evangelism.[33] Gifford has compared the social commitment of Catholics in Africa to an NGO-isation of Roman Catholicism which, according to him, diminishes true evangelism. The reform of religious life proposed by the first Cameroonian Jesuits attempted to reconcile what is traditionally considered the authentic work of evangelism with the need to care for the poor. Within the Jesuit order in the 1970s, this debate took place in terms of what is properly priestly in Jesuit ministries in our world today. With Arrupe and the thirty-first and thirty-second General Congregations (GCs) of the Jesuits, concerns for social justice increased in the Jesuit order. For these progressive Jesuits, evangelism was synonymous with being a living witness to the gospel by serving the poor: some lost their lives for the people they loved and served.

Methodological Framework

This book reclaims institutional history and its relevance in the writing of the history of African Christianity in the twenty-first century. From a theoretical perspective, this study uses a critical, archaeological,[34] and genealogical approach to analyse the process of creation of a religious institution.[35] To its readers, this study may seem chronological and diachronic, as the different chapters move from Chad, to Cameroon, to the VPAO, and to its African reception. My writing process, however, has

---

[33] Paul Gifford, *Christianity, Development and Modernity in Africa* (Oxford: Oxford University Press, 2016).

[34] This refers to Foucault's archaeological idea that structures are sometimes more important than the history of ideas, and that discourses are 'practices specified in the element of the archive': Michel Foucault, *The Archaeology of Knowledge: And the Discourse on Language* (New York: Vintage Books, 2010), 131.

[35] From his Genealogy, Foucault claims that unlike big universal claims, multiple 'little', 'accidental' causes and reversals ('the unexpected', as it is called in this text) are what matters the most in historical analysis. Cf. Paul Ricœur, *Memory, History, Forgetting* (Chicago, IL: University of Chicago Press, 2004), 192–93.

adopted a retrogressive mode[36] that analyses, backwards, the creation of the VPAO. Its original 'event' is, thus, not the beginning of the process with the arrival of the first Jesuit to Chad in 1935. Nor is it the official recognition of the Chad Mission in 1946. Instead, the founding event of the book is the 'unexpected' Cameroonian reaction to the creation of the VPAO from 1973 to 1978. At this time, Cameroonians rejected, for the sake of Africanisation, the proposition of being led by White missionaries in the name of universality or catholicity. They also resisted the new Jesuit jurisdiction they belonged to because the map of this jurisdiction was identical to that of French colonial states in Central and West Africa.

Work in the archives revealed that several 'little causes' led to the final outcome (VPAO), each of which could be studied separately. They included the independence movement and Christian missions worldwide and in Francophone West Africa, the Second Vatican Council, the election of Arrupe and its particular impact on Jesuit work in Africa, the call for a moratorium on Western missions in Africa, and the emergence of postcolonial discourse.[37] All these 'little causes' appear in this study as the context that situates the creation of the VPAO within the broader context of African and World Christianity in the 1970s. Without these 'little causes', the creation of the VPAO would not have been a historical event in itself.

The organising narrative of the book also draws on Michel Foucault's opening chapter in *The Order of Things*. In it, the French philosopher comments on Diego Velazquez' seventeenth-century painting *Las Meñinas*.[38] By the time he painted *Las Meñinas*, Velazquez had been working for the Spanish court for about thirty years, painting portraits of prominent members of the royal family. In *Las Meñinas*, however, the painting seems to be representing its own creation. King Philip IV and Queen Mariana only appear through a mirror, while the centre stage of the painting seems to be occupied respectively, and depending on perspectives, by Princess Margarita, her maids (*Meñinas*), Velazquez himself, or by a dog. As a result, *Las Meñinas* leaves its audience wondering who the real subject of the painting is. Thus, the historical repositioning of the Jesuits in Africa in this book is, I argue, in itself a historical re-creation.

[36] Marc Bloch, *The Historian's Craft*, 1st American ed. (New York: Knopf, 1953), 45.
[37] Julian Go, *Postcolonial Thought and Social Theory* (New York: Oxford University Press, 2016); Achille Mbembe, *On the Post-Colony* (Berkeley: University of California Press, 2001).
[38] Michel Foucault, *The Order of Things: An Archaeology of the Human Sciences* (New York: Vintage Books, 1994).

Writing institutional history in the way this book does can seem at odds with recent developments in a field of history dominated by social and global history. Cultural historians and anthropologists might also, and rightly so, claim that this institutional history on a religious order, the Jesuits, exclusively comprised of men, may leave the reader with the feeling of going back to writing a 'big men' history. As such, it might not address, for example, what John and Jean Comaroff have called 'the everyday' and 'the domestic', those 'counterpositioned' realities which often destabilise established historical accounts.[39]

Such concerns are legitimate. The scope of the book is naturally limited in time and focus: it does not pretend to address all issues. Like Foucault's argument regarding *Las Meñinas* in *The Order of Things*, however, this study has avoided having a 'king' driving its narrative. Rather, it examines and discusses different characters. Some are more powerful than others. Each character appears, disappears, and reappears as other characters emerge in an ever-evolving historical context with multiple centres of action, the whole building into one overarching narrative.

The Introduction starts with de Rosny and introduces other important characters in the book. Chapters 1 and 2 focus on the founders of the Chad Mission, namely Frédéric de Bélinay and Joseph du Bouchet. Chapters 3, 4, and 5 expand on Paul Dalmais, but also include lesser-known Jesuit Brothers who built the Church of Chad. Chapter 6 focuses on François Tombalbaye and Dalmais. Chapter 7's central point is the encounter between Henri Véniat and Cameroonian Archbishop Jean Zoa. It also highlights the voice of a little boy witnessing that encounter. Pedro Arrupe is the main focus in Chapters 8 and 9. Yet, in response to Arrupe's policy, these chapters also give voice to Cameroonian Jesuits, including renowned figures like Engelbert Mveng, Fabien Eboussi Boulaga, and Meinrad-Pierre Hebga. They also include lesser-known Jesuits such as Nicolas Ossama and Emmanuel Teguem, a working-class Jesuit Brother. The Conclusion addresses the competing memories of Mveng and de Rosny.

This book suggests that the shift from the history of strongmen to social history, if too radical, might lead to a polarisation in which the latter paradigm might be an overcorrection of the former. Choices in human societies, and I believe in schools of history, might lead to radicalism if left between the oppressive patriarchal old model and the revolution of masses and non-conformists. In an already restless continent like Africa, a middle

---

[39] Jean and John Comaroff, *Of Revelation and Revolution: The Dialectics of Modernity on a South African Frontier*, vol. 2 (Chicago, IL: University of Chicago Press, 1997), 5.

ground can be found between those two extremes and create space for institutional history in which the voices of those in the margins are heard in response to those in power.

With this new approach, I offer the argument that institutions alone, not big men or popular masses, might guarantee continuity and stability. The immediacy of daily concerns fed by political instability and the lack of basic needs is already too common in the unsettling lives of Africans. Maybe a certain dose of 'longue durée' (long duration), the continuity of institutions, would better serve those in the margins whose primary aspiration is peace and stability. The Church already provides such continuity and stability when it operates as the only functioning, and stabilising, institution in some localities in Africa.

Competition, according to Comaroff and Comaroff, applies to 'diverse local Christianities', with a 'tradition of dissent with its trust in the practical power of revealed truth'.[40] This competition, they argue, means 'that the revitalization of the African soul required a revolution in habits'.[41] In places where non-conformist competition applied, David Barrett has shown that while such competition led to renewal, it also evolved into religious schisms.[42] It is a legitimate question to ask whether or not Africans need more division, or greater stability. Barbara Cooper's account of the Sudan Interior Mission (SIM) shows, for example, that schismatic competition can lead to double-mindedness or even conflict among Christians and with other religions.[43]

Competing Pentecostals and Institutional History

Pentecostals, the largest growing Christian group in Global Christianity, are not addressed in this study. However, they represent the biggest challenge to a return to institutional history. Early Pentecostals found solace in a turbulent world by turning their back to it and becoming less politically engaged. The universal gift of the Holy Spirit allowed a fuller participation of disenfranchised members of established churches. These members often challenged their institutional organisation. Pentecostals

---

[40] Ibid., 7.
[41] Ibid., 8.
[42] David B. Barrett, *Schism and Renewal in Africa: An Analysis of Six Thousand Contemporary Religious Movements* (London: Oxford University Press, 1968).
[43] Barbara M. Cooper, *Evangelical Christians in the Muslim Sahel* (Bloomington, IN: Indiana University Press, 2006).

tended to be porous and borderless, moving across denominations and non-denominations alike. Today, their proliferation creates an environment of religious competition.

There is evidence, however, of increased routinisation among recent Pentecostalism in Africa. This routinisation tends to promote Pentecostal big men whose leadership is built around their persona at the expense of other social groups. In fact, African Pentecostalism seems to have borders. Nimi Wariboko sees commonalities in global and African Pentecostalism. He also believes that there is a Nigerian Pentecostalism, proper to the Nigerian religious *imaginaire* (worldview). Though invisible, this imaginaire shapes the political and material world. To study Nigerian society and institutions requires paying attention to this spiritual imaginaire. To understand the redemptive message of Nigerian Pentecostalism is to understand the institutional failures of its politics and institutions.[44] As Wariboko discusses the 'this' and 'that' of miracles in Nigerian Pentecostalism,[45] one sees an effort to systematise Pentecostal theology.

Systematisation is a further indication of the institutionalisation of African Pentecostalism. Historians simply cannot ignore this institutional development and how it broadly shapes society. Birgit Meyer and Robert W. Hefner have shown that as Pentecostals evolve to become megachurches, they become the focus of the attention of politicians, and often there emerges an ecclesiastic corporatism. As Hefner puts it, 'megachurches mean followers, and their numbers tempts politicians and pastors to dream of power-bloc deals'.[46] Meyer further highlights the modernity, wealth, and prosperity gospel, and global outreach of African Pentecostal pastors, while the same are ministering to the born-again poor.[47]

This corporatism makes the study of religious institutional history necessary. The ongoing unchurching or de-parochialisation, which is the opposite side of this corporatism, can only be explained through the

---

[44] Nimi Wariboko, *Nigerian Pentecostalism* (Rochester, NY: University of Rochester Press, 2014), 280–82.
[45] Ibid., 101–03.
[46] Robert W. Hefner, 'Introduction: The Unexpected Modern-Gender, Piety, and Politics in the Global Pentecostal Surge', in *Global Pentecostalism in the 21st Century*, eds Robert W. Hefner and Peter L. Berger (Bloomington, IN: Indiana University Press, 2013), 16.
[47] Birgit Meyer, 'Christianity in Africa: From African Independent to Pentecostal-Charismatic Churches', *Annual Review of Anthropology* 33, no. 1 (2004): 447–74 – here, p. 448.

analysis of parochialism.⁴⁸ To write history in the context of growing, often uncontrolled competition in a troubled continent which aspires to democracy and stability is, from a methodological perspective, one of the challenges addressed in this book.

The Jesuits primarily represent a 500-year-old institution that is both global and local, and national, regional, and international. From its transplantation in Africa in the 1970s, different agendas have competed: big men have been carefully controlled and moderated by the long-held traditions of their institution as well as by ongoing competing agendas among the leadership. Some historians might find my use of longue durée history reminiscent of the colonial time in which this school of history emerged, or even neocolonial in nature for being French in its origin. Yet although Lamin Sanneh, for example, believed that the Annales School of History 'downgraded human agency in favor of general trends and systemic factors',⁴⁹ his description of the success of Western missions on African soil is portrayed in terms of the longue-durée work by which the missionaries helped preserve African cultures in a world where the same cultures and peoples were being destroyed.⁵⁰ In this study I have chosen to emphasise the importance of continuity and suggest the importance of historians of Africa taking institutions and decision-making processes seriously.

The creation of the VPAO emerges as a historical anomaly in both the context of the continuous Africanisation of the Church from the 1920s and the tradition of Jesuit accommodation in mission.⁵¹ Studying it through the lens of Africanisation moves its Africanisation from the field of theology and philosophy to that of institutional history. As such, it pays particular

---

48 Samuel Nelson and Philip S. Gorski, 'Conditions of Religious Belonging: Confessionalization, De-Parochialization, and the Euro-American Divergence', *International Sociology* 29, no. 1 (2014): 3–21.
49 Lamin O. Sanneh, *Abolitionists Abroad. American Blacks and the Making of Modern West Africa* (Cambridge, MA: Harvard University Press, 1999), 20.
50 Lamin O. Sanneh, *Translating the Message: The Missionary Impact on Culture* (Maryknoll, NY: Orbis Books, 1989).
51 According to Paul Ricœur, the difference between what is historical and what is merely sociological lies in the fact that the historical is not the invariants within a changing phenomenon, but rather change itself. Structures and institutions are objects of history only insofar as they are changing, and a historical 'event' would be that moment of the emergence of conjecture and of the unexpected, which is what I call here 'historical anomaly'. Cf. Ricœur, *Memory, History, Forgetting*, 192–93.

attention to the 'underlying structures that formed the context for the thinking' of Africanisation.[52]

To understand how one moves from a religious phenomenon (which the creation of the VPAO was) to a historical event, one has to look to Michel de Certeau.[53] Like Foucault, de Certeau speaks to the historical period of this study. Both stand separate from historiographical schools in which religious history was something 'belonging to past societies (and surpassed, thanks to progress)'.[54] They also recognise that 'knowledge can have a transforming effect on the power structures that give rise to it'.[55]

As de Certeau rightly argues, 'the Jesuits deliberately place themselves within the field of civil practices. As partisans of adaptation, as the principal legislators of "civility", of "honesty", of "stately duties", even of "honor" or of a "legitimate self-respect" in Christian morality, they try to proportion to these practices a deviation that in every instance is relative to a social task'.[56] That social positioning of the Jesuits makes the study of their organisation as well as their accommodationist missionary practices simultaneously a religious and a political task.

Sources and Structure

The Annales School of History started to develop in the 1930s when the first Jesuits were going to Chad. Michel Foucault's major works were published in the 1970s, when the VPAO was created. For the Annalists and for Foucault, it was also a time of intellectual scepticism. As a Jesuit writing Jesuit history,

[52] According to Foucault, 'the history of ideas – where this means what is consciously going on in the minds of scientists, philosophers, et al. – is less important than the underlying structures that form the context for their thinking. We will not be so much interested in, say, Hume or Darwin as in what made Hume or Darwin possible.' Cf. Gary Gutting, *Foucault: A Very Short Introduction* (Oxford: Oxford University Press, 2005), 33.

[53] 'What is an event', de Certeau asks, 'if not what must be presupposed, in order for an organization of documents to be possible? The event is the means thanks to which disorder is turned into order. The event does not explain but permits an intelligibility. It is the postulate and the point of departure – but also the blind spot – of comprehension': Michel de Certeau, *The Writing of History: European Perspectives* (New York: Columbia University Press, 1988), 96.

[54] De Certeau, *The Writing of History*, 23. In contrast, and without denying their debt to the *Annales*, de Certeau and Foucault attempted to rescue religion and politics as worthy of historical research.

[55] Gutting, *Foucault: A Very Short Introduction*, 51.

[56] De Certeau, *The Writing of History*, 163.

a healthy dose of Foucault's scepticism has been necessary in engaging with the sources for this book. These included primary materials from the Jesuit archives of Vanves (France), Rome, Douala (Cameroon), Nairobi (Kenya), and the 'Fonds Dalmais' in N'Djamena (Chad). These were complemented by the diocesan archives in Yaoundé (Cameroon), government collections in CEFOD (Chad), the archives of the Christian Assemblies of God of N'Djamena, and hundreds of pages of email correspondence and written and tape-recorded interviews with a dozen lay and Jesuit interviewees who were witnesses of part of this history.

The limitations of these sources cannot be overlooked. The book has but a few African voices in chapters related to Chad. Literature on the history of the Catholic Church in Chad is extremely rare. Enforced delay in recruiting Chadian Jesuits accentuated the lack of African Catholic voices in Chad during the period studied in this book. Chadian voices on the history of the Church in Chad were drawn from missionary records. Only in Chapters 6 and 7 do we have more Chadians articulating their views. Records of their views are found mainly in official newspapers.

As the focus of the book moves from Chad to Cameroon, more African voices shape the narrative of Chapters 8 and 9. These African scholars were primary theologians and philosophers. As a result, African historians have sometimes overlooked their views as non-representative. Their training in the West, and their focus on deconstructing Western paradigms of Africa might raise some questions on the true 'Africanness' of their thoughts. However, overlooking the voices of Mveng, Eboussi, or Hebga would simply be incomprehensible for anyone writing the history of the Catholic Church in Francophone Africa. They articulated the best African reception of and response to Global Catholicism in the 1970s.

Ultimately, to understand the making of postcolonial Africa, a careful analysis of the process of Africanisation is needed which incorporates the transition from French Catholicism and colonialism (Part I) to the postcolonial mission (Part II) and the debate around the issue of Catholicity (Part III). Africans questioned the relevance of this Catholicity. They claimed that if the Church in Africa was to be truly African, it should not only de-Westernise; it should also challenge the enlightened notion of universality and the negative perception the Enlightenment created towards African cultures and peoples.

If there was confusion at the beginning of the mission (Chapters 1 and 3), it is because a mission made entirely of French men was settling in a West African country, Chad, exactly at a time when the Church was pushing for Africanisation and local politics were moving towards greater African self-determination. Therefore, what was the purpose of a mission to civilise in this particular context? It was still French and Roman in its purpose. The fight to contain Islam (Chapter 4) and the work to convert Chad's southerners (Chapter 5) were top-down priorities with global implications. They were, however, relatively foreign to the ordinary life of Chadians. And when Chadians finally reacted to this missionary agenda, it led to Chad's Cultural Revolution with the backdrop of Africanisation (Chapter 6).

That Africanisation had already taken place in Cameroon in a very significant way. Cameroon's Africanisation first emerged in Chad during the ordination of Bishop Véniat in 1962 (Chapter 7), at the beginning of the Second Vatican Council, and with the election of Pedro Arrupe as superior general of the Jesuits in 1965. In his attempt to restructure Jesuit missions in West Africa, the new superior general directly addressed the issue of Africanisation. He made speeches on the inculturation of the gospel and appointed a Cameroonian, Meinrad-Pierre Hebga, as major superior (Chapter 8).

Yet, this institutional change did not last. With the creation of the VPAO in 1973, a Frenchman replaced Hebga as superior. This shift triggered a strong reaction from Cameroonian Jesuits. They described the move as a spiritual neocolonialism (Chapter 9). Africans might have become politically independent, and the Church might have become Black in its membership and leadership, but by the end of the 1970s, Africans still felt as if they were not at home or well represented in the structures, and even the spirituality of the Church was in question. Their version of Africanisation was rejected, and they themselves were ostracised. In contrast, a European diluted version of Africanisation was celebrated both in the Church and in Cameroonian politics in the figure of Éric de Rosny.

In the Conclusion of this book, 'mission terminée?' loses its question mark and becomes a fact. The respective fates of French missionary Éric de Rosny and Cameroonian Engelbert Mveng, two contemporaneous and prominent Jesuits in French West Africa, and the political and cultural recuperation and rejection that surrounded their deaths in independent Cameroon, show the lasting impact of competing Catholicisms on the African Church, its potential and its paradoxes. This book confirms that the history of the Christian Church in Africa is a movement that expands through progressions and regressions. It is the story of different, if not competing, interpretations of the same tradition(s).

This study ends in 1978, with the African reception of the VPAO as a neocolonial entity because of its French dominance and the juridical end of the Jesuit mission from France in both Chad and Cameroon. Yet today, through a process of deterritorialisation,[57] the VPAO could be said to have succeeded in creating a new religious internationalism on African soil and an intercultural space in which the Jesuits developed a new sense of belonging and a new network of friendship and apostolic discernment and commitment. What seemed so neocolonial in its beginnings might have redefined African Christianity in ways that transcend nation-states and 'compel people to look beyond their natural boundaries and comfort zones'.[58]

---

[57] According to global historian Lynn Hunt, 'deterritorialization, which some consider to define globalization, challenges the sovereignty of nation-states, which are after all built upon a notion of control over territory': Lynn Hunt, *Writing History in the Global Era*, 1st ed. (New York: W.W. Norton & Company, 2014), 55.

[58] Dana L. Robert, *Christian Mission: How Christianity Became a World Religion* (Malden, MA: Blackwell, 2009), 177.

PART I

The Jesuit Project in West Africa: French Catholicism and Colonialism in Chad, 1935–58

Introduction

This Part focuses on the early years of the mission (1935–46), when its actual nature was in a period of confusion. The mission was initiated by a single individual, Frédéric de Bélinay (1875–1958), without a mandate from his Jesuit superiors. It was formally approved without it being clear whether it was intended to evangelise or civilise.[1] The inclination of the pioneers of the mission, this chapter argues, was towards Frenchification.[2] This was the process by which missionaries helped to negotiate the remaking of French identity and moral prestige in the context of the end of the French empire and a decreasing Catholicism at home. This new missionary outreach increased the self-worth of the missionaries. It also gave them global purpose as they embarked on a conquering movement aimed at keeping African colonies under French political and cultural influence. The Jesuit mission in Chad, the chapter argues, shared the civilising nature of all Catholic missions in the 1930s. The missionaries, however, adapted this civilising mission to the unique context of France and Chad after the Second World War. This context was shaped by French strategic interests in Africa and the Middle East, and the urgent need to contain secularising trends in Chad that were already 'infiltrating' French towns and cities. The Jesuit missionaries in Chad were part of a broader project which the French government claimed worked towards 'pacification' of the region and maintaining the colonial established order.

In the 1930s, Chad became the battleground for global ideologies, religions, and politics. A Muslim-majority country for centuries, Chad witnessed a new move southwards of Islam. This resurgence of Chad's Islam coincided with the beginning of renewed efforts to Christianise the

---

[1] Alice L. Conklin, *A Mission to Civilize: The Republican Idea of Empire in France and West Africa, 1895–1930* (Stanford, CA: Stanford University Press, 1997).

[2] Daniel Abwa uses the term 'francisation' in his *Commissaires et Haut-Commissaires de La France Au Cameroun (1916–1930)* (Yaoundé: Presses Universitaires de Yaoundé, 1998). Frenchification in this text is an English translation of Abwa's term.

southern part of the country. It began with the arrival of the first Protestant missions in 1920, closely followed by Catholic missionaries in 1929.

Prior to the 1920s, the Capuchins, from the eighteenth century, and the Holy Ghost Fathers, from the nineteenth, had missioned to Central Africa. With the early French colonial expeditions known as 'Mission Marchand',[3] 'Mission Maistre', and 'Mission Foureau-Lamy',[4] Chad had become part of the Catholic Apostolic Vicariate of Ubangi. The Sudan United Mission launched its mission in the same region in 1904. The decree of creation of the Apostolic Vicariate of Khartoum in 1913 assigned Chad to Italian Comboni missionaries, alongside the Priests of the Sacred Heart (Dehonians) and the Holy Ghost Fathers. The mission of the latter expanded further south, around northern Cameroon and the Chadian region of Bongor. As the First World War ended, Australian Lutherans settled in Sudan, including, from 1923, among the Massa, the Toupouri, and the Moundang of Chad and Cameroon.[5] By the eve of the Second World War, Catholic and Protestant missionaries had successfully settled in Chad and northern Cameroon.

Europe, in the 1930s, saw the rise of Italian Fascism. The growing influence of this ideology in Italy had ramifications in Libya, which constitutes the northern frontier of Chad. France, likewise, was facing its own internal uncertainties. Unprepared for containing the rise of both Fascism and Nazism, Catholic France was losing its working class to Communism. It was also weakened abroad by increased nationalism that threatened the French empire in China, India, and soon across Africa. This collapse of France's political empire destroyed some of its missions in Asia.

The rise to power of Marshal Philippe Pétain (1856–1951) restored some confidence both among France's political elite and in the Church. But his regime also represented the calm before the storm. France was ravaged at the beginning of the Second World War, ceding its leadership to a new super power. The United States was a clear winner of this war and, as such, a new competing power to reckon with.

---

[3] General Baratier, *Souvenirs de La Mission Marchand* (Paris: Grasset, 1941); Pierre Pellissier, *Fachoda et La Mission Marchand, 1896–1899* (Paris: Perrin, 2011).

[4] All of which took place between 1890 and 1898. See: Ferdinand Foureau, *Documents Scientifiques de la Mission Saharienne: Mission Foureau-Lamy* (Paris: Masson et Cie, 1903).

[5] François Pierret, *Les Débuts de la Bonne Nouvelle Au Tchad, 1920–1951* (Archives of the Jesuit Historical Institute in Africa; Nairobi: n.p., 1971).

France also faced British competition in the region. Heinrich Barth in 1845, and Lieutenant Clapperton before him (1822), explored Central Africa during the first half of the nineteenth century.[6] The British blockage in Nigeria as well as Islamic *razzia* in the nineteenth century might help explain the late return of Catholic missions to Chad. This delay, however, created a false perception of Chad as far too savage and primitive a place for missionaries to dare to evangelise. For instance, initial reports on the region by André Gide portrayed a region in the wildest and most exotic terms proper to nineteenth-century European romanticism.[7] For late British observers, however, the region around Lake Chad was ruled by powerful and respected leaders.[8] These leaders secured the commercial routes towards the Sahara, and were inclined to establish lasting commercial ties with England and the Near East.[9]

Chad provided the shortest pilgrimage route towards the Middle East for West Africans. As stated by Jay Spaulding and Lidwien Kapteijns, 'in the early nineteenth century, a northern Nigerian pilgrim bound for Mecca could have travelled from Lake Chad to the Red Sea with the permission of only three governments: Wadai (following the annexation of Baghirmi), Dar Fur (following its annexation of Kordofan), and Sinnar (or the Turkish regime that replaced it in 1821)'.[10] Even in the Muslim-dominated far north region around Faya-Largeau, agricultural projects were promoted alongside a French military garrison which lasted beyond Chad's independence in 1960.[11]

Besides being latecomers in Chad and West Africa when compared to other Catholic missions in the region like the Spiritans, the Capuchins, the Pallottines, and the Dominicans, the question addressed in Part I of

---

[6] Heinrich Barth, *Travels and Discoveries in North and Central Africa. From the Journal of an Expedition Undertaken under the Auspices of H.B.M's Government, in the Years 1849–1855* (Philadelphia, PA: J.W. Bradley, 1859).

[7] Matt Reeck, 'The Paradoxes of Description in André Gide's *Voyage au Congo and Le Retour du Tchad*', *South Central Review* 36, no. 1 (Spring 2019): 82–103 – here, pp. 85 and 90.

[8] Ibrahima Baba Kake and Elikia M'bokolo, *Histoire Générale de l'Afrique, Des Missionnaires Aux Explorateurs*, vol. 7, 12 vols (Tournai: Casterman SA, 1978), 54.

[9] Ibid., 56.

[10] Jay Spaulding and Lidwien Kapteijns, 'Land Tenure and the State in the Pre-colonial Sudan', *Northeast African Studies* 9, no. 1 (2002): 33–66 – here, p. 44.

[11] Judith Scheele, 'Ravens Reconsidered: Raiding and Theft among Tubu-Speakers in Northern Chad', *African Studies Review* 34 (2018): 135–55 – here, p. 138.

this book is why French Jesuits decided to start a new mission in the very remote Saharan region of Chad in the 1940s, exactly at a time when both French Catholicism at home and France's standing in the world were in deep crisis. Thomas Pakenham has established that two reasons why the French government moved into Saharan Africa in the 1890s were 'to redeem France's humiliation in Europe' and 'to develop new overseas markets for France'.[12] As this section of the book argues, the same spirit was behind France's new missionary outreach in the 1940s: to reassert France's imperial ambitions in the 1930s and redeem it from the humiliation of the Second World War and the collapse of its colonial empire.

Chad's region of Moyen-Logone was heavily populated, and France sought to use this for its own economic gain. It represented a reserve workforce for the French companies in Central Africa. The administrative region of Mayo-Kebbi alone had more than 300,000 inhabitants, and other groups included the Sara (in Logone) and the Massa (in Mayo-Kebbi); these ethnic groups formed the basis of Chad's agrarian population.[13] Because it was a well-watered region, the Logone and Mayo-Kebbi were developed and became what French colonists called 'Le Tchad Utile' (Useful Chad). Colonial administrators created a cotton-growing economy in the region under the monopoly of La Compagnie Cotonnière Equatoriale Française (COTONFRAN).[14] This cotton-oriented economy brought little benefit for the well-being of ordinary Chadians.

This redeeming mission ultimately led to enduring French domination in Chad and Central Africa that outlasted African independences. On both fronts, France perceived Chad as a strategic ally against Communism and Islam. Catholic missions, in this context, served as the cultural component of the battle for the soul of French civilisation. The mission to evangelise and the mission to civilise had become synonymous with Frenchification. This Frenchification agenda attempted to co-opt the political Africanisation of Chad into the Union Française (French Union). It also slowed down ecclesiastical Africanisation of the kind then promoted by the Vatican.

---

[12] Thomas Pakenham, *The Scramble for Africa. The White Man's Conquest of the Dark Continent from 1876 to 1912* (New York: Random House, 1991), 359–61.

[13] Jean Cabot, 'La mise en valeur des régions du Moyen-Logone', *Annales de Géographie* 341 (February 1955): 35–46 – here, p. 44.

[14] Lori Leonard, 'Women Who Changed into Men: A Gendered History of Precarity in "Useful Chad"', *Africa* 89, no. 3 (2019): 521–40 – here, p. 526.

As Jesuit Father de Bélinay explored Chad in 1935, France was confronted with the rise of radical communist and fascist ideologies at home. De Bélinay was also concerned with France's standing in this changing world. The first part of this book shows that the mission of Jesuit pioneers in Chad is to be understood in the context of an uncertain and confused France and its desire to reassert its prestige and power abroad. For these French missionaries in Chad, the civilising aspect of traditional Catholic missions had a stronger political and geostrategic component. Chad was the battle line for competing civilisations. The survival of the France that de Bélinay knew depended on strengthening traditional Roman Catholicism in France and abroad.

In these three chapters, we see that the initial goal of the Jesuit mission in Chad was to evangelise while at the same time maintaining and promoting French interests.

CHAPTER 1

Era of Confusion: The Vatican's or France's Wider Agenda? 1935–46

A mission to evangelise or a mission to civilise? In Paris, in 1935, Jesuit Father Frédéric de Bélinay met Lieutenant Mazodier. The officer had just spent two years in Chad as part of the colonial expedition. He lamented not having seen a single priest during his two years in Chad. De Bélinay was so moved by the story that he volunteered to go to Chad, alone, as an evangeliser. Mazodier's experience reminded de Bélinay that vast portions of humanity were still untouched by the gospel. He had a duty to evangelise them. The primary concern that motivated de Bélinay, as evidenced in his correspondence, was the fate of the French soldiers who, like Mazodier, had been serving the empire. Like these soldiers, de Bélinay's mission in Chad included protecting French interests in Central Africa.[1] He seemed not at all concerned by the Vatican's call to Africanise the Church. The mission to evangelise was a mission to Frenchify.

Himself a veteran of the First World War, de Bélinay is said to have travelled 3,400km by camel. He visited troops from Fort-Archambault to Borkou, near the Tibesti mountains on the Libyan frontier. His Jesuit superiors confirmed what was initially a personal initiative three years later, in 1938. That year, de Bélinay settled in Fort-Lamy (today's N'Djamena, the capital of Chad). He spent most of his time visiting the soldiers, although little is known about his actual work with them. Yet, as this chapter shows, de Bélinay earnestly mobilised France's Gaullism to make Chad a strategic priority. Muslims were on the move southwards and the Americans were coming. Losing Chad to any of them, he believed, would be catastrophic for France and for stability in Central Africa.

---

[1] Two volumes on de Bélinay were written but never published. I found manuscripts in the Jesuit archive in Douala. J. Fortier, *Frédéric de Bélinay: Pionnier des missions du Tchad*, vols 1–2, 2 vols (Tchad, 1988).

This chapter focuses on these early years of the mission, from the exploratory period of de Bélinay starting in 1935 to the mission's formal approval by the Vatican's Congregation for the Evangelisation of Peoples in 1946. It describes the initial steps of de Bélinay in Chad as a time of great confusion in the empire out of which emerged a steady process of Frenchification. Father de Bélinay was in Chad to evangelise. Yet, he carried with him the hopes and anxieties of his homeland. Not only did he see Chad's appeal as a divine call to bring the gospel primarily to French soldiers stationed in Chad, but he was also focused on defending France's strategic interests in the region against the rise of American influence. This approach anticipated the sidelining of the Vatican's urgent priority to Africanise Church leadership.

In his attempt to reconcile the needs of the unevangelised Chadians and the needs of the French soldiers, de Bélinay's mission to evangelise became increasingly synonymous with a mission to Frenchify. He argued for the urgent need to send an army of French missionaries to Chad. These missionaries, he believed, would lead the cultural struggle against the triple threat facing France in Central Africa: the spread of Islam, Communism among its class of Évolués, and American liberal Protestantism. Father de Bélinay's framing of the mission was reflective of the rebranding of French political and religious conservatism at home. From Vichy to Gaullism, Christian missions became the cultural arms for restoring France's prestige abroad after the war.

This was also a time when French Catholicism was struggling at home. The Catholic identity of France's working class was eroding. Its missions in China and India were clouded with uncertainty. In this context, going to Chad represented a new Asia, a new Jerusalem for the Jesuits. They discovered a new adventure that, they hoped, would once again ignite their conquering spirit and missionary zeal. The success of the new enterprise challenged them to address, on a spiritual ground, the humiliation suffered in the Second World War for themselves and for France.

From his own account, this new missionary adventure increased de Bélinay's self-worth. It also gave him a new purpose at the service of his Church and his country. De Bélinay understood service to the Church in line with a new Francis Xavier (1506–52) or a new Charles de Foucauld (1858–1916) of the African Sahara. Service to his country aimed not only at serving its colonial soldiers as chaplain, but also at convincing French officials of the triple dangers of Islamism, Communism, and, above all, Americanism. De Bélinay's mission to evangelise was, therefore, a mission to civilise, in the sense of restoring France's prestige and defending its strategic interests in Central Africa.

With the example of de Bélinay, the Jesuits in French Africa in the 1940s started their mission like middlemen, negotiating France's relevance in the new global order. This order was still French and had to remain so in France's African colonies. It was, however, globally American in reality. This explains why French missionaries would also be anti-American in the context of Chad, where the political order was also becoming irresistibly African.

De Bélinay and his colleagues negotiated the relevance of France in Chad in three steps. First, their religious 'pacification' continued the military 'pacification' of Chad that started in the 1890s. This pacification cemented Chad's loyalty to France amidst the collapse of its empire in the 1940s. Secondly, by adopting a downgraded *mission civilisatrice* and pushing for an anti-elite agenda in their fight against what they perceived as secularising trends in Chadian society, the missionaries failed to foster a Chadian nationalism while French politicians were entertaining a new citizenry for Chadians. This citizenry was never fully realised.

Thirdly, this time of confusion helped to secure, in the long term, a peaceful transition from colonialism to Chad's independence. It also preserved France's stronghold on Chad. With no internal dissent in Chad, the opposition to Islam, Communism, and liberal American Protestantism served the geopolitical and strategic interests of France against its regional competitors. Consequently, the Jesuit Chad Mission remained French-oriented and in line with the purpose of Wider France. It also stayed within a certain distance from a key Vatican priority: the building of a Chadian clergy and leadership in the Church.

Mission to Colonise and the Rise of French Jesuit Progressivism

In the mid-twentieth century, most African countries were moving towards independence. The Vatican was also speeding up the indigenisation agenda in the Church in an effort to secure its survival in Africa after the eventual collapse of colonial empires. Paradoxically, an all-European Jesuit organisation was settling in Chad and other surrounding French colonies. Most of the Jesuit missionaries were French. They were leaving their homeland in the context of the weakening of France's colonial empire abroad and of French Catholicism at home.

As we have seen, the Jesuit story in French West Africa began in the 1930s, in the years leading up to the Second World War and its immediate aftermath. De Bélinay (1875–1958) endeavoured to explore Chad for an evangelisation project among French military personnel stationed in this Sahelian country. At home, in France, the political and religious situation was shifting dramatically. From the Nazi jail where he wrote *The Historian's Craft*, Marc Bloch, one of the founders of the Annales School of History and whose work shaped French historiography during the second half of the twentieth century, witnessed, according to one account, 'the collapse of France and everything in which he believed'.[2] The rise of Fascism in Western Europe had wiped out the enlightened ideals of the French Revolution.

The impact of the victory in 1918 had been short for France. The defeat in 1940 seemed to be worse, as it came with the collapse of the entire French empire. The French elite, powerless as German troops patrolled over French cities, towns, and villages, had bitterly come to realise the damage done to France's pride and moral prestige by the Vichy regime's collaboration with the Nazis. Paradoxically, this regime also believed that the future restoration of France depended on the awakening of its colonies.[3] The cooperation with the Nazis, the treason of the regime's most admired Marshal, Philippe Pétain, and the humiliation of defeat in 1940 had caused great disenchantment among its security and administrative personnel.[4] Pétain had embraced the National Revolution and replaced the traditional 'Liberté-Égalité-Fraternité' (Freedom-Equality-Fraternity) with 'Travail-Famille-Patrie' (Work-Family-Nation), which appealed to Conservative Catholics.[5] It was also an appeal to the 'True French' French citizens – including those who lived in the colonies – who believed that France's prestige had been destroyed and its moral standing in the world weakened.[6]

---

[2] Marc Bloch, *The Historian's Craft*, 1st American ed. (New York: Knopf, 1953), Introduction, viii.

[3] Cf. Pascal Blanchard and Gilles Boëtsch, 'La France de Pétain et l'Afrique: Images et Propagandes Coloniales', *Canadian Journal of African Studies* 28, no. 1 (1994): 1–31 – here, p. 3.

[4] Simon Kitson, 'From Enthusiasm to Disenchantment: The French Police and the Vichy Regime, 1940–1944', *Contemporary European History* 11, no. 3 (August 2002): 371–90.

[5] Ruth Ginio, 'Marshal Petain Spoke to Schoolchildren: Vichy Propaganda in French West Africa, 1940–1943', *The International Journal of African Historical Studies* 33, no. 2 (2000): 291–312 – here, p. 292.

[6] '[Pétain's] new regime quickly endorsed an ideology that came to be known as the "National Revolution". Travail, Famille, Patrie replaced the old Republican values –Liberté, Egalité, Fraternité. The first step of this so-called Revolution was to return France to the "true French". That translated as action against Jews, Freemasons, and Communists': Ruth Ginio, 'Marshal Pétain Spoke to Schoolchildren: Vichy Propaganda in French West Africa,

Among those disappointed at the end of the Second World War was the head of the Catholic Church in French Africa. Apostolic prefect Marcel Lefèbvre of Dakar is known for his role as the papal legate in French Africa and the only Catholic schismatic bishop out of the Second Vatican Council. He witnessed, with great concern, the fall of Pétain during the Second World War and the subsequent rise to power of General Charles de Gaulle and his France Libre. For Lefèbvre, Pétain had not only been a revered victorious warrior. He was also a symbol of the Catholic revival in France during the interwar period.

In his biography on Lefèbvre, Bernard Tissier de Mallerais quotes the papal legate on the fears he expressed. De Gaulle, Lefèbvre said, 'brought back everything that Marshal Pétain had driven out of France. Everything was once again ruined; and the movement for Catholic and Christian order was decapitated.'[7] For Lefèbvre's France, the threefold unity between faith, work, and love of family was at stake. He linked, in a paradoxical association, American-inspired liberal Protestantism and Communism. Lefèbvre believed that the two ideologies were infesting France and threatening France's long-held traditions and beliefs.[8] They also represented a direct threat for Francophone Africa.

There was some basis to Lefèbvre's fears. By the end of the war, the Catholic political and religious order in France was, indeed, in serious peril. A decade earlier, in the 1930s, there had been tensions and sometimes competing agendas between the colonial administration and French missionaries in Africa. Both sides, however, had remained united at least on three fronts: their patriotism, their aversion to having French colonies taken over by another power, and the rise of an African nationalism that would endanger France's hold over its colonies and the entire missionary enterprise.[9] Now, in the 1940s, the context was entirely different. Politically, Pétain and the empire had almost collapsed. General de Gaulle's image was still ambiguous for French allies across the Atlantic and some sectors of the Catholic establishment in France. In the Church, authorities from the Vatican were beating the drums of indigenisation in Africa. This was happening exactly at

---

1940–1943', *The International Journal of African Historical Studies* 33, no. 2 (2000): 291–312 – here, p. 292.

[7] Bernard Tissier de Mallerais, *The Biography: Marcel Lefebvre* (Kansas City, MO: Angelus Press, 2002), 146.

[8] Ibid., 146–47.

[9] Kenneth J. Orosz, 'The "Catechist War" in Interwar French Cameroon', in *In God's Empire. French Missionaries and the Modern World* (Oxford: Oxford University Press, 2012): 233–56 – here, p. 251.

a time when the strength of the Church in France was in serious crisis, and its focus seemed to shift inwards from overseas expansion.

In the middle of the war, in 1943, French priests Henri Godin and Yvan Daniel published a book that connected the crisis of the Church in France with a kind of reversal of the global missionary enterprise. They observed the growing secularising trends, especially among the working class, and wondered whether a change was long overdue for France: would the 'Fille aînée de l'Eglise' (elder daughter of the Church) be at the receiving end of the missionary enterprise? Would France become a mission country (*La France pays de mission*)? (France: A mission country?)[10]

There is no evidence that the authors had any intimate knowledge of Marc Bloch's work or the work of the Annales School of History. Yet, one cannot but notice a clear similarity in the way Godin and Daniel framed the de-Christianisation of France.[11] They talked about the milieu as an 'environmental paganism' that was swallowing France and its popular masses.[12] This milieu was not only geographical, splitting rural and urban France. It was also an ambiance of depravity of love in which Christians were dead drunk with 'spectacles', while showing no signs of guilt or emotion in the face of corruption and injustice: 'On n'y regrette rien, n'y sent aucune contrition' (people there have no regret; they feel no contrition).[13]

Even more concerning for the likes of Lefèbvre, liberal ideology and what they perceived as the downsides of liberalism seemed to be embraced by France's postwar Roman Catholicism.[14] Lefèbvre saw this period as a time of betrayal for traditional Catholicism and for French civilisation. His radical conservatism grew gradually as he witnessed how one pope after another seemingly turned away from the fight against Modernism in favour of a more progressivist and democratic agenda.

The contrast between Lefèbvre's conservatism and French Jesuitism was stark. Before the Second Vatican Council embraced the *aggiornamento*, the French Jesuits were already leaders of Catholic progressivism. *La nouvelle théologie* had prepared them for this moment; years of

---

[10] H. Godin and Y. Daniel, *La France, pays de mission?* (Paris: Les Editions de l'Abeille, 1943). All translations from French to English in this study are mine.

[11] Paul Coulon, 'De la France, pays de missionnaires à la France, pays de mission', *Histoire et Missions Chrétiennes* 9 (March 2009): 3–8.

[12] H. Godin and Y. Daniel, *La France, pays de mission?* (Paris: Les Editions de l'Abeille, 1943), 37.

[13] Ibid., 41.

[14] Bernard Sesboüé and Florian Michel, *De Mgr Lefèbvre à Mgr Williamson. Anatomie d'un schisme* (Paris: Lethielleux/DDB, 2009).

exile and sidelining of theologians like Henri de Lubac by the Vatican had prepared them to shape the ecclesiology of the council. Initiated by French Jesuits such as Gaston Fessard, Victor de Fontoymont, or Teilhard de Chardin, Jesuit progressivism culminated, in 1965, in the election of a progressive, Pedro Arrupe, as superior general of the Jesuits.

Jesuit progressivism, however, represented a shift from the conservatism of the Society of Jesus after its restoration (1814). A conservatism that continued with Jesuit leadership in France until the mid-forties. Norbert de Boynes, Vicar General of the Society of Jesus in Rome during the Second World War, and other Jesuit leaders like Joseph du Bouchet embodied Jesuit conservatism in France. Not surprisingly, as younger generations of Jesuits emerged in France, du Bouchet was sent to Chad in 1947. He became the first apostolic prefect and one of the founders of its Church. He also joined Lefèbvre and other French bishops to shape Church policies for the decades to come. In Chad, this policy was clearly conservative, averse to the clerical Africanisation promoted by the Vatican.

Du Bouchet's conservatism found a powerful ally in Africa. As head of the Church in French Africa, Lefèbvre viewed the 'neo-liberal' shift of the Church as synonymous with American Protestantism. At the core of the liberal agenda was competition, which some Protestant scholars framed in terms of schism and renewal.[15] The liberal trend within Catholicism, Lefèbvre feared, would trigger the end of French civilisation. According to Yves Congar, Lefèbvre believed that France would become like an 'Indian reservation' in the middle of an American Protestant civilisation.[16] The dangers of this liberal agenda were equal only to those of Communism and Islam, and drew a similar battlefield in the Jesuit Chad Mission.

Competition between traditional and liberal Roman Catholicism was only the beginning. This tension escalated after the Second Vatican Council. Lefèbvre became the last Church leader standing for traditional pre-Vatican II Roman Catholicism. He had become conservative to the point that even a conservative Catholic like General de Gaulle seemed too liberal for him. In truth, de Gaulle was a centrist Republican, and a moderate Catholic who had studied with the Jesuits and kept excellent relationships with them. One of his most loyal generals, Philippe Leclerc, became one of the pillars of the early years of the Jesuit mission in Chad.

[15] David B. Barrett, *Schism and Renewal in Africa: An Analysis of Six Thousand Contemporary Religious Movements* (London: Oxford University Press, 1968).
[16] Yves Congar, *La crise dans l'église et Mgr Lefèbvre* (Paris: Cerf, 1976), 64–65.

For better or for worse, the beginnings of the Jesuit mission in Chad grew out of a shattered French Catholicism. Chad served as a refuge for its traditionalism. The agenda of missionaries sent to Chad reacted to the threats presented to this traditionalism by both liberal Catholicism and Islam. As a result, the mission became an opportunity for the French political elite and missionaries to reassert and reinvent themselves. From the exploratory period of the mission to its formal recognition by Rome in 1946, conservative Jesuits and Gaullists worked hand and hand to establish the Church in Chad. Their main difference was that the head of the Fourth Republic was able to integrate communists in his governing coalition in Paris. In Chad, however, the anti-Communism of the missionaries was uncompromising.

Rebuilding the prestige of France took the form of political Frenchification through the Union Française. The religious and cultural agenda of the Union attempted to cut off the secularising trend that sprouted from the traditional *mission civilisatrice*. France's Catholicism might have been in crisis in France; yet, it was a key element of the country's African outreach from the 1940s to the late 1970s.

The Second World War had made Chadians key allies of Gaullism. From the 1920s, the so-called 'Pacification' of Chad by the French that had started in 1898 was officially over. When France collapsed under German tanks, Chadians were the first to enlist in support of de Gaulle's France Libre. Following the war, the military garrisons that had served for the pacification of Chad in the late nineteenth century were turned into bases for France to reassert its supremacy over its equatorial colonies. Attending to the spiritual needs of this French military personnel was a key factor that triggered the creation of a Jesuit mission in Chad.

By the early 1930s, French missionaries went to Chad to sustain the cultural 'pacification' of the country. This project was a continuation of the *mission civilisatrice*, although it attempted to strip the civilising mission of its secularising trend. It was also a time when French Africa was moving towards political self-determination, and when several popes were moving the Church towards Africanisation of its personnel and structures. As they arrived in Chad, early French Jesuit missionaries were convinced that back home, a communist infiltration in society was the biggest threat to France's way of life. Therefore, if left unchecked in French Africa, which they considered the African extension of the homeland, the communist threat would destroy the French political and missionary empires.

How strong the risk of Chad becoming communist in the 1940s actually was, however, remains unclear. The sources available from this period, primarily from the government, the Jesuits, and other Catholic and Protestant missions, reveal a country that was strongly dominated by Muslims in its northern part. It was increasingly Christianised in the south, although the southern region was still shaped by Chadian traditional religiosity.

Having settled earlier than the Jesuits, Protestant churches had built catechetical schools, and had their first Chadians ordained for ministry in 1944. Similarly, since the 1920s, the Vatican had also opted for the rapid Africanisation of Church personnel and hierarchy. It saw this as the best strategy for securing the survival of the Church after the end of the colonial empires. Yet, this Vatican approach opened a veiled competition with French Jesuits in Chad. They cared less about the Africanisation of Church personnel. They gave priority, instead, to the building of a Chadian Church spared from the worms that threatened French Catholicism and the secularising trend of African nationalism which was taking place among Chadian Protestants. Alongside French soldiers and colonists, whose morals and beliefs were not trusted by the missionaries, the latter would form a spiritual army with the primary goal of converting Chadians to Christ. They would do so by developing popular religious programmes aimed at social transformation. Behind their religious aims, those programmes also served as a means to uproot any trace of Communism and Islam, or at least contain both from spreading southwards.

Chad's Loyalty to France amid a Turbulent Empire

From 1945 to 1948, the unrest in the French colonial empire increased the sense that it was the end of an era. There is no better description of the situation than the one made by historian James E. Genova:

> The empire was in ebullition. Riots erupted in Algeria. Confrontations in 1945 between Vietnamese nationalists and French troops in Indo-China progressed to full-scale war by the end of 1946. Insurrection swept Madagascar in 1947, and as early as 1943, demonstrations in French West Africa had obliged the head of the provisional government, General Charles de Gaulle, to sack the governor–general and appoint officials acceptable to the local political elites.[17]

Genova describes the collapse of the French global empire from Senegal to Madagascar and Algeria to Vietnam. He also shows how French officials planned to transition from their one-sided dominant

---

[17] James E. Genova, 'Constructing Identity in Post-War France: Citizenship, Nationality, and the Lamine Guèye Law, 1946–1953', *The International History Review* 26, no. 1 (2004): 56–79 – here, p. 57.

position to a more cooperative one that fitted the political evolution of French colonies towards independence. It became increasingly clear after the war that the basic question was how would France maintain its influence after the collapse of its African empire. According to Genova, from 1943, Frenchification was similar to 'Afro-localisation'. The government of de Gaulle sacked the French leadership in the colonies to appoint other French officials 'acceptable to the local political elite'.[18]

The French political agenda in Africa and that of the Vatican looked quite similar. Yet, Elizabeth A. Foster has also shown the degree of anxiety that the Vatican agenda raised among the French conservative elite. They believed that 'the church was betraying its European base by cultivating African clergy or manifesting support for anticolonial movements'.[19] From France's perspective, the political Africanisation had to be co-opted. This meant cultivating African national leaders who would be favourable to France. This agenda clashed with ecclesial Africanisation. Although missions received subsidies from the French government, having French missionaries replaced by non-French, whether Europeans or Africans, was perceived with great suspicion. It rang alarm bells among some intellectuals like François Méjan, who believed that the Vatican was actually working against French interests in Africa.[20]

In her two major books,[21] Foster and other historians such as Charlotte Walker-Said and Giuliana Chamedes[22] all see the disruptive nature of Church organisations in colonial Africa during the interwar period and

[18] Ibid.
[19] Foster, *African Catholic: Decolonization*, 84.
[20] François Méjan, *Le Vatican contre la France d'Outre-Mer?* (Paris: Librairie Fischbacher, 1957).
[21] Elizabeth Foster, 'A Mission in Transition', 257–77; *Faith in Empire: Religion, Politics, and Colonial Rule in French Senegal, 1880–1940* (Stanford, CA: Stanford University Press, 2013); *African Catholic: Decolonization*.
[22] Charlotte Walker-Said, 'Christian Social Movements in Cameroon at the End of Empire: Transnational Solidarities and the Communion of the World Church', in *Relocating World Christianity: Interdisciplinary Studies in Universal and Local Expressions of Christianity* (Leiden: Brill, 2017), 189–212; *Faith, Power and Family: Christianity and Social Change in French Cameroon*, Religion in Transforming Africa (Woodbridge, UK: James Currey, 2018); Elizabeth Foster and Giuliana Chamedes, 'Introduction: Decolonization and Religion in Modern French History', *French Politics, Culture & Society* 33, no. 2 (2015): 1–10; Giuliana Chamedes, 'The Catholic Origins of Economic Development after World War II', *French Politics, Culture & Society* 33, no. 2 (Summer 2015): 55–75.

right after the Second World War. Since Pope Benedict XV's *Maximum Illud* and Pope Pius XI's *Rerum Ecclesiae*,[23] the Vatican had pushed for ecclesial Africanisation. The Vatican's ecclesial Africanisation differed from de Gaulle's Afro-localisation in that the Vatican meant to raise an African leadership and not, as was the case in Chad, a European leadership acceptable to Africans. Like France, however, this new leadership was promoted on the sole condition that it would remain loyal to the Vatican.

This Vatican agenda anticipated what French politicians were planning in the mid-forties. French missionaries going to Africa in this context were confronted with the challenge of double loyalty. Their evangelising mission was directed by Vatican authorities that since the First World War had been mainly concerned with securing the survival of a Catholic Church that was truly African and still loyal to Rome. Yet, the missionaries employed to implement this agenda were French patriots concerned with Frenchification.

France's 'pacification' agenda in Chad argued that French colonialism was a moral necessity. The Islamic Razzias and jihad had ravaged non-Muslim populations and reduced classes of populations in Chad to slavery. Chadians who resisted this Islamic push had taken refuge in naturally secure zones in the mountains. To colonise Chad was therefore interpreted as a necessary task to end these wars and protect vulnerable Chadians. By the beginning of the First World War in 1914, French domination already expanded over a vast territory covering almost all the territory of Western and Central Sudan,[24] from Senegal to Ubangi-Chari.

Situated at the centre of the Great Sudan, the French military base in Chad was highly strategic.[25] It served as a military support for the

---

[23] Benedict XV, 'Maximum Illud. De Fide Catholica per Orbem Terrarum Propaganda,' *AAS* 11 (30 November 30, 1919): 440–55; Pope Pius XI, 'Rerum Ecclesiae', *AAS* 72 (28 February 1926): 65–83; Roger Onomo Etaba, 'Maximum Illud, de Benoît XV, et l'oeuvre missionnaire au Cameroun (1890–1935): Entre anticipations, applications et contradictions', *Présence Africaine* 172 (2005): 125–45; .

[24] This refers to the historical 'Great Sudan', which was divided into Eastern, Central, and Western Sudan. The first comprised the middle Nile basin, which was colonised first by the Egyptians and then by the English; the second comprised the Lake Chad basin and the countries east of the lower Niger, which were colonised by the French, and the third comprised the countries from the Atlantic (i.e. what is now Senegal) to lower Niger.

[25] For strategic reasons, France had intermittently maintained a military base

project of the Wider France, which celebrated the apotheosis of French overseas expansion after the First World War.[26] Not only had France kept the totality of its colonies in 1919, but it also inherited other territories from its German rival.[27] In the late 1920s, as the first Catholic missions settled in Chad, the pacification of Chad added a cultural and spiritual component. To pacify, to civilise, and to Frenchify were all parts of the mission to evangelise.

Social Unrest in Chad and a Downgraded 'Mission Civilisatrice'

From the 1930s to the 1940s, the social situation in Chad did not make it the most desirable place for Europeans, even zealous missionaries, to either adventure or retire. This decade was marked by drought, famine, and social unrest. The unravelling of Chad's social order led to internal migrations and exposed the failures of French colonial policies. Yet by the end of the decade, as the Second World War began, Chadians rallied around the French governor, Felix Eboué. He was an ally of Charles de Gaulle who opposed the Vichy regime, which was ruling in France at that time.

The Vichy regime, in addition to being an embarrassment for French long-held ideals, was also both xenophobic and paternalistic towards Africans.[28] Yet, by entering the war, Chadians were the first to join the African military coalition led by 'General Leclerc'.[29] Those Chadians in military service also discovered a world beyond the Sahara. They saw for

---

in Chad from September 1900. Cf. Ministère de la France d'Outre-Mer, *Le Tchad* (Paris: Agence de la France d'Outre-Mer, 1950), 6.

[26] Raoul Girardet, 'L'apothéose de la "Plus Grande France": L'idée coloniale devant l'opinion française, 1930–1935', *Revue Française de Science Politique* 18, no. 6 (December 1968): 1085–114 – here, p. 1086.

[27] Girardet, 'L'apothéose de la "Plus Grande France"', 1094. The 'Wider France' also advocates for a 'humanising' French colonial system. In fact, André Gide published the first anti-colonial book in France during that same period. See: André Gide, *Voyage au Congo: Suivi du retour du Tchad* (Paris, 1929). While these early publications condemned the 'abuses' of the colonial system, they nevertheless did not question the colonial ideology as such.

[28] Majhemout Diop et al., 'Tropical and Equatorial Africa under French, Portuguese and Spanish Domination, 1935–45', in *Histoire Générale de l'Afrique*, vol. 8, 8 vols (Paris: UNESCO, 1999): 58–75 – here, p. 66. Governor Eboué was a black man from French Guiana.

[29] His full name was Philippe François-Marie de Hauteclocque (1902–47). He changed his name to protect his family during the war. In: André Martel, 'L'Afrique Française Libre: Support d'effort de guerre française et Allié,

themselves regions so far only described to them by merchants and pilgrims. Crossing North Africa, they fought for the liberation of France and other regions in Western Europe.[30]

Participating in the liberation of France came with some benefits as far as the perception of Africans among Europeans was concerned. African soldiers also assessed how far African participation in the politics of the metropole could go. The two global wars had tested the loyalty of indigenous members of the empire towards France.[31] Parliamentary and public debates turned towards the imminent future of these members. For Marshal Philippe Pétain and the Vichy regime, the French colonies were the territorial extension France needed in order to maintain any relevance in world affairs once the war ended.[32] However, while African lands, gunmen, and natural resources appealed to the metropole, the extension of French citizenship to Africans remained unpopular among the French elite. Africans, even and especially the most educated, regularly experienced 'racist attitudes, and discrimination'.[33]

The rise to power of Charles de Gaulle reframed Franco-African relations. The end of the war created new narratives around immigration to France among Africans. The African soldiers who fought during the war often faced resistance from French society when they attempted to naturalise there, but were privileged by the colonial administration when they returned home. The economic advantages they received from France as 'Anciens Combattants' (war veterans) also made some of them more averse to African nationalism.[34] France took advantage of this sentiment by inviting French colonies and territories to join the newly created Union Française. The terms of this offer, however, remained as ambiguous as the so-called *mission civilisatrice*. In Chad, especially, de Gaulle's Frenchification came with a downgraded *mission civilisatrice*.

1940–1942', in *Le Général Leclerc et l'Afrique Française Libre, 1940–1942* (Paris: Fondation Maréchal Leclerc, 1987), 87–105.

[30] Ministère de la France d'Outre-Mer, *Le Tchad*, 3.

[31] Girardet, 'L'apothéose de La "Plus Grande France"', 1087.

[32] Ruth Ginio, 'Vichy Rule in French West Africa: Prelude to Decolonization?' *French Colonial History* 4 (2003): 205–26. The resistance led by Charles de Gaulle shared the same belief that French colonies were key for the restoration of France.

[33] Ginio, 'Vichy Rule in French West Africa', 216; Genova, 'Constructing Identity in Post-War France', 5.

[34] Mann, 'Immigrants and Arguments in France and West Africa', 375–76.

The proposed transition towards the Communauté Française (French Community), which de Gaulle made in Brazzaville in 1944, effectively made the shift from colonial rule towards political self-determination less urgent. The policies put in place to reaffirm France's domination over its colonies became a response to a sense of general malaise in the French empire. This malaise was doubled by an aspiration for France's restoration.[35] For General de Gaulle, Francophone Africa represented a reserve of loyal servants able to rebuild France. These were an important factor for keeping the dream of the empire alive.[36] The French control over Chad's natural resources, military, and diplomacy continued. It was even reaffirmed in the early 1960s, after independence, with the Franco-Chadian partnership treaties.[37]

To embrace French colonies while refusing their residents the right to citizenship also meant promising them self-determination while denying them independence. French political leaders such as the Minister of the Colonies George Mandel vowed to respect indigenous cultures. These government officials never expected, however, that African colonies would immediately become independent.[38] The Brazzaville Conference of 1944 reaffirmed this trend. It laid the foundations for France's relationship with its African colonies after the war. The Brazzaville Conference also rejected 'any possibility of evolution outside the French Empire'. It stated clearly that the possibility of 'the constitution of self-government in the colonies, even in the distant future, [was] to be excluded'.[39]

For Africans, there were loopholes in the new partnership to exploit to their advantage. The early defeat of France at the beginning of the war, the competing ideologies and propagandas opposing the Vichy regime, de Gaulle's resistance to it on African soil, and the self-awareness of the African intellectual elite sowed the seeds of an African resistance to French colonialism. Catholic missions in Africa had to choose between the two loyalties, unless, as was the case in Chad, Catholics were less involved in the politics of political nationalism.

---

[35] Editors, 'Le malaise du monde', *Revue Politique et Parlementaire* 559 (September 1946): 176–77.
[36] André Martel, 'L'Afrique Française Libre', 102.
[37] Gali Ngothe Gatta, *Tchad, la grande guerre pour le pouvoir, 1979–1980* (N'Djamena: Centre Al-Mouna, 2007), 166–68.
[38] Foster, *Faith in Empire*, 172.
[39] Quoted in: Diop et al., 'Tropical and Equatorial Africa under French, Portuguese and Spanish Domination, 1935–45', 74.

Catholic Missions amid the Collapse of the French Empire

Frédéric de Bélinay, the founder of the Jesuit Mission in Chad, looked desperately at the communist 'invasion' in French villages in the early 1950s. Like him, most of his French Jesuit colleagues understood their Chad Mission as a service to God and to their homeland, France, and its interests in Sahelian Africa. The collapse of colonial empires across Africa had alerted the Vatican to the urgent necessity of Africanising. Not surprisingly, and although for different motives, the clerical Africanisation which the Vatican put in place emulated the political Africanisation.

The renewed interest of the Vatican in indigenisation was based on fear. Since mission and colonialism had seemed to work hand and hand, the Vatican feared that the sudden collapse of the latter could trigger the collapse of the Church as well. The survival of the Church depended on raising an African clergy and leadership in the Church alongside the political African elite. But for a country like Chad, where there was no Catholic Church established until the 1930s, the Africanisation enterprise would take longer than elsewhere in Africa. French Jesuit missionaries, who were among the first evangelisers of Chad, were increasingly caught between two loyalties.

There was loyalty to the Vatican and its calling for Africanisation. One pope after another had pushed for the building up of an African clergy that would secure the continuity of the Church after the end of European colonial empires in Africa. The 1914 war had just ended when Pope Benedict XV published his missionary encyclical *Maximum Illud*, which called for the indigenisation of the Church personnel and hierarchy.[40] The papal document also followed President Woodrow Wilson's blueprint for peace negotiations. From Wilson's fourteen points emerged a new consciousness of internationalism in Christian missions.

In this context, the 'missionaries overwhelmingly supported the idea of self-determination of peoples'.[41] With indigenisation, the new internationalism became 'two sides of the same coin'.[42] During the interwar period, the Roman Catholic Church confirmed this trend towards indigenisation with

---

[40] Benedict XV, Encyclica epistola 'Maximum Illud. De Fide Catholica per Orbem Terrarum Propaganda', *AAS* 11 (Rome: 30 November 1919).

[41] Dana L. Robert, *Christian Mission: How Christianity Became a World Religion* (Malden, MA: Blackwell, 2009), 65.

[42] Dana L. Robert, 'The First Globalization: The Internationalization of the Protestant Missionary Movement between the World Wars', *International Bulletin of Missionary Research* 26, no. 2 (2002): 50.

'Rerum Ecclesiae' (1926),[43] followed in 1951 by *Evangelii Praecones*.[44] In 1957, three years prior to the independence of most French colonies in Africa, Pope Pius XII published another missionary encyclical, *Fidei Donum*.[45] Again, that encyclical pushed for an increase in mission personnel in Africa. It urged 'that a carefully trained Catholic elite be formed at once from the multitudes already converted'.[46]

Pius XII aimed at addressing the shortage in mission personnel and their lack of material sustenance. Across the continent, Africans were ordained to the priesthood and to the episcopate,[47] a historical moment that coincided with the rise of African nationalisms. However, this shift from a colonial mindset in politics and in the Church to an increased African consciousness brought to light the paradoxes of the *mission civilisatrice*. Different Catholicities effectively shaped competing agendas in the Church in French West Africa.[48] Moreover, European missionaries 'found that they could not countenance the logical outcome of their own vaunted civilizing mission: a church directed by Africans'.[49]

For some of the French missionaries working in Chad, loyalty to their own country and its ideals shaped the civilising mission of their work.[50] They gave Chadians an education that was good enough for them to become catechists in the Church or auxiliaries in the colonial administration. The education of Chadians was not good enough to allow them to aspire to leadership in the Church or true self-determination. In addition to clinging to power, another reason why the European missionaries delayed the Africanisation of the Church in Chad was a contextual one.

[43] Benedict XV, 'Maximum Illud. De Fide Catholica per Orbem Terrarum Propaganda'; Pius XI, 'Rerum Ecclesiae', 28 February 1926.
[44] Pius XII, 'Evangelii Praecones', *AAS* 510 (1951): 497–528.
[45] Pope Pius XII believed that 'the Church should be solidly established among other peoples, and a hierarchy given to them chosen from among their own sons' (Pius XII, 'Encyclica epistola *Fidei Donum*', *AAS* 49 [Rome: 1957]: 225–48 – here, p. 244).
[46] Ibid.
[47] Jean-Paul Messina, *Jean Zoa, Prêtre, Archevêque de Yaoundé: 1922–1998* (Paris: Karthala, 2000), 56.
[48] Alice L. Conklin, *A Mission to Civilize: The Republican Idea of Empire in France and West Africa, 1895–1930* (Stanford, CA: Stanford University Press, 1997), 1–2.
[49] Foster, *Faith in Empire*, 170–3; Foster and Chamedes, 'Introduction: Decolonization and Religion in Modern French History'.
[50] Foster, *Faith in Empire*, 12.

There were not that many Chadian candidates for priesthood because of a limited number of lettered men and a Christian culture. The rise of European nation-states in the 1930s and its consequences for Europe and the world also caused European Jesuits to distrust nationalist ideologies everywhere.[51] According to R. Pierce Beaver, while missionaries often took credit for stimulating nationalism after the First World War – because they saw nationalism as a necessary step towards internationalism – that situation changed during the interwar period. The havoc of two world wars had convinced missionaries of the dangers of nationalism. In response, they crafted and promoted a well-controlled supra-nationalism.[52]

The new internationalism and the new global Catholicism promoted a spirituality that claimed respect for indigenous people. This spirituality of respect also came with a Catholic supra-nationalism and was supported by an ecclesiastical apparatus that, paradoxically, also suppressed national sensibilities for the sake of universality and Catholicity. According to Beaver,

> The supervision of the Sacred Congregation of the Propagation of the Faith, the international basis of support provided by the Society of the Propagation of the Faith, the world-wide hierarchy, the liturgical uniformity of the Roman Rite, the identical seminary system everywhere and the discipline of the rules of the various international orders all tend to suppress the national identification of the Roman Catholic missionary and to emphasize his supranational character.[53]

Several religious international congregations, especially the Holy Ghost Fathers, had carried out the French Catholic agenda in Africa.[54] While their proposed supra-nationalism was not challenged on the basis of national ideologies during the colonial period, this situation changed with the Jesuits in West Africa, especially in Cameroon, where the first Cameroonian Jesuits had a national and Africanist-oriented understanding of their place in the Church.

In addition to the inherent Gallicanism that presided over the beginning of the Jesuit Chad Mission, there was also the combination of national politics in Europe and the rapid evolution of the political situation in

---

[51] In R. Pierce Beaver, 'Missions and the New Nationalism', *Journal of Church and State* 3, no. 2 (November 1961): 149–71 – here, p. 155.
[52] Ibid.
[53] R. Pierce Beaver, 'Nationalism and Missions', *Church History* 26, no. 1 (March 1957): 22–42 – here, p. 24.
[54] Adrien Remy, *Les Spiritains face à l'indépendance du Cameroun* (Yaoundé: PUCAC, 2012).

Africa. After the experience of European Fascism, the rise of African nation-states and the spread of communist ideas within them after the war made the French Jesuits in Chad particularly averse to a Catholic elite that embraced African nationalism. How, then, could European missionaries effectively comply with the Vatican elitist agenda in Africa without giving in to African nationalisms? In Chad, the Jesuits avoided this dilemma by opting for a popular-oriented type of Christianity, breaking away from the Vatican's approach.[55] Among them, there was always an unreadiness to be led by Africans because they remained confident of their own superiority.

De Bélinay, Islam, and American Protestants in Chad

The arrival of de Bélinay in Chad in 1935 and the official recognition of the mission by Propaganda Fide in 1946 coincided with the beginning of the decolonisation movement across Africa. Yet, the Jesuits largely remained silent on the political environment of Chad at the time of their arrival.[56] There is, however, evidence of not only some form of ideological continuity, but also logistical support for the mission coming from colonial officials. The military, especially, played a role in the planning of the mission and in parts of its execution. De Bélinay and other first missionaries in Chad had a military background. General Leclerc chose the place for the construction of the cathedral of Fort-Lamy and supported it financially. His wife was present the day the cathedral was inaugurated. Some trips by Jesuit officials also had logistical help from military officials in Chad.

There was also a divide between some colonists who did not want Christian missions to settle in Chad. For them, missionaries taught indigenous people how to think. Some other missionaries wanted Catholic missions to educate Chadians to facilitate their integration as members of the Union Française.[57] For its part, the French government temporarily supported the Jesuits'

---

[55] Cf. Jean Luc Enyegue, 'The Jesuits and Popular Education in Chad, 1946–1975' (African Studies Association Annual Meeting, Chicago, IL, 2018), 35.

[56] Having made few comments about the improved conditions for Chadian society due to education, health services, road building, etc., Jacques Fédry's introduction to the arrival of the Jesuits in Chad skips forward from the early 1930s to 1952, leaving untouched almost two decades of nationalist history. Cf. A. Hallaire and J. Fédry, *Naissance d'une église africaine: Lettres et chroniques du Pays Sarh* (Paris: Karthala, 1998), 13–14.

[57] On F. de Bélinay, cf. French Jesuit archives (AJ), 'Dossier personnel', Boxes 1457, 1458, and 1459; J. Fortier, *Frédéric de Bélinay. Pionnier des missions du Tchad*, vols 1–2, 2 vols (Fort-Lamy: Imprimerie du Tchad, 1958).

educational projects in Chad. France's support for religious education sought, primarily, to protect its strategic interests in Chad while, at the same time, softening its image among the colonised people.

French colonial policy in Africa used a dual discourse. It claimed to support the further integration of African countries and people into the French Union. Such an assimilationist interpretation considered the goal of Christian missions as being 'to mold Africans into loyal Catholic French subjects'.[58] Similar interpretations existed in the ways France dealt with Muslims in Africa. Its policies aimed at making Muslim West Africans 'as good Moslems as Frenchmen'.[59] For French officials, therefore, educating Chadians primarily meant making them useful for the general interests of France.[60] However, in a different discourse, education in French colonies also aimed to promote indigenous cultures and the rights of African peoples. In theory, education sought to promote indigenisation. In practice, however, it became known as Frenchification.

An international conference on colonial education was held in Paris in 1931. In theory, the conference aimed at 'adapting' the schooling system in Africa to 'local needs'.[61] Yet, the African Évolués elite class and colonial administrators worked to make education as similar as possible to France's. Curricula were adapted to those of the metropole. Students received equivalent, if not similar, diplomas.[62] Frenchification, it appears, helped to link Chad's national identity to the idea of making Chad part of the Union Française.[63]

The Union also diminished Chad's ability to assert its selfhood as a nation.[64] The more the metropole embraced French colonies, the more

---

[58] Foster, *Faith in Empire*, 11.

[59] Benjamin Soares, '"Being as Good Muslims as Frenchmen": On Islam and Colonial Modernity in West Africa', *Journal of Religion in Africa* 39, no. 1 (2009): 91–120 .

[60] Catherine Coquery-Vidrovitch, 'Colonisation ou impérialisme: La politique africaine de la France entre les deux guerres', *Le Mouvement Social* 107 (1979): 51–76 – here, pp. 54 and 75.

[61] Harry Gamble, 'La crise de l'enseignement en Afrique Occidentale Française (1944–1950)', *Histoire de l'Éducation* 128 (2010): 129–162 – here, p. 130.

[62] Ibid., 130.

[63] It might be worth recalling that the very idea of extending French citizenship to indigenous people from French overseas territories enjoyed a high level of approval among all social and political layers. Cf. Genova, 'Constructing Identity in Post-War France', 59 and 70.

[64] Thomas Martin has shown that from 1919, Albert Sarraut's assimilationist policies in French colonies deliberately moved from an established policy that colonies should be self-supporting to a policy that favoured the active

it contributed to delaying their self-determination. From 1925, socialist governments in France pushed for secular education in schools while adjusting to a communist agenda that supported anti-imperialism and the right of nations to self-determination. In that sense, the cause of the delays to African self-determination can be attributed to conservative governments, the ultimate leader of which was General Charles de Gaulle.[65] The Brazzaville Conference excluded Africa's self-determination.[66] It also vowed to maintain, and even improve, 'traditional' – and by this it actually meant 'rural' – educational structures.[67]

For Chadians, to go to war alongside French and other African soldiers also meant visiting, for the first time, the home of their colonial masters and that of the men and women who were 'invading' their villages to evangelise them. For a country that seemed isolated geographically and that faced a plethora of social challenges, Chad, as part of the Great Sudan, became increasingly appealing for Christian missions in the mid-twentieth century. As they settled in Chad, not only did Christian missionaries advance their specific form of Christianity, but their very presence also made Chad a microcosm of global Christianity. Missions opened Chad not only to its African neighbours, but also to the Church worldwide.

Chadian historian Maioulam Mbairougol has established that the first contact that Chad had with Christianity was in the seventeenth century. Back then, the Capuchins attempted to evangelise Chad in 1663.[68] The Capuchins' failed experiment left a vacuum that was not filled until after the First World

---

    participation of the state in the economic development of the colonies. He believed such state involvement was important as a means to secure France's imperial security and to bind the rising indigenous elite to the colonial state. Cf. Thomas Martin, 'Albert Sarraut, French Colonial Development, and the Communist Threat, 1919–1930', *The Journal of Modern History* 77, no. 4 (December 2005): 917–55 – here, p. 926.

[65] Cf. Maurice Vallet, 'Le laïcisme dans l'enseignement actuel', *Etudes Religieuses* 189 (5 November 1926): 257–81 – here, p. 262.

[66] Quoted in: Diop et al., 'Tropical and Equatorial Africa under French, Portuguese and Spanish Domination, 1935–45', 74.

[67] 'Colonial education will avoid [...] harming traditional structures because it is essential that peoples develop according to their own genius [...] Education will generally conform to the methods and curricula of France, adapted to Africa, with a large part devoted to handicrafts, agricultural and household initiation and physical education. It will be the least bookish possible, well established in the life of villages': David E. Gardinier, 'Les recommandations de la Conférence de Brazzaville sur les problèmes d'éducation', *Brazzaville* (January–February 1944): 170–80.

[68] Maioulam Mbairougol, 'Implantation et impact des missions protestantes

War. In 1920, an American-based missionary group, the Lutheran Fraternal Mission, led by Norwegian pastors Kaardal and Berge Revne settled at Lere (Chad).[69] Prior to Chad, they had brought the gospel message to parts of Cameroon and Nigeria.[70] From the United States Paul Metzeler, leading the Mid-Baptist African Mission, arrived in Chad in 1923 and settled in Fort-Archambault. Other Protestant groups included the Assemblies of God (1925), led by an Australian pastor, John Olley; the South Sudan Mission, with Americans, Canadians, Swiss, French, Dutch, and Germans (1926); and the Brothers' Evangelical Church (1935).[71] By 1962, most of the Protestant missions had created national churches under Chadian leadership.[72]

On the Catholic side, de Bélinay never used the term Africanisation. Yet, by obtaining the Vatican's official approval of the mission in 1946, he initiated the creation of Chad as an autonomous ecclesiastical jurisdiction.[73] De Bélinay and his Jesuit colleagues in French Africa were, in this initial stage, middlemen negotiating the rise of a new global order. This order was still French in Chad, more strongly American – therefore leading to anti-American sentiment among French missionaries – and increasingly African.

Standing up to Islamic and American Influence in Chad

Writing from Algeria in December 1945, de Bélinay warned the French Governor of French Equatorial Africa (AEF) against the ongoing 'invasion of American Protestant missionaries'.[74] His complaints were an echo of

---

dans le Logone Occidental au sud du Tchad: 1926–1997' (MA thesis in History, University of Ngaoundéré, 2009).

[69] Reverend Kaardal's full name is not mentioned in the original document, yet there is a reference to J. I. and Sophie Kaardal as founders of the Lutheran Church in northern Cameroon around the same period. It is not impossible that the same couple went north to evangelise southern Chad. Kim-Eric Williams, 'Cameroon', in *Dictionary of Lutheran and the Lutheran Traditions* (Grand Rapids, MI: Baker Academic, 2017).

[70] Ibid.

[71] Maioulam Mbairougol, 'Implantation et impact des missions protestantes', 100.

[72] Islam in Chad was equally diverse, with influences from Sudan, Libya, Egypt, Nigeria, and northern Cameroon.

[73] Granito di Belmonte and Fumasoni-Biondi, 'Erigitur Nova Praefectura Apostolica Arcis Lamy (in Tchad) et Societatis (Prov. Lugdunensi) Committitur', *AAS* 11 (1947): 216–17.

[74] Frédéric de Bélinay, 'Lettre au Gouverneur de l'AEF', in ANOM-FM-1AFF-PO: 2180/5: 'Evangélisation du Tchad, 1945–1947'. In a letter to General de

what French missionaries and colonial authorities in Chad had expressed a few months earlier about Islam. On 17 August 1945, Paul Joseph Biechy, apostolic vicar of Brazzaville, wrote to Henri Laurentie, director of political affairs in the ministère des Colonies. Having observed the complete absence of Catholic missionaries in Chad, Biechy urged Laurentie, at the request of Governor Rogué of Chad, to implement what his predecessor René Pleven had envisioned.

Pleven had argued that it was imperative to block (*faire barrage*) the 'invasion' of Muslims in Chad.[75] For both Biechy and Pleven, this barrage was so important that France's highest interests in the region were at stake. The Algerian War, Pleven argued, had made clear what the Muslims in French Africa were up to.[76] They were a threat to regional stability and the 'pacification' France had given to its entire colonial project in Chad and the surrounding regions.

Given the regional influence of Chad, France could not let that 'invasion' go unchecked. A note from the office of the Governor of the AEF could not be clearer:

> The territory of Chad is 'key' from the political, economic, and military point of view (notably military aviation, as we have seen during this war). However, we have made too little effort to make this territory one of the essential elements of the African equilibrium. To the three-fold African position (economic, political, military) of the Territory, a cultural position must be added. Of Chad's 2 million inhabitants, half are 'Arabisants' and half 'pagans'. It is here that the advanced bastion of Christian influence must be created to balance foreign influences from East and West.[77]

Gaulle, de Bélinay reiterated the same opinion a few months later, insisting upon the Christianisation of Chad as a necessity for peace in the region. Cf. F. de Bélinay, 'Lettre au Général de Gaulle, 11 Octobre 1945'.

[75] Mgr P. Biechy, 'Lettre au Ministre des Colonies, Direction des Affaires Politiques, 17 Août 1945', in ANOM-FM-1AFF-PO: 2180/5: 'Evangélisation du Tchad, 1945–1947'.

[76] Ibid. A year later, a confidential note from the Oblates of Mary Immaculate to the Minister of Overseas Affairs raised a similar alarm (14 August 1946).

[77] 'Le territoire du Tchad est une "marche" au point de vue politique, économique, militaire (notamment aviation militaire: on l'a vu au cours de cette guerre). Or nous n'avons encore réalisé que trop peu d'efforts pour faire de ce territoire un des éléments essentiels de l'équilibre africain. A la triple position africaine (économique, politique, militaire) du Territoire une position culturelle doit s'ajouter au plus tôt. Sur 2 millions d'habitants, il y a au Tchad moitié d'arabisants et moitié de "païens". C'est donc ici que doit se

This is the clearest definition of the goal of Christian missions in Chad as elaborated by a government official. The colonial office believed Chad to be strategically important, not only because of its military contribution alongside France during the Second World War, but also because its strategic situation in the heart of Africa made Chad indispensable for regional stability and for the defence of French interests in the region.

There is a paradox in the governor's declaration. He is warning against an ongoing Muslim 'invasion'. He also acknowledges that half of Chad's population were 'Arabisants'. These 'Arabisants' grew out of the *Sanusiyya* Muslim fraternities, as opposed to the *Tijaniyya* fraternity, which was more tolerant of the colonial project.[78] For Chad's so-called 'Arabisant' Muslims, though, the invaders were the French. It was their multi-century Arabo-Islamic civilisation that was threatened by the French invaders.

The 'Arabisants' in Chad were a class of Muslims who wanted Arabic to be the official language of Chad. They also fought for a reconciliation with the Pan-Arabo-Islamic world and rejected Western (and Christian) civilisation. They advocated for a literary interpretation of the *Qur'an*, and the restoration of a global Islamic community, or *Umma*.[79] In this particular context, the so-called 'invasion' might have been the growing influence that Wahhabism and political Islam from Algeria, Egypt, and Mecca had on Chad following the Second World War.[80] Though still a minority in the 1950s, Chad's 'Arabisants' were more religiously enthusiastic than other Muslim groups existing in Chad.

Since the eleventh century, the Islamisation of the kingdom of Kanem had deepened diplomatic and economic contacts with Egypt. This diplomatic outreach was accompanied by the creation of a *madrasa* in Cairo in 1242 for Chadian pilgrims to Mecca.[81] In the sixteenth and seventeenth centuries, the Baguirmi and Wadday kingdoms of Chad made Arabic the official language of their administrations. Abéché became the capital of this Arabisation agenda, moving beyond the mere adoption of the Arabic

---

    créer le bastion avancé de l'influence chrétienne pour équilibrer les influences étrangères venant de l'Est et de l'Ouest.' Cf. ANOM-FM-1AFF-PO: 2180/5: Frédéric de Bélinay, 'Lettre à Henri Laurentie, October 24, 1945'.

[78] Claude Arditi, 'Le Tchad et le monde arabe: Essai d'analyse des relations commerciales de la période précoloniale à aujourd'hui', *Afrique Contemporaine* 3, no. 207 (2003): 185–98.

[79] Henri Coudray, 'Langue, religion, identité, pouvoir: le contentieux linguistique franco-arabe au Tchad', *Centre Al-Mouna* 1 (1998): 19–69 – here, p. 42.

[80] Arditi, 'Le Tchad et le monde arabe', 202.

[81] Ibid., 21.

language to embrace its culture. 'Arabisants' showed growing contempt for other Muslims with either Turkish or Africanised (the *Tijaniyya*) cultural components. King Saboun of Wadday confirmed this Arabising trend in the nineteenth century. He multiplied the construction of Arabic schools in his kingdom and encouraged his subjects to receive their religious training in Egypt and Mecca.[82]

The agenda of the 'Arabisants' was moving towards frontal collision with the French agenda. As Henri Coudray acknowledges, the separation of African Muslims from the Pan-Arabic movement could summarise the French agenda in Muslim Africa in the mid-twentieth century. To achieve that goal, France weakened and ultimately wiped out Turkish influence in the north-eastern part of the region. They supported the Kanuri over the 'violent' Tuareg, claiming to liberate the former from the latter. They also approved, initially at least, the growing influence of Italy in Libya.[83] Additionally, French authorities opened bilingual French-Arabic *madrasas* in Chad, often led by a French person with knowledge of the Arabic language. To protect the effectiveness of this approach, French authorities denied entry to Egyptian teachers and funds. Some of Chad's 'Arabisants' were jailed or murdered.[84] Those living in places like Borkou, Ennedi, and Wadday rejected French education and violently opposed French colonialism.[85] Even now, they still see the French presence in Chad in light of the past Judeo-Christian crusades against Islam.[86]

Beyond the fight against Pan-Arabism, another battlefield for French officials in Chad was their fight against perceived liberal Americanism. This second front was the result of postwar global politics. America's embrace of human rights and its good relations with anti-colonialists exposed French colonial abuses. That the Chad Mission seemed too close to the colonial regime helps to explain a certain anti-American attitude among the missionaries. De Bélinay had written to de Gaulle about the 'urgency to establish a mission in Chad', given the ongoing 'invasion of American Protestants'.[87] His request received the endorsement of the

---

[82] Ibid., 22–23.
[83] Knut S. Vikor, 'An Episode of Saharan Rivalry: The French Occupation of Kawar, 1906', *The International Journal of African Historical Studies* 18, no. 4 (1985): 708–13.
[84] Coudray, *Langue, religion, identité, pouvoir*, 28–29.
[85] Arditi, 'Le Tchad et le monde arabe', 186.
[86] Assaïd Gamar Sileck, 'Bilinguisme: les véritables enjeux', *N'Djamena-Hebdo* 76 (25 February 1993): 8.
[87] 'Archives of the former Jesuit Province of Lyon' (hereafter, M-Ly.). Here,

French governor of Central Africa.[88] Once he was confirmed as head of the mission, de Bélinay kept urging the French colonial authorities to speed up the sending of French personnel to Chad. Catholic women and children, he wrote, were being left without priests. People dying in hospitals were not receiving the sacraments. Sending young French personnel, he concluded, would have a devastating impact on the American-led Protestant 'invasion'.[89]

De Bélinay's letters to French colonial authorities are to be read in the context of the growing influence of political 'Arabisants' and American Protestants in Chad. Within this backdrop, early Catholic missions in Chad were part of France's regional and global diplomacy. The emphasis on the foreignness of Eastern ideologies and the Islamic religion and the dualistic description of the context offered by de Bélinay were clear indications of an international environment that was decisively shifting towards the Cold War.

Having French men and women on the ground also helped to limit the influence of Italy coming from Libya and Sudan. The *francité* of missionary personnel was therefore a necessary condition to advance this regional agenda. To find the French missionary personnel that Chad's Catholic enterprise needed, the Capuchins came from Abyssinia and settled at Doha and Moundou. However, according to the ministère des Colonies, the Capuchins were not well equipped to make the region impermeable to the influence of Islam.[90] To replace them, the administration turned to the Holy Ghost Fathers and the White Fathers. Colonial officials believed both congregations were 'specialized in the apostolate in the Muslim world and in dealing with Islamic influence'.[91] A confidential note from Bishop Yves Plumey, head of the mission of the Oblates of Mary Immaculate in northern Cameroon, confirmed the need to have young French missionaries working hand in hand with colonial officials in the Islamised regions of

---

Box 1457: F. de Bélinay, 'Lettre au Général de Gaulle, 11 Octobre 1945'.

[88] ANOM-FM-1AFF-PO: 2180/5: Lettre du Gouverneur Général de l'AEF, au Ministre des Colonies, Direction des Affaires Politiques, 18 Septembre 1945: 'Je partage entièrement le point de vue du Département, quant à la nécessité d'opposer à l'extension de l'Islam au Tchad, une barrière chrétienne française [...]'.

[89] M-Ly. Box 1457: Frédéric de Bélinay, 'Lettre au Gouverneur de l'AEF', January 1946.

[90] ANOM-FM-1AFF-PO: 2180/5. Le Gouverneur Général de l'AEF, 'A Monsieur le Ministre des Colonies, 17 janvier 1946'.

[91] Ibid.

Chad and Cameroon. This collaboration was also necessary to contain the American influence accelerated by Protestant missions.[92]

For the purpose of securing French personnel for the Mission, Jacques Maritain, the French ambassador to the Vatican, was tasked by Georges Bidault, the French minister of foreign affairs, to negotiate with Propaganda Fide for the sending of French missionaries to Chad.[93] Although Mr Laurentie preferred having the Oblates taking charge of the entire Chad project, Propaganda Fide preferred the Jesuits.[94] In response to the request for more French personnel in Chad, de Gaulle personally approved the sending of Jesuit Father Frédéric de Bélinay to Chad, until Propaganda Fide settled the matter.[95]

Conclusion

The strategic concerns of French Catholic missionaries in Chad were similar to those of the political project of 'Wider France'. For example, as Bishop Carlo Salotti of Propaganda Fide determined, the Jesuits believed that 'the apostolate of the mission was a civilizing apostolate'.[96] Civilising the indigenous was therefore a common goal for both the colonial state and European missions. Missionaries and colonial administrators in Chad agreed on those common challenges. On top of those were Islam and atheistic materialism.

---

[92] ANOM-FM-1AFF-PO: B. 10313. Une note confidentielle de la Mission des Oblats au Nord Cameroun, envoyée au Ministre de la France d'Outre Mer (14 August 1946).

[93] ANOM-FM-1AFF-PO: 2180/5: Henri Laurentie, 'Lettre à Monseigneur Biechy, 9 November 1945'. See also: Jacques Maritain, 'Lettre au Ministre des Affaires Étrangères Georges Bidault, 24 June 1947'. In: ANOM-FM-1AFF-PO: 2180/5: 'Evangélisation du Tchad, 1945–1947'.

[94] ANOM-FM-1AFF-PO: 2180/5: M. Jean Bourdeillette, Chargé d'Affaires de France près le Saint Siège, 'Á son Excellence Monsieur George Bidault, Ministre des Affaires Etrangères, Direction d'Afrique-Levant, 12 janvier 1946'.

[95] ANOM-FM-1AFF-PO: 2180/5: Laurentie, Directeur Politique du Ministère des Colonies, 'A Monsieur le Gouverneur Général de l'AEF, 27 novembre 1945'.

[96] In *Osservatore Romano*, 6 September 1931. As formulated in the prayers for African missions by Propaganda Fide, Africa was still the 'land of idolatry' and 'darkness' until the 1940s. Cf. 'Preces pro Missionibus, 1940': 16–18, in ARSI, *Opuscula impressa I*. Box: P.F. 1003.

Even the religious agenda of the first Jesuits in Chad could not break from the civilising one. In the person of the founder of the mission, de Bélinay, and in each of his successors, the religious aspect of the *mission civilisatrice* was front and centre. Each was part of French traditional Catholicism, which was in crisis at home. And they exported their fear of a new Catholic progressivism via the mission field. These Jesuits found allies in their conservatism among French bishops in Africa. For Lefèbvre, for example, the infiltration of the liberal agenda in the Catholic Church was as dangerous as Communism and Islam. The three ideologies represented existential threats to French civilisation. Going to mission, to evangelise, was synonymous with Frenchification.

From a geopolitical perspective, the French background of the pioneers of the Chad Mission and their closeness to the colonial agenda increased concerns for an aggressive Islam that was already destabilising North Africa. Communism was 'infesting' Vietnam and the rising nationalist elite across Africa. American Protestants were advancing on Chad's villages and towns. All these factors made the Jesuits less inclined to support Chad's rising elite, which was suspected of secularising inclinations. It also delayed the Vatican elitist agenda for the African Church in Chad.

Consequently, there was some confusion on the primary goal of the mission. The Chad Jesuit Mission remained French-oriented and with a certain distance from a key Vatican priority: the building of a Chadian clergy and leadership in the Church. The Catholicity of these Jesuit pioneers was a diluted Gallicanism that allied with the politics of Frenchification. Their Catholicity was simultaneously corrective of traditional French Catholicism in two ways.

Contrary to the stark separation of Church and state required by the French *laïcité*, under de Bélinay mission and state shared the same ideological goals in Chad. On the other hand, the Jesuit Chad Mission, well aware of the ongoing rise of secularising trends among the popular masses in France, opted for the evangelisation of the popular masses in Chad. This populism took place at the expense of – even in opposition to – the rising Évolué class of Chadians as well as the politics of indirect rule the colonists applied to the Islam-dominated regions of Chad. The religious endeavours of the Jesuits in Chad aimed to serve as a stabilising force for the French African empire in the context of transition towards a more polarised world. In this polarised world, France's anti-Americanism in Africa made it part of the Bloc of the non-Aligned. Ultimately, French interests were what mattered the most to France and its representatives abroad.

CHAPTER 2

Founding Era: The Conservatism of Frédéric de Bélinay, Jesuit Pioneer in Chad, 1946–58

On 15 June 1945, Propaganda Fide extended the 'personal jurisdiction' of de Bélinay up to the tenth parallel, leading to the official approval of the Jesuit Mission of Chad in February 1946. A year later, in 1947, the Apostolic Prefecture of Fort-Lamy was created. Du Bouchet, a former provincial of Lyon (r. 1937–43), was appointed the first apostolic prefect. He was joined by one of his former novices, Louis Forobert, in 1948.[1] Under du Bouchet, the territory was divided into two additional missions. The Jesuits directed the mission of Fort-Archambault, and the Oblate Fathers directed the mission of Fort-Lamy.[2] The Capuchins would remain at the head of the Chari Mission until 21 May 1951, when the Jesuits took over its eighteen parishes.

As the previous chapter showed, De Bélinay was a forceful defender of France's geostrategic interests in Central Africa against a rising American influence and the double threat of Communism and Islam. Joseph du Bouchet, in contrast, was sent to Chad primarily to carry out the Vatican's agenda of ecclesial Africanisation. This chapter shows that instead of fully pursuing the Vatican's progressive vision of clerical Africanisation, du Bouchet joined the circle of Lefèbvre, René Graffin, and other French missionary bishops in Africa by delaying the development of a Chadian clergy. For du Bouchet, and in continuity with de Bélinay, Chad was a blessing for France's broader strategy in the Middle East, an opportunity to expand the evangelising mission of the Jesuit Province of Lyon, and a retirement place amid the rise of a younger generation of French Jesuits at

---

[1] Archives of the Jesuit Historical Institute in Africa (A-JHIA): 'Décès Du P. Louis Forobert', *NPAO* 222 (21 February 2009): 9–13. Not classified.
[2] Ibid.

home. Like de Bélinay before him, du Bouchet embarked on a conquering movement aimed at spreading the gospel while keeping African colonies under French political and cultural influence.

Addressing the conservatism of the Jesuit pioneers of the Chad Mission in this chapter also means revisiting recent Jesuit historiography. Thomas Banchoff, José Casanova, and others have demonstrated the existence of a certain conservatism in the Society from its restoration in 1814 to the Second Vatican Council (1963–65).[3] When analysing the post-Vatican II period, there is ongoing discussion over whether or not Pedro Arrupe created a 'new' Society that broke away from this conservatism.[4] Some historians believe that while Arrupe was reforming the Society, the 'old' conservatism was threatening the unity of the Jesuit order. In Spain, a number of Jesuits calling themselves the 'Vera Society' almost created a Jesuit schism.[5]

In France, however, as the chapter demonstrates, the Jesuits did not wait until the 1970s to reform and embrace modernity. Cracks had already appeared in this conservatism in the 1940s, exactly when the Chad Mission was created. Thus, a number of questions arise: what happened to the old guard as a younger generation of French Jesuits rose to power in France? How did its fate shape the French Jesuits' outreach towards Africa after the Second World War? And how did this conservatism affect the Vatican's agenda of Africanisation?

In this chapter, some French conservative Jesuits left France and opted for the overseas missions. The conservatism of the Jesuit pioneers in Chad is an example of shifting dynamics in global Jesuitism in the mid-twentieth century. It shows that as Jesuit progressivism emerged in France during and after the war, it also outsourced the old guard. Some conservative Jesuits like de Bélinay and du Bouchet were sent to Africa, where their conservatism contributed to delay part of the Vatican's agenda to Africanise Christianity. Discussing these pioneers in this chapter helps to demonstrate how some conservative French Jesuits moved from the centre of power in France to become powerful Church-builders in Africa.

---

[3] Thomas Banchoff et al., *The Jesuits and Globalization. Historical Legacies and Contemporary Challenges* (Washington, DC: Georgetown University Press, 2016), 14.

[4] Thomas Worcester, 'A Restored Society or a New Society of Jesus?' in *Jesuits' Survival and Restoration* (Leiden: Brill, 2015), 24–25.

[5] Urbano Valero, *Pablo VI y Los Jesuitas. Una Relación Intensa y Complicada, 1963–1978* (Bilbao: Mensajero, 2019), 94–96.

During the war, French Jesuits had gone through their own transition. For the first time in history, a Frenchman, Norbert de Boynes, was elected Vicar General of the Society of Jesus in Rome (r. 1942–46). He held the highest Jesuit office in the world.[6] His positions concerning the political situation in France and the intellectual revolution that was happening among French Jesuits placed de Boynes among the defenders of the status quo. For example, at a time when Jesuits like Belgian Pierre Charles were developing a twenty-first-century Catholic missiology,[7] one which encouraged ecumenical dialogue[8] and denounced racism and colonialism,[9] de Boynes urged French Jesuits to remain loyal to the established order. Politically, the political order he seemed so reluctant to criticise was the Vichy regime which French missionaries in Africa like Marcel Lefèbvre seemed to admire.

As vicar general, de Boynes resisted projects aimed at writing a history of Jesuit missions in 1943. The Society, he then argued, lacked professional historians able to carry out such a delicate mission.[10] This intellectual unpreparedness on the part of the Society at a critical time in history coincided with the anti-intellectualism of the Jesuit pioneers in Chad. To a certain extent, it was also reminiscent of the resistance of some Jesuits to modernism. Anti-intellectualism in Chad was a key reason why only small numbers of Chadians sought to enter the priesthood.

Yet, in a sign of openness under a shifting context, de Boynes allowed the publication of at least an outline of a history of Jesuit missions.[11] It is possible that de Boynes was acting out of prudence. He seemed to believe that the Society was simply not prepared, in the 1940s, to effectively address the two global ideologies that were turning France apart and, with it, threatening the Church which both Nazism and Communism despised. However,

---

[6] Alexius A. Magni, 'R.P. Norbertus de Boynes a R.P. Alexio A. Mgni Ut Vicarii Generalis Partes Ad Tempus Agat Constituitur', ARSI (11 April 1944).

[7] Pierre Charles, *Principes et méthodes de l'activite missionnaire en dehors du catholicisme* (Louvain: AUCAM, 1932); Pierre Charles, 'La missiologie', *Revue Congo* 1 (1929): 658–63.

[8] Pierre Charles, *Robe sans couture: Essai sur le Luthéranisme Catholique* (Bruges: Charles Beyaert, 1923).

[9] Pierre Charles, 'Colonisation', *Revue Missionnaire des Jésuites Belges* XI (March 1936): 101–12; Pierre Charles, *Racisme et catholicisme* (Tournai: Casterman, 1939).

[10] Norbert de Boynes, 'Lettre au P. Lopetegui, 3 février 1943', in ARSI, *Opuscula impressa I*. Box: P.F. 1003, I.

[11] Ibid.

de Boynes's critics, including Jean Lacouture, see him primarily as a conservative Jesuit. Unlike others of his French colleagues, such as Victor Fontoynont, Henri de Lubac, Gaston Fessard, or Teilhard de Chardin, who were the face of Catholic renewal in Europe, de Boynes remained, with the likes of Joseph du Bouchet, a strong defender of the established political and ecclesiastical order in France. In addition to putting progressive French Jesuits on standby vis-à-vis the Vichy regime and in keeping them in the margins of the Society, he was also a strong believer in universalism and the superiority of Western civilisation and its form of Catholicism.[12]

Understanding the tension between conservative and progressive Catholics, both in France and in Africa, is important for understanding Africa's reception of global Catholicism in the 1970s, which is discussed in Chapters 8 and 9. As these chapters will argue, early African Jesuits, most of whom had studied in Lyon, opposed this universalising trend of Western Christianity and its imposition on them. Often the progressives on African issues, who were willing to push for the creation of a Church that was genuinely African, were ostracised, just as the French Progressive Jesuits of the 1940s were before them.

Therefore, this chapter argues, while the Jesuit Chad Mission shared the civilising nature of all Catholic missions in the 1930s, it also adapted to the unique context of France and Chad immediately after the Second World War. This context was shaped by French strategic interests in Africa and the Middle East, and the sense of urgency they gave to containing secularising trends in Chad that, back home, were already 'infiltrating' French towns and cities. This chapter addresses the missionary vocation of the Jesuit pioneers in Chad, and shows that their conservatism was rooted in a tradition that allied France's military establishment to conservative politics and conservative Catholicism.

Further, the missionary approach of the Jesuit pioneers in Chad was based on the fear of the transfer of France's secularising trend in the mid-1940s to the French empire in Africa. De Bélinay expressed this conservatism in racial terms and in uncompromising language that considered all non-Christian religions and ideologies as 'false religions'. Those false religions were to be fought against before they destroyed true religion and Western civilisation. This Western civilisation, even in the context of Chad, was a prerequisite for the effective Christianisation of Africans. To Africanise meant to translate French Christianity into a form that made it accessible to a Chadian audience that knew little French in the 1940s.

[12] Jean Lacouture, *Jésuites: Les Revenants*, vol. 2 (Paris: Seuil, 1992), 351.

Figure 2 Joseph du Bouchet with a French colonial official, Archambault, 1954 (Archives JHIA, Nairobi).

The Church in Chad in 1935

In 1935, Frédéric de Bélinay was welcomed in Fort-Lamy, the colonial capital of Chad, by a French family named 'les Jamet'. While staying here, he received a visit from Father Sourie of the Missionaries of the Sacred Heart of Jesus (Saint Quentin).[13] Sourie belonged to the Apostolic Vicariate of Nkongsamba, in the Mungo region of Cameroon.[14] This group of missionaries had travelled on from Cameroon in 1935 and settled in the Chadian town of Kélo. Sourie and de Bélinay discussed the possibility of founding a new Catholic mission, and de Bélinay offered to go further north, into

---

[13] On the chronology of these early years of the mission, see: Charles Vandame, *Cinquante ans de la vie de l'Eglise Catholique au Tchad* (Paris: L'Harmattan, 2012), 11–12. I was not able to find more biographical data on Sourie.

[14] Pater Gerebern, *Pioniers 25 Jaar in de Ubangimissie Der Belgische Capucijnen* (Antwerpen: Franciscaansche Standaard, 1935), 41–42.

Muslim-dominated Chad. Instead, Sourie went further south, where he founded a mission in Yagoua, in the far northern region of Cameroon. He also started to tour some more remote areas in Chad, including Ennedi, Borkou, and Tibesti, in the 'more-or-less Islamized region'.[15]

En route to Yagoua, there was a settlement called Bongor, located in the Middle Logone region, which was the most important settlement of the Mayo-Kebi prefecture, populated by the Massas (or Bananas). The Jesuit missionaries saw in this 'very primitive people' an ideal opportunity for conversion. Bongor had a large population, including many children, and the people were sedentary and lived off agriculture. Men proudly wore goatskins that gave them a majestic look. Women decorated their noses and lips with all kinds of cabochons of wood and metal and carried little silver trays on their lower lips.[16]

Before leaving Bongor, Sourie asked de Bélinay to anoint a sick man who was a former seminarian from Yaoundé (Cameroon). The movement of missionary personnel across national boundaries, in this particular case between Chad, Ubangi (known today as the Central African Republic), and Cameroon, was a sign that the geographical isolation of Chad did not preclude it from being connected to regional and even global trends within Christianity. This regional fluidity of missionary boundaries represented an opportunity for regional collaboration. Chad's religious map was not so different from others in the region such as northern Cameroon, northern Nigeria, and Ubangi. Just like in those countries, early Jesuit accounts divided Chad along three religious divides. There were Muslims and Christians, each with a dual component: Catholics and non-Catholic Christians, 'true' Muslims (*Sanusiyya* 'Arabisants') and what the Jesuits considered 'superficial' Muslims (mostly *Tijaniyya*). There was a large portion of ethno-religionists, especially among the Sara people. Different Christian denominations competed to evangelise these ethno-religionists.

In demographic terms, the Jesuits counted 'true Muslims' (400,000), 'superficial Muslims' (580,000), and the Sara people (640,000).[17] By the time of the official recognition of the Chad Mission in 1946, very few Chadians had been converted to Christianity. Protestant missionaries, the Capuchins, and the Oblates all made little progress in terms of

---

[15] A-CEFOD. Fonds Dalmais: 'Ministère de Noël à Bongor', *Lettres du Tchad* 11 (January 1948): 5.
[16] Ibid.
[17] 'Le Tchad', *JAF* 1 (1953): 39–40.

conversions.[18] This lack of success made it difficult to develop a well-trained Christian community. Without trained Christians, the Vatican's agenda of clerical Africanisation was harder to implement.

The Church in Chad, 1919–35

As mentioned at the start of Part I, the Catholic missionaries had not settled in Chad until 1929, some time after their Protestant counterparts. French missionary Gabriel Herriau, of the Holy Ghost Fathers, was the first. Coming from Bangui, he built a Mission at Kou. Three years later, in 1932, he and two other Brothers had to abandon the mission due to the spread of trypanosomiasis.[19] Within the Catholic Church, Chad was part of two separate apostolic vicariates: Khartoum (northern Sudan) and Fumban (Cameroon).[20] The Capuchins from Canada and the Sacred Heart of Jesus (Saint Quentin) missionaries from France had control over its territory.[21] The situation changed with Rome's decision to send in two additional religious movements in 1946 – namely, the Oblates of the Immaculate Heart of Mary and the Jesuits.[22]

For Chadians who joined Protestant missions, their training period was shorter than the traditional training of Catholic priests, and they quickly became leaders of their churches and their countries.[23] Some of these church leaders, such as N'Garta Tombalbaye, were politically more engaged than the Chadian Catholics: Tombalbaye was later to became the first president of independent Chad.[24]

[18] Ibid. 39.
[19] Eglise de Pala, '70 ans de l'arrivée du premier missionnaire à Kou, l'Eglise du Tchad passe de 5 à 7 diocèses', *Bulletin Diocésain de Pala* 115 (January 1999): 7–8.
[20] A. Hallaire and J. Fedry, *Naissance d'une église africaine: Lettres et chroniques du Pays Sarh* (Paris: Karthala, 1998), 7.
[21] Godefroy Clovis Dévost, *Les Capucins canadiens au Tchad* (Montréal: Éditions de l'Écho, 2003).
[22] Granito di Belmonte and Fumasoni-Biondi, 'Erigitur Nova Praefectura Apostolica Arcis Lamy (in Tchad) et Societatis (Prov. Lugdunensi) Committitur', *AAS* 11 (1947): 216–17.
[23] Jacob F. Ade Ajayi, *Christian Missions in Nigeria 1841–1891: The Making of a New Elite* (Ibadan: University of Ibadan Press, 1965); William E. Phipps, 'The Influence of Christian Missions on the Rise of Nationalism in Central Africa', *International Review of Mission* 57, no. 226 (April 1968): 229–32.
[24] Arnaud Dingammadji, *Ngarta Tombalbaye: Parcours et rôle dans la vie politique du Tchad (1959–1975)* (Paris: Harmattan, 2007).

This rise of Protestants into politics had its roots in the mission strategy most Protestant missions adopted. Protestantism often favoured the 'three selfs' approach to missions, developed by Henry Venn and Rufus Anderson, which promoted self-governance, self-support, and self-propagation. According to Venn and Anderson, the goal of the mission was to 'advance the gospel' and 'build the Church in every land as self-governing, self-supporting and self-extending unit of the church universal'.[25] With basic literacy, Protestant Christians had the tools to be among the leading figures of Chad's Christian nationalists. This language of self-determination was well suited to the political context in Chad as the country made its way towards independence, but it was not part of the Catholic vocabulary. In fact, in 1955 the Vatican condemned the three-self theory as a Catholic practice altogether.[26]

The late arrival of Catholic missionaries, in contrast, left them without an educational infrastructure that could have helped prepare a Catholic nationalist elite (had the missionaries wished to train one) or even a Catholic clergy. Unlike in Mesopotamia[27] or Iraq and Lebanon, where in the 1930s they had arrived late to a Muslim-majority region and developed schools that had immediate impact among the political elite,[28] in Chad the Jesuits chose to focus their educational efforts on the Chadian popular masses. They made this choice, initially at least, as part of a religious crusade against Islam and the threat of atheistic materialism. Focusing on the popular masses was a necessary step in a country that badly needed an educational infrastructure for its youth, but it nevertheless made it harder for the Jesuits to arrive at a point where the Chadians were ready for Catholic priesthood. Those they trained in their schools were able to be catechists, but they were not, however, well-trained enough to be candidates for priesthood in the Society of Jesus. It takes time and a lot of investment to train a Catholic priest. The Chad Mission suffered for the lack of the country's well-prepared candidates in order to pursue the Vatican's agenda of clerical Africanisation. Another factor might have been the French-centred nature of the mission of early Jesuits in Chad.

[25] Cf. Max Warren, ed., *To Apply the Gospel: Selections from the Writings of Henry Venn* (Grand Rapids, MI: Eerdmans, 1971).
[26] Pope Pius XII, 'Lettre Encyclique ad Sinarum gentem', *AAS* 47 (1955): 5–14.
[27] Kristian Girling, 'Jesuit Contributions to the Iraqi Education System in the 1930s and Later', *International Studies in Catholic Education* 8, no. 2 (2016): 179–92.
[28] Franck Salameh, 'A Man for Others: The Life and Times of Lebanese Jesuit Henri Lammens, 1862–1937', *The Journal of the Middle East and Africa* 9, no. 2 (2018): 213–36.

Frédéric de Bélinay: Missionary at Heart, Frenchman First

Born of a noble family in Liginiac, Corrèze (France) in 1875, Frédéric de Bonafos de Bélinay attended high school in Bellevue (Moulins). From there, he moved to Saint-Cyr, the elite military academy of France. He was twenty-three when he joined the Jesuits in 1898,[29] at exactly the time of the so-called 'pacification' of Chad that inaugurated French colonialism in the region. Having completed his theological studies, de Bélinay was enrolled in the French army as a lieutenant during the First World War. At the end of the conflict, he received military honours in the French army.[30] After the war, he returned to the Jesuit community, where he held different ministries, respectively in Saint Etienne, Aix-en-Provence, and Grenoble. Later, in 1931, an encounter with Lieutenant Mazodier,[31] who was returning from Chad, triggered F. de Bélinay's call to serve as a missionary in Chad.[32] Yet, he remained a Frenchman first, convinced of France's greatness and its enlightening role among the nations. Protecting France's colonial interests would, unsurprisingly, collude with his mission to evangelise.

De Bélinay decided to go to Chad in the midst of the glorification of the 'Wider France'. This mission was a personal calling, and an opportunity to rekindle his missionary life as a Jesuit. In a note to his provincial from Fort-Lamy in Chad, 1938, de Bélinay wrote:

> All my religious life, woven with failure and lamentable health, I always felt like an ungrateful son, a dead weight [...] I could see myself appearing one day before St Ignatius, covered with confusion for my barren life [...] Finally, this blessed opportunity of Chad presented itself, and I felt encouraged to risk the adventure – for it was one – and now I feel the infinite joy of having accepted this mission.[33]

---

[29] Cf. M-Ly. 'Personal Files'. Boxes 1457, 1458, and 1459. This is the personal file on Father Frédéric de Bélinay. File 1457 also contains a memorandum from the Central Archives of Military Justice on de Bélinay. The next files, 1458–59, contain five manuscripts with the notes and preliminary work of Joseph Fortier on his biography of Father de Bélinay.

[30] It is important to notice that de Bélinay's service in the army was not without incident. He was accused of 'intelligence with a foreign power' – in this case, Great Britain – but was later absolved from any wrongdoing. Cf. 'Dossier B. 1457'.

[31] Joseph Fortier, *Frédéric de Bélinay: Pionnier des missions du Tchad*, vol. 1 (Tchad, 1988).

[32] M-Ly. Box 1457: 'Frédéric de Bélinay'.

[33] M-Ly: Box 1457: 'Personal Files'.

The nature of the source for this information, de Bélinay's 'personal file', and the fact that the provincial was at the receiving end of his letter are clear indications that de Bélinay was not making a mere 'pious' and 'humble' representation of his Jesuit life. His words, instead, should be taken almost literally. In this note, he talked about his 'failure', twice about his 'barren life', and of his 'confusion'. He also mentioned his 'lamentable health', and explained how Chad represented the dream of his life. The 'Dossier' has ample evidence of his 'poor health'. On several occasions, the provincial and his consultors also discussed de Bélinay's advanced age and wondered whether or not he was physically fit enough for such a mission.

De Bélinay saw Chad as an opportunity for his self-realisation. In the Jesuit catalogues, prior to his going to Chad, when he was not teaching in a school, he had always had 'housekeeping' roles in Jesuit communities. While these 'community jobs' were very important within the Jesuit organisation, they might not have been the ideal missions for this former army officer. In Chad, however, this 'barren life' would come to an end. Frédéric de Bélinay would become a leader, a founder.

There is a spiritual dimension to de Bélinay's calling. One can grasp it by looking at the Jesuit tradition. Saint Ignatius of Loyola, the founder of the Jesuits, never considered his own poor health or age handicaps to doing God's work.[34] Neither were long distances or harsh climatic and sociopolitical situations a missionary impediment for Francis Xavier and others who, like him, took the roads and the seas to unknown destinations to spread the gospel message. The Formula of the Institute, the fundamental law of the Jesuits, states that those who would join the Society should promise to go wherever the pope may be pleased to send them, whether 'among the Turks or to other infidels, even to the land they call India, or to any heretics or schismatics, or to any of the faithful'.[35] As historian Jean Lacouture framed it, the first Jesuits

> all burned for departure, to the Holy Land, to martyrdom [...] Jerusalem, the earthly Jerusalem, was their overriding goal. Such was their desire to share their faith, to live it in their flesh and their blood, that the site of Christ's Passion counted for more with them than any dangers that might lurk there.[36]

---

[34] Ignatius of Loyola, *A Pilgrim Journey: The Autobiography of Ignatius of Loyola*, trans. Joseph N. Tylenda (San Francisco: Ignatius Press, 2001), 37.

[35] Ignatius of Loyola, *The Constitutions of the Society of Jesus*, trans. George E. Ganss (Saint Louis, MO: The Institute of Jesuit Sources, 1970), Formula of Paul III, 7.

[36] Jean Lacouture, *Jesuits: A Multibiography* (Washington, DC: Counterpoint, 1995), 57–58.

It was not the only thing de Bélinay had in common with Charles de Foucauld, who, a few years earlier, had evangelised Algeria. Both were also military men. To be a soldier like de Bélinay was valued in Chad. The Chad Mission benefitted from its military connections. In the aftermath of the war, as mentioned in the first chapter, the sense that Francophone Africa had a role in defining France's national identity and had shared in its struggles contributed to making French generals very popular.[37] The generals represented a stabilising force amid the 'malaise'. They were celebrated at home and abroad as representatives of France's recovered prestige. In the Chad Mission, General Philippe Leclerc was that hero, even for Jesuits like de Bélinay.

A victorious general of the Second World War alongside de Gaulle, Leclerc inspired the first major project of the mission. He wanted the cathedral of Fort-Lamy to be built. He chose its future location and he supported it financially.[38] Correspondence between Henri Rostan d'Ancesume, provincial of Lyon and direct superior of de Bélinay,[39] and the office of the overseas ministry reveals a coordinated effort by both parties to make sure they were on the same page in Chad. Some of the provincial's trips to Chad were planned with the help of the same office. The military actively helped to organise the Chad Mission on the ground, and the Jesuits were always concerned about how their mission could help the French military attachés to Chad.[40]

De Bélinay, like de Foucauld, was also in a religious war. The vocation of de Bélinay was brewed from a conservative pot that for most of the early twentieth century had tied French Jesuits to the French military establishment. He believed in the Christian values of family, order, and work; yet, while other missionaries like Lefèbvre had expressed scepticism about de

---

[37] And as the French–Indochina War escalated, about 70,000 soldiers from Africa enlisted to preserve the French colonial empire. Cf. Michel Bodin, 'La géographie du recrutement des soldats africains (1944–1954)', *Guerres Mondiales et Conflits Contemporains* 189 (1998): 123–34.

[38] M-Ly. 102/1: Joseph du Bouchet, 'Lettre à Monsieur l'Abbé Louis, Aumônier de l'Hôtel National des Invalides, Fort-Lamy, le 15 février 1948'.

[39] 'Henri Rostan d'Ancezune', *Compagnie* 362 (November 2002): 179.

[40] M-Ly: Box 102: J. du Bouchet, 'Letter to the Provincial, March 15, 1948' in Archives of the French province (Vanves), Coll. 'Ancienne Province de Lyon' (M-Ly), Box 102. This box contains (1) Letters of Joseph du Bouchet, 1936–43; (2) Letters of Provincial Auguste Décisier, 1943–49; (3) Letters of Provincial Henri Rostan d'Ancézune, 1949–51; (4) Letters of Provincial André Ravier, 1951–57.

Gaulle in these early years of the Fourth Republic, de Bélinay pragmatically allied with de Gaulle to advance his mission in Chad.

In France, the religious ground had been shifting towards the left since the late 1920s. Jesuits such as Antoine Dieuzayde, Albert Valensin, Eugène Roche, and Henri Lalande reacted to the Bolshevik Revolution by embracing Catholic left-wing populism. Some of them became chaplains of the 'Action Catholique Spécialisée' (Specialised Catholic Action) in different cities across France.[41] For conservative Jesuits like de Bélinay, therefore, going to mission represented an opportunity to fight this liberal trend and not leave its 'false religions' unchallenged.

Formal Approval of the Mission and the Fight against 'False Religions'

At the beginning of the Chad Mission, the Jesuits in the Middle East were working to create a pluralistic society. In such pluralistic societies, the rights of religious minorities were respected.[42] In Chad, however, the early Jesuits were less interested in accommodating non-Christians or whatever they perceived as 'false religions'. The ideological inclinations of the pioneers had greater weight in this uncompromising approach than the broader agenda of their founding province, Lyon. As already mentioned, Chad's mission was de Bélinay's personal initiative, and the response from the provincial of Lyon to de Bélinay's missionary project was not immediately positive.

Chad was mentioned for the first time in a consult of the province of Lyon on 7 March 1945. The consultors were open to the idea of founding a mission there, but they also understood that accepting such a mission would be very challenging. On 14 January 1946, the provincial informed his consultors that the French government was considering the Oblates for the Chad Mission. The provincial believed that de Bélinay, in his fifties, was not fit for that kind of enterprise. He was also afraid that very little was known about the remote country de Bélinay planned to evangelise. After three years of difficult negotiations with his superiors, and thanks to the support of some government and colonial officials in Paris and in Chad,

---

[41] Bernard Giroux, 'L'action catholique à l'ombre de la Grande Guerre. L'exemple de quelques aumôniers de la Jeunesse Étudiante Chrétienne', *Revue d'Histoire de l'Eglise de France* 99, no. 1 (January 2013): 95–114 – here, pp. 96–98.

[42] Franck Salameh, 'A Man for Others', 220.

de Bélinay's mission was finally approved. He voluntarily explored Chad from 1935 to 1937, and he was confirmed as military chaplain in 1938.[43]

On 21 March 1946, Bishop Celso Costantini, then secretary of the Congregation for the Propagation of the Faith, announced the creation of the Apostolic Vicariate of Chad. He appointed de Bélinay head of the vicariate. Following Costantini's decree, the Jesuit consultors of Lyon approved de Bélinay's appointment. The next year, in 1947, the vicariate was made into an apostolic prefecture. Through that decision, the Jesuits also took charge of 'the entire territory of the colony', while the Oblates of Mary Immaculate who, up to this point, had been missioning in the western part of the colony, moved south, to the northern region of Cameroon.[44]

The Jesuits were put in charge of the rest of the territory of Chad submitted so far to the Vicariate of Khartoum. This territory had previously been entrusted to the Fathers of Verona, Italians. They never occupied it.[45] The territory of the Jesuit Fathers represented four-fifths of Chad, an area twice the size of France. The northern part included Tibesti and Ennedi, a huge desert, and mountainous areas sown with oases. It was traversed by the nomads and extended to the border with Libya. The southern part, with Fort-Archambault as its base station, included the edges of the Chari river and its tributaries, Barh Sara and Aouk, on the border of Oubangui-Chari. It was populated mainly by the Saras. Between the two regions there were vast and quite fertile regions, strewn with numerous villages. Huge deserted savannahs, the haunts of all African animals, from lions, giraffes, and elephants to gazelles and wild guineafowl, made the region as beautiful as its climate made it hellish.[46]

For five months – that is, from May to the end of October – the rains made the tracks impassable, especially in the south. To reach Fort-Archambault from Fort-Lamy, Father Barjon had to wait three weeks during the month of October. A convoy of boats carrying skirmishers would take at least ten days to cover six to seven hundred kilometres. In

---

[43] Joseph Fortier, 'Chad', in *Diccionario Histórico de la Compañía de Jesús*, vol. 1 (Madrid/Roma: IHSI/UPComillas, 2001), 745. Vandame, *Cinquante ans de la vie de l'Eglise Catholique au Tchad*, 11.

[44] M-Ly. 149: 'Correspondance du Provincial avec la mission du Tchad, ou à propos du Tchad, 1947–1958'. In this box, note especially 'letters of du Bouchet', and a 'financial file from 1968–1972'. Revd Jean-Baptiste Janssens appointed J. du Bouchet as regular superior of the mission on 1 July 1947.

[45] A-CEFOD. Fonds Dalmais: 'Quelques précisions sur la mission', *Lettres du Tchad* (November 1946): 1.

[46] Ibid.

November, Father Scherantz would take the waterway, the roads being still cut by the floods.[47] In total, between fifteen days and a month was needed to travel from France to Chad.[48]

Other factors made the provincial even less enthusiastic. The French Jesuits had more urgent matters to deal with. The difficulties experienced in their missions in Asia and concerns about the rise of totalitarian regimes in Europe as well as Communism represented the real enemies.[49] According to de Bélinay, these regimes and their ideologies represented the 'false religion'.[50] France and the world were under their immediate threat.

Late in his life, de Bélinay wrote about how these regimes had a 'hatred of God and his Church', and were causing 'atrocious persecutions and martyrs in China today'.[51] He remembered Hitler, Mussolini, Stalin, and all these

> Communists now mingled in all our villages, houses, families, governments, and factories [...] The apostles of God, the true Catholics, struggling with an agent of Satan to win and retain the assent of a bewildered, and ignorant man, unconscious of the importance of the issues, obsessed and interested only by his affairs, his cattle, his bank account, his loves and resentment.[52]

These notes from de Bélinay's retreat might well have reflected the state of the world in 1954. Amid the Cold War, the Vatican suspended the experiment of worker priests in France for fear of communist infiltration.[53] China was undergoing a Cultural Revolution, communist in nature and particularly

---

[47] Ibid., 2.

[48] Ibid.

[49] The French anti-communist crusade was proclaimed by Albert Sarrault, minister of the colonies, on 22 April 1927, when he said: 'Le communisme: voilà l'ennemi!' (Communism: that's the enemy!). See: Raoul Girardet, 'L'apothéose de la "Plus Grande France": L'idée coloniale devant l'opinion française, 1930–1935', *Revue Française de Science Politique* 18, no. 6 (December 1968): 1085–114 – here, p. 1106.

[50] M-Ly. Box 1457: *Écrits divers*. 'Vue d'ensemble sur la vraie religion; Précis de la Foi Catholique'. Retreat notes, 7 July 1954.

[51] Ibid.

[52] M-Ly. Box 1457: Box 1457: *Écrits divers*. 'Vue d'ensemble sur la vraie religion; Précis de la Foi Catholique'. Retreat notes, 30 June 1954. He is reflecting on these ideologies in France, after his mission in Chad has ended, yet while considering an eventual return.

[53] Guillaume Cuchet, 'Nouvelles perspectives historiographiques sur les prêtres-ouvriers (1943–1954)', *Vingtième Siècle. Revue d'histoire* 87 (July 2005): 177–87.

violent for Christians. World Christianity was in disarray amid relentless attacks from nationalist leaders who regarded missions as tools for Western domination.[54] The Maronite Lebanese could look up to missionary Henri Lammens as 'a mentor and mender of their muzzled history', yet the Muslim Lebanese considered his work primarily as a form of colonialism.[55]

Therefore, French missionaries in Chad perceived Communism primarily as a 'godless' ideology. It had almost destroyed France and Europe and continued dangerously to penetrate its villages and overseas territories. French colonists in Chad represented the evil 'apostles' of this 'false religion'. According to the Jesuits, the Évolués, the elite class of Chad, were their primary victims. The communist threat which the Évolué class represented in Chad reminded the Jesuits of a situation in China where Communism had led to the extinction of the Church.[56]

The conservatism of Jesuit pioneers in Chad was perceptible in the warlike language they used as they approached non-Catholic religions and ideologies. At a time when most African countries aspired to independence, this conservatism was further expressed by its work to keep central and western Francophone Africa French at any cost. Like the majority in France, de Bélinay went to Chad believing that Africa had a positive role to play for the restoration of post-Second World War France.[57] Presenting the Chad Mission to a French audience in 1956, his younger colleague Paul Dalmais urged French Catholics to appreciate the strategic importance of Chad for the future of France.[58]

---

54 Dana L. Robert, 'Shifting Southward: Global Christianity Since 1945', *International Bulletin of Missionary Research* 24, no. 2 (April 2000), 53.
55 Franck Salameh, 'A Man for Others', 220 and 232.
56 According to R. G. Tiedemann, 'the government sponsored the Catholic Three Self-Movement of 1950–1951 to establish a self-governing, self-supporting, self-propagating Church free of all foreign influence. The state obtained its objective with the establishment of the National Patriotic Association, CCPA, in 1957 and the consecration of government sponsored bishops in 1958. Officially, the Chinese Catholic Church had severed all links with the Vatican': Adrian Hastings (ed.), *A World History of Christianity* (Grand Rapids, MI: Eerdmans, 1999), 406.
57 A dissertation by Alison Joan Murray suggests that this favourable trend of the French public towards Africans was carefully planned during the interwar period, as French state-sponsored movies framed the empire as a strategic necessity for the greatness of France, 'a tired and war-torn nation in need of renewal' (Alison Murray, 'Framing Greater France: Images of Africa in French Documentary Film, 1920–1940' [PhD dissertation, University of Virginia, 1998], ii).
58 Paul Dalmais, 'L'avenir religieux du Tchad', *Etudes* (January 1956): 39–51.

Most missionaries going to Chad were familiar with the French and Chadian political environments, with their shared ambiguities. They shared those ambiguities. De Bélinay believed that the 'godless religion' that was destroying France was God's punishment for the White race ungratefully turning its back on God. He wrote:

> God, the Catholic Church, have favoured the white race for 2000 years. Her ingratitude, her revolt against J.C. [Jesus Christ] in the name of science, creates for her the worst threat (spoken by J.C. to Marg. Marie) [Jesus Christ to Marguerite-Marie Alacoque] of late that our race falls back into the wrath of God, Blacks, Yellows, Indians, etc. Do you know that the Catholic Church is the only one to serve as a temple to the good God? Neither Muslim mosques, nor Hindu temples, nor Jewish synagogues, nor Protestant temples, which do not believe in the real presence of Jesus in the Eucharist, claim to be the dwelling place of God.[59]

That de Bélinay wrote this in the 1950s is a reminder of why Vatican II had to happen, and fast! His mind was still working according to the logic of *extra ecclesiam nulla Salus* (No salvation outside the Church). Since science is to blame for everything, he doubled down on the anti-modernist agenda that had characterised the Catholic Church for more than a century, and the Jesuits from their restoration in 1814 until the 1940s, when younger French Jesuits started contesting this conservatism.

The somewhat racist references to Not only does de Bélinay 'Blacks, Yellows, and Indians' cannot be overlooked. They equally seemed to represent the hand of God in punishing the ungrateful privileged White race that had abandoned its Maker. As God used Israel's enemies in the Old Testament to punish Israel for its rebellions, God is now using Black, Reds, and Yellows to teach secularised France, the White race, and the entire Western civilisation a lesson. Lefèbvre could have said these words. He would, indeed, resurrect this mindset after the Second Vatican Council. Before this council opened its doors, de Bélinay had gone home, hopefully to the Heavenly Father he honestly desired to serve. This time, he had greater accomplishment to show forth. He had opened vast regions of Chad to the gospel.

De Bélinay suffered from neurasthenia. His Jesuit superiors believed he was not fit to return to Chad. On 14 September 1946, Charles Margot was appointed vice-superior of the mission. In October of that same year, a Procure of the Mission was opened for the purpose of supporting the

---

59   M-Ly. Box 1457: In 'Frederick de Bélinay, Ecrits divers, 1875–1958'. 'Marg. Marie' in this context is a reference to Saint Margaret Mary Alacoque (1647–90), pioneer of the devotion to the Sacred Heart of Jesus.

missions of the Near East and Chad. A new mission newsletter, *Lettres des Missionnaires,* replaced *Courrier* to inform the Jesuits and the families and friends of the missionaries about the mission. Jesuit communities across France were mobilised for that same purpose. These newsletters served as a recruitment tool for the Jesuit provinces of France.

While returning to Chad from one of his medical check-ups, de Bélinay wrote to his provincial, fully committing himself to the Mission:

> When I left Chad, I thought it was over. Today, I have a desire to return, despite all the annoyances of climate, and insects. I am convinced that all anticipated difficulties could be overcome [...] [I have] the intimate conviction that this return is not an adventure. At 62 years, there is nothing more [for me] to spare.[60]

Not only does de Bélinay confirm his determination to pursue the Chad Mission, he also hints at his spirituality of martyrdom. At sixty-two, he was still younger than the life expectancy of European missionaries in Chad.[61] De Bélinay understood that his time in Africa might be close to an end. Safeguarding the future of the mission, he believed, consisted in obtaining its official approval by the proper Vatican authorities. He travelled again to France in 1945 to share his thoughts with his Jesuit superiors and to gain their support for his new project.

The consultors' meeting of 23 September 1945 confirmed de Bélinay's desire to return to Chad. At de Bélinay's request, the consultors also agreed to assign Claude Scherantz (1893–1970) to that mission. Joseph du Bouchet, de Bélinay's immediate successor in Chad, opposed de Bélinay's return. Disappointed with this decision, the founder of the mission spent the rest of his life in France praying, organising support groups, and raising funds for the mission.

Conclusion

On 10 November 1958, Frédéric de Bonafos de Bélinay received the newly ordained Bishop Paul Dalmais of Fort-Lamy. F. de Bélinay showed signs of great joy and peace. The next day in the morning, he received Holy Communion, his last. Forty-five minutes after Dalmais had given him his blessing, de Bélinay died in peace. He was eighty-three. The pioneer of the Jesuit Mission and one of the founders of the Catholic Church in Chad had just received his viaticum from the new leader of the Church in that

---

[60] M-Ly. Box 1457: 'Frédéric de Bélinay, 1875–1958'.
[61] Most of them died in their late seventies; other pioneers of the missions like Charles Jacquet lived until they were in their nineties or more.

country. Both were French, and more than twenty years had passed since de Bélinay first set foot in Chad.[62] Upon his arrival as the head of the mission in 1946, Joseph du Bouchet had continued de Bélinay's work of establishing the institutional basis for the mission. With him, the Jesuits finally launched concrete mission work in Chad. Yet, the mission was still entirely French in 1958, two years before Chad's independence. Dalmais' appointment could be seen as a sign: the ecclesiastical Africanisation was no match for the political Africanisation.

There was almost no actual mission work to show for de Bélinay's decade in Chad. He was initially a military chaplain, then he became a missionary explorer, and finally he was the founder of the largest Jesuit mission in West Africa. De Bélinay expressed his love for Chad and explored its minerals in an attempt to make the mission economically self-sustaining. He also vowed – and this remained a wish until he returned to France – to have some catechetical translations done in one of the local languages. By the time he was forced to retire in Paris, he had found neither gold nor silver in Chad. Nor had he ever had the opportunity to learn any of Chad's languages. The Vatican's agenda of Africanisation was never part of either his vocabulary or his immediate agenda.

However, this exploratory period of the Chad Mission is worth studying. With it, one can gain a better understanding of the historical context of the Church in France, but also of the religious background and the spiritual and ideological motivations of Jesuit missionaries who were sent to Chad in the 1940s. Like de Bélinay, most of them lived through or fought in the two world wars. They once believed in nationalism, although as a necessary step for internationalism. Amid the increased secularisation of France, they perceived godless nationalism to be a danger to the ideals of the country they loved and to religion.

As the next chapter will show, these missionaries, faced with the Vatican's demand to Africanise the Church, remained attached to a spirituality of respect for indigenous cultures and religions. However, they were also averse to the rise of national leaders in the Church, which they associated with the Évolué class and the threat of Communism. Their military background prepared some of these missionaries to become, like Charles de Foucauld, the new fathers of the Sahara Desert.

---

[62] SL 457: J. du Bouchet, 'Frédéric de Bélinay, 1875–1955', *Courrier de la Province de Lyon* 108 (1958), 9. SL is the code used in the archive (Vanves) for a periodical used by the members of the province of Lyon: *Courrier de la Province de Lyon*.

CHAPTER 3

Colonial Era: Joseph du Bouchet and the Building of the Jesuit Mission in Chad, 1947–58

On 1 November 1947, Joseph du Bouchet arrived in Fort-Lamy. He had just been appointed apostolic prefect of Chad.[1] To welcome him, his colleague Charles Margot gathered the entire colonial elite of the city. Military honours followed du Bouchet's arrival. A solemn mass was celebrated on the site of the future Cathedral of Notre Dame. By noon, the European Fraternity of Fort-Lamy had received du Bouchet. The next day, on the Commemoration of All the Faithful Departed, he presided at another eucharistic celebration in the cemetery where Commandant François Lamy, explorer and conqueror of Chad, was buried.[2]

The French military establishment in Chad stood by du Bouchet's side. Madame Leclerc, wife of the famous general who led French Sub-Saharan African troops in the Second World War, sat in the front row.[3] She was the main benefactress for the construction of the new cathedral. A few months later, on 15 February 1948, du Bouchet wrote to the national chaplain of the veterans in Paris, asking for their support for the Chad Mission. Since Chad was an important French military base, some veterans in Paris had been there and were willing to throw their support behind the mission.[4]

---

[1] According to the 1981 edition of Canon Law, 'a vicariate apostolic or a prefecture apostolic is a certain portion of the people of God, which for special reason is not yet constituted a diocese, and which is entrusted to the pastoral care of a Vicar apostolic or a Prefect apostolic, who governs it in the name of the Supreme Pontiff': *The Code of Canon Law: A Text and Commentary* (New York: Paulist Press, 1985), 371.

[2] On Lamy, see: François Joseph Lamy, *Le Commandant Lamy d'après sa correspondance et ses souvenirs de Campagne, 1858–1900* (Paris: Hachette, 1903).

[3] 'Histoire d'une cathédrale', *JAF* 1 (1965): 16–25.

[4] M-Ly. 149: J. du Bouchet, 'Lettre à Monsieur l'Abbé Louis, Aumônier de l'Hôtel National des Invalides, February 15, 1948'.

Figure 3 Bishop Joseph du Bouchet visiting Archambault, 1951 (Archives JHIA, Nairobi).

During du Bouchet's welcoming ceremony on the site of the cathedral of Fort-Lamy, the new head of the mission noticed the presence of some 'brave Blacks'. Amid traditional songs and dancing, these Africans brought many gifts. With the help of three interpreters, some of them asked for blessings to be given to their rosaries and themselves.[5] Among these Africans, the head of the Cameroonian immigrant 'colony' in Fort-Lamy offered a welcoming address to du Bouchet.[6] Other Cameroonians quickly put themselves forward to become Jesuits.

J. du Bouchet's arrival officially ended the exploratory period of the Chad Mission (1931–46). To mark that rupture, du Bouchet denied the return of the founder of the mission, Frédéric de Bélinay, to Chad. His predecessor, he believed, would be more useful to the mission if he remained in Paris.[7] Moreover, the official recognition of the mission by the Vatican, and the subsequent ecclesiastical organisation of the mission that followed, seemed to initiate a brighter horizon for the Africanisation of its personnel and leadership which the Vatican was pushing for. In practice, having a sitting bishop in Chad was a positive step towards recruiting and training a local clergy and lay personnel for the mission. Such a step was necessary to make the Church in Chad truly Chadian in its religious practices, its personnel, and its leaders.

[5] M-Ly. 149: J. du Bouchet, 'Lettre au Provincial, March 15, 1948'.
[6] A-JHIA: Charles Margot, 'Mes chers noirs', *Lettres du Tchad* 4 (February 1948): 2. Not classified.
[7] M-Ly. 102/1: J. du Bouchet, 'Lettre au Provincial, September 22, 1948'.

Yet, this chapter argues, du Bouchet continued with de Bélinay's conservatism. He closed the door to African vocations from Cameroon. He, instead, requested more missionaries from Lyon for the Chad Mission. Du Bouchet was advised by Bishop René Graffin of Yaoundé, and might have listened to Papal Legate Lefèbvre. He finally showed no interest in the Vatican's progressive policy of Africanisation. Not surprisingly, the Vatican priority efforts to raise an African clergy in Chad stalled. The new apostolic prefect was part of the colonial establishment in Chad, the head of a church that was still colonial.

Under du Bouchet, however, partial Africanisation of the Church was achieved on three other fronts: the creation of Chad as an autonomous ecclesiastical jurisdiction, the evangelisation through the incorporation of African art and architectural features in the construction of mission chapels, and a focus on catechetical and biblical translations. Africanisation was primarily a theological and liturgical task, while the recruitment of African Jesuits and the rise of an African leadership in Chad were delayed. With du Bouchet, the Africanisation agenda had become a form of vernacularisation. The Vatican's elitist agenda could wait for another generation, yet its broader evangelising agenda was realised with little cost for the future of Chadian Catholicism. The Vatican had nothing to lose by overlooking this silent dissent from the Jesuits in Chad.

Outreach to the French youth

That du Bouchet overrode the Vatican was not accidental. Young men in Chad were not well prepared enough to become priests. And du Bouchet was left, at least initially, to count on the French youth for the pursuit of the mission. In *Lettres du Tchad*, the Mission's newsletter, du Bouchet wrote about the French youth on 2 April 1948:

> A new and young public, so to speak, is eager for newness, for mission to the savages, for primitive missionary life, and for Christianity. This stimulates them, creates enthusiasm, and answers their secret expectations, and takes them out of their mediocrity ...[8]

This conception of the French youth being inclined to newness was du Bouchet's first shared belief with Bishop Marcel Lefèbvre. Lefèbvre often decried the youth of France for their love of spectacle, saying that at the

---

[8] M-Ly. 149: J. du Bouchet's report of the situation of the Chad Mission (seventeen pages), 2 April 1948.

same time they paid no mind to church attendance and were remorseless in the face of the horrors of social justice. To create enthusiasm for the mission, J. du Bouchet played to this eagerness for novelty that the young people had to call them to arms. He also offered an interesting rhetorical gradation, as he made a distinction between the 'mission to the savages', 'primitive missionary life', and 'Christianity'. Through this social classification of religion, ranging from what he saw as the worse to the better, he affirmed Christianity to be not only superior but also necessary to free the 'savages' from primitivism.[9]

The French *mission civilisatrice* also shared this vision. In practice, French Catholicism in Chad was at war with the country's 'primitivism'. Du Bouchet concluded his appeal with an *ad hominem* argument. By calling French young men 'mediocre', he shamed and simultaneously taunted them to embrace the new religious adventure upon which he had embarked. In his appeal to the youth, he might have thought of himself as the new Francis Xavier of Chad.[10] The salvation of 'primitive' Africans went alongside the awakening of the French youth from their tepid mood and, eventually, this awakening would help secure their own salvation. Going to Africa was necessary for the salvation of Africans. It was equally good for the rebuilding of France's morale, the spiritual awakening of its youth, and its re-Christianisation.

J. du Bouchet's focus on the youth was part of a broader home-mission strategy in France. Since the creation of the French Catholic Youth Association in 1886, engaging young people in the re-Christianisation of France had been a priority for French Roman Catholicism; this outreach towards the youth was reinforced during the interwar period. The Jeunesse Ouvrière Chrétienne (JOC: Christian Youth Workers) was created in 1926. The Jeunesse Agricole Catholique (JAC: Catholic Agricultural Youth) and the Jeunesse Estudiantine Chrétienne (JEC: Catholic Student Youth) were both created three years later, in 1929. These Catholic youth associations intended to develop 'instruction among the working classes', a task many

---

[9] As Paul Kollman has observed, that kind of speech 'constitutes discursive positions of European self and non-European other, to classify Christian practice, and to classify practitioners and those to whom such practitioners were sent': Paul Kollman, 'At the Origins of Mission and Missiology: A Study in the Dynamics of Religious Language', *Journal of the American Academy of Religion* 79, no. 2 (June 2011): 442.

[10] In Francis Xavier, 'Letter to his Companions Living in Rome', in *The Letters and Instructions of Francis Xavier*, Series I – Jesuit Primary Sources, English Translations, no. 10 (Saint Louis, MO: Institute of Jesuit Sources, 1992), 66–67.

Catholics saw as 'a necessity, driven by the order to (re-)Christianise French society. The aim was to slow the propagation of competing ideologies which, potentially or actually, threatened the church's influence in France'.[11] Catholic youth associations became partners in the mission field for the Jesuits in Chad, as recruiting local vocations had become almost impossible.

Failed Attempts to Recruit Indigenous Vocations

While appealing to the youth in France, du Bouchet, initially at least, also considered recruiting indigenous vocations, since this was an essential requirement of the Africanisation project the Vatican authorities were pushing for. Unfortunately, du Bouchet's attempt to recruit indigenous vocations did not last long. Two months after his arrival, du Bouchet discussed with his provincial and religious superior in Lyon the possibility of admitting a Cameroonian named Maurice Mbarga into the Society of Jesus. This letter appears to be the only evidence of any attempt by du Bouchet to open the Jesuit order to Africans.

Mbarga, who, from missionary sources, was already a priest, represented an excellent opportunity for the Chad Mission. He could cover extended areas of the Church ministry in Chad, including the administration of the sacraments of baptism, holy matrimony, and especially that of reconciliation. He could also serve as a stimulus for young African vocations in the Sahelian country. That possibility was shot down immediately. The French apostolic vicar of Yaoundé, René Graffin (r. 1943–61), a Spiritan[12] who was Mbarga's ecclesiastical superior, advised du Bouchet against such an admission. He portrayed Mbarga, and another unnamed Cameroonian candidate who came with him, as 'opportunistic'.[13]

There is evidence of a certain anti-Cameroonian sentiment in the rhetoric of the missionaries working in Chad early on in the mission. In the Letters of Charles Margot, Cameroonian immigrants in Chad are described as

> a few hundred, mainly government, bank, or trade employees, of a somewhat primitive, though superior primitive culture. They are proud to be a homogeneous race, proud to the point of disregard for others, and

---

[11] Marie-Pierre Wynands, '(Re)Christianizing the Popular Classes. The Catholic Church and Faith Training, 1921–1939', *Revue Française de Science Politique* 66, no. 2 (2017): 43–61 – here, pp. 44 and 47.

[12] Another term for 'Holy Ghost Father'.

[13] M-Ly. 149: J. du Bouchet, 'Letter to the Provincial, November 22, 1948'. I was unable to find any record on Mbarga in the diocesan archives of Yaoundé.

with almost unhealthy susceptibility [...] However, taken apart, most Cameroonians have valuable qualities and, better understood, would be true friends and faithful auxiliaries.[14]

Other reasons eventually motivated the opposition of Yaoundé's apostolic prefect to the admission of Mbarga and his colleague. Some African bishops resented the fact that their African seminarians or priests might join the Society of Jesus, even if such vocations later proved to be very successful for the future Jesuit Province. For example, on 24 December 1971, a letter mentions contacts between the provincial of Paris and Cardinal Zoungrana of Ouagadougou (Burkina Faso), concerning the admission of Jean Ilboudo. Ilboudo later became the first African provincial of West Africa (1996–2000), and general assistant for Africa in Rome (2000–08). The same letter alludes to another seminarian of Koumi, Martin Birba, who depended on Bishop Tapsoba, and wanted to join the Society of Jesus.[15]

Discouraged by the cases of Mbarga and his Cameroonian colleague, du Bouchet never again considered recruiting seminarians or ordained priests from neighbouring countries. In contrast to the Capuchins, the Jesuits in Chad seemed to ignore local and regional missionary dynamics. As later experiences confirmed, accepting vocations from neighbouring countries could have benefitted the nascent Church of Chad. For example, southern Cameroonians proved to be excellent missionaries in northern Cameroon, which was geographically, sociologically, culturally, and religiously similar to Chad. The best-known case was the work of Simon Mpeke (1906–75) among the Kirdi of northern Cameroon.[16] Jean-Marc Ela (1936–2008), a disciple of Mpeke who became a prolific African theologian, was also very successful in the region.[17] These missionaries offered an alternative to the French approach. Ela became one of the African pioneers of liberation theology, breaking away from Western-centred theology and ecclesiology.

[14] Margot, 'Mes chers noirs'.
[15] A-Pa. 162: 'Correspondence with the Vice-Province of West Africa, 1972–1973'.
[16] Grégoire Cador, *L'héritage de Simon Mpeke: Prêtre de Jésus et frère universel* (Paris: Lethielleux: Desclée de Brouwer, 2009). Mpeke was one of the first Cameroonians ordained as a priest in 1935.
[17] Some of Ela's books include: Jean-Marc Ela, ed., *Voici le temps des héritiers. Eglises d'Afrique et voie nouvelle* (Paris: Karthala, 1981); Jean-Marc Ela, *Ma foi d'Africain* (Paris: Karthala, 1985); *Le cri de l'homme africain: questions aux chrétiens et aux églises d'Afrique* (Paris: L'Harmattan, 1980).

Failing to pursue a regional approach to recruiting African Jesuits represented a missed opportunity. The admission of a priest could have supplied, for Chad, the well-trained Catholic flock that was necessary for Jesuit training. Margot also acknowledged that Cameroonian immigrants in Chad were an 'enormous support for the nascent mission, well trained in Christian liturgy, and able to help train others'.[18] Having lived longer in a 'true Christianity', Margot added, these Cameroonian immigrants understood Christian liturgy, and became the liturgical basis for several Jesuit parishes in Chad.[19]

Cameroonians were not the only well-trained Christians living in Chad. There were also Congolese and Ubangians. They were advanced in their knowledge of letters, and they had been moulded by missionaries for long enough to have become 'good auxiliaries for White missionaries'.[20] But instead of trying to find vocations from among the African diaspora in Chad, du Bouchet sent a request to Lyon for more French missionaries.

Another factor might lie behind the non-admission of Africans into the Society in Chad and in French Africa overall. In 1949, the apostolic vicars of Francophone West Africa, all of them French missionaries, gathered in Brazzaville. Lefèbvre presided over the meeting. Their goal was to offer a 'unified way of action' that would be common to the four Francophone vicariates in Central and West Africa.[21] Based on the later decision of Lefèbvre, as a schismatic bishop, to reject the *aggiornamento* of the Second Vatican Council, it is possible that the Brazzaville encounter led to a more conservative shift in the missionary approach of Francophone Africa.

Evidence of such a claim comes from the realisation that when du Bouchet returned from Brazzaville, he stopped any attempts to recruit Africans, and immediately requested more French missionaries for Chad.[22] Moreover, during the ordination to priesthood of François Ngaïbi (1957), the first Catholic priest in Chad, the Capuchins who had trained

---

[18] Margot, 'Mes chers noirs', 2.
[19] Ibid.
[20] Ibid., 3.
[21] Plenary session of the apostolic vicars and prefects of French Equatorial Africa in Brazzaville, reported by du Bouchet in a letter to the provincial, 31 May 1949. There are more letters between Lefèbvre, then superior general of the Fathers of the Holy Spirit, and Janssen, superior general of the Jesuits, concerning the control of a geographical area in the north of Chad. Propaganda Fide settled that dispute in favour of the Jesuits. Cf. M-Ly. 174–77: 'Registre des consultes, 1931–1976', Consult minutes (8 January 1951).
[22] M-Ly. 149: J. du Bouchet, 'Letter to the Provincial, June 13, and July 27, 1949'.

him complained that the apostolic prefect wanted everything to be done in Latin. He even refused indigenous music, although liturgical songs were already translated into Ngambay.[23]

Request for More Personnel from Lyon

From available sources, it seems that no more effort was made, under du Bouchet, to encourage local Jesuit vocations in Chad. Yet, more missionaries were needed. The Jesuit Province of Lyon, unfortunately, was not in a position to fully satisfy du Bouchet's request. In July 1951, the provincial of Lyon formally asked Revd Jean-Baptiste Janssens (1889–1964), superior general of the Jesuits, to allow the arrival of two Brothers of the Venice-Milan province.[24] This request was remarkable in its own right. The French government had been, up to this point, resisting the presence of non-French missionaries in its African territories. Especially prohibited in Chad were the Italians.

There is no evidence that this prohibition had anything to do with the fear of the Vatican's threat on French interests in Africa, as François Méjan would later suggest.[25] Instead, Italy represented a threat because of its historical relationship with Libya, a direct regional strategic adversary to France's interests in Chad. Although with no clear justification, up to this point the Spanish Jesuits were not allowed either. Ultimately, du Bouchet's request for missionary personnel was also a clear admission of the bigger challenge that the Chad Mission represented.

In 1946, when it assumed the direction of the Chad Mission,[26] the province of Lyon totalled 510 Jesuits. They worked in five high schools, training houses for younger Jesuits, and spiritual and social centres. Another 113 of them were scattered around the globe as foreign missionaries.[27] More than twice as large as France, Chad was a geographic, cultural, and religious

---

He repeated that request on a regular basis, until the subject was brought to the attention of the general.

[23] Michel Guimbaud, 'Mgr Gaumain, Souvenirs' (10 March 2010) <http://www.freres-capucins.fr/IMG/pdf/Gaumain.pdf> [accessed 16 April 2017].

[24] M-Ly. 174–77: Consult minutes (9 July 1951).

[25] François Méjan, *Le Vatican contre la France d'Outre-Mer?* (Paris: Librairie Fischbacher, 1957).

[26] 'With the exception of the administrative regions of Mayo Kebi and Logone, evangelized one by the Oblates of Mary, and the other by the Capuchins'. Cf. 'Le Tchad', *JAF* 1 (1953): 39.

[27] Pierre Emmanuel, 'Lyon', *JAF* 1 (1953): 11. The province of Paris, which later

challenge.[28] Its 2.5 million souls spoke different languages. And the country was seen foremost as an isolated land, hot and dry, with a spreading, conquering Islam, the progress of which the Jesuits vowed to stop.[29]

Nevertheless, the Jesuits also became aware of the shifting demographics in global Roman Catholicism. Commenting on the papal missionary intention of 1951, Jesuit priest H. Haeck acknowledged the substantial growth of Roman Catholics in Africa. The membership of the Church had shifted from about 1.2 million in 1900 to 14 million in 1950. During the same period, the number of priests in Africa rose from 1,735 to 9,402. But the increase in the number of priests and sisters was proportionally inferior to that of the broader membership of the Church.[30] Facing these religious and demographic shifts, it became imperative for the Jesuit leaders in Lyon to either accelerate the training of a local clergy in Chad, as the Vatican was urging, or find a way to send more missionaries to the African mission. As already noted, they opted for the latter. Six years later, in 1957, the Vatican could not have been clearer about the urgency of sending more missionaries to Africa:

> We are aware, Pope Pius XII wrote, that seeds of trouble are being sown in various parts of Africa by the proponents of atheistic materialism, who are stirring up the emotions of the natives by encouraging mutual envy among them and by distorting their unhappy material condition in an attempt to deceive them with an empty show of advantages to be won, or to incite them to seditious acts [...] Any delay or hesitation is full of danger [...] For this reason, it is imperative that help should be given now to the shepherds of the Lord's flock in order that their apostolic labours may correspond to the ever-growing needs of the times.[31]

---

    evangelised Cameroon and Côte d'Ivoire, had similar numbers: 630 Jesuits in total, with 154 of them as missionaries. Cf. 'Paris', *JAF* 1 (1953): 17–19.

[28] M-Ly. 102/2: A. Décisier, 'Lettre du 30 avril 1946'.

[29] 'Le Tchad', *JAF* 1 (1953): 39. Ten years later, the Jesuits opened a parish in Fort-Lamy, Kabalay, with a membership of about 65,000, not counting members from villages who were attached to Kabalay. This parish was also responsible for the education of about 7,000 young men and girls, and 30 catechumenal training centres: André Martin, 'Kabalay, croissance chrétienne', *JAF* 1 (1963): 40.

[30] Cf. the Jesuit archives of Vanves (France), under: 'Revues de presses et faits divers' (Press Reviews and News Items), hereafter B-Af.C. Here, B-Af.C. 2/1.1. H. Haeck, 'Revues de presses et faits divers'. L'intention missionnaire de 1951.

[31] That call to increase missionary personnel in Africa was reiterated by Pope Pius XII in his encyclical *Fidei Donum*, *AAS* 49 (1957): 225–48, here 239ff.

On the eve of independence, the task of sending more missionaries to Africa was more urgent because of a threefold competition. In the case of Chad, in addition to Islam, Protestant missions had been strengthening their presence.[32] Likewise, materialistic atheism, spread by European immigrants, was gaining ground among the young African elite also known as the Évolué class.[33] According to the Jesuit consultors in Lyon:

> The task in Chad is overwhelming and demands enormous sacrifices for the Province. Was it a wise decision to accept it in the first place? There is no guarantee the mission could receive 50 new missionaries for the next fifteen years. [J. du Bouchet] is considering asking the Propaganda Fide to ask another French missionary corporation to take over half the territory.[34]

The doubt among the leadership of the Lyon Province raises questions about the preparation of the Chad Mission as related to the overall apostolic planning of the province. Initial consultation meetings had focused on whether or not to grant permission to de Bélinay. However, there really never was any serious deliberation about the implications of accepting the Chad Mission as such, and about the resources the province might need for its success. That the challenge arose six years later is not surprising. The Chad Mission, it has been said, was primarily the initiative of a single Jesuit before both its needs and the international context in Asia made the African mission attractive to many others. On the other hand, the Middle East had been part of French missionary outreach for almost a century. Extending the Near East mission to the whole territory of Chad might have been a step too far. The territory was extremely vast, and Chad, with its harsh climate, was not easily accessible. It was, indeed, in the middle of the African Sahel, beyond the Sahara, and far away from the Middle East.

Yet, after six years on the mission, and given the insistence of the Lyon Jesuits who were already in Chad, the province consultors addressed the pressing demand for more missionaries. The petition for more missionaries and the recognition of the enormous sacrifices being made meant that the actual mission work on the ground needed more personnel. Du Bouchet might have closed the door to clerical Africanisation, which the Vatican was pushing for. In spite of this, however, he and his European colleagues

---

[32] According to Paul Dalmais, Protestant missionaries first arrived at Léré in 1920. See: Paul Dalmais, 'Mission du Tchad', *JAF* 3 (1959): 33–34.

[33] B-Af.C. 2/1.1: 'Revues de presses et faits divers'.

[34] M-Ly. 175: 'Consult minutes, October 31, 1951'. On 3 December 1951, the consult confirmed the challenges of the mission; see: 'Consult minutes, December 3, 1951'.

Figure 4 André Meynier (left) just after his arrival as a young scholar in Archambault, 1954, with Brother François Catt and Father Victor Waton (Archives JHIA, Nairobi).

seemed to be making substantial progress in the field of vernacularisation. This seemed a good development for the Church in Chad. And the Vatican had nothing against that either.

Construction and Art as Evangelisation

When the superior general of the Jesuits, Vladimir Ledochowski, decided to make Chad part of the Middle East Mission, Joseph du Bouchet was still provincial of Lyon. He was, in fact, very excited and enthusiastic about the new challenge. In a letter to the members of his province on 25 December 1936, du Bouchet received 'with great joy' the father general's decision.[35]

---

[35] M-Ly. 102/1: 'Lettres circulaires J. du Bouchet'.

Two other letters from the general, on 15 and 25 August 1937, confirmed the conversion of the Muslims as the apostolic priority of that mission. André Décisier, who succeeded du Bouchet as provincial of Lyon, echoed the new commitment of the Lyon Province towards the Middle East. Recent doubts about Chad seemed to have been dispelled as well.

In a visit to Beirut, Décisier, while vowing to continue the commitment of his province in the Middle East, also specified the purpose of the mission. Its works, he said, would be strictly limited to 'spiritual matters'.[36] Referring to Chad as a 'pagan land', 'forgotten', 'located in the confines of Egypt', a reminder of the *Hic sunt leones*, Décisier expressed his hope that the Chad Mission would strengthen 'our [France's] strategy' in the Middle East.[37] Despite its roughness, he concluded, Chad would bring great vocational and spiritual benefits to the province and its members.[38]

From a territory where 'no altar, or cross was planted in 1946',[39] the missionary report of 1955 registered an increase in mission work. Part of this success came from the institutional evolution of the mission as an apostolic prefecture and the admirable construction works that the Jesuit Brothers were carrying out.[40] The brothers themselves saw their social stature improve in the African mission field. Their very presence and their work also had an impact on African society.

Pictures from the mission describe a transfer of knowledge through the use of art that went along with changes in architecture, worship, and evangelising methods. Describing one of the chapels the Brothers had built, Jesuit priest Roland Pichon wrote:

> The chapel of Bediondo was already African by its pillars made of Palmyra palm branches. It is much more so now thanks to [Brother] Augustin Vala, who wrote the history of salvation on her walls for his African brothers. This work began last Christmas, [and] included several pictures of Biblical scenes: the Cana wedding, the Resurrection of Lazarus, Pentecost, and the Vatican Council, where among the bishops of all colours represented, one can recognise Bishop [Henri] Véniat.[41]

---

[36] M-Ly. 102/2: A. Décisier, 'Lettre du 30 avril 1946'.
[37] Paul Dalmais, 'Mission du Tchad', *JAF* 3 (1959): 32.
[38] M-Ly. 102/2: A. Décisier, 'Lettre du 30 avril 1946'.
[39] This was an exaggeration that later became part of the Jesuit narrative, making them the 'founders' of the Church in Chad. I have shown the existence of Catholic missions that existed before the arrival of the Jesuits.
[40] 'Nos Frères du Tchad', *JAF* 3 (1955): 27–30.
[41] Roland Pichon, 'Bediondo, le salut sur les murs', *JAF* 1 (1964): 41. Bishop Henri Véniat will be discussed in the next section of this chapter.

In Chad, Christian symbols often redefined the landscape. Church buildings mixed modern Western architecture with Chadian features. Crosses were planted on street corners. Public paintings of the nativity scene or Christmas cribs took centre stage in villages and markets. Some of the churches were baptised with names of famous Western Jesuits and, later on, with names of the martyrs of Uganda.

The use of construction and painting as a means to evangelise is a well-established Catholic practice. Cardinal Celso Costantini, head of Propaganda Fide who had been instrumental for the institutional recognition of the Chad Mission, believed in the power of art to evangelise. However, he insisted that as they go to mission, 'missionaries should not transport France, Spain, and Italy with them'. On the contrary, 'the three vital principles [of mission] are: evangelise, not colonise; respect the art and culture of the country; and remove foreign forms from sacred art'.[42]

Moreover, according to Jesuit historian John O'Malley, 'liturgy, broadly understood, is the fundamental context for Christian appropriation of the material culture' at the receiving end of Christian missions.[43] The Jesuits had previously used that evangelising method in other places such as colonial Mexico or Ethiopia. Each time, the Jesuits would use art and architecture to instruct on Christian doctrines. However, because the workers were Indians or Ethiopians, these often gave new meaning to artistic productions in ways that were not necessarily orthodox.[44] In practice, art served as a means for local appropriation of Christianity.

As the Jesuits trained Chadians in construction and agricultural techniques, there was hope among them that Chadians, in contact with European Brothers, would join the Society, but that they would do so primarily as Brothers:

> At your contact, Brothers, Chadian Brothers will arise one day! Brothers, we are already thinking. But to respond, we need light and strength, which normally require an old Christian soil. Of these new Christian churches,

---

[42] Andrew F. Walls, *The Missionary Movement in Christian History: Studies in the Transmission of Faith* (Maryknoll, NY: Orbis Books, 1996), 176.

[43] John W O'Malley, *Four Cultures of the West* (Cambridge, MA: Belknap Press of Harvard University Press, 2004), 181.

[44] Here are two references on the matter: Eleanor Wake, *Framing the Sacred: The Indian Churches of Early Colonial Mexico* (Norman, OK: University of Oklahoma Press, 2010); María-José Friedlander and Bob Friedlander, *Hidden Treasures of Ethiopia. A Guide to the Remote Churches of an Ancient Land* (New York: I. B. Tauris, 2015).

which the [European] Brothers have raised up by their labours and their prayers, others will rise and, like them, will follow the Lord.[45]

In this abstract, Father Pichon acknowledges the delay in recruiting African vocations while simultaneously expressing the hope that the work the Jesuit Brothers were doing in Chad would inspire indigenous men to become Jesuit Brothers. It is not clear whether this was an innocent and yet realistic assessment of the situation in Chad, or a veiled admission that the Jesuits expected local vocations to be limited to Chadians becoming Brothers, and not Fathers. As a matter of fact, the first Chadians to become Jesuits were Brothers. A twofold explanation can be given for that state of affairs.

The practical nature of the work the Brothers were doing in Chad put them closer to the common people. This proximity facilitated a better knowledge of the Brothers and a better understanding of their lifestyle. Further, to become a Jesuit Brother did not require advanced degrees in philosophy and theology, which were necessary for vocations to the priesthood. Becoming a Brother was therefore easier for a Chadian than becoming a priest.

Prioritising Chadian vocations among the Brothers had real consequences for the Africanisation of Chad's Christianity. While Brothers could advance the bottom-up works of evangelism through vernacularisation, catechisation, and construction, they could not constitutionally become leaders either in the Church or in the Society of Jesus, as the Vatican would have wished for. Only priests could become Jesuit superiors: African bishops were chosen from among African priests. All the first bishops in Chad had been French leaders of the Jesuit mission or other missionary congregations. They were all Westerners. Not surprisingly, the delay in promoting vocations to the priesthood in Chad led to delays in the Africanisation of leadership. This put the Jesuits in Chad in opposition to a key priority of the Vatican: that the Church in Africa be led by Africans. By 1951, a few Spanish Brothers were finally welcomed as builders. Adding to that exception, a Spanish father was to be in charge of them.[46]

A final link between art and evangelism in the Jesuit Chad Mission was seen in the use of music. Although he had prohibited the Divine Office from singing and forbidden the use of musical instruments in Jesuit houses,[47]

---

[45] P. Pichon, 'Bediondo, le salut sur les murs', 30.
[46] M-Ly. Boxes 174–76: 'Consulte Lyon, 1931–1970', Consult minutes (3 December 1951).
[47] Thomas Frank Kennedy, *Music and the Jesuit Mission in the New World* (Saint Louis, MO: Seminar on Jesuit Spirituality, 2007), 2.

Ignatius of Loyola encouraged their use in Jesuit schools. Like theatre, the Jesuits pioneered the use of music for catechesis and evangelisation in the sixteenth century as part of their commitment to the education of the youth.[48] This tradition was deployed in Jesuit missions across the globe. T. Frank Kennedy has analysed the specific case of Paraguay, where the Jesuit opera often included ballets, dance, and other spectacular performance, which not only transmitted the creedal contents of Catholic official doctrine but also left performers and spectators with a certain religious effervescence and the feeling of having experienced the supernatural.[49]

In Chad, Father Bernard Duperray developed a similarly active or practical method of learning. In a context where verbal communication was still impossible because of lack of translations, the missionaries applied visual art and music for alphabetisation, to teach catechesis, and to communicate the gospel message. Pierre Njé-Ra-Koula, the Chadian monitor of the parish school of Chagwa, taught his kids and his pupils how to conjugate the verb 'to run', by inviting them to actually run around the class, repeating: 'I run in the classroom, you run in the classroom, etc'. These active methods could, however, be confusing:

> Here is a brush-haired kid, his eyes constantly lit by an enticing idea, which, to conjugate the verb 'to have a slate', cries out loudly: 'I'm a slate, you're a slate', provoking the hilarity of the Fathers, whose ears do not lose anything from the lesson, through the brick walls.[50]

Another innovation launched by Father Duperray was the learning of Ngambaye and French at the same time. It was called 'the syllabic method: *ba*, it is the river; *Bi*, sleeping; *Bo*, big or big; *Bû*, ashes. Father Fortier, in Moïsala, used this method to compose a syllabus of Mbaye, and to teach catechists how to read'.[51]

Singing was a very effective learning technique for the fathers. As Duperray would say: 'when one knows one song, he would repeat it ten times'. Children generally sang French popular songs: 'songs and poems

---

[48] John W. O'Malley, Gauvin A. Bailey, and Steven J. Harris, *The Jesuits II: Cultures, Sciences, and the Arts, 1540–1773* (Toronto: University of Toronto Press, 2006), 452.

[49] Thomas Frank Kennedy, 'Jesuits and Music: The European Tradition, 1547–1622' (PhD Musicology, Santa Clara, CA, University of California Santa Clara, 1982), 202–03.

[50] *Lettres du Tchad* (1949).

[51] Fortier, *Les débuts de l'évangélisation au Moyen Chari, Diocese de Sarh (Les Pionniers) (1946–66)*, vol. 1 (Sarh: n.p., 1991), 54.

learned by heart [...] are heard on the paths that surround the Mission; they are found on the football field where, every evening, children played a game, barefoot of course'.[52] In Duperray's method, 'religious instruction is based on image and singing. Children sing the entire Bible and the life of Jesus. And that teaching technique has a lasting effect'.[53] These practical methods were so effective that even the cook of the Jesuit community became a schoolteacher, an evangeliser, in his free time.[54]

Conclusion

The first part of this book has provided the historical background of the Jesuit mission in Chad. This context, it appears, aligned the mission to France's *mission civilisatrice* through a process of Frenchification that limited the mission personnel to French citizens. It also consistently delayed the Vatican's priority of clerical Africanisation. The Jesuit pioneers in Chad, as evidenced in the first chapter, understood their mission primarily in the context of wider France, rather than the Vatican's focus on indigenisation or clerical Africanisation. In the second and third chapters, the analysis of the conservatism of Frédéric de Bélinay and Joseph du Bouchet again aligns both Jesuits with conservatives among French Jesuits and within the post-Second World War Roman Catholic Church in Francophone Africa.

As Chapter 3 demonstrates, Father du Bouchet's call to the French youth and his request for more European missionaries while delaying admission of Africans to the Society meant that the beginnings of the Church in Chad was tantamount to a transplantation of French Catholicism onto African soil. It also expanded the French Jesuits' Middle East missions and their war against atheistic materialism. Within the African context, this approach made du Bouchet the early pioneer of the papal encyclical *Fidei Donum* (1957). The encyclical called more European missionaries to be sent to Africa, exactly at a time when Africa had reached its political independence and was moving towards ecclesial Africanisation.

That du Bouchet led the Chadian Church to this outcome was not surprising. According to Jean Lacouture, du Bouchet was averse to change, even as provincial of Lyon.[55] Jesuit Pierre Raisson, who wrote his obituary, described du Bouchet as a 'righteous man' who sometimes reached

---

[52] Ibid., 53–54.
[53] Ibid., 53.
[54] Ibid.
[55] Lacouture, *Jésuites: Les Revenants*, vol. 2, 357–58.

the 'extreme limits of righteousness'. He was a spiritual man who could also be very cold and rigid. Yet, Raisson concluded, 'if he was wrong, it was because he lacked light, not because he was against the light'.[56]

At the end of his term as provincial, du Bouchet was sent, to the surprise of all, to mission. Chad was, for a man of his experience, a new beginning. And after a time of hesitation, du Bouchet embraced his new mission with great enthusiasm, although he lacked the practical skill to lead such a mission. Further, as demonstrated in this chapter, he joined other French bishops in Africa whose conservativism du Bouchet naturally embraced. Under the leadership of Lefèbvre, French Africa became the last refuge of Church leaders who could not strive in France after the Second World War. They were often ideologically to the right of de Gaulle and, as such, to the far right of the rising French Catholic left. Inside the Society, de Bélinay and du Bouchet represented – although not at the level of Lefèbvre – the face of this remnant of the right wing. They were men used to being in power who, having lost it in France, could still master and keep it in Chad.

Not surprisingly, the pioneers of the Jesuit Chad Mission launched a transplant of French Catholicism into French Africa. This transplant was more reminiscent of the colonial and pre-Second World War's *mission civilisatrice* than in alignment with the changes Africa's decolonisation demanded. As a result, de Bélinay, du Bouchet, and their Jesuit colleagues ignored and delayed the Vatican's agenda of Africanisation of the leadership of the Church in Chad.

With the refusal to accept vocations from neighbouring countries, du Bouchet put his hope in having new personnel primarily from France and Europe rather than fostering the African vocations needed to build a Church that was genuinely African. The Vatican itself seemed to approve this approach with the later publication of *Fidei Donum* in 1957. Moreover, even as the first Jesuits in Chad hoped that the Chadians might become Jesuit Brothers, the Brothers, by virtue of the limitations in the scope of their ministry – for they were not priests – would still have left the Chadian Church dependent on missionary personnel. The arrival of more of the latter could not effect the Africanisation of leadership that the Vatican was pushing for.

Therefore, not only did the missionary approach under du Bouchet delay the Africanisation of the Church leadership in Chad, it also secured

---

[56] Pierre Raisson, 'Le Père Joseph du Bouchet, 1890–1970', *Jésuites* (1971): 177–79.

those leadership positions for French missionaries for decades to come. In fact, the end of the 1950s coincided with the establishment of Fort-Lamy as a diocese. J. du Bouchet was retiring. With no Chadian clergy, Paul Dalmais, another French missionary, was appointed as the diocese's first Bishop in 1957.[57]

Under J. du Bouchet's leadership, however, the new Jesuit global commitment was invested in building a local Church in Chad which, although strongly French in those beginnings, was still rooted, nevertheless, in the hope of de-Frenchification. Moreover, in order to Africanise this Church, the work of the pioneers consisted in a bottom-up approach that focused primarily on construction work, catechisation, and shaping the religious landscape of Chad with Christian symbols.

---

[57] M-Ly. 175: 'Consult minutes, July 15, 1957'. He was ordained bishop a year later.

PART II

The Outward Mission: Education and Competing Catholicisms

Introduction

The process of Frenchification that started with de Bélinay and du Bouchet was implemented through specific policies. These combined the twofold objectives of evangelism and social development. Part II of this book argues that social progress was considered a form of evangelism in the Chad Mission. The Jesuits, drawing from their old traditions in the field of education, applied different strategies among the Muslim populations and ethno-religionists. It explores how the combination of social development and Frenchification helped to advance the political and ecclesiastical agenda of Africanisation.

The Jesuit mission also faced the cultural and political challenge of Chad's Cultural Revolution, which the Jesuits addressed by drawing from their traditional mission strategy of accommodation. In Chad a Church was established in its own right, with its own bishops, seminaries, and schools, while remaining independent from neighbouring Cameroon and Ubangi. Africanness took the form of grassroots evangelism and was led, in this initial stage, by Jesuit Brothers, who also launched the first inculturation project and raised the prospect of African Jesuit vocations. Ultimately, the creation of ecclesiastical Chad and its French ties set up the foundations of the modern Chad state as an ally of France and a stabilising force in a region at the crossroads of competing global ideologies and religions.

In the early stages of the mission, before independence had been achieved, Chadian Muslims asserted their African identity by rejecting Western education, which they considered to be contrary to their beliefs and irrelevant for their already-established Muslim political elite. The Jesuits developed a vast educational project for Chad's Muslim populations which was designed to convert moderate Muslims while pushing back against Pan-Arabism, which was seen in France as a direct threat to French interests in the region.

For the ethno-religionists of southern Chad who converted to Christianity, the political outcome of the Jesuits' vast educational project was paradoxical. Christian political leadership at independence was the result of a Western education. This education favoured their being auxiliaries in the colonial administration, and then leaders of independent Chad. Yet, unlike other Christian missions in Africa, whose educational initiatives led to the birth of African Christian nationalism, Jesuit education in southern Chad simply came too late to create an infrastructure that could foster nationalism among Catholics. The anti-elitism of the Jesuits in Chad was not designed to create a Catholic elite that would oppose French colonialism. They left that opportunity to their Protestant counterparts, who became leaders of independent Chad.

The education of Chad's southern ethno-religionists was the largest in scope and content. It aimed at developing 'Le Tchad Utile' (Useful Chad), and it favoured Chad's southern elite to govern a pro-French independent Chad. With French in its curricula, the education received from the Jesuits seemed to reinforce the Frenchification agenda. It was also deliberately anti-elite, confirming a trend seen elsewhere in Francophone Africa. Within this system of auxiliaries and loyalty, school teachers became key actors in the *mission civilisatrice*, and were sometimes more zealous in their implementation of its Frenchification agenda than the colonial administrators.[1] Consequently, Jesuit early education in Chad continued to serve the project of 'Wider France' more than it fostered Chad's political nationalism. It also set up the basis of development-oriented Christianity alongside an evangelising project that combined Bible translations, catechism, and the practice of sacraments. The anti-elitism of the Jesuit Chad Mission became a hindrance for the implementation of the Vatican's agenda of clerical Africanisation.

Later, the outward work of the mission grew substantially at a grassroots level. The Jesuits built chapels adapting to the local vernacular, translated the catechism – the first catechism and grammar in the Sara language was published on 26 August 1949 – and the Bible, and published dictionaries with grammars. The Jesuits built chapels adapted to local vernacular and integrated Chadian culture into the liturgy.

The rise to power of François Tombalbaye, a Protestant leader, was the manifestation of political and ecclesiastical Africanisation and would test France's Jesuit Mission in Africa. Tombalbaye's launching of a Cultural Revolution promoted a return to Chad's traditions and cultures in an attempt to Africanise the country's politics and churches, yet, in the long term, it was clearly averse to an Africanised Protestant leadership in Chad opposed to syncretism. In broad terms, the Cultural Revolution seems

---

[1] Peggy R. Sabatier, 'Charles Béart, "Bon Père" or "Le Colonialisme Incarné?": Colonial School Director and the Ambiguities of Paternalism', *Proceedings of the Meeting of the French Colonial Historical Society* 4 (1979): 141.

Figure 5 The young scholar André Martin teaching the Catechism to children in Archambault, 1953 (Archives JHIA, Nairobi).

to have benefitted the Jesuits and Chadian Catholics. The Brothers successfully accommodated the country's traditional *yondo* initiation, while delaying the more threatening (for the president) clerical Africanisation.

The subsequent persecutions of Protestant churches led to the decapitation of their African leaders. This challenged the leadership of the Catholic Church to react. Whether one finds the Catholic archbishop of N'Djamena, Paul Dalmais, to be cowardly or simply too cautious in dealing with this major crisis, it delayed clerical Africanisation and spared the Catholic Church the worst of François Tombalbaye's regime.

CHAPTER 4

Era of Civilisation: Popular Education and Islamism

Joseph du Bouchet had just settled in as the leader of the Church in Chad when, on 25 September 1946, the governor of French Equatorial Africa vowed to give the education of indigenous children 'extreme attention'. Education, he said, was essential to French colonial interests in Africa, and would improve the human skills and behaviours of the Chadian youth. Catholic missions, especially the Jesuits, were entrusted with this task of educating Chadians, as 'loyal auxiliaries' to the colonial administration.[1] For it to be successful, however, there would be a need for government subsidies.[2]

Having young French missionaries working in the Muslim-dominated north of Chad was of paramount importance. Like the missions in the Muslim areas of the northern region of Cameroon were already doing, led by Bishop Yves Plumey, the Catholic missions in northern Chad focused on promoting social services first. Only then did they begin the work of evangelising Muslims: the twofold goal was to impede the infiltration of Pan-Arabism and Pan-Islamism in Chad and the surrounding French possessions. These ideologies, they believed, posed a direct threat to France's geostrategic interests in the region.

As this chapter will show, the Jesuits were on familiar ground, as they drew on their long tradition of educating children. Jesuit education in Chad not only served as a form of evangelism, but it was also a tool for Frenchification or ultra-Gallicanism – that is, the overseas transplantation of France's Catholicism. In its focus on the popular masses and resistance

---

[1] Peggy R. Sabatier, '"Elite" Education in French West Africa: The Era of Limits, 1903–1945'. *The International Journal of African Historical Studies* 11, no. 2 (1978): 247–66 – here, p. 247.
[2] ANOM-FM-1AFF-PO-2180/5: 'Note de l'office du gouverneur général de l'AEF au ministre de la France d'Outre-Mer, 25 Sept. 1946'.

of the elite, this strategy set the Jesuits in Chad apart from traditional interpretations of the role of Christian missions in raising African nationalism. The same anti-elitism, however, might have further delayed the clerical Africanisation of the Church in Chad. Despite some converts among the young Muslims showing clear evangelising skills, there is no evidence of these being interested in becoming priests.

Unlike their contemporaneous missions in the Middle East, where the Jesuits tried to use colonial ties to create a pluralistic society, the primary goal of the Jesuit mission in Chad, in this initial stage, was to contain Islam. They saw Islam as a threat to France's geopolitical interests and stability in the region. In that sense, their mission aligned with France's diplomatic attempt to isolate Chad's Islam from the broader *Umma* and Pan-Arabism.

Muslim northerners resisted this strategy. They initially perceived Jesuit education as a foreign intrusion in their political affairs. Yet, they later allowed their children to attend Jesuit schools on the basis of post-independence political pragmatism: having a Western education was key to staying in power after independence. While the Jesuits might not have contributed to directly raising Chadian nationalism among the Muslims, they did in fact train a Muslim elite in postcolonial Chad. Analysing different Jesuit strategies for overcoming Muslim resistance to their education shows some secularising trends, as some of the missionaries adopted an apostolate of presence and focused on social progress rather than evangelism.

Early Jesuit Ministries to African Children

Initially, in Chad the Jesuits focused on educating the poor instead of the elite. The most important Jesuit missions in Africa during the time of Saint Ignatius were to the kingdoms of Ethiopia and Congo. There is no evidence I can find about their commitment to education in Ethiopia until their expulsion in 1632.[3] In Kongo, however, it is said that three orphans of the Collégio dos Orfãos of Lisbon, founded in 1548, accompanied Jesuit

---

3   See: Wendy Laura Belcher, 'Sisters Debating the Jesuits: The Role of African Women in Defeating Portuguese Proto-Colonialism in Seventeenth-Century Abyssinia', *Northeast African Studies* 13, no. 1 (2013): 121–66; Isabel Boavida, Herve Pennec, and Manuel Joao Ramos, eds, *Pedro Paez's History of Ethiopia, 1622*, trans. Christopher J. Tribe, vol. 1, 2 vols (London: Ashgate, 2011); Philip Caraman, *The Lost Empire: The Story of the Jesuits in Ethiopia* (Notre Dame, IN: University of Notre Dame Press, 1985).

Diogo Gomes (1520–55) to his mission there.[4] These children, also known as the 'Meninos da Doutrina' [Boy Catechists], were primed to teach catechism to other children overseas.

In Central Africa, the first book known in the Bantu language was the Kikongo catechism by Mattheus Cardoso (1624).[5] This catechism discourages men to have children outside their legitimate marriage. In 1642, Angolan-born Jesuit Antonio do Coucto published his *Gentilis Angollae in fidei mysteriis eruditus: Opusculum Reginae Fidelissimae Mariae I jussu denuo excussum*, which was re-edited twice, in 1661 and 1784.[6] The text is in triple columns of Latin, Kimbundu (an Angolan language), and Portuguese. It is arranged in the form of dialogues on the commandments of the Lord and of the Church, the Lord's Prayer, each of the seven sacraments, the Trinity, and purgatory.

In the southern part of the African continent, the Jesuits also paid special attention to children in their mission strategy. The missionaries focused on boys, 'believing that they would understand the faith more quickly and would convert easily'.[7] Elitists, they started by converting in the court and convincing elders that having access to their boys was necessary for the mission and their social progress. They built a school for children which trained about 510 children between 1879 and 1897.[8] Advancing their work of translation, a Bechuana catechism written by Father Terörde served to instruct children at Grahamstown (now in South Africa).[9]

In the Gulf of Guinea, a nineteenth-century document by Antonio Zarandona, procurator for the missions of the Jesuit Province of Spain, gives a central role to the evangelisation of children. Zarandona prepared the document as a framework for the Jesuit mission in Fernando Po (1857–72),[10] which is part of today's Equatorial Guinea. Once in Fernando Po, Jesuit missionaries were to open 'a special school for

---

4   Mattheus Cardoso, *Le Catéchisme Kikongo de 1624*, trans. François Bontick (Brussells: Académie Royale des Sciences d'Outre-Mer, 1978), 18–19.
5   Ibid., 19.
6   Antonio Do Coucto, *Gentilis Angollae in Fidei Mysteriis Eruditus: Opusculum Reginae Fidelissimae Mariae I Jussu Denuo Excussum* (Lisboa: Olisipone, 1784).
7   Aquinata N. Agonga, 'Hoping Against All Hope: The Survival of the Jesuits in Southern Africa (1875–1900)', in *Jesuits' Survival and Restoration: A Global History, 1773–1900*, ed. Robert Maryks (Leiden: Brill, 2015), 476.
8   Ibid., 472.
9   Ibid., 473.
10 Antonio Zarandona, 'Proyecto de una Misión a las Islas Españolas del Golfo

children, without neglecting the adults'.[11] The education of boys became the most important ministry for the Jesuit mission (1857–72), often at the expense of girls and adults.[12]

This strategy backfired just as it did in the Zambezian court, because the Jesuits faced strong resistance from the parents. It became clear to Father José Irísarri, who was the superior of that mission, as well as his superiors in Spain, that the mission of the Society in Fernando Po was suffering because of their 'tradition of not dealing with women'.[13] For them, this situation was due, partly, to the lack of a female branch of the Society or a women's congregation that could help them with the education of the girls.[14] Where such a female congregation collaborated with the Society, like the Ursulines in North America,[15] Japan,[16] or Münster,[17] Jesuit ministries to women and children often increased. For instance, although the Jesuits' own reports from Fernando Po did not clearly identify the nature of the resistance they faced – except that there were Protestants – their successors in the mission, the Claretian Fathers, named Protestant missionaries and mothers as leaders of this resistance.[18]

---

de Guinea. Presentado en la Dirección de Ultramar Por A-Z, El 4 de Mayo de 1857', n.d., AHA. C 458, n. 8570009.

[11] Ibid.
[12] On this topic, see: Jean Luc Enyegue, 'The Jesuits in Fernando Po, 1858–1872: An Incomplete Mission', in *Jesuits' Survival and Restoration: A Global History, 1773–1900*, ed. Robert Maryks (Leiden: Brill, 2015), 466–86.
[13] Archivo Provincial de Toledo, in: Archivo Histórico de Alcalá (AHA), C-67.
[14] Ibid.
[15] Alanna Catherine DeNapoli Morris, 'Female Missionaries in The Jesuit Relations: A Study of the Creators of the Ursulines Seminary in Quebec' (A Thesis Submitted in Partial Fulfillment of the Requirements for the Masters of Theological Studies, Weston Jesuit School of Theology, 2005), 3–4.
[16] Haruko Nawata Ward, 'Naitō Julia and Women Catechists in the Jesuit Mission in Japan and the Philippines', in *Putting Names with Faces: Women's Impact in Mission History* (Nashville, TN: Abingdon Press, 2012), 249.
[17] Simone Laqua-O'Donnell, *Women and the Counter-Reformation in Early Modern Münster* (Oxford: Oxford University Press, 2014), 4–5.
[18] The list of missionaries in Fernando Po at the arrival of Usera in 1843, prior to the Jesuit mission: Miss Clarke, Mrs Saker, Mrs Prince, Mrs Sturgeon, Mrs Bundy, Mrs Norman, Mrs Ennis, Mrs Gallimore, Misses Stewart, Davis, Couper, and Vitou. Cf. Jerónimo M. Usera y Alarcón, *Memoria de la isla de Fernando Poo* (Madrid: T. Aguado, 1848), 27–28. Another reference on the issue: Jean Luc Enyegue, 'The Adulteresses Were Reformers: The Perception and Position of Women in the Religious Fight of Fernando Poo,

Figure 6 A child praying in front of a wall painting by Fr André Martin, Archambault, 1953 (Archives JHIA, Nairobi).

The renewed focus on children after the restoration of the Society (1814) coincided with a new political and religious environment. Politically, the nineteenth century was a century of greater awareness of children rights. The International League recognised children as the centre of pedagogy, following new developments in child psychology and biology.[19] From a

---

1843–1900', in *Encounters between Jesuits and Protestants in Africa*, eds Robert Maryks and Festo Mkenda (Boston: Brill, 2017): 215–32.

[19] Carmen Labrador, *El sistema educativo de la Compania de Jesus. Continuidad e innovacion. Ante el cuarto centenario de la Ratio Studiorum* (Madrid: UPComillas, 1987), 27–29.

religious perspective, from the end of the seventeenth century up to the nineteenth, new religious orders and congregations were created all over Europe with the education of children as their central mission.[20]

This apostolate suffered a setback during the suppression of the Jesuits (1773–1814) and the French Revolution's capitalisation of public education over Catholic education. Confronted with revolution, the Church restored the Jesuits as a counter-revolutionary force aimed at stopping the spread of modernism in Europe. In order to do so, education took the front seat in the apostolate of the Restored Society and its missions around the world.[21] In the Philippines, for example, which shared its educational policy with the Central African region of Fernando Po, a decree from the general governor on 1 October 1859 left the direction of the municipal school, also known as 'Escuela Pía' [the Pious School] to the Jesuits.[22] At the same time, the 'Junta Superior de la Instrucción Primaria' [The National Board of Primary Education] proposed the creation of a normal school to train teachers in order to address 'the urgent need to reform primary education'.[23]

As they settled in Chad in the mid-twentieth century, the Jesuits did not depart from this old tradition of educating the youth as a means of evangelisation. Education became key for their agenda to conquer Chad for Christ's Kingdom by endorsing conservative Gallicanism and anti-elitism in a downgraded *mission civilisatrice*.

Wrapping Gospel Education with Anti-Elitism and Anti-Nationalism

Scholars have traditionally linked the rise of African nationalism to the intellectual training nationalist leaders received in Christian schools. A focus on the impact of Christian education on the nationalist elite has often overlooked its primary religious goals and influence, especially on the masses and on the 'implantation' of local churches. In Francophone Africa, schooling helped the mission to evangelise, to fight against Communism, and to raise a Catholic clergy. As Éric Lanoue suggests,

[20] José Malaxecheverria, *La Compania de Jesus por la instruccion del Pueblo Vasco en los siglos XVII y XVIII* (San Sebastian: Gariby, 1926), 223.
[21] Frias Lesmes, *Historia de la Compañía de Jesús en su Asistencia moderna de España* (Madrid: Razón y Fe, 1923), 733.
[22] Pablo Pastells, *Misión de la Compañía de Jesús de Filipinas en el siglo XIX*, vol. 1 (Barcelona: Tip. y Lib., 1916), 13–14.
[23] Ibid., 53.

even the ordination of the first African Catholic bishops like Bernard Yago (1916–97) of Côte d'Ivoire served as a 'symbol' for transition from a missionary to an 'implanted' Church.[24] These leaders of the Church were, however, also perceived as national figures and often had effective political influence. By impeding ecclesiastical Africanisation in Chad, the Jesuits seemed to move in opposition to this trend, both politically and ecclesiastically.

In Chad, French Jesuits wanted to preach the gospel; yet as they shifted their education policy from favouring the elite to focusing on the masses, they also pushed back against nationalism. Jesuit education in Chad aimed not so much to raise Christian nationalists as to evangelise the masses. They also wanted to contain the already rising Christian political elite, which showed early signs of secularism. The Jesuits tried to limit the spread of Islamisation in the north of Chad, the rise of a nationalist, secularist, and materialistic ideology in the south, and, to a lesser extent, Protestant-Americanism.

Until the time of independence, however, Muslim populations from the north, known as 'Arabisants' in Jesuit sources, who held political power in northern Chad, believed that their children did not need Western education, be it public or religious, to be politically influential. All Western education was perceived as a pagan intrusion in their political affairs. As a result, their nationalism was a defence of the purity of their religion. It grew out of a continuous resistance to Western education, which to the Muslim populations seemed a threat to their political privileges as well as a proselytising enterprise.

There is little evidence that, before independence, Western education contributed to increasing the nationalistic instinct among the Muslims. Yet, this education empowered slaves and non-Muslims, who went on working for the first administration of independent Chad and ruling over Muslim northerners. Only then did northern populations realise that maintaining their political influence in the power struggles following the independence of Chad depended on their children receiving a Western education. It also depended on showing their loyalty to France.

[24] Éric Lanoue, '"Le temps des missionnaires n'est plus!": Le devenir postcolonial de l'enseignement catholique en Côte d'Ivoire (1958–2000)', *Cahiers d'Etudes Africaines* 43 (2003): 99–120 – here, pp. 102–03.

The Jesuit Downgraded *Mission Civilisatrice* in Chad

As a colonial power, France sought, primarily, to protect its strategic interests in Chad while, at the same time, softening its image among the colonised. This orientation of France's colonial policy in Africa used a dual discourse. It claimed to increase the integration of African countries and their peoples into the Union Française (French Union). To succeed in this would mean upgrading the education of Africans to meet the standards of French citizenry. At the same time, paradoxically, the French also promised to promote indigenous cultures and the rights of African peoples. Interpreting France's education policy in Africa from the perspective of France's colonial interests, it appears that both public education and the public funding of private education in Chad in the late 1920s coincided with the project of the 'Wider France'. This project followed the end of the First World War and culminated at the end of the Second. The 'Wider France' celebrated the apotheosis of French overseas expansion and its civilising mission.[25]

The civilising nature of France's colonial project and the latter claim of promoting indigenisation were therefore aligned with the goals of Catholic missions in Chad. This Frenchification of the indigenous members of the empire was urgent as part of their integration into the cultural mould of France. It also helped to maintain the relevance of a declining France on the world stage.[26]

The Frenchification of the empire was accompanied by an educational project. An international conference on colonial education was held in Paris in 1931. This conference promoted the aim of 'adapting' the schooling system in Africa to 'local needs'.[27] In practice, however, the African Évolués elite class and colonial administrators worked to make education as similar as possible to France's. Curricula were adapted to those of the metropole. Students received equivalent, if not similar, diplomas.[28]

---

[25] Raoul Girardet, 'L'apothéose de la "Plus Grande France": L'idée coloniale devant l'opinion française, 1930–1935', *Revue Française de Science Politique* 18, no. 6 (December 1968): 1085–114 – here, p. 1086.

[26] Girardet, 'L'apothéose de la "Plus Grande France"', 1094. The 'Wider France' also advocates for a 'humanising' French colonial system. See Gide, *Voyage au Congo: Suivi du retour du Tchad* (Paris, 1929). While these early publications condemned the 'abuses' of the colonial system, they did not question the colonial ideology.

[27] Harry Gamble, 'La crise de l'enseignement en Afrique Occidentale Française (1944–1950)', *Histoire de l'Éducation* 128 (2010): 129–62 – here, p. 130.

[28] Gamble, 'La crise de l'enseignement en Afrique Occidentale Française (1944–1950)', 130.

Frenchification, it appears, helped to link Chadian national identity to the idea of making Chad part of the Union Française. The very idea of extending French citizenship to indigenous people from French overseas territories enjoyed its highest approval among all social and political layers during this period.[29] However, this unionist policy also diminished Chad's ability to assert its selfhood as a nation.

Historian Thomas Martin showed that from 1919, Albert Sarraut's assimilation policies in the French colonies deliberately departed from the established policy that colonies should be self-supporting. They promoted, instead, a policy that favoured the active participation of the state in the economic development of the colonies. Sarraut believed that such state involvement was important as a means to secure France's imperial security and the loyalty of the rising indigenous elite to the colonial state.[30] Embracing French colonies, therefore, contributed to delaying the colonies' self-determination.

In the interwar period, especially from 1925 onwards, socialist governments in France pushed for secular education in schools while adjusting to a communist agenda. The communist agenda supported anti-imperialist forces and the right of nations for self-determination. In that sense, the cause of the delay of African self-determination can be attributed to conservative governments, of which General Charles de Gaulle ultimately became the leader.[31] Their fight against Communism coincided with their pushback against Africa's self-determination. The Brazzaville Conference of 1944 first exposed de Gaulle's doctrine about the Union Française and African self-determination. This seemed as paradoxical as the 'Wider France' in its educational orientation. As previously mentioned, the conference excluded 'any possibility of evolution outside the French Empire, [as well as] the constitution of self-government in the colonies even in the distant future'.[32] The educational project of Brazzaville also vowed

---

[29] Cf. Genova, 'Constructing Identity in Post-War France: Citizenship, Nationality, and the Lamine Guèye Law, 1946–1953', *The International History Review* 26, no. 1 (2004): 56–79 – here, pp. 59 and 70.

[30] Cf. Martin, 'Albert Sarraut, French Colonial Development, and the Communist Threat, 1919–1930', *The Journal of Modern History* 77, no. 4 (December 2005): 917–55 – here, p. 926.

[31] Cf. Vallet, 'Le laïcisme dans l'enseignement actuel', *Etudes Religieuses* 189 (5 November 1926): 257–81 – here, p. 262.

[32] Quoted in: Majhemout Diop et al., 'Tropical and Equatorial Africa under French, Portuguese and Spanish Domination, 1935–45', in *Histoire Générale de l'Afrique*, vol. 8, 8 vols (Paris: UNESCO, 1999): 58–75 – here, p. 74.

to maintain, and even improve 'traditional' – it actually meant 'rural' – educational structures:

> Colonial education will avoid [...] harming traditional structures because it is essential that peoples develop according to their own genius [...] Education will generally conform to the methods and curricula of France, adapted to Africa, with a large part devoted to handicrafts, agricultural and household initiation and physical education. It will be the least bookish possible, well established in the life of villages.[33]

The political vision of Wider France, followed by that of the French Union, the Eurafrique, which later became the Union pour la Méditerranée (Mediterranean Union), shaped educational programmes in Chad in the 1950s. For French officials, to educate Chadians meant foremost to make them useful for the general interests of the metropole.[34] Similarly, France aimed at making Muslim West Africans 'as good Muslims as Frenchmen'.[35]

The strategic concerns of French missionaries in Chad were therefore similar to those of the political project of the 'Wider France'. For example, as Bishop Salotti of Propaganda Fide determined, the Jesuits believed that 'the apostolate of the mission was a civilizing apostolate'.[36] Civilising the indigenous was therefore a common goal for both the colonial state and European missions. On the other hand, the Catholic mission and the colonial administration in Chad agreed on their common challenges. Those challenges included not only Islam and Communism but also indigenous religious practices. All these challenges immediately became the main concerns for the Jesuits in Chad. The Jesuit educational project approached these challenges differently in different contexts: they used one system with the Muslims of the north, and another when working with the

---

[33] David E. Gardinier, 'Les recommandations de la Conférence de Brazzaville sur les problèmes d'éducation', *Brazzaville* (January–February 1944): 170–80.

[34] Catherine Coquery-Vidrovitch, 'Colonisation ou impérialisme: La politique africaine de la France entre les deux guerres', *Le Mouvement Social* 107 (1979): 51–76 – here, pp. 54 and 75.

[35] Benjamin Soares, '"Being as Good Muslims as Frenchmen": On Islam and Colonial Modernity in West Africa', *Journal of Religion in Africa* 39, no. 1 (2009): 91–120.

[36] In *Osservatore Romano*, 6 September 1931. Africa was still the 'land of idolatry' and 'darkness' until the 1940s. See: 'Preces pro Missionibus, 1940': 16–18, in ARSI, *Opuscula impressa I*. Box: P.F. 1003.

southern ethno-religionists. Chad was, for the Jesuits, the New Jerusalem, central to their broader Near East religious and diplomatic outreach.

Chad: The New Jerusalem

During his acceptance speech on 6 May 2007, the newly elected French president, Nicolas Sarkozy, discussed a project of 'L'Union pour la Méditerranée' (Mediterranean Union) as a pillar of his foreign policy. For some observers, Sarkozy's Union pour la Méditerranée aimed primarily at offering Turkey an alternative union to its most desired European Union, to which Sarkozy believed Turkey did not belong. For the Turkish government, though, Sarkozy's project was a reminder of a painful past: the defeat of the 1920s and the total collapse of their empire.[37]

North and Sahelian Africa served as the grounds of this humiliating defeat. Another interpretation of Sarkozy's Union pour la Méditerranée is that it was the recycling of an old agenda for French colonial right-wing parties known as the 'Eurafrique'. Facing the decline of its colonial empire and the rise of anti-colonialist superpowers and nations after the Second World War, the idea of 'Eurafrique' intended to create a strategic and economic Third Bloc between Europe and Africa. It was, indeed, a neocolonial project directed at the exploitation of Africa's natural resources and geographical landscape to strengthen Europe's geopolitical position and guarantee its independence from both the USA and the USSR.

The Eurafrique also aimed to weaken a rising African anti-colonialism.[38] To achieve its goal, especially in North Africa and the African Sahel, the Eurafrique, or the Françafrique (the French implementation of the project among its former colonies),[39] had to address three immediate threats with a religious component. Most importantly, in northern Chad was Pan-Islamism and Pan-Arabism. Communism, and to a lesser extent Protestant-Americanism, were their biggest threats in southern Chad.

According to Claude Artidi, by the beginning of the twentieth century there were about fifty Libyans who controlled commerce in the Chad region of Wadday.[40] Alongside the Libyans were Syrians and Egyptians

---

[37] Dorothée Schmid, 'La Turquie et l'Union pour la Méditerranée: un partenariat calculé', *Politique Étrangère* 1 (2008): 65–76.

[38] Papa Dramé and Saul Samir, 'Le projet d'Eurafrique en France (1946–1960): quête de puissance ou atavisme colonial?' *Guerres Mondiales et Conflits Contemporains* 4 (2004): 95–114.

[39] François-Xavier Verschave, *La Françafrique: Le plus long scandale de la République* (Paris: Stock, 2006).

[40] Claude Artidi, 'Le Tchad et le monde arabe: essai d'analyse des relations

in Abéché, Mao, Moussoro, and Fort-Lamy, all places where the Jesuits strategically opened their first mission stations. By the time they settled in Fort-Lamy in the 1940s, Syrians, Lebanese, Greeks, and Armenians coming from Sudan had settled in the Muslim-dominated areas of large cities in Chad.[41]

The Jesuit mission in Chad was, indirectly, part of this French agenda. The reference to 'Jerusalem' by Jean Lacouture is important to establish a connection between the project of the Wider France and the Jesuit Chad Mission.[42] The French Jesuits considered Chad to be part of their broader Middle East strategy, and Chad was part of a Greater Sudan that appealed to Catholic and Protestant missionaries alike.[43] Until 1946, the annual catalogues of the Jesuit Province of Lyon listed Chad as part of the Mission d'Orient (the Middle East Mission).

Moreover, the association of Chad with the Middle East was part of a broader, and quite complex, Mediterranean strategy for the French Jesuits in the context of their new global commitment.[44] This Jesuit strategy seems to anticipate Sarkozy's 'Projet pour l'Union de la Méditerranée'. The apostolic cohesion of the Jesuit French assistancy – and the Lyon Province in particular – relied on what was then called its 'Mediterranean vocation'.[45] Key to that vocation was its support of the Church in Greece,

---

commerciales de la période précoloniale à aujourd'hui', *Afrique Contemporaine* 3, no. 207 (2003): 185–98 – here, p. 192.

[41] Ibid., 198.

[42] Jean Lacouture, *Jesuits: A Multibiography* (Washington, DC: Counterpoint, 1995), 57–58.

[43] J. H. Boer, *Missionary Messengers of Liberation in a Colonial Context. A Case Study of the Sudan United Mission*, 2 vols (Amsterdam, 1979); Richard Gray, 'Christian Traces and a Franciscan Mission in Central Sudan', *Journal of African Studies* 7 (1967): 392–93; A. S. Kanya-Forstner, 'French Missions to the Central Sudan in the 1890s: The Role of Algerian Agents and Interpreters', *Paideuma* 40 (1994): 15–35; Dorothea McEwan, *A Catholic Sudan: Dream, Mission, Reality* (Roma: Stabilimento Tipografico Julia, 1987).

[44] John T. McGreevy, *American Jesuits and the World: How an Embattled Religious Order Made Modern Catholicism Global* (Princeton, NJ: Princeton University Press, 2016), 219.

[45] The term 'assistancy' represents a governing structure of the Jesuit order. It also highlights its tendency to localise while remaining Rome-centred at its core. In its first volume, the *Journal of the Assistancy of France* displays this tension between the local and universal [Roman]: 'The Jesuits, scattered throughout the world, are assembled in Provinces according to the place of their origin or their apostolate. At the head of each one, a Provincial depends

Turkey, Syria, Lebanon, and all of North Africa. The most important element of this vision was the strengthening of the work of the Jesuits in the Muslim world.[46]

Chad, which was part of the Greater Sudan, and a majority Muslim country, clearly belonged to that region.[47] This French strategy in the Muslim world was directed from Paris and Lyon, and also from Rome. Starting in 1936, Revd Vladimir Ledochowski (1866–1942), the superior general of the Jesuits, created the 'Mission du Proche Orient' (Middle East Mission). It aimed at uniting different French missions from Syria, Egypt, and Armenia under one 'regular superior', who would reside in Syria and act as major superior.[48] It is therefore important to understand the Jesuits' approach to education in northern Chad through this lens.

Education to Contain Islamisation

At its conception, the goal of the Jesuit educational project towards Muslim populations of Chad was not religiously neutral. Nor was it, in its initial definition, a secularising enterprise. Instead, its original purpose was to convert Muslims. Then, after Vatican II, it shifted towards fostering peaceful cohabitation with them, not by changing textbooks as such, but by developing friendship and personal relationships with Muslim leaders. Several factors contributed towards this change in the orientation of Jesuit education in Chad.

---

directly on the General who, from Rome, appoints him. These Provinces, in their turn, were grouped in eight Assistancies. The creation of the Assistancy of France coincided with the early years of the Society of Jesus [in the sixteenth century]. [After the suppression and the restoration of the order in 1814], in 1820, a new "Province" of France was created. It was gradually divided, with the Province of Lyon governing the entire south. In 1852 the southwest was grouped around Toulouse, while in 1863, under the name of Champagne, the northeast formed a fourth province. In 1952 was born the Province of Madurai (India), formerly a mission entrusted to Toulouse': *Jésuites de l'Assistance de France* (*JAF*) 1 (1953): 2.

46 'Tchad', *JAF* 1 (1953): 11–12.
47 Ministère de la France d'Outre-Mer, *Le Tchad*.
48 M-Ly. 102/1: 'Lettres circulaires de Joseph du Bouchet', A-Pa. 185: 'Compte-rendus des consultes de la Province, 1933–1947'. In the Jesuit archives in Vanves (France), 'A-Pa' refers to the archives of the former Jesuit Province of Paris.

The Vatican expresses concerns about the Islamic threat

There is evidence that the Vatican perceived Islam as a threat not only to the establishment of new Christian communities in the African Sahel, but also to Christian communities that were already established in the southern regions of Chad, Cameroon, and the Central African Republic. In 1937, a papal missionary for Africa highlighted the missionary potential of the one hundred million Africans. They were ready, the pope said, 'to discard their native cults and to enroll in a better religion'. However, 'the choice presented to them lies between Mohammedanism, Communism, and Christianity'.[49]

In West Africa, there were 1,181 primary schools with 80,413 pupils, and 95 secondary schools with 6,888 students. In Central Africa, there were 7,588 primary schools with 413,821 pupils, and 378 secondary schools with 18,657 students.[50] The primary task of these schools became to establish Roman Catholicism as a credible and strong alternative to Islam and Communism. The support of the colonial administration, and the vast agenda of church-building projected this strength, while Roman Catholicism's approach towards accommodating traditional religionists made it acceptable to some Chadians.

The reason for Chad's appeal and the pope's missionary call was strategic. Bishops Yves Plumey and Jean Zoa, as well as Jesuit historian Engelbert Mveng, found the pope's motivation in 'rumours' in Vatican circles that some French colonial officials wanted Chad to become entirely Muslim.[51] Reinforcing the Chad Mission was therefore a top priority for the Vatican, not only to stop that colonial Islamisation project, but also to protect younger churches from Cameroon and the Central African Republic from what Rome considered 'the threat of Islam'.[52] To achieve that goal meant investing heavily in education. It meant converting the northern populations of Chad that had resisted Islam for centuries, and in southern Chad it meant converting the so-called 'animists', while protecting them from Communism.[53]

---

[49] Cf. 'Mission intention for July and August: Schools for Africa', *Jesuit Missions* (July–August 1937).

[50] Ibid.

[51] Yves Plumey, *Mission Tchad-Cameroun, l'annonce de l'évangile au Nord-Cameroun et au Mayo-Kébbi* (Italie: Editions Oblates, 1990); see E. Mveng and J. Zoa's preface to the book, pp. iv–vi.

[52] Jesuit archives in France, 'M-Ly. 102/1' and 'A-Pa. 185'.

[53] Paul Dalmais, 'L'avenir religieux du Tchad', *Etudes* (January 1956): 39–51 – here, p. 51.

The Jesuit Mission attempts to contain this threat

Early on, when the Chad Mission was launched, Chad was part of a broader evangelising strategy of the French Jesuits towards the Middle East. The goals of this strategy gave a religious purpose to their work in Chad. French Jesuits going to the Middle East believed that 'the charity of deeds exercised through the corporal and spiritual works of mercy will draw these Blacks to our Catholic schools and Jesus Christ of Nazareth, Model of Character, and the integrating magnet in our Catholic curriculum, will then draw them to Himself'.[54] In a visit to Beirut, André Décisier, successor of du Bouchet as the Jesuit provincial of Lyon, vowed to continue the commitment of his province in Chad and the Middle East.[55] He reaffirmed the purpose of the mission, and limited its work 'strictly on spiritual matters'.[56] Concerning Chad, a 'pagan land', 'forgotten', 'located in the confines of Egypt', that mission would strengthen 'our [France's] strategy' in the Middle East.[57] Despite its roughness, Décisier concluded, Chad would bring great vocational and spiritual benefits to the province and its members.[58]

The Muslim political elite of the north rejects Western education

Mario Joaquín Azevedo, a leading scholar in the historiography of education in Chad,[59] writes that 'formal education did not reach Chad until the first missionary school was established in the south in 1820'.[60] While this date cannot be confirmed, and most scholars' chronology holds that Christian education was developed in Chad a century later, in the 1920s, with the arrival of the first Protestant and Catholic missions, it is undoubtedly the fact that the pace of educating young Chadians slowed down during the 'pacification' of Chad, from the 1890s.[61] Azevedo argues that during the

---

[54] Ibid.
[55] Joseph du Bouchet was the first apostolic prefect of Chad, from 1947 to 1958, two years prior to Chad's independence. See Granito di Belmonte and Fumasoni-Biondi, 'Erigitur Nova Praefectura Apostolica Arcis Lamy (in Tchad) et Societatis (Prov. Lugdunensi) Committitur', *AAS* 11 (1947): 216–17.
[56] M-Ly. 102/2.
[57] Paul Dalmais, 'Mission du Tchad', *JAF* 3 (1959): 32.
[58] M-Ly. 102/2. A. Décisier, 'Lettre du 30 avril 1946'.
[59] This chapter owes most of its information about the history of education in Chad from the precolonial period to Azevedo.
[60] See: Mario Joaquín Azevedo, *Cameroon and Chad in Historical and Contemporary Perspectives* (Lewiston, NY: E. Mellen Press, 1988), 147–48.
[61] I was not able to find any data accounting for the results of this first educational

precolonial and colonial periods, 'both resistance to "Western contamination" and the nomadic and semi-nomadic lifestyles of its inhabitants' rendered Western education in northern Chad 'virtually non-existent'.[62] Therefore, until the 1920s, the only educational structures available to Muslim children were religious ones. *Qur'anic* primary schools taught religion and Arabic literacy. Even years after independence, he believes, the general trend of education in northern Chad had not improved.

Now, when compared with the southern region, the curriculum in northern Chad was still poorer after independence, and school attendance was weak.[63] Existing Muslim secondary schools, such as the École de Mohammed III, modelled themselves on the Arab Islamic schools in Egypt.[64] More telling was that 'as late as 1960, the inhabitants of Abéché [seen as the capital of Islam in Chad] considered schools to be sources of "cultural impurity", and refused to send their children to the French-Arab high school built by the French'.[65] Muslim leaders preferred to send their slaves rather than their own children to schools providing a Western education.

This short survey shows that the established political elite of northern Chad did not need a Western education to be politically influential until about ten years after independence. Resisting Western education, however, did not mean that Muslim children were illiterate. According to Azevedo, Islamic and mosque schools dominated education in northern Chad. Imams in mosque schools often taught theology and Arabic. This curriculum was enriched by 'jurisprudence, and related subjects such as interpretations of the *Qur'an*, the traditions and sayings of the Prophets, oratory, the biography of the prophet, and Arabic grammar'.[66]

---

initiative in Chad. And I cannot answer questions about the class of people who received that education. Nor can I give an account of the impact they might have had in Chadian society, and whether or not they played a long-term political role in planting the seed of the later rise of Chad's nationalism.

[62] Azevedo, *Cameroon and Chad in Historical and Contemporary Perspectives*, 149.

[63] For example, 'while children in the south attended primary schools for six years, in the north, children abandoned school after a maximum of only three years. With the institutionalization of a one-school year, the average school attendance rate in the south was 50 percent of the eligible children, while the highest attendance rate in the north (namely, in Guéra) was equivalent to the lowest rate in the south, that is, only 28 percent': ibid.

[64] Ibid.

[65] Ibid., 150.

[66] Mario Joaquim Azevedo, *Chad: A Nation in Search of its Future* (Boulder, CO: Westview Press, 1998), 92.

In order to confirm how systematic schooling among Muslims in Central Sudan was, Ousmane Kane shows that from the interpretation of the *Qur'an* derived other studies such as memorisation (*hifz*), exegesis (*tafzir*), and the art of its psalmody (*tajwid*).[67] Those studies affected the whole life of the Muslim, as did jurisprudence and even commerce, which were all regulated with the ultimate goal of perfecting the religious life of the believer.[68]

For northern political elites, to have Western education was not, therefore, synonymous with being 'civilised'. Instead, it meant being religiously impure. Western education, they believed, was antithetical to true Islam. Slaves from the north who received that Western education were certainly empowered politically in the long term. Yet, until independence, both public and religious education across Chad remained at the level of primary education.

The Reaction of the Jesuits to the Northerners' Resistance

The Jesuits complained about the resistance they faced from Muslim leaders. In 1963, three years after independence and during the Second Vatican Council, Jesuit missionary André Worbe wrote:

> So far, the [Western] school has practically not taken up with these Arabs. They are very proud people, with a strong contempt towards any other population that they consider merely slaves. The Arabs have long considered that the need to learn was for others, not them, who were the chosen race of God. Today they are a little frightened to see themselves victims of a reversal of the master by the slave [...] and the most pragmatist and lucid among them would like to catch up the delay that has accumulated.[69]

Worbe shows that while Western education – which was primarily Christian – might not have played any role in the rise of Chadian nationalism, it nevertheless presented a political challenge to Muslim northerners after independence.

According to Worbe, delaying the education of Arab children was starting to have a negative impact on the political influence of the northerners. Those they previously considered mere slaves were rising to become the ruling elite of independent Chad after going to Western

---

67 Ousmane Kane, *Beyond Timbuktu: An Intellectual History of Muslim West Africa* (Cambridge, MA: Harvard University Press, 2016), 76.
68 Ibid., 82.
69 André Worbe, 'School for Muslims', *JAF* 1 (1963): 45–46.

schools: 'In a country like Chad', Worbe wrote, 'education is key for business management and access to well paid jobs.' The former 'slaves' holding those positions had begun to 'colonise' the land of 'free men' – that is, the Muslims – for 'the southern Sara occupied the commanding posts in the prefectures of the northern breeders'. As a result, the desire for education started to become a genuine desire for sociopolitical progress among some Muslim parents.[70]

The year 1963 also represents the opening of the Second Vatican Council. Following the Council and its favourable outreach to non-Catholic and non-Christian traditions, the goal of the Jesuit presence in the Muslim world evolved and focused on fostering peaceful interreligious cohabitation.[71] In Chad, the Jesuits started presenting their educational project in religiously neutral terms. That attitude was absent in the earlier years of the mission. It came late and grew out of both the new approach to religious pluralism championed by Vatican II and the reaffirmation of an independent Chad as a secular state modelled on the French constitution.

Facing both a secular independent state and the interreligious outreach of Vatican II, the Jesuits decided to build schools for Muslim children. Some missionaries like Juan Luis Martélez taught in northern public schools as 'volunteers', sometimes hiding their identity as priests.[72] Others, like Julien de Pommerol, Henri Coudray, and Charles Vandame, deepened their study of Islam, leading to numerous publications.[73] These efforts

---

[70] Ibid., 46.
[71] In preparation for the Roman Synod of 1974, the then superior general of the Jesuits, Pedro Arrupe, insisted on the need for Jesuits to be opened to other religions and cultures. He had presented the same argument to African Jesuits in Douala, Cameroon, in 1972. See: ARSI. Arrupe 1009/570: 'The Contemporary World: Its Challenges to the Missionary Church' (1973). Published in *Omnis Terra* 4 (November 1973): 29–40. This is Arrupe's 'General Theory of Evangelization', in preparation for the 1974 Synod of the Bishops on Evangelization. Also: ARSI. Arrupe 1009/567. 'The Missionary Apostolate in Africa Today'. Adaptation of the address of Father Pedro Arrupe, General of the Society of Jesus, delivered at the Conference of the Jesuit Major Superiors, Douala (Cameroon), 22–26 March 1972.
[72] Juan Luis Marteles, 'Sembrando la Palabra y sirviendo a los hermanos', 2006. It was not an official policy for the Jesuits to hide their religious identity while living and working among Muslims in Chad. The case of Marteles was unique, and related to his personal vocation.
[73] Julien de Pommerol, *Dictionnaire Arabe Tchadien-Français* (Paris: Karthala, 1999); *L'arabe Tchadien. Emergence d'une langue véhiculaire*

aimed to dissipate any misconceptions about the presence of Christianity among Muslims.

Leading Jesuit scholars in Chad started offering neutral or non-syncretistic interpretations of their work. These scholars presented Christianity as a tool for social progress, as 'something other than a foreign sect which recruits followers among the animists'.[74] Rather, Christianity was concerned about the wholeness of the human being in both body and spirit. Its task was 'to increase the education of boys and girls, to contribute to the training of those who will work in the years to come to the human, economic and social, material and spiritual development of the Chadian nation'.[75]

One might also notice a generational shift at this stage between the early conservatives and younger generations of Jesuits like anthropologist Claude Pairault. Pairault came to suggest that the goal of Jesuit education among Muslim children was one of social progress alone, free from any direct religious intent. His Jesuit friend the historian Joseph Fortier confirmed this idea. Fortier insisted 'missionaries avoided proselytism in their schools'. And according to him, the religious education Christian children received in Jesuit schools often could not pass the test of time and political unrest:

> Catechetical schools were opened in parishes, and as a channel to attract prospective Christians from population groups that have resisted Islam. Most of the neophytes, however, converted to Islam when they migrated to N'Djamena after the civil war. Pierre Faure opened a cultural centre in Abeche. Missionaries avoided proselytism in their schools.[76]

Fortier reaffirms the religious neutrality of Jesuit schools as far as Muslim children were concerned. He also alludes to a concern about the perseverance of Muslims who converted to Roman Catholicism. When Muslims gained power following the Civil War, many of these Christians reconverted to Islam.[77] Finally, his reference to Pierre Faure's work in

---

(Paris: Karthala, 1997); *J'apprends l'arabe Tchadien* (Paris: Karthala, 1999); *Grammaire pratique de l'arabe Tchadien* (Paris: Karthala, 1999).

[74] Claude Pairault, 'Au bout du Tchad', *Jésuites 3* (1960): 43–46 – here, p. 46.
[75] Ibid.
[76] Fortier, 'Chad'.
[77] Another Jesuit confirmed this trend of Catholic converts becoming Muslims, not because of their economic empowerment, but because memorising Western programmes seemed too overwhelming for their children. Cf. José Luis Ferrer Soria, *Naissance et épanouissement d'une jeune communauté chrétienne au Tchad* (Paris: Éd. Centres Sèvres, 1976), 22.

Abéché introduces his reader to the concept of 'cultural centre'. This new concept also claimed its religious neutrality:

> Father Faure, abandoning all proselytising ideas, opened his home and his heart to young Muslims. His house is really their home. They feel at home, without any embarrassment. Evening classes, boarding schools, sports groups, a library, and a cultural centre make the Abéché Mission a home open to all. Christian values penetrate by osmosis into the hearts of these boys. Some young Muslim pupils have devoted two and three hours of each day to do free classes for adults, evening classes.[78]

The key words signalling the religious shift in Jesuit missionary strategy among Muslims are 'abandoning all proselytising ideas'. Moreover, cultural centres multiplied across Chad and, later, across the entire West African mission field. These were informal educational centres, which the Jesuits established in popular and economically poor areas. They provided a library, reading space, and classrooms for support courses directed at struggling students. Children were trained to a basic level in languages, technology, theatre, etc. After the success of the Abéché centre, new 'cultural centres' were built in Jesuit missions in Chad (Kyabe and N'Djamena), and more recently in Burkina Faso, Congo Brazzaville, Senegal, and Togo.

Educational Tools to Stop Islam and Protect Christian Communities

In 1960, Pairault completed an ethnographic investigation tour at Boum Kébir in the central region of Chad. Boum Kébir represented a proud Muslim society that still understood its identity as antithetical to Western civilisation. The Jesuit educational project, according to Pairault's account, faced strong resistance from Boum Kébir. In that region, the Jesuits had been very successful in converting non-Muslim populations among the Dangaléat, the Sara-Kenga, and the Hadjeray of Guéra, which had resisted Islam for centuries.[79]

---

[78] Paul Dalmais, 'La mission du Tchad et les chrétiens de Fort-Lamy', *Mitte Me* 11 (1966): 26–27.

[79] Literally, the Hadjera are people living 'in the mountains'. They are located in north and north-east Chad. Muslims among them served as interpreters and local chiefs during the colonial period. See: Augustin Mathieu, 'Au Pays Hadjeray', Lettres du Tchad (June–July 1957): 2. Augustin Mathieu, 'Renforts pour la Mission des Hadjeray', *Lettres du Tchad* (October 1959): 4. Peter Fuchs, *La religion des Hadjeray* (Paris: L'Harmattan, 1997), 216–17.

Giving an account of his experience, Pairault wrote: 'The first conflict I experienced was, and still is, about grammar'.[80] No Black or White men who were not Goulaiti – Boum Kébir's inhabitants – had ever spoken the language of Boum Kébir. And not a single Goulaiti had ever learned to speak French, except two immigrants from Djibouti and Vietnam.[81] In order to improve communications with the Goulaiti, Pairault decided to test other didactic tools of communication. These included photography, films, and audio recording. In that single tour, he took more than 1,500 pictures, 2,000 feet of films, and a few kilometres' worth of magnetic tapes.[82] Yet, Pairault believed, 'none of these tools could really give full account of the true essence of Boum Kébir's society'.[83]

On a strictly pedagogical level, children in northern schools relied on memorisation, repetition, and oral and written examinations on the interpretation of the surahs. The most successful among these students, instead of receiving a secular diploma, received the title of *goni* (master of the *Qur'an*).[84] These techniques contrasted with those used by the Sara of southern Chad. Here, 'experience, admonition, storytelling, and observation generally guaranteed the transmission of knowledge and values from one generation to the next'.[85]

The Jesuits primarily conceived their work not as a purely neutral and secular enterprise directed at the Muslim north, but as a strengthening of Christian communities living amid Muslim majorities, fostering new converts among the popular masses that had resisted Islam and the Muslims. The claim for neutrality in the interpretation of their mission grew out of the orientation of the Vatican II and Chad's independence as a secular state.

Chad's Islam and Pan-Arabism

There is a point that needs to be made about the connectivity of Chad's Islam with the broader global *Umma* and recent research on Islamic studies in Africa. Islamic scholar Scott S. Reese has argued that 'one of the great ironies of European empire is that far from disrupting this

---

[80] Claude Pairault, 'Au bout du Tchad', *Jésuites* 3 (1960): 44.
[81] These immigrants, according to Pairault, came as *tirailleurs* (French sharpshooters or African mercenaries) during the Second World War.
[82] Pairault, 'Au bout du Tchad', 44.
[83] Ibid.
[84] Ibid.
[85] Azevedo, *Chad: A Nation in Search of its Future*, 92.

connectivity among believers, imperial rule in many ways enhanced it'.[86] However, the case being made in this book is that the main goal of French colonists was to isolate Chadian Muslims from the global Pan-Islamic movement. Chad had been connected to the Middle East since the pre-Islamic period, and this connection had remained uninterrupted. In fact, Chadian 'Arabisants' defied France's attempt to interrupt their connection with the global *Umma* by boycotting the colonial educational agenda and rejecting their proposed bilingualism.

In the 1940s, French colonial authorities attempted to replace Arabic *madrasas* with French-Arabic (bilingual) *madrasas*, in order to push back against the Pan-Islamism and Pan-Arabism of Chad's Muslim populations. According to Islamic scholar Ousmane Kane, Pan-Islamism had its roots in Saudi Arabia. It served as King Faysal's arm to spread Wahhabism and so push back against the Pan-Arabism pursued by the Egyptian Nationalist leader Nasser.[87] Both ideologies had followers in Sub-Saharan Africa. And neither was acceptable to France.

In 1947, Faki Oulech, who had just completed his studies in Khartoum and Cairo opened a *madrasa* in Abéché (Chad). Oulech's *madrasa* modelled the Egyptian one. In response, the French opened an École Normale (Teacher Training College) in the same city, similar to the *madrasa* of North Africa, but under the direction of a Frenchman who was an 'Arabisant' sympathiser. Abéché's Muslims boycotted the French initiative. In response, the colonial government proposed that Oulech merge his *madrasa* with the École Normale, which the latter rejected. Faki Oulech was accused of rebellion, arrested, and expelled from Abéché and Chad.[88]

Oulech's case shows the difficult task French authorities, and thus the Jesuits, faced as they tried to Frenchify Chadian Muslims. It also proves that Islam in Chad was not simply a mere adoption of a foreign import. Oulech had made his own synthesis from different forms of Islam existing in Chad. He had received his training from competing Arabic and Egyptian schools. Yet, one might also recognise a *Sanusiyya*-Libyan influence in both the political orientation of his struggle, and his insistence on purity. With the support of Libya, under Turkish influence, the *Sanusiyya* had been adopted

---

[86] Scott S. Reese, 'Islam in Africa/Africans and Islam', *The Journal of African History* 55, no. 1 (2014): 20–21.

[87] Ousmane Kane, 'L'"islamisme" d'hier et d'aujourd'hui: Quelques enseignements de l'Afrique de l'Ouest', *Cahiers d'Etudes Africaines* 52, nos 206/07 (2012): 545–74 – here, p. 555.

[88] Henri Coudray, *Langue, religion, identité, pouvoir: Le contentieux linguistique franco-arabe au Tchad*, vol. 1 (N'Djamena: Centre Al-Mouna, 1998), 26.

by the Wadday kingdom of Chad in the nineteenth century,[89] in a diplomatic effort aimed at securing the Benghazi-Kufra-Abéché trade route.[90]

Following the collapse of the Ottoman Empire, some Muslim leaders in West and Central Africa embraced a reformist agenda that emphasised the return to the tradition of Prophet Mohammed and rejected an Africanised, acculturated version of Islam.[91] France also picked sides in this struggle by opting to support the *Tijaniyya* against the *Sanusiyya*. In Chad, the *Sanusiyya* embraced both Pan-Arabism and Pan-Islamism as the best solution for re-Islamisation or Islamic revival and moral renewal. They instructed their followers in Arabic and jurisprudence, and rejected any compromise with colonial education. According to Kane, however, France had embraced the *Tijaniyya* to counter the Turks who had decapitated the leader of the *Tijaniyya*.[92] And alongside their alliance with the *Tijaniyya*, they also teamed up with the Kanuri against another *Sanusiyya* group: the nomadic Touareg.[93]

Two examples provided by the Jesuit newsletter *Nouvelles de la VPAO* show how the Jesuits interacted with those groups. Spanish Jesuit José Luis Marteles had settled in Faya-Largeau, a nomadic centre for *Sanusiyya* followers.[94] There, he taught philosophy, history, and geography in a public high school attended mostly by Muslim children. Henri Coudray was missioning in Abéché to teach at the French École Normale.[95] Coudray was joined by Lebanese Sisters of the Sacred Heart. Their mission was to train school teachers who were bilingual in French and Arabic. The Italian Jesuit Brother Gianni Zucca covered the areas of N'Djamena, Moussoro, and Kanem, while French Serge Sémur did pastoral work in rural Guéra.[96]

---

[89] Jean-Louis Miege, 'La Libye et le commerce transsaharien au XIXe siècle', *Revue de l'Occident Musulman et de La Méditerranée* 19 (1975): 136.

[90] Jean-Louis Triaud, 'Les "trous de Mémoire" dans l'histoire africaine. La Sanûsiyya au Tchad: Le cas du Ouaddaï', *Revue Française d'Histoire d'Outre-Mer* 83, no. 311 (1996): 5.

[91] Fabienne Samson, 'Les classifications en Islam', *Cahiers d'Études Africaines* 52, nos 206/07 (2012): 335–36.

[92] Kane, 'L'"islamisme" d'hier et d'aujourd'hui', 560.

[93] Finn Fuglestad, 'Les révoltes des Touaregs du Niger (1916–1917)', *Cahiers d'Études Africaines* 13, no. 49 (1973): 82–120.

[94] Julien Brachet and Judith Scheele, 'Les années écroulées: Vestiges, développement et autonomie à Faya-Largeau, Tchad', *L'Homme* 215/16 (December 2015): 279–305.

[95] A-PAO. N-PAO 2 (1 May 1975): 9.

[96] A-PAO. N-VPAO 11 (20 September 1976): 5.

As for the strategies they applied, both Marteles and Coudray understood the shifting ground of the mission field. While the traditional mission was meant to convert pagans (and Muslims) to Christianity, the new mission instead sought to prioritise the development of all, including Muslims. Both Jesuits also had a political role as tensions increased between the north and the south. For his part, Marteles reached out to Muslim military leaders and the southern elite as he attempted to reconcile the two sides of the Civil War. Coudray, in contrast, still considered the Muslims as the 'church of the margins' (*l'Église du dehors*). He was also the official representative of Agence Française de Développement (AFD: the French Development Agency) in Abéché. Not surprisingly, his work and that of all French missionaries among Chad's Muslim populations from the north focused on developing the so-called bilingual projects. These projects were promoted by the French government from the time of colonialism onwards, and rejected by Chad's Muslims.[97] Jesuit settlements in northern Chad followed *Sanusiyya* bastions, developing bilingual programmes aimed at mitigating the Arabising trends of the Muslim reformists. Most of their early publications were works on grammar and Chadian Arabic-French translations and dictionaries.[98]

Conclusion

Having officially settled in Chad in 1946, amid the political unravelling of the French empire and the rise of African nationalism, the Jesuits used education to execute a religious agenda. Their educational project in Chad was oriented mainly towards the evangelisation of the popular masses. They saw education not only as a means of converting the masses to Catholic doctrines and practices, but also as a barrier against the spread of Islam southwards; at the very least, they sought to use it to foster peaceful cohabitation with the Muslim north of the country. While most Muslim leaders from the north rejected the Jesuit outreach towards them as foreign, pagan, and even colonial, there were a few cases of success as well.

---

[97] A-PAO. H. Coudray, 'Nouvelles d'Abéché', N-VPAO 34 (1 May 1979): 2.

[98] Julien de Pommerol, *Dictionnaire Arabe Tchadien-Français* (Paris: Karthala, 1999); Pierre Palayer, *Dictionnaire Kenga* (Tchad) (Louvain: Peeters, 2004); *Grammaire du Dadjo d'Eref* (Paris: Peeters, 2011); *Lexique de plantes du pays Sar, plantes spontanées et cultivées* (n.p., 1977); *Eléments de grammaire Sar* (Tchad) (Pol, 1970); Jacques Hallaire, *Au confluent des traditions de la savane et de la forêt. Étude thématique des contes Sar* (Moyen-Chari, Tchad) (N'Djamena: CEFOD, 1987).

For example, Chief Madengar of Bekamba, a veteran of the Rif War in Morocco (1925–26),[99] was a Muslim and a polygamist. He allowed three or four of his children to become Christians. One of them, Benoît, started teaching catechism to other children. By 1956 he had trained a group of ten who were baptised at Easter, and another ten were baptised in 1957.[100]

The conversion of Benoît and his Brothers represents a clear success in the Jesuits' outreach to Muslim populations in Chad, and in their attempt to evangelise them. It also reinforces a key aspect of the evangelising strategy in Chad: a grassroots approach that would often reach children first and then, through them, their parents and the rest of society.

Chief Madengar is also evidence of the shifting dynamics among Muslim leaders towards Christianity. He was a chief and a soldier. Both positions made him an ally of the colonial state; he had spent time in Morocco, so had experience outside Chad, and might have appreciated a new political reality and a different approach to being a Muslim. His approval of Jesuit education for his children and their conversion situated him among the 'Arabisants' whom the Jesuits had targeted from the beginning of their mission.

Madengar's change of mind contrasts with other Muslim leaders who resisted Western education for both religious and political reasons during the decolonisation period. However, after independence, some of them made a strategic decision to have their children baptised and have a Western (often Christian) education, in the hope that they could maintain their political privileges in modern Chad. This entente would last until the beginning of the Civil War in Chad, when Christian-Muslim relations were at their worst.

Some Chadian Catholics felt vulnerable in the face of the new friendly relationships the Jesuits were developing with the Muslims. Understandably, these Christians were already haunted in their villages and towns by the noisy boots and cries of Islamised northern rebels during Chad's Civil War (1965–79). Yet, the new approach towards Muslims was a second strategic decision the Jesuits had made that eventually assured the survival of the Catholic Church in Chad, regardless of the political shifts on the ground.

---

[99] For most historians, this was the beginning of Morocco's nationalist movement. See: C. R. Pennell, 'Ideology and Practical Politics: A Case Study of the Rif War in Morocco, 1921–1926', *International Journal of Middle East Studies* 14, no. 1 (February 1982): 19–33.

[100] Joseph Fortier, *Les débuts de l'évangélisation au Moyen Chari, diocèse de Sarh (Les Pionniers), 1946–1966*, vol. 1 (Sarh: n.p., 1991), 32.

The first of these decisions was the accommodation of the *yondo*, the Sara initiation rite. Similar accommodating attempts had cost the Jesuits their missions in Asia and led to the suppression of their order in the eighteenth century. In Chad, however, and as the following chapters show, the Vatican did not interfere. These actions made the Jesuits look moderate in the eyes of an aggressive political regime that targeted all Christians, especially of Chadian descent, who dared to openly oppose its Cultural Revolution. This shift in tone was also a reflection of a new era. The Second Vatican Council had inaugurated a new approach in Catholic outreach to non-Catholics. Friendship, human development, and interreligious dialogue took precedence over direct evangelism among the Muslims. A young and more progressive generation of Jesuits was ready to lead this project.

CHAPTER 5

Era of Accommodation: Mission towards the Southern 'Ethno-Religionists'

The lack of a well-trained youth might explain the conservatism of the Jesuits pioneers discussed in the previous chapters, as well as their reluctance to foster a Chadian clergy. Analysing their educational project in Chad, one can see a certain conservatism among the Muslims in the north, and, as this chapter argues, among ethno-religionists in the south. The anti-elitism of Jesuit education in Chad might have succeeded against Communism in the south. This strategy, however, also worked against the promotion of a Chadian clergy and leadership.

Among the ethno-religionists in the south, the Jesuits launched a massive educational and catechetical programme, aimed primarily at converting non-Christian Chadians to Christianity. The programme built the foundations of an African Church which the Vatican wished to be authentically Chadian, but which became, at least for a time, an example of ultra-Gallicanism. To comprehend ultra-Gallicanism, one has to understand the export of French Roman Catholicism in missions overseas. This export often happened in coordination with the French government, although with a diluted *laïcité* (secularism), if not an aggressive grassroots anti-secularism agenda. In southern Chad, this ultra-Gallicanism meant creating a Frenchified Church in its governance, school programmes, and catechetical contents. The Church aggressively pushed back against elitism and its atheistic materialistic trend. Gradually, social progress, including the opening of schools and hospitals, became a kind of evangelisation in its own right.[1]

This chapter continues the discussion on Jesuit educational tradition. This tradition inspired the roots of the vernacularisation of the Church in Chad. Among the strategies employed for this vernacularisation were an

---

[1] ANOM-FM-1AFF-PO-2180/5. B10313: 'Une note confidentielle de la Mission des Oblats au Nord Cameroun, envoyée au Ministre de la France d'Outre Mer (14 août 1946)'.

anti-communist campaign in Chad and a shift towards the poor and the masses. This missionary approach challenges the perception of the elitism of Jesuit education worldwide that has dominated recent historiography. Jesuit elitism, or populism in this case, was shaped by a mixture of a top-down strategy and continuous adjustment to conditions in the mission field. The opposition to nationalistic, secularist, and materialistic trends among the southern Christian Évolué class made the Jesuit enterprise in Chad intentionally religious and openly suspicious of Christian elitism.[2] Facing what they considered 'a threat' to Christianity and religion in southern Chad, European Jesuits launched a vast educational project aimed at curtailing this trend.

A review of this educational project reveals the innovative pedagogical tools used by the Jesuits in the education of everyday Africans in Chad, including the use of technology, skilled construction work, agricultural techniques, singing, and painting as means of transmitting practical and religious knowledge. Yet this also meant a setback to the Vatican's agenda of clerical Africanisation. Anti-elitism hindered the effective training of a Chadian clergy. In these early years of the mission, young men from Jesuit schools in Chad could have been good catechists, but not good enough to become Catholic priests or Jesuits.

Anti-Communism: A Common Jesuit Concern in the North and South

Among the non-Muslim populations of southern Chad, the Jesuits identified two main challenges to their educational project. There was the secularist trend of the Évolués elite class, which the Jesuits, faithful to the pope's directives, vowed to stop and to avoid reproducing. According to the papal mission intention of 1937,

> A more insidious enemy is Communism, whose single-minded objective is to turn the Black into Reds. We have the challenge. We know the prize: One hundred million souls. Our program of Catholic education has been tested and found not wanting. That is, not wanting in anything but schools and the personnel and means with which to sustain them.[3]

---

[2] Not only was President François Tombalbaye expelled from his Protestant denomination, but the chief of the northern rebellion (FROLINAT), Dr Abbah Siddick, was himself a proclaimed atheist (Robert Pledge, 'Chad: France's African War', *Africa Report* [1 June 1970]: 16).

[3] Editors, 'Mission intention for July and August: Schools for Africa', *Jesuit Missions* (July–August 1937), 185.

On the other hand, the masses were left out of both *Qur'anic* and Western education, yet the education of these people was key to the long-term success of the religious goals of the Jesuits.

The rapid literacy growth in the south of Chad – compared to the more Muslim north – was not primarily the result of missionary education; it was a consequence of public policies from the French government. One reason is that, as said earlier, Christianity effectively took root in Chad later than in other African countries. Protestant (1920) and Catholic missions (1929) barely had an educational infrastructure in place until after the Second World War. Another reason is that, by the end of the War, 'the sparse education available within Chad was restricted entirely to the primary levels'.[4]

Therefore, one can conclude, the literacy gap between those who received primary education from Western schools and those who attended Islamic schools was not so wide. The same applied to their relative competences or their ability to become colonial employees. French officials effectively used northerners who attended Islamic schools in the administration of the north as they did with educated southerners in their own region. The political advantage shifted towards the south only after independence, with François Tombalbaye's administration (1960–75).

Unlike in the north, education in the south 'was patterned after the French curriculum and emphasised French mastery'.[5] Schools were entirely funded by the government. Private schools, including Catholic

---

[4] According to Azevedo, 'It was not until 1945 that the first secondary school was established in N'Djamena, and by 1959 only three secondary schools had been established throughout the colony. At the time of independence in 1960, there were only 225 primary schools in the country (35 of them private), still only 3 secondary schools, and 9 technical schools with a combined enrollment of 55,160. Thus, at the time the colony achieved its independence, only 11 percent of the school-aged population in Chad received any formal education [...] At the time of independence, there was no university education available in the country. In 1968, all 202 Chadian university students were attending school abroad, mainly in France and Belgium. In 1963, the government founded a National School for Administration in N'Djamena and the National School of Telecommunications in Sarh, followed by the establishment of the University of Chad in 1972. It was not until 1972 therefore that higher education was available within the country': *Cameroon and Chad in Historical and Contemporary Perspectives*, 48.

[5] Ibid. It was not until the mid-1920s, a century after the first missionary school, that investment in public education started improving.

ones, received government subsidies.⁶ Following independence, a substantial increase in public education occurred when the Tombalbaye regime 'established secondary schools in each prefecture, except Biltine, increasing the number of secondary schools to 20'.⁷

While the reluctance of the northerners to allow their children a formal education was 'dismaying to the French', the Sara were much more receptive to it.⁸ As a result, most Chadian government officials were southerners, particularly from among the Sara ethnic group. The fact that the Sara people had received a Western education boosted their long-term political fortunes. Azevedo believes that 'by the time the north finally realized the broader implications of its educational disadvantage, François Tombalbaye (himself a member of the Sara ethnic group) had systematically excluded the north from all positions of influence in the new republic'.⁹

Azevedo's main assumption was that 'the main goals of the colonizer in Chad were to extend the French empire, maintain law and order, and promote economic production in line with the aspirations of the colonizer'.¹⁰ In the north, these goals were achievable through indirect rule. Muslim leaders with no Western education effectively took care of all political and economic tasks during the colonial period. In the south, in contrast, where the indirect rule did not apply, French officials concentrated on the economic development of the country. They considered southern Chad 'Le Tchad Utile' (Useful Chad).¹¹ Likewise, from the time of their arrival

---

⁶ 'A record of educational progress is documented by official enrollment figures over the years which followed. By 1928, 3,431 students were enrolled in public schools and 6,000 in Christian schools. Twenty-five years later, in 1953, 13,290 students were enrolled in public schools, 2,852 in Catholic schools, and some 281 in the few Protestant schools. By 1972, the overall rate of attendance among Chadian school-age children had reached 22 percent, with 183,840 students in primary schools and 9,418 in secondary schools. Only four years later, the number of students in both primary and secondary school had climbed (to 321,382 in the secondary schools), and 600 students were attending the University of Chad': Azevedo, *Cameroon and Chad in Historical and Contemporary Perspectives*, 148.

⁷ Ibid.

⁸ Azevedo, *Chad: A Nation in Search of its Future*, 31.

⁹ Azevedo, *Cameroon and Chad in Historical and Contemporary Perspectives*, 137.

¹⁰ Azevedo, *Chad: A Nation in Search of its Future*, 31.

¹¹ Ibid. In fact, historian Thomas Martin has effectively shown that there was a direct link between French colonial economic development and the communist threat, especially in the 1920s (Thomas Martin, 'Albert Sarraut, French

Figure 7 Wearing his school uniform, Ila, a young Chadian pupil, discovers his country on a globe, 1955 (Archives JHIA, Nairobi).

in 1946 to the end of the Tombalbaye regime in 1975, the Jesuits heavily invested in the education of southerners, most of whom became Christians. Yet they still viewed the existing Christian elite as a threat.[12]

The threat of Communism was the primary concern of the Jesuits among Christian southerners.[13] Between the two competing ideologies of Islam and Communism that threatened their mission in Chad, the Jesuits seemed more favourably inclined towards Islam than Communism. Jesuit Paul Dalmais of N'Djamena, who believed Protestant converts constituted the 'elite class' of Chad, once said it would be better for Chad to become entirely Muslim than be dominated by secularised Christian Évolués.[14] He shared the view of some colonial officials that this Christian elite was

---

Colonial Development, and the Communist Threat, 1919–1930', *The Journal of Modern History* 77, no. 4 [December 2005]: 919–20).

[12] Archives of the Province of Lyon in Vanves: Box M-Ly 102/1–2.

[13] Paul Dalmais, 'L'avenir religieux du Tchad', *Etudes* (January 1956): 51; 'Mission du Tchad', *JAF* 3 (1959): 32. Pius XI, 'Mission Intention for July and August: Schools for Africa', *Jesuit Missions* (July–August 1937).

[14] Paul Dalmais, 'Le Tchad, mission stratégique', *Vivante Afrique* 203 (June–July 1959): 3. Dalmais is not expressing an anti-Protestant opinion here. He

increasingly dangerous for the future of Chad. Dalmais, however, differed with the colonists on the reasons for this threat and the urgency of taking care of it. While government officials opposed Christian missions for 'helping indigenous people to think',[15] Dalmais, in contrast, worried about their departure from Christian values, their potential anti-clericalism, and their exaggerated taste for material goods.[16]

The nationalism of the Christian Évolués made them enemies of the colonial state, while their materialism made them vulnerable to Communism and, therefore, potentially antithetical to the teachings of the Catholic Church. Some of the nationalist leaders had become sympathetic to Communism and actively opposed Western Christianity.[17] François Tombalbaye, who later became the first president of Chad, was one of these Christian Évolués.[18] He broke with his Baptist Church in 1950 to create a new Church, and once in power (1959–75), he launched a Cultural Revolution that ended up persecuting Christians, expelling some and possibly murdering others.[19] Therefore, the choice to focus on the masses and the substance of Jesuit education in Chad intended to avoid this secularising trend. That was the reason why the Jesuits wanted to make that particular mission primarily 'spiritual'.

---

is critical of the secularising and materialistic nature of the Christian elite in Chad, most of whom happened to be Protestants.

[15] A. Hallaire and J. Fedry, *Naissance d'une église africaine: Lettres et chroniques du Pays Sarh* (Paris: Karthala, 1998), 13–14.

[16] Dalmais, 'Le Tchad, mission stratégique', 3.

[17] Jesuit archives of the French province, Box 1457: 'Frederick de Belinay, 1875–1958'. Especially in Box 1457: *Écrits divers* and 'Vue d'ensemble sur la vraie religion; Précis de la Foi Catholique'. Retreat notes, 7 July 1954.

[18] Arnaud Dingammadji, *Ngarta Tombalbaye: Parcours et rôle dans la vie politique du Tchad (1959–1975)* (Paris: Harmattan, 2007); Tombalbaye, 'A cause du succès spectaculaire du Yondo, LA TARTUFFERIE RELIGIEUSE AUX ABOIS'; Agence France-Presse (AFP), 'Tchad: Tombalbaye assimile la coopération avec la France à "une nouvelle forme de colonialisme"', *Le Monde* (13 December 1973), 2.

[19] Pasteur Burgera, 'L'affaire des missionnaires d'Andoum', *Canard Déchaîné* 0053 (18 February 1975): 5; Pierre Faure, *Monseigneur Paul Dalmais dans la Guerre du Tchad: Document pour l'histoire* (Paris: n.p., 2003); Editorial, 'Suédois au pied du mur', *Canard Déchaîné* 0053 (18 February 1975): 6; Illiya Romba, 'Ils ne sont pas morts', *Canard Déchaîné* 0052 (5 February 1975) 1 and 4; N'Garta Tombalbaye, 'Conférence de presse du Président Tombalbaye à Paris', *Canard Déchaîné* 0047 (23 November 1974) 3.

Focusing on the Southern Popular Masses

In 1963, the city of Fort-Lamy represented a confluence of religions, a mosaic of languages and customs. With nearly 100,000 inhabitants, Fort-Lamy was host to a large Jesuit parish. The Jesuit parish of Kabalay supported 65,000 souls from the urban centre, and many more from surrounding villages. The mission schools of Fort-Lamy totalled 5,000 pupils, compared to the 650 who attended the Félix Eboué Public High School. In both the mission school and Félix Eboué, as well as in the other and only technical high school of the city, the Jesuits provided pastoral help as chaplains. They also opened thirty catechetical schools, while Catholic Action worked with hundreds of young people and adults.[20] All these ministries, according to the former head of the mission, Charles Vandame, aimed to create 'a Christianity for the popular masses'. Vandame defined the goal of these schools as 'to build a just, fraternal and prosperous society, marked by the values of the Gospel, with respect for the local culture'.[21]

By focusing mostly on illiterate Chadians, the Jesuit project indirectly delayed the political emancipation of Catholics. Several missionary practices explain this delay. Although the Jesuits were present in big cities like Fort-Lamy and Fort-Archambault, the focus of the Jesuit educational project in southern Chad was primarily rural, agricultural, and away from political centres. The Catholic Youth Association (CYA) 'promoted by François Cordonnier and Louis Forobert, trained young people living in rural areas in agricultural techniques. This project led to the opening of several Centres for Professional Agricultural Training in Monkara (Koumra), Diamra, Mongo, Guéra, Bendana, Bediondo, and Ngaro'.[22] By 1967, this rural project had reached up to 200 villages. Sixty of these villages had literacy activities, 50 had communal barns, another 50 had artesian wells, and 20 had model hens.[23]

In that same year, 1967, the Bureau of Agricultural Production launched the 'Mandoul Operation' in the Koumra-Bédiondo-Moïsala region. With the help of the CYA, this project invested large economic and human resources in rural cooperatives for the production of cotton. The CYA trained the members of these cooperatives to build Christian households,

---

[20] André Martin, 'Kabalay, croissance chrétienne', *JAF* 1 (1963): 40.
[21] Charles Vandame, *Cinquante ans de la vie de l'Eglise Catholique au Tchad* (Paris: L'Harmattan, 2012), 13.
[22] Joseph Fortier, 'Chad', in *Diccionario Histórico de la Compañia de Jesús*, vol. 1 (Madrid/Roma: IHSI/UPComillas, 2001), 746.
[23] Ibid.

Figure 8 Felix, boy catechist and interpreter, stands behind Fr André Martin, Archambault, 1953 (Archives JHIA, Nairobi).

especially 'among the former uprooted students who repelled the work of the land'.[24] The rural focus of Jesuit education corroborates the fact that the political emancipation of Chad was not its intended goal.[25] Cotton, the main agricultural product from these farms, was good for France, but not necessarily for Chad. Cotton for export generated income for Chadian taxes. It did not put food on their tables,[26] nor did it provide them with medical care.[27]

If there were any political goals at all related to the Jesuit education of the southerners, they were primarily for the benefit of the 'Wider France', rather than for Chad's immediate emancipation. The literature taught in Jesuit schools promoted Frenchification. As part of a survey on reading in Chad, in 1963, the Jesuits distributed a questionnaire to their students. The most frequent answers to the question inquiring about their favourite

[24] Ibid.
[25] I found no evidence of such a claim in Jesuit writings.
[26] Jacques Boisson, *L'histoire du Tchad et de Fort Archambault* (Besançon: Editions du Scorpion, 1966), 170.
[27] Marie-Antoine Painchaud, 'Histoire du diocèse de Moundou' (n.p., 1985), 61–62.

books were, 'Victor Hugo (at the head of many), Alphonse Daudet (especially for the Lettres de mon moulin), Molière, and La Fontaine, followed by a certain number of obscure French authors'.[28]

As a result, new Catholic converts were not ready during the decolonisation period to push back against France. Moreover, that lack of political readiness, coupled with the Jesuits' tolerance for syncretistic practices, shaped the Catholic reaction to Tombalbaye's Cultural Revolution a decade after independence. They suffered its tragic consequences less than their Protestant counterparts, who were more politically engaged and less tolerant to syncretism.

Although an important aspect of it, 'Wider France' was not the only goal of the Jesuit educational enterprise in Chad. A more complete picture of their work shows a broader commitment to religious priorities, rather than a mere pursuit of France's colonial goals. The work of the Jesuits in the south during the first decade of their presence in Chad (1946–56) focused mostly on building churches and schools. By the end of 1951, they had built eighteen parishes. Jesuit Brothers also built the 'Cultural Center of Lamy for high school pupils'.[29] Two Jesuit brothers in particular, Francisco Laraya and Joseph Auger, were responsible for building three primary schools in Archambault, as well as the cathedral of Archambault (1959) and churches in Koumra (1955), Moïsala (1956), Bousso (1958), and Kyabé (1959), in addition to a seminary and a high school. The combination of these construction works and the formal education they provided in those schools aimed at improving the lives – bodies, minds, and spirits – of their Church members.

In 1951, the apostolic prefect of Chad, du Bouchet, expanded the Jesuit educational project by opening an École Normale. His goal was to train schoolteachers and 'to promote social progress and the evangelisation of the youth'.[30] The Territorial Assembly – that is, Chad's first parliamentary body – partially sponsored teachers' salaries. These salaries, however, remained insufficient for Catholic schools; from Fortier's account, in 1959, the difference between teachers' salaries in public and private schools was 25 per cent, leading to deficits in Catholic schools, which lost most of

---

[28] Victor Waton, 'Auteurs préférés des jeunes', *JAF* 1 (1964): 45.
[29] Fortier, 'Chad', 745–51.
[30] Fortier, 'Chad'. 746. Normal schools played an important role in promoting the secularist ideology in France (cf. Vallet, 'Le laïcisme dans l'enseignement actuel', 262–63). Aware of that influence of normal schools, du Bouchet might have decided to promote a Christian normal school that would train less antagonising teachers for the Church.

their teachers. The École Normale was closed in 1966.³¹ In the fifteen years during which it operated, Fortier recalled, the École Normale

> had trained more than 300 teachers who worked for the four dioceses of Chad. In 1961, there were 4,807 pupils (1,600 of them girls) in the 17 Catholic schools of Fort-Lamy alone. In 1966, 17,290 children were in Catholic schools, a 10 per cent of the total school population in Chad: 5,300 from Fort-Lamy diocese, and 3,760 for Fort-Archambault. In 1977, there were still 3,400 pupils in Catholic schools of the diocese of Fort-Lamy (and 3,730 in Sarh), despite the suppression of catechetical schools in 1977; but by the end of the civil war in 1982, a quarter of all private school teachers had joined public schools.³²

This situation shows that six years after independence, the system of Catholic education in Chad was still dependent on government subsidies. Therefore, instead of the Jesuits helping Chad train its national leaders, their educational project actually depended on the support of those leaders who were already in power. Their support of the Jesuits formed part of government policy, yet the most immediate interest the Jesuits had in accepting such collaboration was that it gave them a unique platform from which to evangelise.

The Religious Impact of the Centres for the Formation of Catechists

Schools were an effective tool for evangelisation, yet not the only one the Jesuits used in southern Chad. Another Jesuit initiative in the south involved the creation of the Centres for the Formation of Catechists (CFCs). These centres trained catechists to assume parish responsibilities in the Jesuit dioceses of Sarh and N'Djamena. A centre typically comprised 30 households with a population of about 200. According to Roland Pichon, every village had a catechism adapted to the literacy level of its members. Often, this catechism was elaborated in the form of questions and answers. Catechists who could not read or write but had 'a very good memory' had to memorise the catechism.

As far as the content of the message was concerned, catechumens learned about the *Missio Dei*, Christian liturgical symbols, and worshipping practices, including the practice of the sacraments.³³ Moreover,

---

[31] Fortier, 'Chad', 746.
[32] Ibid.
[33] Roland Pichon, *Un Jésuite persona non grata* (Paris: Harmattan, 2008), 38–39.

the Jesuits made every effort to adapt this catechetical training to local traditions. For example, the traditional initiation rite of the Sara people, the *yondo*, which later became the cornerstone of Tombalbaye's Cultural Revolution,[34] was reinterpreted according to the Christian understanding of the rite of baptism. According to Pichon, the mission itself 'had become the place where the true Yondo was practiced'. The Jesuits interpreted it as the 'passing from the mortal condition to the eternal life of the children of God'.[35]

In the CFC, young people learned how to spell and recite, and the rudiments of calculation.[36] There were three parts in the catechism for catechumens, which were extended over three years. First, they had to memorise routine prayers like the Lord's Prayer, the Ave Maria, Prayer to the Holy Spirit, etc. Then, they would learn the history of ancient Israel as it appears in the Old Testament. And finally came the life and teachings of Jesus in the New Testament, the life of the Church and its sacraments, and the Creed.[37] Jesuits like Jacques Hallaire also published prayer pamphlets and hymnals.[38] He and others like Jacques Fedry translated texts from the New Testament, which they used for the annual spiritual retreat of the catechumens.[39]

Both the colonial and independent administrations considered each CFC a village in its own right, with its own tax collection system and a cotton market.[40] Young people who took part in this training left their villages, their daily routine, their family, their plantation, to become

---

[34] N'Garta Tombalbaye, 'Les principes de l'initiation au Yondo ainsi que ceux du Christianisme et de l'islam s'accordent', *Agence Tchadienne Presse* 3054 (30 April 1974): 1–5; Tombalbaye, 'A cause du succès spectaculaire du Yondo, LA TARTUFFERIE RELIGIEUSE AUX ABOIS'.

[35] Pichon, *Un Jésuite persona non grata*, 41.

[36] André Meynier, 'Formation de catéchistes à Kyabe', *JAF* 4 (1962): 43–44.

[37] Hallaire and Fedry, *Naissance d'une église africaine*, 22.

[38] Ibid., 26.

[39] Ibid; Jacques Fedry and Pascal Djiraingue, *Prières traditionnelles du Pays Sara* (Sarh: CEL, 1977).

[40] Interview with Revd Agide Galli, Gallarate (Italy), October 2013. Agide Galli (born 1928) arrived in Chad in 1965 to assume the direction of this centre. He later became the second Jesuit provincial of a West African province (1979–83), then assistant to the Jesuit General Peter-Hans Kolvenbach for African affairs (1983–94). He later returned to Chad as director of the major seminary for the training of diocesan priests. He was one of the founders of the Jesuit mission in Togo, where I collaborated with him for two years from 2006 to 2008. His work with the catechists in Chad, he confessed, was the thing he was most proud of in his entire Jesuit life.

studious schoolchildren for many weeks. This shift from formal education to informal education, especially in rural areas, became urgent as the government withdrew its subsidies after independence. It also contributed to sedentarising populations who, for centuries, had been threatened by slave raids carried out by the Baguirmi and the Wadday from the north.[41] The Sara were grouped in administrative units and performed common rituals, including the *yondo*, which gave them a sense of unity. With the Church, they were part of building a new agricultural economy and developing new architecture for their people. Increasingly equipped with buildings, churches, schools, residences, etc., the missions started considering construction works and building maintenance as an integral part of their unique educational and evangelising enterprise.[42]

In 1955, a missionary report described the early stage of this architectural evangelisation in these terms:

> Like Brother Catt, Brother Bonnevay embraced the work in rural areas. In three years, 14 homes have emerged, a new garden with innumerable orchards. He has recruited maneuvers, and by the example of his work he made workmen out of them; all became his friends, and many, in contact with his soul, became Christians [...] In Bousso, a beautiful garden, about yards, is cultivated to improve the life of ordinary people. And soon a church, the most beautiful house to house the Lord, will rise.[43]

As these Jesuit Brothers were building houses for worship, they concomitantly helped to build the minds and touch the souls of the masses. Their ultimate goal was not a political one. Theirs was the rise of a 'beautiful house to the Lord', where a local Christian community could pray and worship.[44]

Pedagogical Skills Used in the CFC

Candidates for baptism were required to know the entire catechism, and to be able to respond to three to four hundred questions. Their responses had been memorised and repeated again and again, individually and in small groups. Charles Margot compared this learning process to a 'concert', in which catechism was sung by a choir of young people under the leadership

---

[41] Mario Joaquim Azevedo, *The Roots of Violence: A History of War in Chad* (London: Routledge, 2005), 18.
[42] Henri Véniat, 'Le R. P. Véniat nous parle du Tchad', *Jésuites* 1 (1960): 42.
[43] Editors, 'Nos Frères du Tchad', *JAF* 3 (1955): 27–30.
[44] Ibid.

of a catechist.⁴⁵ Many catechists were primary school children. Some of them were not yet baptised. They could speak their mother tongue and read and write in French. And they knew how to seek and catch the attention of the adults.⁴⁶

Each year, an exam was offered, and the catechumens who passed it received several awards according to their progress in the course. The awards included a medal for the first year, a Christian image for the second, and a cross for the final year.⁴⁷ To keep the catechumens focused during the learning sessions, the priest or the catechist used pictures of the gospel scenes, also called 'images Bernadette' in Charles Margot's letters. In addition to the pictures, they also used agricultural metaphors and projections during the night. This technique was known as 'Chinese shadows'. It consisted of having the catechist stand with a lamp behind a white shield and pass pictures and paintings through slides. A film projector could also be used thanks to the power from the battery of the missionary's car.⁴⁸

Catechetical centres across the Chad Mission aimed at training Chadian 'pastors'. These were agricultural monitors for rural areas and preachers. In Moïsala, a financial support from the apostolic vicar of Dakar, Marcel Lefèbvre, helped create a catechetical centre like those of Koumra and Archambault.⁴⁹ For two years, young men aged between about sixteen and twenty were taught French, reading, writing, and arithmetic. They also received practical training in agriculture.⁵⁰

The goal of the catechetical schools was to have these young men become pastoral agents in their home villages. They preached the gospel and offered mentorship to others on agricultural matters.⁵¹ Although situ-

---

45 Charles Margot, 'Nos Noirs', *Missi* 10 (October 1948): 238.
46 Ibid., 238.
47 Hallaire and Fedry, *Naissance d'une église Africaine*, 22.
48 Ibid.
49 Bishop Marcel Lefèbvre, we shall recall, is known for breaking with the Roman Catholic Church after Vatican II, which seemed too liberal for him. His influence in Francophone African missions was enormous before the Council. See: Bernard Sesboüé and Florian Michel, *De Mgr Lefèbvre à Mgr Williamson. Anatomie d'un schisme* (Paris: Lethielleux/DDB, 2009); Dossier, 'Vers la fin du schisme? Levée de l'excommunication des évêques lefebvristes. Textes et réactions', *Documentation Catholique* 2419 (1 March 2009): 235–55.
50 Joseph Fortier, *Les débuts de l'évangélisation au Moyen Chari, Diocèse de Sarh (Les Pionniers), 1946–1966*, vol. 1 (Sarh: n.p., 1991), 56.
51 Fortier, *Les débuts de l'évangélisation au Moyen Chari, Diocèse de Sarh (La Relève), 1966–1978*, vol. 2 (Sarh: n.p., 1991), 202.

ated in a Muslim-dominated area, Fort-Lamy, the capital of Chad, hosted large groups of Christian immigrants. In their three parishes, the Jesuits had schools for girls and boys, chaplaincies for schoolchildren and high-school pupils, scouting and guidance, and other Catholic youth associations, such as the Coeur Vaillants, the Catholic Student Youth (JEC), and the Christian Youth Workers (JOC). They offered classes for about a thousand adult employees. There was also a medical school and a nursery which served Catholics, Protestants, 'ethno-religionists', and Muslims. In the Muslim region of Mongo, Father Cavoret opened a youth centre for young people who had been left behind by the educational system; here, they were also offered classes.[52]

Conclusion: Rigobert of Chad, Schoolboy Evangeliser

In 1964, Rigobert, a Chadian boy whom the Jesuits called 'the Black Samuel', said he had received a calling to join the Jesuits. He said he directly heard God's voice calling him: 'Rigobert, Rigobert! Go and join the Fathers!' Then Rigobert, like the young Samuel in the Bible (1 Sam 3:4), came to see Father Joseph Franc to inquire whether or not there was a place for such a calling in the Society.[53]

As a primary school teacher, Rigobert was certainly a talented man. Yet, he had not earned a primary school certificate. His request to join the Jesuits was turned down. It is not clear whether or not the title 'the Black Samuel' was meant to be sarcastic, as in, 'in 1964, this was the best candidate from Chad who could apply to become a Jesuit'. The fact is, the missionaries in Chad had already turned down other candidates who had a better education, choosing, therefore, not to follow the Vatican's directives.

Rigobert serves as a good example of the issues in Jesuit education in southern Chad discussed in this chapter. He was a fine product of the bottom-up work the Jesuit missionaries had been doing there, and had received the best education the Jesuits could offer. The missionaries had sustained a religious schooling system that provided a primary-level education to thousands of Chadian children. These children, sometimes before their baptism, became translators, then school teachers, and finally evangelisers in their own right. Yet, none of these children were admitted to the Society of Jesus until the first Chadian Brothers in the 1970s.

---

[52] Dalmais, 'La mission du Tchad et les chrétiens de Fort-Lamy', 26.
[53] P. Franc, 'Fort-Archambault, Samuel Noir', *JAF* 2 (1964): 48.

The story of Rigobert is thus relevant for Jesuit historiography in two ways. First, contrary to what scholars usually assume, Jesuits' prioritising of secondary and higher education did not necessarily lead to their disengagement from elementary and primary education, and from educating the poor. Jesuit foundational texts and the early historiography of the Society situate the origins of Jesuit pedagogy in the biography of Ignatius and the early modern period in Spain. His own childhood education influenced his worldview. The education led him to make the instruction of children a core element of his self-understanding and of Jesuit identity and mission. Jesuit strategies in their missions in Europe, Africa, America, and Asia show the continuous and permanent role of children in the Jesuit missionary enterprise. In Chad, children were not only the evangelising targets of Jesuit missionaries; they were also collaborators in missions as translators and catechists.

Second, traditionally, in urban areas and places where a formal educational network already existed, the Jesuits developed secondary and higher education. In contrast, elementary and primary education developed in peripheral areas that were not affected by urbanisation, as well as in missions overseas, especially where such a network of primary education did not exist.[54] From the time of Saint Ignatius to the Restored Society, the Jesuits remained committed to ministering to (and through) children, and saw this as a central tool for preserving their own identity, spreading the gospel, and effecting social and cultural change.[55]

As the Jesuits settled in Chad, they used this rich tradition of educating the youth and the poor as a core element of their mission strategy. Yet, unlike other places in Africa where Christian missions sought to train a nationalist elite, the Jesuits in Chad resented Christian elitism and worked against its growth. In their practices, art, the development of architecture, literacy, singing, translating catechisms, and the Bible all became common as they sought to bring the gospel message to the poor. Evangelisation, practical and social works, and charity were synonymous. Their work on and with the popular masses again fell short in its promotion of a Chadian clergy and ecclesial leadership. Some missionaries, nevertheless, seemed to believe that the Christianisation of Chad was 'rushed'.

In 1960, a Jesuit proudly described the success of their educational project in Chad. In Fort-Archambault, for example, he counted 780 boys

---

[54] Aldo Scaglione, *The Liberal Arts and the Jesuit College System* (Amsterdam: John Benjamins, 1986), 19–20.

[55] Malaxecheverría, *La Compañía de Jesús por la instrucción del Pueblo Vasco en los siglos XVII Y XVIII*, viii–x.

Figure 9 Dalmais during a visit to Kyabé, 1954 (Archives JHIA, Nairobi).

who were educated by 12 African instructors and only 1 European missionary. Of these boys, 128 received a Christian baptism. Most children from Protestant families who attended the school were not baptised. He considered them to be as good as those studying in France and Egypt.[56] African personnel had grown in quantity and quality. While their education was as good as in civilised France, it seems it was still too soon to have the students become Jesuits. This situation betrayed the reality of what had been, all along, a downgraded *mission civilisatrice*.

The education of girls was most difficult for the Jesuits, in part because they are an all-male religious order. However, the few initiatives they took in that direction emulated the *sixa* in Central Cameroon. Jesuit education in Chad aimed at giving young women the care and education that would prepare them primarily for household tasks. Young brides, still catechumens, were 'promised' to Christian boys. They were then prepared for baptism at the mission during the months preceding the celebration of holy matrimony. This accelerated and intensive catechumenate generally gave excellent results.[57]

[56] Anonymous, 'Missionnaires de l'Assistance de France: Tchad', *Jésuites* 4 (1960): 36–38.
[57] P. Robinne, 'Tchad, Damandji, un missionnaire révise ses méthodes', *Jésuites* 4 (1961): 40–41.

The nineteenth-century concept of the domesticity of women was alive in mid-twentieth-century Chad. It is not because Jesuit missionaries in Chad did not believe in women and their capacity to carry on the work of the Church. Evidence in Chad suggests otherwise. What was happening was a structural handicap. An all-male sixteenth-century organisation was building a Church in a cultural context where foreign men did not have access to Chadian women in order to minister to them. The Jesuits overcame this handicap by building catechetical schools where they promoted a grassroots evangelisation led by married couples and children. They also reinforced monogamy among people who were traditionally polygamous.

In 1961, a year after Chadian independence, the religious focus of the Jesuit work became more inclusive. The Jesuits in Chad now belonged to a secular state. Preparations of the Second Vatican Council were ongoing. The Jesuits became more understanding towards modernity and its secularising trends, as younger generations of Jesuits took over the mission. Jesuit Father de Robinne was the first to warn against the 'dangers of quick Christianisation'. He blamed education for making Christianity a mere social phenomenon, lacking both doctrinal and spiritual depth. With independence, the demand for education had increased to fill positions in the newly Africanised administration. The first generation of Jesuit missionaries was replaced by younger European Jesuits with a different understanding of what the Church should be, and a renewed optimism following the election of Pope John XXIII in 1959.

The Vatican Council was about to start. In this particular context, the secularising trend, Father de Robinne feared, might have been just that. He feared that the old world was being replaced with a new and rapidly evolving one calling for radical change in the Church. Was this *aggiornamento* going too fast for the bishops from Chad who went to the Council? They were all Westerners. And there is evidence that the Jesuit French bishops from Chad agreed with the Vatican was timely about the need to vernacularise Catholicity. However, they disagreed with the Vatican regarding these bishops being replaced by African Church leaders at this particular time. Leadership Africanisation was to be delayed.

Moreover, the contrast between the late colonial period and the early years of Chad's independence shows a clear shift in the Jesuit approach to educating Chadians. Their initial goal was primarily religious. Yet, as they embraced the teachings of Vatican II and the political context of independent Chad, the education they offered became less intentionally syncretistic. The education also became more religiously neutral, especially among Muslim populations. Securing peaceful cohabitation with Chadian Muslims became a priority for the Jesuits in Chad.

CHAPTER 6

Era of Revolution: Bishop Paul Dalmais and Chad's Cultural Revolution, 1958–75

In one of his sermons given in 1964, Jesuit Father Raymond de Fenoyl preached of the necessity 'to love one's country with all his heart, even more with his arms'.[1] His words had a different resonance for the Jesuits listening to him. Some of them heard an echo of an old maxim of their founder Ignatius of Loyola: that love must be put into actions rather than words.[2] For others, the question was what did it mean to love Chad with one's arms, four years after independence? De Fenoyl was newly appointed superior of the Chad Mission in replacement of Dalmais who, in 1958, was appointed archbishop of Fort-Lamy.

The episcopate of Dalmais (from 1958 to 1979) helps us to understand the complex situation of missionary Christianity immediately after the independence of Chad. Born in Lyon, France, in 1917, Dalmais joined the Jesuit order on 17 October 1936. He was ordained to the priesthood in the Cathedral of Lyon on 31 July 1949 and joined the Chad Mission two years later. On 16 February 1955, he was appointed superior of the Jesuit Chad Mission. He became bishop of Fort-Lamy, today's capital city of N'Djamena, on 13 April 1958. He retired as archbishop of N'Djamena in 1980, and went back to the Jesuit community in Congo Brazzaville. Exhausted and sick, he returned to Lyon in 1991, where he died on 23 July 1994.[3]

---

[1] Reported by Revd Charles Vandame, 'Anniversaire national', *JAF* 2 (1964): 46–47.
[2] Ignatius of Loyola, *The Spiritual Exercises of St Ignatius of Loyola*, trans. George E. Ganss (New York: Vintage, 2000), 'Contemplation to Attain the Love of God' and 230.
[3] Cf. Jean Géli, 'Ordination de Mgr Paul Dalmais', *JAF* 3 (1958): 35.

Dalmais led the Church in Chad in the context of the Chadian Rite Controversy and Chad's Cultural Revolution (1973–75). In previous chapters, Catholic missions had failed to raise an African political and religious elite. Chad Protestantism, in contrast, already had a well-trained Chadian leadership. This chapter argues that the rise to power of President François Tombalbaye, a Protestant, and the subsequent persecution of Christians (especially Protestants) during his Cultural Revolution confirmed Jesuit missionaries' pragmatic approach to Chad's traditions and their aversion to a Christian elite in Africa.

Once political power had shifted from Europeans to Africans, the lives of African Church leaders were less safe than those of their European colleagues. African political leaders imprisoned, exiled, and murdered leading African ecclesiastics. European missionaries, in contrast, were simply expelled. The cost for Africans in leadership was greater than that of Europeans holding the same positions. As a result, Africanising the Church did not guarantee preservation of the Church after African independence.[4]

Tombalbaye of Chad, like Sékou Touré of Guinea, claimed to be decoupling the politics and religion of his country from neocolonialism. Formerly a deacon in the Baptist Church, Tombalbaye represented the worst nightmare for his former religious peers, whom he persecuted to death. This chapter shows that by delaying the Africanisation of Church personnel and leadership in Chad, the Jesuits limited the persecution of Chadian Catholics. The Jesuits shared the Vatican's concerns for survival and even revised the latter's strategy of Africanisation.

The Chad Mission shows that the Africanisation of leadership did not necessarily guarantee the preservation of the Church against hostile African governments. In Chad, the more Africanised a Church was, the worse it suffered under Tombalbaye's persecution. The worst retaliation Western missionaries could suffer during this time was expulsion from the country. In contrast, dozens of Africans who were leaders of Protestant churches were tragically murdered.

As Tombalbaye began his Cultural Revolution in the 1970s, he launched a systematic persecution of his former Protestant co-religionists. He also entertained a polemical, yet cordial, relationship with Dalmais. The clash of Christianities in Chad could not be overstated: an African Protestant

---

[4] Following leaders like Alioune Diop or Léopold-Sédar Senghor in Senegal, who tried to decouple Christianity from colonialism. See: Elizabeth Foster, *African Catholic: Decolonization and the Transformation of the Church* (Cambridge, MA: Harvard University Press, 2019).

president opposed to Western and African-elite Protestants. Meanwhile, the way European Catholic leaders accommodated Chadian traditions, the hybridity of their Christian practices, and the lack of an African Catholic elite in the Church spared its members from the worst of Tombalbaye's intra-Christian crusade.

Bishop Dalmais' silence during the persecution seemed cowardly and was very controversial at the time. It also attests to the delicate balance metropolitan bishops in Africa had to find in the face of oppressive regimes. This chapter analyses the first major clash of Christianities in Chad. Unlike de Gaulle and the Jesuits, who were Catholics, Tombalbaye was a Mid-Baptist deacon who had broken ties with his old Western-dominated Church to create his own.

The Rise of Dalmais and His Episcopal Ordination: A New Hope for Africa?

In 1951, Dalmais arrived in Fort-Lamy. He had just concluded one of his several 'acrobatic travels' in the African Sahel. The *Transsaharienne* was the name given to the itinerary missionaries took from Lyon to Chad. They would fly from Lyon to Algiers, then take different flights respectively to Béchar, Adar, Gao, Niamey, and Kano, and ultimately land in Fort-Lamy.[5] Once in Fort-Lamy, Dalmais took a 'whale-boat' towards Fort-Archambault. The boat broke down eight days later. Dalmais, terribly sick, was left lying on the banks of the Chari river, a few kilometres away from Bousso, one of the first stations of the Jesuit Chad Mission.[6]

The new head of the Chad Mission walked to the mission station, where Jesuit Father Louis Forobert welcomed him. According to Father Victor Waton, each of the missionaries' trips in the West African Sahel was 'an adventure'.[7] For while Propaganda Fide considered Chad 'really a beautiful mission country', Chad was also 'perhaps the hardest in the world'.[8] Therefore, it appealed to 'the worthiest of ambitious desires and generous vocations'.[9]

---

[5] A-CEFOD. Fonds Dalmais: 'Voyage du Père Forobert', *Lettres du Tchad* 8 (October 1947): 2–8.
[6] Victor Waton, 'Mgr Paul Dalmais, 1917–1994'. Obituary note in 'Library of Arrupe Jesuit Community, N'Djamena'.
[7] Ibid.
[8] A-CEFOD. Fonds Dalmais: 'Quelques précisions sur la mission', *Lettres du Tchad* (November 1946): 2.
[9] A-CEFOD. Ibid.

Dalmais himself acknowledged this harsh reality when he said that in Chad, one would more easily come face to face with a lion[10] than with a European, not to mention a priest! In an immense region extending north of the 10th parallel to Tibesti, with a population of 1.6 million according to the census of 1947, the Jesuits joined the Capuchins in Chad. The task was urgent. Chad was the last Sahelian African country still untouched by the Christian message.[11]

The mission territory took on the shape of an octopus. Its head was in Mongo; one tentacle was at Fort-Lamy (about 400km west), while others were at Bokoro (220km west), Ati (160km north), and Mangalmé (120km north-east), and later at Melfi, Korbol, Nielim, and Chari in the south.[12] Of the 1.3 million inhabitants in the Jesuit Mission's territory in 1948, 1.1 million were Muslims; 120,000 were 'Traditionalists', with about 100,000 practising the 'Margaye' religion.[13]

A year later, in 1949, only 2,000 to 3,000 were Catholics, while there were about 3,000 Protestants.[14] The decree of 17 May 1951 fixed the limits of ecclesiastical jurisdictions in Chad. Mayo-Kebbi was assigned to the Oblate Fathers, the Logone Region to the Capuchins, and the rest of the territory to the Jesuits. The different congregations cooperated to implement this decree. The Oblates took over Bongor, which had been a Jesuit mission. The Jesuits took over Moïsala and Koumra, previously mission stations. Of the 23 Jesuits in Chad in 1951, 7 were in their thirties, and were actively learning Chadian languages. This number grew to 31 in 1954 and 35 in 1955. Among them was the future leader of the mission, Charles Vandame.

A year into Dalmais' term as head of the mission, in 1957, there were a total of 41 Jesuits in Chad. The mission was expanding rapidly with the opening of new missions in Dadouar, Kalabai, and Kyabé. Among the newcomers were Joseph-Raymond Perrier in Baro and Roger Vialle in Dadouar. Several Venetian Jesuits arrived in 1958, among them Giovanni Montavani and Conrad Corti. The latter both had medical training.

On Sunday, 13 April 1958, Dalmais received his Episcopal ordination. The appointment and ordination were likely a reward of a successful short term as superior of an expanding mission. By 1959, the mission counted 40 priests, 5 scholastics, and 11 Jesuit Brothers. New missions were opened in

---

[10] A-CEFOD. Fonds Dalmais: 'Mission du Tchad', in *Courrier* 1 (1947): 1.
[11] A-CEFOD. Ibid.
[12] Ibid.
[13] A-CEFOD. Fonds Dalmais: Joseph Auger, 'Aperçu sur la mission du Tchad', *Lettres du Tchad* 12 (November 1949): 4.
[14] Ibid.

Danamaji, Largeau, and Bediondo. All these Jesuits were living in sixteen communities spread across the territory of the mission.

The celebration of Dalmais' ordination had a regional representation. The French archbishop of Bangui (Central African Republic), Joseph Cucherousset (1907–70), presided over the celebration. Bishops Yves Plumey (1913–91), a Frenchman, and Thomas Mongo (1914–88), a Cameroonian, both came from Cameroon. Nigerian John of the Cross Anyogou (1898–1967), auxiliary bishop of Onitsha, represented Catholics from his country. They concelebrated with Cucherousset.

The ordination mass offered a clear picture of a rapidly shifting Catholicism in Africa. Mongo and Anyogou were Africans. François Ngaïbi, the first Chadian Catholic priest, was there. Ngaïbi was from the Doba region. The Holy Ghost Fathers in the 1920s and the Capuchins of the province of Toulouse from the early 1930s had missioned in Doba with a clear inclination towards Africanisation. They sang in Mbay in their liturgies and had young Chadians serving mass with them dressed in cassocks like young seminarians. Some of these young men soon became catechists, including Ngaïbi, who, with seven other children, went to Bangui for training. Ngaïbi was a catechist in 1948 when he was received by the Capuchins. He went to France to be trained by the Oblates, and was ordained as a priest by Bishop Marcel Lefèbvre in 1957.[15]

During the celebration, Jesuit missionary Jean Géli reported the attendance of about five thousand Christians, including Africans and Europeans.[16] Dalmais addressed the crowd in Ngambay and Sangho, their own languages. This was a sign of the progress the missionaries had made in their knowledge of Chad's culture and languages. Dalmais himself understood this moment as one that awakened 'hopes of an entirely Catholic African Church'.[17]

It is not clear, however, what Dalmais meant by 'new hopes' in this context. The Vatican encouraged the sending of more European missionaries to Africa in 1957. From the Vatican's perspective, this wave of European missionaries was meant to support the momentum of an African Church on the rise with additional personnel and economic resources. On the other

---

[15] <http://www.freres-capucins.fr/IMG/pdf/Gaumain.pdf> [accessed 22 October 2018]. Following Ngaïbi, Louis Draman from Moundou was ordained in 1970, and two others in 1975.

[16] Jean Géli, 'La consécration de Mgr. Dalmais, premier évêque du Tchad', *Jésuites* 3 (1958): 35–38.

[17] Ibid.

hand, for the French missionaries working in Africa, 'hopes' might have been synonymous with supporting the work they were already doing.

An African interpretation also acknowledged, at least implicitly, the strengthening of their hold on the leadership of the Church. For Africans who attended this celebration, it is unlikely that they perceived Dalmais' ordination as 'new hopes'. Dalmais, a Frenchman, was ordained by a fellow French missionary bishop, who was a papal legate. They were surrounded by other French bishops from Cameroon and the Central African Republic.

The Africans who were present, and not the sizeable French old guard, might have been the real hope. It might also be the case that Dalmais' reference to new hopes simply acknowledged the rise of multicultural Catholic leadership in Africa. Depending on particular contexts, foreign missionaries and Africans would share the presiding roles, sometimes as a minority, and sometimes in the majority. Dalmais recognised the fait accompli, that the European monopoly over leadership positions in the Church was over. This situation was, indeed, hopeful for the Catholicity of the Church.

The different interpretations of Catholicity among Africans and Europeans were not necessarily mutually exclusive. Chad was a young Church still in need of support in terms of personnel and financial resources. Unable to promote Chadian personnel within the Church, the missionaries asked for more reinforcements from Europe. Pope Pius XII's encyclical letter *Fidei Donum* was therefore a godsent opportunity for them that confirmed the strategy the Jesuits had adopted from 1951. The presence of African Church leaders such as Mongo, Anyogou, and Ngaïbi was, however, unmistakable. A French bishop could still ordain a French missionary in Chad in 1958, yet in Nigeria and Cameroon, history was moving decisively towards the Africanisation of leadership in the Church.

A story like that of Chad was becoming rare. Since the Africanisation of the leadership in the Church was taking effect in Africa, it was up to Chad to try to catch up. The Vatican went along with this new development in the Church of Chad. The pope had appointed all the bishops attending the ordination. The war on Communism and the containment of Islam in Chad was an interest shared by the Vatican, French missionaries, and the rising African Catholic elite. While different interpretations of Catholicity might compete in modern Chad, unity was preserved around the pope, the spreading of the gospel message, and the Catholic crusade against 'false ideologies'.

A Religious Warrior Amid the Cultural Revolution

Dalmais had once considered himself a 'religious warrior'. He was a soldier under the banner of the cross whose mission was to stop the spread of Islam in Chad and Christianise what he called its 'animist' inhabitants. In an article in *Etudes* (1956), he expressed his concern about the increasing secularism and materialism of the Christian Évolués elite class in Chad. This class, he believed, was Protestant.[18] Their influence was growing in Chadian society.

For instance, in 1959, in the region of Western Logone alone, there were already 49 Chadian Protestant men and women who were nurses, and 9 medical doctors, for a Baptist population of 10,866.[19] In 1968 these numbers had increased: 60 Chadian pastors, 425 catechists, 25 women nurses, and 15 medical doctors over a Baptist population of 15,436.[20] Catholics had nothing of the kind in their ranks. Dalmais' worry was not as much about the capacity of this Christian elite to effect a social agenda as it was about its proximity to colonists whose commitment to faith and religion was dubious.

Guided by his fear of secularism, Dalmais concluded that it would be better if more Chadians became true Muslims than 'Christians of that kind'.[21] He studied the work of Protestant churches in Chad. As superior of the mission, he sometimes encouraged the Jesuits to collaborate with them. In some cases, the arrival of the Jesuits displaced Protestant missionaries who preferred a relocation away from Catholic influences. A non-identified Jesuit wrote in 1946:

> Hearing my settlement in Mongo, the Protestant Swiss Pastor, who had asked for a plot of land, renounced it. He is not without merit: he is currently, with his wife and six young children, in a remote village, at the foot of Mount Guéra, lost in an arid and isolated region. He is also returning to Switzerland and I wonder if he will come back.[22]

---

[18] Paul Dalmais, 'Le Tchad, mission stratégique', *Vivante Afrique* 203 (June–July 1959): 3.
[19] Maioulam Mbairougol, 'Implantation et impact des missions protestantes dans le Logone Occidental au sud du Tchad: 1926–1997' (MA thesis in History, University of Ngaoundéré, 2009), 87.
[20] Ibid., 91.
[21] Dalmais, 'L'avenir religieux du Tchad'.
[22] A-CEFOD. Fonds Dalmais: 'Mission du Tchad', *Courrier* 1 (1947): 2.

Parting ways also avoided any friction or double-mindedness among denominations and their followers. In neighbouring Cameroon, for example, the French governor, Jean-Baptiste Marchand, put in place policies of denominational isolation to prevent public disorder caused by 'overzealous catechists infringing on one another's territory and engaging in fiery denunciations of rival denominations'.[23] These behaviours often scandalised Africans and led to the closing of some churches.[24]

In this case, the isolation of the Protestant family in Guéra, Chad, seemed self-imposed. It was motivated either in order to avoid double-mindedness among the converts[25] or to preserve missionaries' children from 'corrupted' behaviours from indigenous children. The latter was clearly a racist objective. *Courrier du Tchad* already described the complexities of race in the Chad Mission in 1947:

> The Protestant mission has a beautiful building but not a proper temple. Her school is run by 3 European teachers, and a Savoyard woman teacher who really loves France. There is a boarding school for the mulatos, whose teacher has asked me to do everything I can for them. They are, indeed, much to be pitied, being neither Black nor White and despised by everybody. By the way, they are the poorest of all.[26]

The reference to the race of the nun – a Savoyard who 'nevertheless loved France' – and to the mixed-race children underlines the importance of the race factor in the pursuit of the mission.[27] The Savoyard people, who spoke French and shared French culture, had often been considered 'Italian' because of the Piedmont-Sardinian influence over them and their

---

[23] Kenneth J. Orosz, 'The "Catechist War" in Interwar French Cameroon', in *In God's Empire. French Missionaries and the Modern World* (Oxford: Oxford University Press, 2012), 241.

[24] Jonathan Fox and Ephraim Tabory, 'Contemporary Evidence Regarding the Impact of State Regulation of Religion on Religious Participation and Belief', *Sociology of Religion* 69, no. 3 (Fall 2008): 245–71 – here, p. 247.

[25] According to Frank A. Salamone, 'the double bind refers to a situation in which a person in authority has sent out mixed messages to a subordinate about the appropriateness of behavior in a specific situation': Frank A. Salamone, 'Mixed Messages at the Mission', *Anthropos* 86, nos 4–6 (1991): 488.

[26] A-CEFOD. Fonds Dalmais: 'Mission du Tchad', *Courrier* 1 (1947): 3.

[27] There were about 25,000 Arab Choa living in 300 villages across the Chari river in 1973. While their settlement in the region can be traced back to 425 BC, they were conquered by the Kanem-Bornou in the seventeenth century. Christian Bouquet, 'Genèse et Évolution de l'habitat Rural Dans Le Bas-Chari Tchadien', *Etudes Rurales* 70 (June 1978): 52.

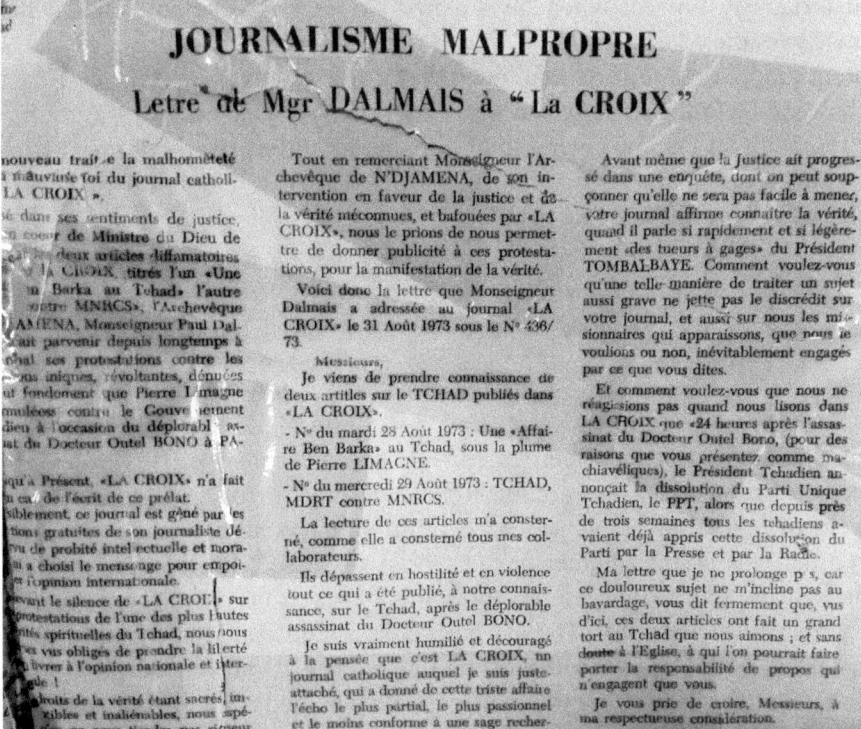

Figure 10 Bishop Dalmais' response to *La Croix*, 31 August 1973, in defence of Tombalbaye (Archives JHIA, Nairobi).

rulers.[28] Their history of migrations had created an important Savoyard diaspora in the nineteenth century, and most Christian families encouraged their children to join missionary congregations.[29] Moreover, 90 to 95 per cent of the Savoyard clergy came from rural areas, and the Savoyard economy was 79 per cent agricultural.[30] With Chad being almost entirely rural with a Catholic ethnic diversity, being a Savoyard was a clear asset for a missionary in Chad.

Collaborating with Protestants, however, remained secondary among Dalmais' concerns. In addition to atheistic materialism, he saw Islam as the most important challenge for the Chad Mission. The nature of his relationship with other Christians and Muslims was a record he wanted

[28] Jacques Lovie, *La Savoie dans la vie française de 1860 à 1875* (Paris: Presses Universitaires de France, 1963), 2.
[29] Ibid., 21.
[30] Ibid., 7 and 21.

historians to correct when he directed Pierre Faure to write down his own version of Chad's Civil War. Faure, a friend of Dalmais, wrote a monograph in 2003, available in the Jesuit archives in Vanves, from some of Dalmais' personal notes. Faure was at pains to set the record straight about Dalmais' version of his role during the Civil War in Chad.[31] Dalmais' relevance in the history of Christianity in Chad, however, was shaped by the Cultural Revolution.

The First Chadian Rite Controversy and Jesuit Accommodation (1966)

The political environment of the time, especially President François Tombalbaye's rise to power (1960), his Cultural Revolution (1973–75), and the Civil War that precipitated Dalmais' retirement (1979), ultimately shaped Dalmais' term as archbishop of Fort-Lamy from 1958 to 1979. Six years after the independence of Chad, in 1966, a conflict broke out.[32] This conflict was about whether or not Christians could receive the Sara initiation rite, the *yondo*. Some Protestants believed the *yondo* to be totally contrary to their beliefs. Having their children initiated, they said, was an apostasy. Following their Protestant neighbours, some Chadian Catholics also asked the Jesuits not to baptise people who had been initiated, including their own children.

Jesuit sources first referred to the *yondo* in 1949. In *Lettres du Tchad*, Father Léon Chaine described a popular celebration that involved people of different sexes and generations. Young men returning from this rite caught his attention. Wearing masks, a tail made of animal pells, straw muffs at their hocks, and collections of bracelets on their arms, their bodies were covered with red clay. They had spent sleepless nights in the bushes and joined a secret society with its own language and social codes.[33] According to Chaine, the initiation lasted between two and three months. It was a very harsh and secretive experience. Some of the young men never returned from the bushes. Those who returned were prohibited from giving details about its whereabouts. The goal was to make

---

[31] See: Pierre Faure, *Monseigneur Paul Dalmais dans la Guerre du Tchad: Document pour l'histoire* (Paris: n.p., 2003).

[32] That Jesuit Jacques Hallaire compared this crisis to the Chinese Rites Controversy. See: Jacques Hallaire, 'Drame de conscience au pays Sara', *JAF* 3 (1966): 41.

[33] A-CEFOD. Fonds Dalmais: Léon Chaine, 'Une fête populaire', *Lettres du Tchad* 8 (May 1949): 1.

them mature men, 'killing' the evil spirit (Koi) in them to help grow the good one (N'di).[34]

In 1966, after the Second Vatican Council, the Jesuits again discussed accommodating the *yondo* in Chad. Jacques Hallaire argued that the *yondo* was popular and a 'unifying' practice for the entire country, and that it forged the character of young men. The *yondo* also served to solidify social bonds. It contributed to the social and cultural renewal of society. Given the context of Vatican II, Hallaire wondered if it was possible to take the positive aspects of the *yondo* and Christianise it.[35]

Hallaire and other Jesuits had two sets of solutions. They could create a Christian *yondo*. The downside of that solution, they soon realised, was that instead of remaining a unifying factor for society, the *yondo* would become very divisive across religious lines. They also contemplated asking Christian families to send their children to the traditional *yondo*. The problem there lay in convincing Chadian traditional leaders to strip it of the elements that were contrary to Christian values.

With the help of Matthias Garteri, a Chadian seminarian, and some Chadian lay catechists, the Jesuits organised a campaign. Its objective was to convince villagers that such adaptations were not betraying the spirit of Christianity. Christian children should absolutely reject anti-Christian elements of the *yondo*, even if such a rejection might condemn them to death. However, it was also their obligation and duty to help the 'pagans' improve the *yondo*. Some traditional leaders embraced the compromise. As pressure mounted from the rest of Chadian society, young Catholics stood their ground and a Christianised version of the *yondo* was adopted.[36]

The adaptation of the *yondo* was a major victory for the Jesuits' vernacularisation approach in Chad. By the early 1970s, efforts like the Christianisation of the *yondo* or the Africanisation of the Easter liturgy had become common practice in the Jesuit-controlled dioceses of Chad. A reason for this change also had to do with the rise of a local clergy. Although there were still no Jesuits from Chad, not even in training, the Jesuit bishops running the Church could not ignore pressures from their few diocesan priests and seminarians. The meeting of the Presbyterium of Fort-Lamy, 2–4 February 1972, in which 6 of the 27 priests and seminarians were Chadians, discussed the challenges of the Church in Chad. They adopted a stance on the issue of the 'native' clergy. It aimed at promoting greater participation of Chadians in decision making and in the

[34] Ibid.
[35] Jacques Hallaire, 'Drame de conscience au pays Sara', 41.
[36] Ibid.

government of the Church, in order 'to decolonise' the life and ways of thinking of the Church.[37]

Dalmais and Chad's Cultural Revolution, 1973–75

The Cultural Revolution launched by Tombalbaye quickly shook the foundations of the *yondo* compromise. Tombalbaye took his inspiration from Mobutu Sese Seko's 'Cultural Revolution' in Zaïre. The concept of 'Cultural Revolution', however, first appeared in China. This revolution created autonomous churches and sought to eliminate all foreign influence within Chinese Christianity. It also led to great suffering among Christians: 'Indeed, the period from the mid-1950s to the late 1960s was a time of great suffering for Christianity worldwide. Nationwide mobilisation campaigns such as the Great Leap Forward (1958–60) and the calamitous Cultural Revolution (1966–69), in particular, adversely affected the Christian churches.'[38]

This movement took the name of 'Tchaditude' (Chadianisation). Some saw Chadianisation as a form of 'southernisation' or 'Sara-isation' of Tombalbaye's administration.[39] Tombalbaye himself set the example by being the first to change his name. He dropped the Christian 'François' for the Sara 'N'Garta' Tombalbaye. Christians were, likewise, forced to renounce their Christian names.[40] Cities like Fort-Lamy and Fort-Archambault, centres of Jesuit missions, were respectively renamed as N'Djamena and Sarh, reversing the religious baptism of public spaces the Jesuits had supervised from the time of J. du Bouchet. All adult men who were not initiated had to enlist for the *yondo*.[41]

Years earlier, in 1950, Tombalbaye had been excommunicated from his Baptist Church. Then a deacon, he had decided to start a Church of his own. He built it three hundred feet away from his former Church.[42] Tombalbaye was still young, and a fervent Baptist, when he first met

---

[37] Editors, 'Réunion du diocèse de Fort-Lamy', *JAF* 59 (June 1972): 118.
[38] Adrian Hastings (ed.), *A World History of Christianity* (Grand Rapids, MI: Eerdmans, 1999), 407.
[39] Mario Joaquim Azevedo, *Chad: A Nation in Search of its Future* (Boulder, CO: Westview Press, 1998), 50.
[40] Ibid. For example, people named 'Issa', 'Brahim', or 'Souleymane' could keep their names; it was, however, forbidden to use the Western versions of these – respectively 'Jesus', 'Abraham', or 'Solomon'.
[41] Cf. 'Retour du Yondo', *Canard Déchaîné* 0043 (Oct. 12, 1974).
[42] Emeritus Catholic Bishop Charles Vandame, email message to author, 10 March 2017.

Dalmais.⁴³ By the time Dalmais was ordained bishop in 1958, his younger African friend was prime minister. Two years later, he became the first president of the new Republic of Chad.

The Cultural Revolution ultimately led to an estrangement between the two men. Dalmais saw in those changes an effort 'to decolonise' the nomenclature of the cities and national monuments. For Dalmais, the Cultural Revolution was also an anti-France movement.⁴⁴ The imposition of the *yondo*, as well as a calculated diplomatic shift away from French monopoly by Tombalbaye's government, contributed to his estrangement from Dalmais. From 1971, and alongside a sustained anti-Western campaign, Tombalbaye's government shifted its foreign policy towards a reconciliation with the Muslim world. This move was an attempt to isolate internal dissidents and rebellions from the Muslim north of his country. The reconciliation with the Arab world also produced a crack in the *de facto* monopoly France had on the foreign policy of its former colony. During this anti-French campaign, thirty French citizens, including two Jesuit priests, were expelled.⁴⁵

The official government newspaper, *Le Canard Déchaîné*, acknowledged the expulsion of several Swedish Protestant pastors and their families.⁴⁶ Sources outside Chad also confirmed that Christians faced persecution during the Cultural Revolution. Writing in the missionary newspaper *The Lightbearer* in 1974, Pastor W. H. Teh of Nigeria said that Christians in Chad were living through the worst period of Church history because of the revolution.⁴⁷ Reverend Raymond Buck and Adam Thomas of the Sudan United Mission, announced the 'withdrawal' of Swiss missionaries, and added that a Roman Catholic father had been killed.⁴⁸

---

43   M-Ly. B. 2181: Dalmais' personal notes on the Cultural Revolution of N'Garta Tombalbaye: 'Diaire 1959–1975', (43/2).
44   It is, however, important to note that in 1970, there were 3,500 French soldiers still supporting Chadian security forces (Robert Pledge, 'Chad: France's African War', *Africa Report* [1 June 1970]: 16).
45   'L'Eglise Catholique et la Révolution Culturelle de Ngarta Tombalbaye', in M-Ly. B. 2181. 39/1–8: 'Dossier Paul Dalmais, 1917–1994' – here, 39/1–2.
46   Editorial, 'Suédois au pied du mur', *Canard Déchaîné* 0053 (18 February 1975): 6.
47   W. H. Teh, in *The Lightbearer* (1974): 5. My informants include Les Carew, Steve Gault (the Mid-Africa mission's current administrator for Africa and Europe), and Charles Vandame and Agide Galli (both Jesuits who were working in Chad when the event occurred).
48   Adam Matthew Publications, 'SUM in Nigeria, the Cameroons, Chad,

Witnesses in Chad four decades later still remembered these dark years of Tombalbaye's persecution of Christians. They reported that Christians were tortured, and hundreds lost their lives in several locations in 1974. The Protestant opposition only grew stronger when the president started forcing all non-Catholic Christian denominations in Chad to unite under the banner of the 'Evangelical Church in Southern Chad'. This Evangelical Church in Southern Chad was the only one the government recognised as 'official' for all Protestants.[49]

Dalmais initially interpreted the Cultural Revolution as an anti-France political movement.[50] Meanwhile, the French press framed it as a religious war between Christianity and a Christian president eager to return to the darkness of barbarity and paganism. On 30 December 1974, Jean Grandmougin of radio station France Inter blamed the religiously disordered mindset of the president for the murders. Tombalbaye, he said, was once a faithful Baptist deacon; he was now embracing Voodoo and Hinduism and their 'evil' effects. Historian Christian Bouquet called the Haitian influence on Tombalbaye the 'folie mystique' (mystical foolishness). This was not religious in nature. It was a political and anti-French and anti-Western propaganda that aimed at making every European living in Chad a 'little [Jacques] Foccart', the embodiment of French neocolonialism in Francophone Africa.[51]

Competing Views of Christianity: True Christianity vs Christendom

The president himself complained about the bad press surrounding the *yondo*. In August 1973, he accused 'certain Christians' who opposed the initiation of being complicit with colonialism.[52] Later, he firstly accused *Le Monde* of being complicit in that religious 'tartufferie' (hypocrisy). He

---

Sudan, and other African territories'. Annual Report 1973, published on 3 February 1974. This is the only mention of a Catholic leader being murdered. None of my Catholic sources in Chad confirmed that particular case.

[49] Cf. C. Raymond Buck, 'Consultation in the Chad', in *BMM-Martyrs* (Foreign Secretary, 1974). Page not provided.

[50] Making it a religious conflict would have affected the Church negatively. After all, it was a minority in a Muslim-dominated country.

[51] Cf. Christian Bouquet, *Tchad: genèse d'un conflit* (Paris: Harmattan, 1982), 145.

[52] Jean de la Guerivière, 'Tchad: subversion contre l'initiation', *Le Monde* (11 December 1973): 8; AFP, 'Tchad: Tombalbaye assimile la coopération avec la France à "une Nouvelle Forme de Colonialisme"', 2. Printed copies of *Le Monde* were found in A-CEFOD, 'Journaux'.

claimed they produced missionary propaganda that the *yondo* was ancient paganism and barbarism.[53] Secondly, he reiterated that religion transcends any civilisation. As it adapted when it interacted with other cultures, the president argued, Christianity should do the same now and not oppose the Sara civilisation.[54] In a veiled threat, he continued:

> When in the name of the Christian religion, Western Christians, filled with prejudices and not able to assimilate to our civilisation, want to impose on us their way of life, they are not bringing the peace of Christ into our home. They bring regrettable conflicts [...] Definitively, it is never Christianity that fights against the *Yondo*, but rather 'a certain form of Chrétienté [Christendom]'. Because Christianity [le christianisme] does not [cannot] disrespect what is profoundly human and spiritual. Initiation is the soul of the Sara people. Why would they lose it, and for what?[55]

Tombalbaye differentiated between 'Christendom', a form of imperial Christianity, and Christianity, a religion based on the gospel of Christ. The irony with his interpretation is that while he argued this point, he was simultaneously attacking the Baptist, Bible-oriented religious groups, while it was the Catholics who were, in this particular context of French colonialism, the ones representing the so-called 'Christendom'. In a press conference, published on 23 November 1974,[56] the President explained again that a 'certain form of Christianity' was not Christianity as such, but rather a 'certain Christian civilisation', the one that brought 'torture, lies, homosexuality, murder, exploitation, poverty, coup d'état, etc. in Africa; and the one that caused two world wars. Its main concern was the temporal, not the spiritual world'.[57]

---

[53] Reacting to that 'foreign propaganda', the *Canard Déchaîné* continued to publish abstracts of Tombalbaye's lecture on the *yondo*, which he gave on 29 April 1974 to the Écoles des Cadres of the National Movement for Cultural and Social Revolution (NMCSR). He hoped the French newspapers would have the courtesy to do the same.

[54] N'Garta Tombalbaye, 'A cause du succès spectaculaire du Yondo, LA TARTUFFERIE RELIGIEUSE AUX ABOIS [sic]', *Canard Déchaîné* 0046 (11 November 1974): 1 and 6. Printed copies of the newspaper *Canard Déchaîné* are in A-CEFOD, 'Journaux'.

[55] Ibid.

[56] N'Garta Tombalbaye, 'Conférence de presse du Président Tombalbaye à Paris', *Canard Déchaîné* 0047 (23 November 1974): 3.

[57] Tombalbaye, 'A cause du succès spectaculaire du Yondo, LA TARTUFFERIE RELIGIEUSE AUX ABOIS'.

Tombalbaye believed the only way Christianity would become distinctively Chadian was if it were stripped of its Western, civilising, cultural, and imperialistic components. Biblical Christianity, he argued, was the only one Chadians would accept.

Either Tombalbaye's reaction attested to a truly religious concern, or it reflected what R. Pierce Beaver has called 'a split personality', stating that most nationalist leaders suffered from this.[58] At a time when he was persecuting Evangelical Christians in Chad, the president, ironically, presented himself as the defender of true, gospel-based Christianity. As such, he was also against a form of Christianity tainted by the ideology of Western civilisation, its imperialism, and what he considered its cultural abuses.

Tombalbaye reminded Chadians that their country was under attack by foreigners. On religious grounds, however, one of his allies, Needi Brahim Seid, published an article in *Canard*. He affirmed that the *Yondo* was not a mere moral equivalence to Christianity anymore. It was not even mere religion. It was 'God in liberty' (Le Yondo est Dieu en liberté). It was sacred.[59] Several Chadian Protestant pastors who were close to the President encouraged the creation of national churches. In the regions of Sarh, Maro and Koumra, for example, the Evangelical Church of Chad became the only official Protestant Church.[60] Catholic churches remained untouched by this nationalising process.[61]

---

[58] 'The leaders know that the nation is far from self-sufficient and must have capital and technical assistance from outside. But they feel that this is owed them as a right, or as atonement for wrongs against their people, and they want it on their own terms and without strings attached [...] The masses are strengthened in their religious adherence, but the intellectual is likely to hold affectionately to the old rites within the family circle while his allegiance is to secularism in all other things. He is a split personality': R. Pierce Beaver, 'Missions and the New Nationalism', *Journal of Church and State* 3, no. 2 (November 1961): 149–71 – here, pp. 151–52.

[59] Needi Brahim Seid, 'Ne trahissons pas le Yondo', *Canard Déchaîné* 0048 (7 December 1974): 6.

[60] A-CEFOD. B. CF.B. 01285 CF: Ngaryanan Noudjalbaye, 'L'Eglise Baptiste dans la tempête au Tchad (1973–1975)' (Direction de la Documentation de la Présidence de la République, 1976), 12–13, CEFOD, A-CEFOD. Box: CF.B. 01285 CF.

[61] A-CEFOD. B. 254B: 'Fonds Dalmais'. On 22 November 1974, Parisian Liberal journal *L'Aurore* (The Dawn) explained the difference in treatment between Catholics and Protestants by the fact of Catholic syncretism: 'The Catholic missionaries, it is true, are much more conciliatory. Their flock

A Challenge to the Jesuits

The crisis around the *yondo* presented several challenges to the Jesuits. The experiment had become a deadly weapon that Tombalbaye used against political dissidents.[62] The Christianised version of the *yondo*, which the Jesuits had previously negotiated with traditional leaders, was prohibited and its secrecy reinforced. Those who received it were prohibited from sharing anything about their experience. The crisis exposed a rift among Christian churches in Chad.

In 1973, fourteen Protestant pastors who opposed the Cultural Revolution were allegedly murdered in Banda, near Koumogo. As the media accused the Catholic leadership of its silence, a meeting of Catholic bishops and clergy was convened to discuss a common position regarding the new turn of events. In N'Djamena, the clergy were still mostly European. Dalmais was then Bishop and president of the Conference of Catholic Bishops in Chad. His European clergy were unanimous in denouncing the new policy and alleged political assassinations. They promised to publicly condemn these acts.

However, the Catholic lay personnel of Fort-Lamy, especially the catechists, opposed that approach. They advised prudence and silence. In their view, the European personnel had the luxury of opposing the president, since they only risked expulsion from the country. Leaders of the *yondo* themselves were afraid of political retaliation should a European be victimised by the *yondo*.[63] The consequences for African Christians were worse. The catechists found support from the Capuchin bishop of Moundou. A Canadian, Bishop Régis Belzile, resented the political activism of his French colleagues.[64] In 1979, during the Civil War, he accused

---

often has a triple affiliation: Catholic, animist, and Muslim. In the minds of Chadian Catholics, the keys to the kingdom of God are now available to all, and the gates of heaven are no longer as narrow as in the past. More demanding, the Protestants inevitably drew the wrath of those responsible for the cultural revolution.'

[62] Dalmais discusses his relationship with Tombalbaye in his diary. Cf. M-Ly. Box 2181: 'Dossier Paul Dalmais, 1917–1994'; documents from this collection include: 'Diaire 1959–1975'. See also Pierre Faure, *Monseigneur Paul Dalmais dans la Guerre du Tchad: Document pour l'histoire* (Paris: n.p., 2003).

[63] Robert Jaulin, *La Mort Sara. L'ordre de la Vie ou la Pensée de la Mort au Tchad* (Paris: Plon, 1966), 23.

[64] We already saw with du Bouchet that the Capuchins were not happy with the work of the Jesuits, either because they seemed too Latinised or because

Dalmais of putting the lives of the missionaries at risk because of his indiscretions and pro-French positions.[65]

American Protestant sources reporting the context of the murder of Protestant pastors in Chad are evasive and offer different estimates of victim numbers. Protestants agreed on the fact that the political police were responsible for the deaths of these pastors, some of whom might have been buried alive. Chad's station of the Baptist Mid-Africa Mission suggests that some members of this denomination were among the victims.[66] Les Carew, one of the Baptist Mid-Africa missionaries currently working in Chad, also confirmed the event in a written note to me, and noted that his father-in-law, who is now deceased, trained some of the victims.[67]

None of the sources actually confirms 'Banda' as a crime site. However, these Protestant sources and other informants, including Roman Catholic archbishop emeritus of N'Djamena Charles Vandame, and other Chadians, all agreed that several murders took place. They also insist on the religious motives of these actions. Christians were persecuted because they resisted what these missionaries and evangelists believed to be 'pagan' in the Cultural Revolution. Chadians, in Tombalbaye's framing, believed in a Chadianised Christianity freed from any Western imperialistic influence.

---

they were too political. The latter was the case in the dispute between Dalmais and Belzile.

[65] M-Ly. Box 2181: Pierre Faure, 'Mgr Dalmais dans la Guerre du Tchad: Document pour l'histoire' (2003), 45. That year, Dalmais had attempted to mediate between President Malloum and Hussein Habré. Christians from his own diocese saw it as a betrayal. Cf. M-Ly. Box 2181: RESRAT (Rencontre Sacerdotale et Religieuse des Africains au Tchad), 'Lettre ouverte à Mgr Paul Dalmais' (23 July 1979).

[66] 'Paul Metzler, the statement says, started Baptist Mid-Missions' work in Chad [...] In 1973, the Church in Chad took a strong stand against government-forced tribal initiation rites. At that time, there were hundreds of churches. The believers were severely persecuted, and 13 of our senior Chadian pastors were martyred. Baptist churches were closed, and Baptist Mid-Missions missionaries were expelled. The Chad field remained closed to missionaries until 1975. Within three weeks of military overthrow of the former government, the Baptist churches were reopened. Only a few of the former missionaries returned to Chad – most had taken on ministries in other BMM fields': <https://www.bmm.org/country/chad/> [accessed 22 February 2017].

[67] Email sent on 22 February 2017. I asked Les to give me more information about his wife's parents. He did not answer.

The crisis around the *yondo* escalated in January 1974. As Tombalbaye was concluding an official visit in France, a French journalist asked him whether he was responsible for the murder of the Protestant pastors.[68] He replied that if that were the case, Archbishop Dalmais 'would have opened his mouth!'[69] The president might have been referring to Dalmais' talkative character.[70]

Fearful of the dangers a direct confrontation with the president might mean for Catholic communities, Dalmais decided to respond to the president in a private letter instead. In that letter, he condemned religious and political repression. He sent another note to French newspapers critical of the position of 'prudence and silence' of the bishops.

Concerning Dalmais' 'indifference', one observation can be made. Contrary to what the 'Dossier Dalmais' suggests, the incidents discussed during that press conference did not only occur in late 1973; they were ongoing. Tombalbaye's sarcasm as reported in the 'Dossier' does not appear in *Canard Déchaîné*. The question therefore is whether the 'Dossier' was referring to a particular incident that took place in Banda in 1973, or reacting to the crisis that was actually going on during Tombalbaye's visit in Paris in late 1974. One thing is clear. The persecution against Christians took place during the Cultural Revolution and Protestant churches paid a heavy price.

Escalation of the *Yondo* Crisis

The *yondo* became mandatory in 1973. However, the Baptist Church's opposition to the traditions of Chad and its conflict with Tombalbaye started years before. From the time of their arrival in Chad in 1920, Protestant churches required new converts to renounce their own traditions, which they saw as fetishism. Not complying with that mandate often led to excommunications.[71] Church members and their children were not allowed to take part in the *yondo*. Doing so was seen as an apostasy.[72]

The first confrontation between Baptist churches and Chadian politics arose between 1948 and 1960. This period corresponded with the creation of political parties in Chad. This political context might have led to the

---

[68] M-Ly. Box 2181. 39/3–4: 'Diaire 1959–1975'.
[69] M-Ly. Box 2181: Pierre Faure, 'Mgr Dalmais dans la Guerre du Tchad: Document pour l'histoire' (2003), 30.
[70] Ibid.
[71] Mbairougol, 'Implantation et impact des missions protestantes', 70.
[72] Ibid., 71.

closing of some Baptist churches;[73] however, Dalmais himself acknowledged that converts from Protestant churches constituted the 'elite' of Chad.[74] We could then expect the early persecutions against their churches to come from colonial authorities eager to control Chad's elite. Dalmais' *History of the Catholic Church in Chad*[75] indicates that there were cases of French colonial officials who considered Christian missions a threat. Others officials requested the presence of Christian missions.[76] In his introduction to Jesuit Jacques Hallaire's *Naissance d'une Eglise*, Jacques Fedry wrote that some colonial officials considered churches to be 'evil' because they taught indigenous people how to think.[77] What is missing, however, is any evidence of expulsions or deadly persecutions of Church members coming from colonial officials.

One hypothesis is that the nationalist awareness of the Évolués, who were trained in Protestant schools, made them more critical of Western missionaries. They either left churches or launched attacks against their former mentors.[78] A possible reason for such pressure was that some leaders in African nationalist movements, including Chad's, had become sympathetic to Communism becoming anti-Christian.[79] Another hypothesis is that the political commitment of Chad's new converts put them at odds with the 'apolitical' theologies of their respective churches. Churches might have closed because this elite was either excommunicated from or left them, sometimes to found their own. This might have been the case for Tombalbaye himself, who, as mentioned, was a deacon in the Mid-Baptist Mission Church before his excommunication in 1950.[80]

---

[73] Ibid., 73.
[74] Dalmais, 'Le Tchad, mission stratégique', 3.
[75] An unpublished four-page document located in the library of Arrupe Jesuit Community in N'Djamena.
[76] Paul Dalmais, 'Histoire de l'Eglise Catholique au Tchad' (n.p., 1972).
[77] Hallaire and Fedry, *Naissance d'une Église africaine*, 13–14.
[78] This was the case of nationalist movements across Africa, including the UPC of Cameroon, which, like the PPT of Chad, was affiliated to the RDA. Cf. Auguste Owono-Kouma, 'La riposte des leaders de l'UPC aux vicaires apostoliques du Cameroun. Analyse historico-littéraire de la réaction des nationalistes camerounais à la *Lettre Commune* d'avril 1955', *Histoire et Missions Chrétiennes* 10 (June 2009): 119–39; Richard A. Joseph, 'Ruben Um Nyobè and the "Kamerun" Rebellion', *African Affairs* 73, no. 293 (October 1974): 428–48.
[79] Jesuit archives of the French province, Box 1457: 'Frederick de Belinay, 1875–1958', especially in Box 1457: *Écrits divers* and 'Vue d'ensemble sur la vraie religion: Précis de la Foi Catholique'. Retreat notes, 7 July 1954.
[80] Dingammadji, *Ngarta Tombalbaye: Parcours et rôle dans la vie politique du Tchad*.

Finally, several incidents between missionaries, indigenous evangelists, and traditional leaders might have led to the final clash of 1973–75. A document by Noudjalbaye Ngaryanan (1976), then director of the Documentation Office of the Presidency of Chad, highlighted several of these incidents. There was the case of Baptist pastor and medical nurse Lazare Rimingaye of Koumra. Against the general rules of Baptist hospitals prohibiting their personnel from being involved with the *yondo*, this nurse treated young people who were wounded during these initiations. He was fired. Rimingaye later engaged in a public campaign against his former Church and its members. He was awarded a position inside Tombalbaye's administration.[81]

On 30 March 1973, Baptist Christians from Bessada refused to take part in the funerals of Tombalbaye's brother to avoid apostasising, because of all the traditional rituals that went along with such ceremonies. Ngarsouana, another Christian, refused, for religious reasons, to inherit a *mian-bo*. The *mian-bo* was a traditional stool venerated by his tribe. Ngarsouana had the support of his pastor Gordon Wimer, who took the *mian-bo* and exposed it in public. Such a sacrilege was unacceptable for traditional leaders. Tombalbaye, again, was informed and ordered the issue to be settled in a customary court.[82]

There were official statements from Tombalbaye and his government threatening those who opposed the *yondo*. What follows is a chronology of his declarations from 1973 to 1974 alone. In August 1973, he accused 'certain Christians' who opposed the *yondo* of being complicit with colonialism.[83] In April 1974, as he attacked his political opponents, the president called them 'enemies of the state, and complicit in international imperialism'. They ought to be taken care of at any cost.[84]

A few weeks later, on 30 April 1974, Tombalbaye gave a lecture in which the practice of *yondo* was equated to both Christianity and Islam. The initiation to the *yondo*, his argument went, was a civilisation, a way to

---

[81] Noudjalbaye, 'L'Eglise Baptiste dans la tempête au Tchad (1973–1975)', 5.

[82] Years before that incident, in 1958, pupils from Rachel Metzler's Baptist school were abducted and forcefully brought to an initiation camp. Mrs Metzler armed some of her church members and went into the bush to bring back her pupils. There is no doubt Prime Minister Tombalbaye also knew about that 'profanation'. Ibid. 5–8.

[83] De la Guerivière, 'Tchad: subversion contre l'initiation'; AFP, 'Tchad: Tombalbaye assimile la coopération avec la France à "une nouvelle forme de colonialisme"'.

[84] N'Garta Tombalbaye, 'Nous avons agi conformément à notre Révolution Culturelle', *Agence Tchadienne de Presse* 3036 (8 April 1974): Introduction.

God, in opposition to a 'certain' form of Christianity that brought all the ills to Chad. He urged the people to reject Western Christian names and depressing civilisation.[85] A clearer picture of what Tombalbaye meant by 'a certain form of Christianity' appeared from October 1974 onwards, as *Canard Déchaîné* escalated its attacks on Protestant pastors.

On 14 October 1974, Canard advertised the return of some government officials from the *yondo*. One of them, Mr Laoukoura N'Gantar, president of the National Economic and Social Council, had his picture on the front page. Again, the editorial repeated Tombalbaye's claims that the *yondo* was not contrary to 'true Islam' or to 'true Christianity', since both religions transcend any particular culture. Surprisingly, the same editors added, 'also certain Christians see it as evil, despite the fact that Christianity itself has a social, political, and economic component'.[86] The 20 November edition of the newspaper announced Tombalbaye's upcoming visit to Paris. It re-published Tombalbaye's April lecture on the *yondo*.[87]

Responding to a question about the most difficult challenges facing his Revolution, Tombalbaye replied:

> The attacks against the Cultural Revolution have multiplied by 10, maybe 100. Now we have studied the tactics of the enemy. Thanks to God, we successfully avoided its traps. Generally, our adversaries mix religion and politics. And these two spheres are irreconcilable [...] The curse for our country is that we are extremely religious. We haven't succeeded in separating religion and politics. [88]

Tombalbaye affirmed the incompatibility between politics and religion. While he was specifically targeting those Muslims who believed in Allah while still visiting their 'marabouts', his message was also directed to all religious groups operating in Chad. It would be a mistake, Tombalbaye warned, for some religious leaders to keep mixing religion and politics. Tombalbaye's struggle, as he saw it, was a fight against neocolonialism and the role of Western-based religions in fostering it.

---

[85] N'Garta Tombalbaye, 'Les principes de l'initiation au Yondo ainsi que ceux du christianisme et de l'islam s'accordent', *Agence Tchadienne de Presse* 3054 (30 April 1974): 1–5.

[86] Editors, 'Retour du Yondo', *Canard Déchaîné* 0043 (12 October 1974): front page.

[87] N'Garta Tombalbaye, 'Tombalbaye à Paris le 20 Novembre 1974', *Canard Déchaîné* 0045 (3 November 1974): 1 and 6.

[88] Tombalbaye, 'Tombalbaye à Paris le 20 Novembre 1974', 3.

The Last Conspiracy

Tombalbaye's warnings and his response to the persecution anticipated a follow-up question from another journalist. 'What did the President think', the journalist asked, 'about the most recent information the French news organisation France Inter just published this morning (November 3, 1974)?' The journalist had received that information from Canadian priests.[89] These priests also claimed that hundreds of Christians were tortured or murdered during the initiation. In response, the president denied any responsibility for these things and rejected these accusations. He was not the *mban*, the one in charge of the *yondo*. The people advancing claims about these murders should provide a list of names. Of all those who attended the initiation, Tombalbaye remembered only two, namely Mahamat Nguekidabaye and Adoum Melfi. They took a different road on their way back to N'Djamena, by the river.[90]

Some Protestants supported the government. The main target of these Protestants was the Alliance Évangélique Française (French Evangelical Alliance). Madame Thevenet gave a forceful defence of the president. Her husband, she claimed, founded the Assemblies of God in Chad. She opened two orphanages, two hospitals, and other social centres across Chad. She had been in the country from 1965, following her now deceased husband, who arrived in 1964.[91] She saw many Christians of her Church take part in the initiation and return safe. They were still actively involved in the work of the Church. She also called all her Protestant colleagues who used their religion to advance a political agenda against the 'Grand Comrade' 'liars'. Pastor Widmer and the Alliance Évangélique, Mrs Thevenet continued, were not representative of true Christianity.[92]

---

[89] I could not confirm who these Canadian priests were. It is the only reference to Canadian 'priests' in the series of *Canard Déchaîné* that discussed the *yondo* crisis. It is possible that the journalist was, in fact, referring to Canadian pastors, since some Mid-Baptist missionaries were Canadians.

[90] Tombalbaye, 'Tombalbaye à Paris le 20 Novembre 1974', 3–4.

[91] This is not exactly accurate. Australian pastor John Olley founded the Assemblies of God Mission in Chad, and settled at Moïsala and Doba in 1926.

[92] Editorial, 'Témoignage d'une vraie Chrétienne', *Canard Déchaîné* 0052 (5 February 1975): 1–2. Editorial, 'Mme Thevenet affirme: Tous nos prédicateurs sont revenus sains et saufs de l'initiation', *Canard Déchaîné* 0052 (5 February 1975): 6. Was it coincidental that the same edition of *Le Canard* published a government order settling a dispute between Mrs Thevenet and

Following Mrs Thevenet, *Le Canard* highlighted that Pastor 'Daidanso was still alive'.[93] He was not aware of explicit cases of persecution. Daidanso's name, however, never came up as a victim from religious sources, but only from government documents.[94] *Le Canard* also celebrated several high-ranking officials from the government who seemed to be 'returning from the dead'.[95]

The credibility of Daidanso's testimony, like that of Mrs Thevenet, is not self-evident. Either both individuals had something at stake in defending the government or some of their declarations were proven wrong. To those who, like Tombalbaye and Daidanso, claimed the absence of names as proof of an international conspiracy, some sources actually provided names of Christians who suffered persecution.[96] Some missionaries, including Jesuit Roland Pichon, were expelled.[97]

Canard Déchaîné confirmed the expulsion of several Swedish pastors and their families.[98] Sources outside Chad, already mentioned earlier in this chapter (see p. 158), also confirmed that Christians faced persecutions during the Cultural Revolution:[99] they suffered for their opposition to the Cultural Revolution. For Tombalbaye and his allies, however, these Christians were persecuted because they mingled in Chad's internal

---

other Protestant colleagues? That puts a cloud over the integrity of her testimony. See: *Canard Déchaîné* 0053 (18 February 1975): 5.

[93] Illiya Romba, 'Ils ne sont pas morts', *Canard Déchaîné* 0052 (5 February 1975): 1 and 4. Pasteur Burgera, 'L'affaire des missionnaires d'Andoum', *Canard Déchaîné* 0053 (18 February 1975): 5.

[94] Pastor Daidanso was appointed member of the Evangelical Church of Chad, the only official Protestant denomination recognised by Tombalbaye's government (see *Canard Déchaîné* 0022 [23 February 1974]: 3). In addition to that questionable relationship with the government, the claim that he was the only ordained Protestant pastor is not accurate. At least seven pastors were ordained in the Sudan United Mission alone in 1956. Their names were Tite Dinagmnai, Jean Miangam, Jeremie Djelardje, Philippe Demlamel, Noel Tissa, Zacharie Yangar, and Banglang Joseph (see Mbairougol, 'Implantation et impact des missions protestantes', 83).

[95] Romba, 'Ils ne sont pas morts'.

[96] Mbairougol, 'Implantation et impact des missions protestantes', 76.

[97] Roland Pichon, *Un Jésuite persona non grata* (Paris: Harmattan, 2008).

[98] Editorial, 'Suédois au pied du mur'.

[99] Adam Matthew Publications, 'SUM in Nigeria, the Cameroons, Chad, Sudan, and other African territories'. Annual Report 1973, published on 3 February 1974. This is the only reference of a Catholic leader being murdered. None of my Catholic sources in Chad confirmed that particular case.

Figure 11 Meinrad-Pierre Hebga, SJ, in spiritual direction, Yaoundé 2003 (Archives JHIA, Nairobi).

political affairs. Chad, Tombalbaye argued, had to defend its independence against these latest agents of neocolonialism. While there was no certainty about the exact number of victims, several sources – both written and oral – including the Catholic archbishop emeritus of N'Djamena Charles Vandame, agree that persecutions took place, and on a large scale.[100]

The competing agendas of the different churches in Chad gave more credibility to their accounts than to the government and its propaganda arm, *Canard*. Witnesses concurred that Christians were effectively tortured, and hundreds eventually lost their lives in several locations during the critical year of 1974.[101] Banda, which the 'Dossier' refers to, might have been only one event in a larger-scale persecution.[102]

---

[100] Charles Vandame and Benjamin Bamani, *La joie de servir* (Paris: Sarment-jubilé, 2009).

[101] I talked to several Jesuits from Chad who witnessed the Cultural Revolution, or whose parents told them about the persecutions. Other lay people in Chad confirmed these accounts. The *yondo* is still regarded as 'secret', and it is not appropriate to reveal what exactly happened there. The names of these informants remain confidential for that reason.

[102] From these sources, the Protestant opposition only grew stronger when the president started forcing all non-Catholic Christian denominations in Chad to unite under the banner of the 'Evangelical Church in Southern Chad'. This Evangelical Church in Southern Chad was the only one the government

Dalmais: Scapegoat in the Government Reaction?

In a letter to Gerald Wright on 24 January 1974 but published on 5 February 1975, an anonymous Protestant living in the United States denounced 'the lies spread by some Evangelicals' claiming the murder of up to 5,000 Canadian missionaries. He also called out the myth of the murder of 130 pastors, falsely claiming that at this point there was only one Protestant pastor ordained in Chad: Pastor Daidanso. If the accusations against the government were true, the letter continued, why have the Catholic bishops of Chad, the metropolitan archbishop [of N'Djamena] said nothing about it, or at least mobilised the Roman Curia or the Vatican and the international community for such a ferocious and barbarous persecution against fellow Christians? *Tchad et Culture* is a Catholic journal edited in N'Djamena. Why hasn't it, he wondered, made the slightest reference to all these alleged massacres of Christians, some of them supposedly buried alive because of their loyalty to Christ? Is not the Catholic Church, he concluded, the most powerful and hierarchical Church in the world? Is it afraid to speak in defence of innocent human lives outrageously tortured and massacred?[103]

A response was now expected from Dalmais, who had been called out not once but twice – and through him, the Catholic Church. The anonymous writer of the letter is right about the silence of Catholic sources. There is no reference to the persecution of Christians in the Catholic journal *Tchad et Culture*. The journal, however, celebrated the 'new era' of General Félix Malloum, who overthrew Tombalbaye and his government.[104] Other Jesuit sources in Chad, including *Lettres du Chad* and *Nouvelles de la Vice-PAO*, remained silent about the politics of Chad. Introducing Hallaire's *Naissance d'une église*, Jacques Fedry suggested that the government censured missionaries for the letters they sent, and the missionaries did not want to risk talking about politics in their correspondence.[105]

Dalmais' writings and other Jesuit documents on Chad show that while his conscience might have dictated a public condemnation of

---

recognised as 'official' for all Protestants. See: Buck, 'Consultation in the Chad'. Page not provided.

[103] Anonymous, 'Lettre d'un Chrétien du Tchad à M. Gerald Wright. RR5, Cambridge (GALTT) NR5S6. Ontario-Canada. N'Djamena, Jan. 24, 1974', *Canard Déchaîné* 0052 (5 February 1975): 5.

[104] General Malloum, 'Le 13 Avril 1975, Pour un Tchad nouveau', *Tchad et Culture* 86 (May 1975): 2–3.

[105] Hallaire and Fedry, *Naissance d'une église africaine*, 27–28.

Tombalbaye's actions, he opted, instead, to direct his anger at the president privately. Other bishops, with the support of Chadian Catholic lay evangelists, had tied his hands by insisting that 'prudence and silence' be the official position of the Church. Dalmais' reaction to the negative effects of the Cultural Revolution, however, raises a basic question which historians struggle to answer: how should Catholic leaders, especially those living in Christian minority countries, react to a political regime that promotes an ideology that is contrary to Christian beliefs? Was it appropriate for Dalmais to remain silent, at least publicly, in order to save his own Church, while other Christians were being slaughtered? History, however, shows that Dalmais wrestled with these questions until late in his life. This was the reason he wanted his record on the Chadian Civil War to be corrected.[106]

Rejecting total neutralism, Dalmais tried diplomacy in the face of a violent regime. He kept an open channel with the regime with the hope of making a difference from within, but Tombalbaye burned that bridge during his Parisian interview. Dalmais was not an introvert. Even according to Tombalbaye, Dalmais' silence in this particular context was simply unnatural.[107] From Dalmais' own diaries, he preferred to publicly condemn the slippages of the Cultural Revolution. He refrained from going public, however, because of his position as the head of the Catholic Church in Chad. As such, he decided to comply with the will of the majority among his peers. Against what his own conscience dictated, Dalmais chose to protect the Catholic Church in Chad against persecutions from an unscrupulous president.[108]

---

[106] In 1979, during the Civil War in Chad, Bishop Belzile of Moundou accused Dalmais of imprudence. Dalmais, he said, talked too much, and tended to defend the official positions of the French government. Such an attitude, Belzile believed, was putting the work of the Church at risk. During the same war, Christians accused him of being excessively pro-Muslim, and so against the interests of fellow Christians. This time Dalmais was guilty of collaborating with the Imam of Ndjamena to attempt a peaceful mediation in the conflict that was turning Muslim and Christian communities against each other.

[107] As mentioned previously, if the crimes he was accused of were true, Tombalbaye said, 'Dalmais would have opened his mouth' (Pierre Faure, 'Mgr Dalmais dans la Guerre du Tchad: Document pour l'histoire', 30).

[108] And Church here means 'people of God', bishops, but also the catechists and their families who militated for 'silence and prudence'.

Dalmais finally discussed the matter with the Propaganda Fide in Rome, and Pope Paul VI.[109] In fact, Tombalbaye's persecution was exactly what all the twentieth-century popes had feared amid their concerns about what would happen to the Church should it remain predominantly Western in its personnel if the empire came to collapse and was replaced by a hostile and nationalist government. Building an African clergy and promoting an African leadership in the Catholic Church was the answer given by the Vatican. Therefore, one would expect the Vatican to have pressed Dalmais for answers on that particular front.

During his encounter with the pope, Dalmais was asked about the state of the Africanisation of his clergy. In response, he proposed that married men be ordained. Some Africans and Europeans prelates had, in vain, made similar propositions during the Roman Synod of October 1971.[110] Dalmais also mentioned the case of Japan, where persecutions and the murder of priests had almost completely destroyed the Church. Christians in Chad, he implied, were confronted by a similar threat. The pope replied that while such ordinations were canonically possible, they did not seem opportune to him in view of the present context that valued the celibate life of the priests.[111]

Simply interpreted, Dalmais was giving the pope a solution he knew would be unacceptable to Rome. Reflecting on the celibacy and the ministerial priesthood, Dalmais had already expressed Rome's fear that loosening the rules about the celibacy of priests might erode its theological interpretation.[112] Interestingly, his solution to the pope's question was not addressing the Africanisation of the religious order he belonged to, and which was in charge of the Chad Mission. While the Eastern Catholic Church canonically accepted the possibility of married priests, religious orders like the Jesuits did not. His solution to the pope was, therefore, antithetical to the Africanisation of the Jesuit membership in Chad. For his solution to be taken seriously, the Jesuits would have to change their fundamental rule, which, at this point, was not up for debate.

---

[109] M-Ly. Box 2181. 39/1–8: 'Paul Dalmais, 1917–1994'.
[110] 'Africans Ask Pontiff for Married Priests', *New York Times (1923–Current File)*, 4 July 1970, 13 <https://search-proquest-com.proxy.bc.edu/hnpnewyorktimes/docview/118846174/fulltextPDF/DB94E4ACBB344BBDPQ/1?accountid=9673> [accessed 5 April 2018].
[111] M-Ly. Box 2181: 'Paul Dalmais, 1917–1994', 39/1–8.
[112] M-Ly. Box 2181, 41/1–3: Paul Dalmais, 'Réflexion au Tchad sur le sacerdoce ministériel et le célibat'. Cf. *The Code of Canon Law: A Text and Commentary*. Canon Law, § 277.1.

It is not that Dalmais did not care about a more decentralised Roman Catholic Church. In fact, during the Second Vatican Council, where he first met Cardinal Giovanni Battista Montini, the future Pope Paul VI, Dalmais and other bishops from Chad defended a decentralised Church that would empower local bishops. Joining Dalmais' comfort zone, they also strongly advocated for the de-Latinisation of the liturgy. They complained, for example, that the Roman Rite was 'too foreign' for African Christians.[113] However, Dalmais simply believed that the Church and the Society of Jesus in Chad were not ready for an indigenous government.

Dalmais' position departed from Pope Paul VI's own declarations in Kampala (1969).[114] He was also contradicting the superior general of his religious order. During several trips in Africa from 1970 to 1972, Pedro Arrupe had reiterated the urgent need for Africans, including in the Church, to be in charge of their own destiny.[115] Dalmais, on the contrary, did very little to change that situation, both as the head of the Jesuits in Chad and now as the leader of the Catholic Church in Chad. In a letter to his friend and Jesuit colleague Pierre Faure on 16 April 1976, he wrote:

> I raised with Mgr [Simon] Lourdusamy [1924–2014] the problem of the succession of the bishops when Véniat and I will resign. They seem persuaded in Rome that it is now unthinkable to replace a white bishop with another white bishop. In our conversation, I tried to put this in perspective by asserting with force and conviction that it was not possible [...] 8 or 10 more years may be necessary for an African bishop.[116]

---

[113] M-Ly. Box 2181: Paul Dalmais, 'Le point sur le concile', conference to French Seminarians in Rome (12 October 1963).

[114] Pope Paul VI, 'Excellentissimis Viris e Legatorum Coetu in Ugandensi Republica', *AAS* 11 (1 August 1969): 580–86; Pope Paul VI, 'Homilia in sollemni canonizatione Beatorum: Caroli Lwanga, Matthiae Mulumba Kalemba et viginti sociorum Martyrum Ugandensium', *AAS* 56 (18 October 1964): 907–08.

[115] Pedro Arrupe, 'Allocutio R.P. Petri Arrupe, Praesidis Unionis Superiorum Generalium, Ad Conferentias Episcopales Africae et Madecassensem in Urbe Abidjan', *AR* 15 (22 August 1970): 680–84; Arrupe, 'Apostolatus S. I. in Africa', *AR* 15 (March 1972): 859–78.

[116] M-Ly. Box 2181: Pierre Faure, 'Mgr Dalmais dans la Guerre du Tchad: Document pour l'histoire' (2003), 33. Simon Lourdusamy was an official of the Congregation for the Evangelization of Peoples in 1971, and then from 1973 to 1985. This Roman Congregation is in charge of appointing Catholic bishops.

Literally understood, this quotation is evidence that Dalmais deliberately delayed a priority of the Roman Church. Moreover, speaking to French Seminarians in Rome, Dalmais had also downgraded the contribution of African bishops during the Second Vatican Council. He said, quite accurately, but not without sarcasm: 'Africans did not lead the council; they were well represented!'[117] By that, he meant the current African bishops were second-grade bishops at the Vatican Council.

Conclusion: Oil Politics and the Gospel in Chad

On 12 August 1972, Fort-Archambault was renamed and became 'Sarh'. Writing in the weekly Pan-African magazine *Jeune Afrique*, Jos-Blaise Alima explained the Sara's meaning of 'Sarh', the new name given to 'Fort-Archambault'. It alluded, he said, to a 'concentration camp'. The choice of words was poor. After the war, and especially at a time when Tombalbaye was shifting his foreign policy towards the Arab world, to mention concentration camps was a risky choice. For Tombalbaye, the city was renamed in memory of 'labour camps and the sacrifices imposed on' Chadians who supplied cheap labour in French Equatorial Africa.[118]

In the same volume of the weekly Pan-African magazine, C. Wauthier published an article that linked the rise of 'African Messianic churches' to nationalist movements in their rejection of African traditional cultures.[119] While Tombalbaye had become a leader of one of these churches, other churches in Chad still had strong Western personnel and support.

Tombalbaye's Cultural Revolution can therefore be interpreted in terms of postcolonial nationalism, both politically and religiously. The revolution was officially launched in 1973, at a time when independent Chad felt under siege from France. In addition to having a military base in Chad that seemed complacent amid the advance of the northern rebellion, there was also a resurgence of French cultural influence in the lives of Chadian citizens.

Writing in *Der Spiegel*, Hans Hielscher describes life in an Auberge, a gourmet restaurant in N'Djamena: 'elegantly decorated', Hielscher wrote, 'its chef, of international class, serves you – for a good price obviously – the

---

[117] 'Ce n'est pas l'Afrique qui a mené le Concile. Mais l'Afrique a fait bonne figure!' Cf., M-Ly. Box 2181: Paul Dalmais, 'Le point sur le concile'.

[118] Cf. Archives du Centre d'Étude pour l'Action Sociale (A-CEPAS). Jos-Blaise Alima, 'Tchad: Le deuxième front', *Jeune Afrique* (henceforth *JA*) 605 (12 August 1972): 22–23. Not catalogued.

[119] A-CEPAS. C. Wauthier, 'Les sectes messianiques et les églises séparatistes en Afrique', *JA* 605 (12 August 1972): 52–53.

grape quail, the Strogonoff [sic] filet [...] as in Paris'. 'Twelve years after independence,' he concluded, 'many Europeans behave there as they did in conquered countries. They lack only the chicotte.'[120] Colonialism was back.

In need of help from wherever he could find it, Tombalbaye reinforced diplomatic and cultural ties with Zaïre and its president, Mobutu Sese Seko. He dressed like Mobutu and believed in Mobutu's Zaïrianisation, which he emulated a year later with the Cultural Revolution. He also turned to his Libyan and Sudanese neighbours and the rest of the Muslim world. King Faysal of Saudi Arabia visited the country and promised to build the largest mosque in Sub-Saharan Africa in N'Djamena.

These new diplomatic initiatives were taking place after 1973. In that year, the oil crisis made France and the rest of the world realise their vulnerability and dependence on oil producers. Chad suddenly became a potential oil producer. By 1974, *Canard Déchaîné*'s headlines were triumphant. On 8 January 1974, the front page headline declared: 'Voeu unanime: Pétrole au Tchad en 1974' (Unanimous Wish: Oil in Chad in 1974).[121] Ten months later, on 24 October 1974, Chad's oil miracle was confirmed: 'Ça y est! Du pétrole au Tchad' (Here it is! Oil in Chad).[122]

These headlines were published as Tombalbaye was preparing to visit France. Arab oil producers started leveraging their newly discovered power. They also coalesced around the OPEP and foreign policies supportive of the Palestinians and those that were clearly anti-Israel. Socialism and Islam were celebrated by *Jeune Afrique* as being compatible. France was also taken by surprise as Americans asserted their geostrategic interests following the discovery of Chad's oil. They had funded exploration at the time when France had rejected Chad's requests to do so. The United States could now decide where to have this oil exported; and it could not go through North Africa.

Pressing Chad's government by turning a blind eye on its rebellion and putting pressure on its president was a diplomatic tool to get the most from Chad's black gold. That French Jesuits felt that the Cultural Revolution was anti-French in nature can be interpreted from the lenses of this international context. Tombalbaye felt trapped as the French media questioned

[120] A-CEPAS. Hans Hielscher, 'Les Blancs en Afrique noire: Du colonialisme au néocolonialisme', republished in *JA* 590 (29 April 1972): 18–22 – here, p. 22.
[121] Editorial, 'Vœu unanime: Pétrole au Tchad en 1974', *Canard Déchaîné* 0017 (8 January 1974): front page.
[122] Editorial, 'Ça y est! Du pétrole au Tchad', *Canard Déchaîné* 0044 (24 October 1974): front page.

him on the massacre of Christians. He clearly used Dalmais, his old French friend, the head of the Catholic Church, as a scapegoat.

Chadian Catholics, who had negotiated a compromise on the *yondo* in 1966, had little moral or religious conflict with the Cultural Revolution. They, however, feared for their families, should their Church leaders take a stance against the president's domestic policy agenda. Dalmais felt compelled to remain silent on the abuses of the Cultural Revolution. He succeeded, however, in vernacularising the Church in Chad mainly by securing a compromise with traditional leaders around the *yondo* rite. This compromise was followed by increased adaptation and de-Latinisation of the liturgy. Moreover, the Jesuits compared their syncretism around the *yondo* to the Chinese Rites Controversy. In doing so, they situated their new global commitment within the framework of their missionary tradition.

However, within the context of Chad's Cultural Revolution, a distinctive characteristic was revealed within the Jesuits' rites controversy in Chad. By promoting a bottom-up approach to evangelisation, the resulting syncretism made Chadian Catholics more flexible in the face of persecution. The syncretism of Chad Christianity was unique. As the aforementioned article of *L'Aurore* said, Catholics in Chad were 'simultaneously Catholics, animists, and Moslems'.[123] Moreover, because they lacked an intellectual and religious elite, Catholics suffered less persecution than their Protestant colleagues, who constituted that elite class and were theologically less tolerant of religious syncretism.

---

[123] A-CEFOD. B 254B: *L'Aurore* (30 December 1974).

PART III

The Postcolonial Mission and Catholicity: From Chad to Cameroon, 1962–78

Introduction

In the previous chapters, we see how Muslims from the north, as well as increased government intervention and Protestant competition in the south had pushed the Jesuits to change their evangelising methods and to consider new ways to Africanise. This double pressure led the Jesuits to introduce among them 'new reductions' where Christian families were trained and sent back to their communities. Christians trained in the Jesuit reductions became evangelisers and social-developers in their respective communities. As a result, the Catholic population grew. New chapels were built by Jesuit Brothers who used agriculture and painting to evangelise. Other evangelising methods included the development of rhetoric, singing catechism and the gospel. They also introduced new teaching techniques more accessible to the students.

Chad's cautious Africanisation approach of the mission was justified and confirmed with Pope Pius XII encyclical *Fidei Donum* in 1957. On the eve of African independence, the Vatican asked for hundreds of additional European missionaries for Africa as a last chance to save civilisation.[1] The Vatican's appeal for more missionaries was combined with increased clerical Africanisation in neighbouring countries like Cameroon. And in 1962, the two trends had their first encounter in Chad. That year, Jean Zoa, a young Cameroonian archbishop ordained Henri Véniat, a French missionary, as Bishop of Sarh in Chad. With this ordination, the rebirth of missionary Christianity became the new reality in Chad. The challenges of this rebirth of missionary Christianity for the rising African Catholic elite came to life during this ordination.

These three chapters show the way in which Jesuitism operated in Chad and Cameroon after independence, and the increasing integration of the people into the mission and strategy of Catholicism. Tracing the shift in dynamics with independence in the first chapter in this part of the book, the following chapter, Chapter 8, examines the kind of Africanisation

---

[1] Pope Pius XII, 'L'encyclique "Fidei Donum" (21 Avril 1957) sur la situation des missions notamment en Afrique', *Revue du Clergé Africain* (1957): 321–37.

the first Cameroonian Jesuits wanted, combining African leadership and nation-building with grassroot evangelism. The radical thinking of the first African Jesuits was perceived as a threat in the Vatican, among their European superiors, as well as European missionaries in Africa. These Africans were sidelined as Europeans regained control of the governance of the new Jesuit jurisdiction in 1973. Chapter 9 tells the story of the outward dissent of the first Cameroonian Jesuits including rejection of European leadership, the mapping of Jesuit jurisdictions in Africa, and the very notion of universality that is at the core of Roman Catholicism and the Jesuit organisation. By giving voice to a Jesuit working-class Brother, the chapter addresses the Cameroonians' dissent as part of major problems affecting the Society of Jesus and the Church globally after Vatican II and African independence.

CHAPTER 7

Era of Consolidation: The Rebirth of Missionary Catholicism after Independence, 1962–73

From the beginning of the mission, the Jesuits in Chad had resisted the Vatican's clerical Africanisation. They opted instead to request more French missionaries. This strategy seemed so effective that, on the eve of independence, the Vatican confirmed a new missionary era for the African Church with *Fidei Donum* in 1957. In Chad, at least, missionary Christianity had successfully overcome the nationalist challenge that had driven the Vatican's Africanisation agenda. In 1972, Charles Vandame, head of the mission, and other European Jesuits sought to enhance the statutory jurisdiction of Chad. They were in control; they had made Chad their stronghold.

A similar trend was observed in other areas. In Chad, 'White men were back in the driving seat. They controlled the planification of African economies; decided the careers of African politicians; fixed the prices for raw materials; and had more white populations than before independence.'[1] Postcolonial Chad was born, with Europeans still controlling all areas of Chad's society: the economy, the military, and even the Church.

Two years after its independence, in 1962, a French missionary, Henri Véniat, was ordained bishop of Sarh, the second-largest city in Chad. The ordination itself was a triumphant celebration of the Jesuits' strategy of delaying clerical Africanisation in Chad. Véniat was not the last in a long list of Frenchmen ordained bishops in the Sahelian country. He was the symbol of a rebirth of missionary Christianity. The entire delegation of Chad in the Vatican Council was made of Europeans, as were the large

---

[1] First published in *Der Spiegel* and re-edited by *JA*: Hans Hielscher, 'Les Blancs en Afrique noire: Du colonialisme au néo-colonialisme', *JA* 590 (29 April 1972): 18–22.

majority of African bishops who attended. While these bishops pushed for a progressive agenda in the Council based on inculturation and real openness about clerical celibacy, they nevertheless retained power in Chad.

Véniat's ordination was also the first official encounter between Chad's Westernised Catholicism and Cameroon's increasingly Africanised Catholicism. Africans witnessing the episcopal ordination understood that Véniat might have been the only choice available in a Church still lacking in indigenous clerics. François Ngaïbi was Chad's single Chadian priest. Véniat's ordination, however, symbolically represented the beginning of a new era of rebirth of missionary Christianity in Chad.

Alongside the strengthening missionary Christianity, there was economic and political neocolonialism. This neocolonial cliché disturbed the Jesuits. To avoid the perception of an all-White Jesuits' ghetto in Chad, a closer relationship with the Cameroonian Jesuits was recommended. As we will see in Chapter 9, this dominated the reorganisation of the Society in French Africa and led to the creation of the VPAO.

Véniat's Ordination and Competing Priorities

Born in Paris in 1917, Henri Véniat was already corresponding with French Jesuit missionaries in the Middle East at the age of thirteen. He finally joined the Society in 1937. Having spent a short period in the Middle East, he returned to France in 1938. At the time, de Bélinay was exploring Chad. From 1940 to 1944, Véniat joined the French cavalry fighting in the Second World War. He was ordained as a priest in 1949, and was sent to Chad a year later. Following the Episcopal ordination of Dalmais in 1958, Véniat succeeded him as the superior of the Chad Mission. Four years later, at the age of forty-five, he was ordained bishop of Fort-Archambault. This was twenty-five years after he joined the Jesuits.

The political elite of Chad, including President Tombalbaye, the French ambassador, and the commandant of the French forces in Chad, were among the faithful present during Véniat's ordination. The mostly African Catholic leadership from neighbouring countries was well represented. Presiding over the ordination was a young Cameroonian, Archbishop Jean Zoa (1924–98) of Yaoundé.[2] Alongside Zoa were Jesuit Bishop Dalmais of Fort-Lamy, Capuchin Bishop Samuel Gaumain of Moundou, and François Nzagpé of Cameroon, the first Jesuit to be ordained from West Africa.

[2] 'Henri Véniat, 1917–1998', *Jésuites de France* (1998): 132–35. I received the sacrament of confirmation from Zoa's hand, and served as an altar boy in many of his masses.

Many African seminarians from the region also attended.[3] In Nigeria, and especially in Cameroon, where young Africans had become leaders of their own Church, attending Véniat's ordination left them with the impression of a White ghetto amid a rising African-dominated Christianity. For these Africans, the ordination of Véniat simply reflected a bygone era.

The paradox of the situation became even more evident as Zoa began his homily. He had still been a pagan, Zoa said, only thirty years earlier. The missionary who baptised him was still alive. And there he was, surprisingly, ordaining as bishop one of those same missionaries. The ordination, he concluded, was an opportunity to celebrate the universality of the Roman Catholic Church and to affirm equal respect for all races and cultures.[4] Zoa's careful use of words made one thing clear: if he was still pagan by the time the Catholic Church arrived in Chad (1929), and was now an archbishop of Cameroon's largest diocese, then the Church in Chad could have done better than having him ordaining another missionary bishop. What have the founders of the Church in Chad, including the Jesuits, been doing for forty years?

It did not take long for these Africans to get an answer. The missionary era might have been too old for Cameroonians and Nigerians. It was not in Chad. The missionaries were in 'their' territory, triumphant, somewhat arrogant. As he took the podium to express his gratitude to the participants, a confident and triumphant Véniat directed his first words to the African seminarians, the 'future of the church', to the pupils and lay catechists. Days were coming, he said, when they could envision leading their Church. They simply had to remain 'faithful, generous, and charitable', and not 'mediocre, selfish, and fearful'.[5]

The underlying message of Véniat could not have been clearer. The population of Chad attending the ordination should not have been fooled by what was happening in front of them. They might have been witnessing a Frenchman ordained by an African archbishop. Yet the Church of Chad, this Chadian bishop concluded, was not ready for African leadership, and would remain dependent on the West, both financially and for its leadership, for decades.[6] Both Frédéric de Bélinay and Joseph du Bouchet had already set up a fundraising mechanism in 1946, when the

[3] Editors, 'Sacre de Mgr Véniat', *JAF* 2 (1962): 40.
[4] Ibid., 41.
[5] Ibid.
[6] An article by Paul Dalmais in the Jesuit journal, 'L'avenir religieux du Tchad' *Etudes* (January 1956): 39–51, explained to Catholics in France why they should support that mission.

latter requested the mission be separated from the Middle East. Family donations in support of the Mission effort in Paris or as a gift to individual Jesuits represented another source of income from Europe.[7]

One of the pupils who attended the ordination, however, did not miss its historical symbolism for the Church of Chad. He wrote:

> There were Sara people of all kinds: the Saras of Koumra, Kumogo, Bediondo, Djoli, Kira, Danamadji, etc. There were the Mbays, Moïsala, etc. There were people from Fort-Lamy, Kabalay, Bousso, etc. Above all, there was a Black archbishop, Archbishop Zoa, who had consecrated Bishop Véniat, and a Black Jesuit father [Fr François Nzagpe of Douala]. Both of them came from Yaoundé [...] A strong wind came to chase us but I was very happy because it was the first time I witnessed an episcopal ordination.[8]

This exchange between Bishop Zoa, Bishop Véniat, and a young Chadian boy reveals competing priorities as far as Africanisation was concerned. Having to ordain a missionary bishop was evidently an uncomfortable situation for Zoa and his African peers. It also seems that the young boy enjoyed having Africans so well represented in presiding roles during the liturgy. However, as this chapter argues, the respective episcopal ordinations of Dalmais (1958) and Véniat (1962) sent a signal that even after independence, the French leadership in Chad was there to stay. The transformation of the African Church and society in Chad was being shaped in Western terms. Missionary Christianity had risen stronger from the fears of the late fifties. Then Dalmais, echoing the Vatican's concerns, expressed worries about the future of a Chadian Church without a local clergy. Events in Chad seemed to be taking a different direction. Africans noticed and reacted to it.

Missionaries' Control over Chad's Church

Raising an African clergy for an African Christianity had been the aim of the Vatican all along. Until late in the 1950s, this message seemed unheard in Chad. Yet, a year before independence, in 1959, reality seemed to catch up with the head of the mission. Dalmais felt that a shift was needed from a missionary Church to a Chadian one. His missionary report of that year acknowledged that:

---

[7] Father Luis Lomazzi, 'Aide pour la mission', *JAF* 4 (1962): 38.
[8] 'Sacre de Mgr Véniat', 43.

The political evolution is not without influence on the current state of Christianity. On this point, our late arrival presents a particularly serious handicap: as the country is moving rapidly towards its independence, it does not yet have an indigenous clergy, but one, Rev. François Ngaïbi. He comes, as is natural, from an older mission, that of the Logone. He works there with the Capuchin Fathers.[9]

In the same 1959 report, Dalmais, sounding like an Africanist or a Vaticanist, wrote that 'a new world was on the rise'. The political situation in Chad, he argued, was rapidly shifting, and this change represented an immediate danger for the mission, because there still was not a Chadian clergy.[10] The seminaries were full of students, yet the most advanced among them were still only in the fourth year of high school. Further, secularism was making inroads among the Christian Évolué class, primarily among Cameroonians and Ubangians, but also among Chadian Christians. Most of the secularising Christian class believed Christianity was outdated.

There was renewed interest, Dalmais observed, in authentic African values, with a certain hostility towards White men and anything that pertained to them. In a recent conference, he narrated, a European was talking about two types of civilisations: the ancient and the modern. A Chadian interjected, arguing that there was a third civilisation: the *yondo* of Chad's non-Muslim populations. We have to develop, Dalmais concluded, the kind of African Christianity that would be cleansed from whatever appeared to be foreign to Chad. European civilisation has become synonymous with the civilisation of domination. In their liturgy, songs, religious pedagogy, the missionaries should avoid anything that looks European in nature.[11]

Transforming Chadian society was clearly putting pressure on the Church in Chad. Dalmais was expressing the common anxieties of European missionaries across Africa on the eve of independence. This sense of concern was reinforced in Chad, where missionaries shared the feeling that their efforts to stop the advance of Islam had failed. By 1959, Islam was on the rise, pushed by 'unlettered' African Fakis.[12] If only,

---

[9] In 'Mission du Tchad', *JAF* 3 (1959): 35.
[10] Paul Dalmais first published the article in *Afrique Vivante*, the missionary newsletter of the White Fathers. It was re-edited by *Jésuites*, the newsletter of French Jesuits: Mgr Dalmais, 'Un monde qui naît: La mission du Tchad', *Jésuites* 3 (1959): 31–37 – here, p. 35.
[11] Ibid., 36–37.
[12] Editors, 'Au Tchad', *Jésuites* 2 (1960): 37.

the missionaries wondered, they had inculturated more Chadian songs and liturgies, and raised a Chadian clergy![13]

Within the Church, though, the ghost of 1959 was quickly exorcised. The truth, in the case of Chad, is that missionary Christianity had never been stronger. The fact that Africans were needed in leadership to overcome the rising nationalism was not the only thing the Vatican seemed to have got wrong about Africa. The very fear that missionary Christianity might be vanquished with African independence was also dismissed in Chad. In 1962, as Véniat was ordained, Nigerians and Cameroonians seemed shocked by this White ghetto amid an increasingly African-dominated Christianity.

For Europeans, though, the ordination of Véniat represented a unique hope for the African Church in Chad.[14] However, the reassertion of French authority over the Church of Chad did not mean that the Jesuits were not trying to train a Chadian clergy. In fact, after he replaced du Bouchet as head of the mission, Dalmais launched a programme to train Chadian missionary personnel. This training simply did not yield its fruits soon enough. It faced serious financial challenges.

In 1955, the Jesuits had opened a minor seminary in Bousso. Their first high school, Charles-Lwanga (created in 1960), served to train both lay students and seminarians.[15] Henri Venet, the first director of the seminary, often expressed his admiration for the symbiosis between seminarians and lay students.[16] However, in October 1969, his successor Francis Lecoq suppressed the financial aid the seminarians were receiving. The reason for the new policy remained unclear, especially for a school the Jesuits considered the 'hope of the future African clergy of Chad'.[17] Seven years later, there were no more seminarians left in the school. The hope seemed to vanish. The Capuchins and the Jesuits, 'experiencing difficulties to meet the ever-increasing needs', were forced to appeal to Italian, Spanish, and Canadian Brothers.[18] These Brothers were responsible for expanding the grassroots work of the mission.

---

[13] Ibid., 39–40.
[14] As already said, Véniat was one of many Frenchmen ordained bishops in the Sahelian country. Since 1979, however, only two French Jesuit missionaries have been ordained bishops in Chad: Charles Vandame (1982) and Henri Coudray (2009).
[15] Joseph Fortier, 'Chad', in *Diccionario Histórico de la Compañía de Jesús*, vol. 1 (Madrid/Roma: IHSI/UPComillas, 2001) 'Chad', 746.
[16] Henri Venet, 'Problèmes du séminaire', *JAF* 3 (1964): 44–45.
[17] Editors, 'Au Tchad', *Jésuites* 2 (1960): 36–40.
[18] See: Charles Vandame, *Cinquante ans de la vie de l'Eglise Catholique au*

Jesuit 'Reductions' amid Protestant Competition

Beyond shortcomings in training Chadian leadership for the Church, Jesuit missionaries remained focused on grassroots evangelism. Véniat, particularly, believed in this vernacularisation effort as key to transforming the Church and society. Under Véniat's leadership, hundreds of children were catechised.[19] The missionaries also continued learning local languages, and studying indigenous cultures. They also trained indigenous catechists. They encouraged the Chadian Christians to compose songs in their own languages, inspired by the gospel. And they adapted worship to their local practices.[20] In 1962, there were no copies left of the first edition of the translation of the gospel in the Sara language.[21]

The encounters with Protestants, especially the Baptist Africa-Mid Mission and the Sudan United Mission, represented a constant pressure on the Jesuits to change their evangelising methods, change local behaviours, and consider new ways to Africanise. This impact was especially felt by African families. The very year of Véniat's ordination, Jesuit Guy Abeille wrote:

> We are beginning to have young Catholic households and, at the instigation of the J.A.C [Catholic Agricultural Youth], we would like them to imitate the creativity ['esprit d'initiative'] of the Protestants in the fields of culture, housing, as well as education. That is why we are so impatient to see the Sisters arrive who will do with us what the wives of pastors do.[22]

From Abeille's report, Catholics admired and emulated the example of Protestant families: how they conducted themselves and how they raised and educated their children. The Jesuits quickly shifted their work to translating the Bible as Protestants did, to make the word of God available to Chadian Catholics.[23] Their contact with the Protestants increased their awareness of the need for non-clerical collaboration. They were amazed that there were already Chadian-born Protestant pastors.[24] Additionally,

---

    Tchad (Paris: L'Harmattan, 2012), 19.

19 André Meynier, 'Formation des catéchistes à Kyabe', *JAF* 2 (1962): 43–44.

20 The celebration of Good Friday in 1972 imitated traditional funeral rituals in Chad. See: André Meynier, 'Une expérience d'adaptation au Tchad', *JAF* 54 (February 1972): 37.

21 Jacques Hallaire, 'L'évangile sara: difficulté d'une traduction', *JAF* 1 (1962): 46.

22 Guy Abeille, 'Les Protestants et nous', *JAF* 2 (1962): 45–46.

23 Jacques Hallaire, 'L'évangile sara', 46.

24 Jean Géli, 'La consécration de Mgr. Dalmais, premier évêque du Tchad', *Jésuites* 3 (1958): 35–38 – here, p. 36.

the Jesuits came to appreciate the efficient work of the Catholic Agricultural Youth (JAC) Movement, and the pressing need for religious women in the mission field. Even more curiously, they drew a parallel between the missionary strategies of the Protestants in Chad and their glorious past in the reductions among the Guaraní of Paraguay.[25]

To advance the training of missionary personnel, catechetical schools were created in Komougo, Bedaya, and Bediondo. The Jesuits called those efforts their 'new reductions'.[26] Those 'reductions' occurred at a time when the government of Chad was also concerned about land disputes. On 1 December 1962, the government created new, larger, villages in rural areas, ranging in size from forty or sixty inhabitants per village to about 300 people. Jesuit missionaries received this government policy very well. It helped them compensate the shortage in mission personnel. Instead of the ten to fifteen missionaries previously needed, they now needed only three or four, freeing more personnel for other regions.[27]

The Jesuit 'reductions' in Chad were an addition to other educational projects and were an integral part of their work of evangelisation.[28] They introduced the use of draft animals for agriculture. This was an effort to boost the economic situation of Chadian young Christians in rural areas. By doing so, they raised up their social status.[29] The increase in Church membership also affected church architecture.[30] Photographic evidence shows that while they followed African patterns in the early years of the mission, churches quickly became Westernised, though not systematically.[31] Adaptations in the architecture and the decoration of the interior of church buildings often depended on an individual Jesuit's willingness

---

[25] Ibid.
[26] Jacques Hallaire, 'Evangile et coutumes', *JAF* 1 (1963): 44.
[27] Cf. André Meynier, 'Kyabé, travaux quotidiens', *JAF* 1 (1963): 41–42.
[28] According to Jean Géli, 'Whereas in 1952 there was only one primary school, today (1958) there are more than 20, and a normal school operates with 60 interns. In the bush there are dispensaries, workshops, boarding schools for fiancées': Géli, 'La consécration de Mgr. Dalmais, premier évêque du Tchad', *Jésuites* 3 (1958): 35–38 – here, pp. 36–37.
[29] Jacques Hallaire, '[Introduction de la] culture attelée au Tchad', *JAF* 3 (1962): 47–48.
[30] André Martin, 'Kabalay, croissance chrétienne', *JAF* 1 (1963): 40.
[31] Even as the buildings were becoming externally more Westernised, in Bekamba, for example, we see the Jesuits trying to decorate the inside of the churches with African saints, especially the martyrs of Uganda. Cf. P. Lecoq, 'Eglise en dur', *JAF* 4 (1965): 45–46.

to create a distinctive Chadian Church. Here again, Jesuit Brothers, who worked shoulder to shoulder with ordinary people, became pioneers of architectural vernacularisation.

Brother Augustin Vala decorated the chapel in Bedaya. One of the paintings he made portrayed Catholic bishops gathered in the Second Vatican Council. The pope, John XXIII, was wearing the tiara and had his hand raised in blessing. Two cardinals surrounded him. In front of them was the altar for the mass with the book of the gospel. On each side of the main celebrants there were thirty-six bishops, five of which were Black. In another painting, an African priest was recognisable by his facial scars. About thirty assistants, boys and girls, were kneeling and turned towards him. They presented to the spectators only their necks, the bottoms of their trousers or skirts, and the soles of their shoes.[32]

Brother Vala's painting was a recognition of the global nature of Roman Catholicism and a celebration of Chad as an integral part of it. It also breathed the air of reform that the Vatican Council inspired. The reality of concelebration, the disposition of the altar, the centrality of Scripture, and the diversity of races and genders were all indications of a new era in the Church. It pointed to a transformed society in Chad, one still controlled by Europeans but unashamedly African. Like Vala, Jacob Gabin's painting celebrated the Africanity of the Church in its new African martyrs. He 'was very kind to decorate the wall at the back with a fresco depicting Christ on the cross, surrounded by the twenty-two martyrs of Uganda, since this church is dedicated to them'.[33]

In Chagwa, Brother Pequenot led another initiative. He was 'a master carpenter, architect, bricklayer, and mechanic'.[34] He had never received a formal education in these areas, but learned through practice alone. Chad offered him a unique platform to master his trades. The expectation was that through the Jesuit Brothers, Chadians would receive training in practical professions. The social impact of this learning process, however, was never separated from its religious expectations:

> At your contact, the 1955 report of the mission wrote, Chadian [Jesuit] Brothers will rise one day [...] Of these new Christian churches, which the Brothers have raised up and made grow by their labours and prayers, others will rise who will follow the Lord as they did.[35]

---

[32] Roland Pichon, 'Bediondo, le salut sur les murs', *JAF* 1 (1964): 41.
[33] P. Lecoq, 'Bekamba: Eglise en dur', 45–46.
[34] Ibid., 28–29.
[35] Ibid., 30.

The missionaries added to the Christian evangelisation 'the teaching of manual labour, agriculture and industry'.[36] Pictures taken from the mission field in Bediondo (1964) show how painting and sculpture became effective tools for transmitting practical and religious knowledge.[37]

Jesuits also collaborated with the Société d'Urbanisation du Tchad Urbanisation (STU: Society of Chad) to build 250 residences in Fort-Lamy. They made sure that this urbanisation process did not destroy local traditions and cultures.[38] The contribution of their French lay collaborators, however, was often ambiguous. One lay organisation, the JAC, pushed for the creation of exclusive Christian villages. It encouraged young Christian families to own property, to diversify their economic activities, and to embrace modern agricultural techniques.[39]

However, the missionary ideology of these youth groups may be interpreted as a resistance to the vernacularisation of Christianity. By definition, the JAC consisted largely of young Christians who believed God had spoken in their heart to radically change things in society, especially in villages. While the transformation they sought was primarily moral, they were also 'extremely opposed to everything that looked like paganism'.[40] Some African Jesuits such as Meinrad-Pierre Hebga expressed strong reservations about these lay volunteers. Hebga believed the volunteers overstated their claim of having expertise about African problems, while in fact they showed little understanding and appreciation of African traditional values.[41]

Attempts to Make Chad a 'Major Mission' or a 'Vice-Province'

As the missionaries expanded their grassroots evangelism, they could count on lay volunteers to get the job done. However, there is also a clear indication of their unwillingness to cede actual power. In fact, their position had grown so strong that the Jesuits in Chad took steps to enhance the statutory jurisdiction of the Chad Mission.

---

[36] Henri Joseph Eugène Gouraud, *Zinder-Tchad: Souvenirs d'un Africain* (Paris: Plon, 1944), 150.
[37] Pichon, 'Bediondo, le salut sur les murs', 41.
[38] Pichon, 'Bediondo, le salut sur les murs', 43. Visiting Chad in 1971, twenty-one years after he had been there as a military attaché, Revd Chabert, provincial of France, expressed his admiration for the progress made in urbanisation and the organisation of rural Chad: 'Le Pére Chabert au Tchad', *JAF* 45 (February 1971): 26–27.
[39] Hallaire, 'Evangile et coutumes', 43.
[40] Ibid., 42.
[41] A-Pa. 151: Meinrad-P. Hebga, 'Letter to Jean-Yves Calvez' (6 January 1971).

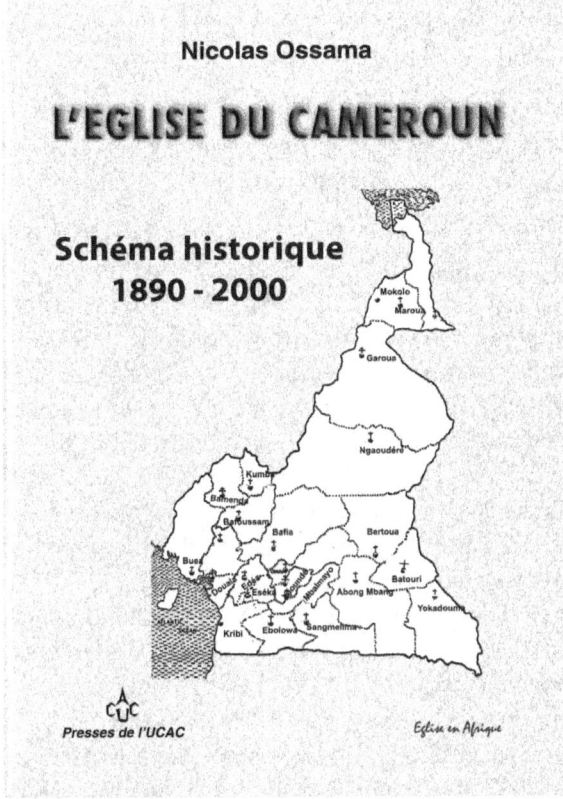

Figure 12 Book cover of *L'église du Cameroun: schéma historique, 1890–2000* by Nicolas Ossama (UCAC, Presses de l'UCAC, 2011).

From 1961, there was growing concern among the leaders of the Chad Mission that despite lay contributions, the missionary personnel were not sufficient to support the work of their mission. Bishop Véniat responded to that shortage by asking for more Jesuits from Spain and North America.[42] Eight years later, in 1969, Charles Vandame, head of the mission since 1968, made a similar observation.[43] Vandame admitted that the Church in Chad had failed to recruit indigenous vocations. Consequently, he called for new ways to address that failure.[44]

---

[42] A-PAO. H. TCH. 19: Henri Véniat, 'Quelques réflexions, problèmes et conclusions' (10 August 1961).

[43] A-PAO. H. TCH. 19: Charles Vandame, 'Réflexions sur quelques problèmes majeurs de l'Eglise du Tchad. A l'occasion du survey' (April 1969).

[44] Ibid.

In the letter of the Chad Mission on 15 February 1971, Vandame described the African situation in very critical terms:

> The current organisation of the Society in Africa evokes the colonial period [...] Such an organisation is no longer satisfactory [...] This situation is no longer tolerated in the territories where the indigenous Jesuits form an important group.[45]

As the head of the Chad Mission, Vandame's words could not have been more paradoxical. He acknowledged that the current forms of Jesuit missions in Africa were as colonial as they could be, and he considered the lack of African personnel intolerable. Key aspects of his solution were the bringing in of more Western missionaries and the institutional evolution of the Chad Mission. As the Jesuits in Chad addressed the question of creating a 'Major Mission' or 'Vice-Province' on 23 July 1971,[46] the main goal of this institutional evolution was not Africanisation as such. Instead, it aimed to have the European personnel of the Chad Mission well represented in international Jesuit forums.[47]

In December 1971, Vandame extended an invitation to Meinrad-Pierre Hebga, the Jesuit regional superior of Cameroon, to discuss 'ways to exchange ideas and personnel'.[48] It was the first invitation of its kind. Hebga visited Chad in January 1972. That same month, the Jesuit consultors of Chad considered whether or not the Chad Mission should be established as an 'Independent Vice-Province of Chad'.[49] The reasons for this institutional change highlighted an acknowledgement of the shifting political and ecclesial realities on the ground.

According to Vandame, Chad, on the political level, 'ha[d] broken its colonial-type dependency to become an independent nation'. Therefore, it was necessary for the Mission to move from the status of mission to the status of vice-province. This change meant the Chad Mission, as it existed, was a colonial mission, a status at odds with independent Chad. Making it autonomous also meant renouncing privileged bilateral ties with France 'in favor of a decolonised religious structure (at the level of formal structures, for in practice we remain foreign missionaries)'.[50] In Vandame's own words, the Chad Mission still looked like a colonial enterprise:

---

[45] A-PAO. H. TCH. 20: *Nouvelles Mission SJ du Tchad* 1 (15 February 1971): 1–16.
[46] A-PAO. H. TCH. 20: *Nouvelles Mission SJ du Tchad* 3 (23 July 1971): 1.
[47] Ibid.
[48] A-PAO. H. TCH. 20: *Nouvelles Mission SJ du Tchad* 6 (3 December 1971).
[49] A-PAO. H. TCH. 20: *Nouvelles Mission SJ du Tchad* 8 (15 January 1972).
[50] Later in 1972, the consult reiterated its belief that 'the current dependence

It is a vast organisation still very European in its apostolic staff, in the origin of its economic resources, in its methods of work, in the catechetical, liturgical, pastoral, and apostolic 'models' which inspire its choices. The Church appears as a foreigner in her own country.[51]

Vandame's consultors made several suggestions to break from these colonial-like structures and practices. Their solutions also explicitly addressed the issue of Africanisation at three levels: replacing each retiring foreign missionary or volunteer with an African, adapting the work of the mission to African needs, and making sure the mission was self-supporting. In Vandame's own words:

> When someone arrives at the end of his contract, ask each time the question: 'can he be replaced by an African?' Where a position of responsibility cannot be Africanised, ask yourself the question: 'is the work to be accomplished adapted to Africa?' Where a work requires resources that cannot be found in Chad, ask the question: 'is the work adapted to Chad?'[52]

The idea of replacing every departing missionary with an African was not actually achievable unless recruits came from other regions. There were no Chadian Jesuits at the time. Moreover, in his second question, Vandame did not say why 'a position of responsibility cannot be Africanised'. Yet, to his credit and that of his advisers, although late in the process, they sincerely considered adapting their work to African realities. They also expected that the jurisdictional evolution of Chad would improve inter-African ties within the African assistancy.[53]

The change of attitude among European missionaries in Chad was also dictated by pressing needs on the mission field. Transformation in society led to transformation in churches. More than a decade after independence, the provinces of Italy and Spain provided additional missionary personnel for the Chad Mission. These provinces eventually became 'reluctant to supply personnel for a mission that officially depended on the Province of France'. For 'it seemed to them a bit absurd, since they had so many other

---

with the Lyon Province was satisfactory': *Nouvelles Mission SJ du Tchad* 13 (5 December 1972).

[51] A-PAO. TCH. 20. 16: 'Compte rendu de la Consulte et de la réunion des supérieurs de maison suite à la consultation demandée par la Père Costes' (29 May 1973).

[52] Ibid.

[53] A-PAO. H. TCH 20: 'Délibérations du Tchad', *Nouvelles Mission SJ Tchad* 8 (15 January 1972).

duties of their own. They would feel more responsive to the Chad Mission, if Chad were to become an independent Vice-Province'.[54] Therefore, having these European personnel replaced by Africans was key to the survival of the Chad Mission. Nothing had been done, however, to promote indigenous vocations in Chad. Where, then, would they find the African personnel they desperately needed?

A Relationship with Cameroon: Extending Chad's Model beyond Chad

There was not unanimity among leaders of the Chad Mission about whether or not the institutional evolution could solve the challenges they faced. According to Vandame, some consultants believed the reasons in favour of an institutional evolution were primarily 'ideological'. Looking at what was going on in the mission field, these advisers insisted, 'the current situation is satisfactory'. Others wondered whether it was appropriate for the Chad Mission to become an independent vice-province with entirely European personnel. Other regions in the continent, they said, where there were already African personnel would not understand 'the establishment of a European ghetto in Chad'. This was especially so in what many considered the postcolonial or post-missionary era.

A credible reason to extend the institutional evolution of the Chad Mission to other African countries – especially Cameroon, Burkina Faso, and Congo Brazzaville, where there were already African vocations and where the Jesuits would share a common language – was that such an extension would supply Chad with much needed African vocations. The French provincials helped advance that approach. André Costes, Odilon de Varine, and Jean-Yves Calvez, then Regional Assistant for France in the Roman Curia, proposed a compromise on these terms:

> They could organise a joint Province Congregation in Cameroon and Chad. This decision would, in no way, bind the future; but it would lead to some progress. The Consult [of Chad] noted that this initiative was likely to stimulate common reflections on our Jesuit life in Africa. It would also strengthen the ties between two neighboring territories.[55]

The French compromise confirmed that the real reason that triggered this institutional debate was a lack of representation of Chad in both the

---

[54] Ibid.
[55] A-PAO. H. TCH 19: 'Délibérations du Tchad', *Nouvelles Mission SJ du Tchad* 8 (15 January 1972). [Emphasis added].

province congregation of France and the GC. Of further note, rather than having written their own letters of support, Costes and Calvez were quoted in *Lettre de la Mission du Tchad*, the communication channel of Chad missionaries.[56] This compromise was significant, because it represented the first 'official' attempt to create a common Jesuit deliberative jurisdiction between Chad and Cameroon.[57]

The attempt to create a common Jesuit jurisdiction between Chad and Cameroon originated from Chad. It was deliberated mostly among Chad, Lyon, and Paris Jesuits. These Jesuits intended primarily to solve Chad's internal problems. Cameroon was not fully integrated in these initial discussions; it only became part of the equation to supply Chad with African personnel, without whom the idea of an independent Vice-Province of Chad would have been, in Vandame's own words, 'intolerable'.[58] The purpose of such a jurisdiction was to provide the Chad Mission with the African representation it needed in its personnel in order to pretend that it was a vice-province in Africa. It was to demonstrate that Chad deserved a voice in Roman and other international Jesuit gatherings. The deliberations that led to the creation of the Vice-Province of West Africa (VPAO) later confirmed that tendency.

The newsletter of the Chad Mission reported additional reasons in favour of upgrading Chad's jurisdictional status in May 1973:

> The appointment of a territorial superior is motivated by the following considerations: specificity of the Chadian problems; the type of apostolic commitment already made; the history of the Jesuit Mission of Chad, the

---

[56] No letter from either Costes or Calvez confirmed that fact. One reason is that most of the internal correspondence between Jesuit superiors is still unavailable for research. Another reason might be that such a letter never existed. There were other ways to communicate such opinions, including visits to France, or from France to Chad. Yet, because the provincials of France received the Letter of the Chad Mission, Vandame would not write this unless he was sure it came from Costes and Calvez, or that both men would agree with it.

[57] The use of 'official' here is important, since the attempt was shared by at least three Jesuit superiors (Chad, France, and Calvez in Rome) with the authority to formulate such a request to the Father General. The first references to such a reconciliation by Vandame and Chabert did not have the same weight. Only one important superior is missing in this debate: the regional superior of Cameroon.

[58] A-PAO. H. TCH. 20: 'La Compagnie en Afrique et Madagascar', *Nouvelles Mission SJ du Tchad* 1 (15 February 1971): 1–16.

great distances, the slowness and the vagaries in the delivery of the mail, and, consequently, the relative estrangement of a Vice-Provincial would leave the Jesuits, without a Territorial Superior, dependent on the Ordinary of the place.[59]

Beyond the logistics of the Chad Mission, Vandame was making another valid point. Leaving Chad with no territorial superior bore the risk of the work of the Society in Chad being shaped by the 'Ordinary' – that is, local bishops. However, the risk of such absorption was avoided from the beginning of the mission. The Jesuits always ensured a Jesuit superior was appointed for the Chad Mission alongside the apostolic prefect. This was the case even though that prefect was a Jesuit.[60] The separation was important in order to secure the independence of the Society in its institutions and protect its work from constant interference by local bishops. The legal boundaries between Jesuit missions and African dioceses were a major concern for Arrupe as well. He directed his assistant, Victor Mertens, to write a draft agreement that would define the nature of that delicate yet unavoidable relationship for the lasting success of the African Jesuit mission.[61]

A closer look at Vandame's note, however, also shows that Chad presented preconditions that made it impossible to appoint a superior from another country if Chad was to remain part of the new jurisdiction. The reference to the 'history of the Chad Mission', the link between the leadership of the eventual new province, and the exclusion of Anglophones were reminders that Chad was, after all, French. These preconditions also excluded African Jesuits from being considered as effective leaders of the Chad Mission and, as a corollary, the VPAO, should the organisation include Chad.

---

[59] A-PAO. TCH. 20: 'Compte-rendu de la Consulte et de la réunion des supérieurs de maison suite à la consultation demandée par la Père Costes', *Nouvelles SJ Tchad* 16 (29 May 1973).

[60] Propaganda Fide appointed apostolic prefects and bishops, while the superior general of the Jesuits appointed the superior of the Chad Mission. When du Bouchet was apostolic prefect, Dalmais was superior of the Chad Mission, and when Dalmais became bishop, Véniat became superior of the Chad Mission; when Véniat became bishop of Fort-Archambault, Vandame became superior of the Mission, etc.

[61] A Latin draft was written in 1970 (Victor Mertens, 'De contractibus cum Hierarchia in missionibus' [June 1970], and a final proposal approved in 1973: cf. Victor Mertens, 'La place et l'attitude des missionnaires étrangers aujourd'hui en Afrique', *Chine–Madagascar* 145 (December 1973): 5–11.

African Jesuits like Fabien Eboussi Boulaga and Hebga had visited Chad. And Hebga met Vandame in several meetings of African major and mission superiors. Yet neither Hebga nor Eboussi could meet the conditions posed by Chad's leadership. Had the same preconditions applied elsewhere, in Cameroon or Côte d'Ivoire, it would have been impossible to have a missionary who had spent his entire apostolic African experience in Chad to be appointed major superior of the VPAO.

Conclusion

The reconciliation with Cameroon began with the choice of Jean Zoa, newly appointed archbishop of Yaoundé, to ordain Véniat. The tension that appeared in this ordination was symbolic of a dual dynamic of the Church in two countries whose destinies were linked. For Chad, though, there is no question about the strength and control of the missionaries in the Church. While the Jesuit leaders in Chad acknowledged the colonial nature of the Church they built, they also showed little indication that they wanted the foundations of this building to be changed.

This chapter has shown that a decade after independence, French missionaries still controlled the leadership of the Church in Chad. They kept it foreign while integrating some new blood from other parts of the continent. As such, they shaped the terms of their relationship with Cameroon, admitting the possibility of greater collaboration while also presenting preconditions that would keep the nature of their organisation unchanged. If Chad could not become an autonomous jurisdiction because of its all-White personnel, it was to keep a level of autonomy within a broader Jesuit jurisdiction. The leader of the Chad Mission, they argued, ought to be one of its missionaries.

Cameroonians had similar conversations during the creation of the Jesuit Region of Cameroon in 1968. They insisted that their major superior be an African. As Chad moved to shape the future of the new regional jurisdiction that was in the making, the clash of the two visions became inevitable, as the next chapter will show. Could Chad transfer its model beyond Chad? And how would it be received?

CHAPTER 8

Era of Experimentation: M.-P. Hebga, First Cameroonian Major Superior, 1968–73

On 27 June 1968, Pedro Arrupe officially created the Region of Cameroon. He also appointed Hebga as regional superior. Informing Jacques Lesage, then provincial of Paris, Arrupe wrote:

> Since the Fathers of our Society were called in 1957 to assist in the work of evangelization in Cameroon, many circumstances have changed: the country obtained its national independence, a local hierarchy was formed with Cameroonian Bishops, and our houses benefit from the presence of a certain number of trained Jesuits from Cameroon, resulting in a new context which calls for a new way of relating this territory to the Province of Paris […] I decide therefore to constitute the territory of Cameroon into a Region and place it under the authority of a Major Superior depending on the Provincial of Paris. I appoint to the post of Superior of the Region Fr Meinrad Hebga, Rector appointed of the Libermann High School of Douala. He will take charge next July 31st [1968].[1]

The political emancipation and Africanisation of both the leadership of the Catholic Church in Cameroon and the membership of the Society were mentioned as factors that had influenced Arrupe's decision. Also significant was Arrupe's trust in Hebga's abilities. He had appointed Hebga to be the rector of Libermann. The difference between the date of Hebga's appointment and his inauguration was only a month. This was a sign of Arrupe's belief in Hebga's readiness for the job.

Concluding his letter, Arrupe blessed the new institution. He also determined the ultimate goal of the new Region, which alluded to Africanisation.

---

[1] Pierre Arrupe, 'Au P. Lesage, 27 June 1968'. CB 231, Paris 68/18. A copy of the official document can be found in the annex.

He expected the Region 'to produce abundant fruit for a deeper rooting of the Society in the traditions and culture of the country, and a greater number of recruitments of indigenous vocations'.[2]

In this chapter, the creation of the Jesuit Region of Cameroon and the appointment of a Cameroonian as its superior represents a typical case of successful Africanisation, as envisioned by the Vatican and demanded by Africans themselves. Challenges faced by the new African leadership in Cameroon, however, also shine a light on the making of postcolonial Africa by establishing parallels between political and ecclesiastical Africanisation. African political leaders like Tombalbaye claimed leadership over their nations yet still remained dependent on France. In the same way, Cameroonian Jesuits obtained the African leadership they had demanded, yet the Jesuit Region of Cameroon was officially dependent on Paris, while Hebga's leadership remained under French supervision.

African Jesuits soon realised that the transition from missionary to African Christianity required more than the Blackening of leadership. For this transition to be transformative and create a Church that was genuinely African, deeper reforms were necessary at the institutional and theological levels, as well as the level of the grassroots efforts of mission. This chapter focuses exclusively on the institutional part of this history, while Chapter 9 will address the Africans' demand for Africanity. In this claim of Africanity, they opposed perceived racism and Catholicity itself.

The chapter argues that in creating the Jesuit Region of Cameroon, the Society of Jesus took the first important step towards the Africanisation of the order in West Africa. The new jurisdiction and leadership projected transformative results for the Church in Cameroon. They checked most of the boxes of Africanisation. School curricula in Libermann High School promoted African Studies, and a Cameroonian regional superior was appointed. The Jesuits assumed charge of an international major seminary in Otélé, with the aim of training an indigenous African clergy. When they left the direction of the seminary five years later, it had a Cameroonian as its director.

Reception of the New Jesuit Jurisdiction in Cameroon

The Cameroonisation of the Society was also ensnared in conflicts caused by both Europeans and Africans. For Cameroonian Jesuits, the new jurisdiction was a natural development of the Church in Africa. The regionalisation of Cameroon was a first step towards it playing a more important role in

---

[2] Ibid.

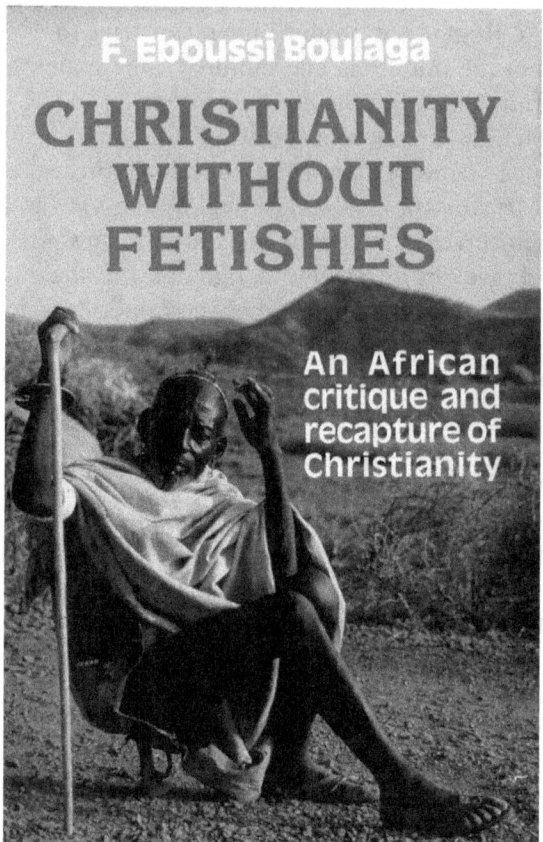

Figure 13 Book cover of *Christianity Without Fetishes: An African Critique and Recapture of Christianity* by F. Eboussi Boulaga (New York: Orbis Books, 1984).

shaping the Society of Jesus in West Africa and beyond. Surprisingly, Bishop Thomas Mongo of Douala, a Cameroonian himself, objected, although not strongly, to the appointment of the new regional superior. The bishop's reaction was unexpected by Jacques Lesage, since Mongo had previously proposed Hebga's name to become director of the seminary.[3]

Mongo's reaction underlines the fact that expectations might not have been the same between Cameroonian Jesuits and Cameroonian bishops. One reason for Mongo's reaction might have been that he favoured the Africanisation of the Jesuit leadership in Cameroon, but only as long as it was taking place outside his diocese. Hebga could be director of the

---

[3] P. Lesage, 'Lettre au R. P. Durand-Viel, le 24 Juin 1968'.

seminary in Yaoundé, but not director of Libermann and regional superior of Cameroon with residence in Douala, Mongo's diocese. His reaction was also common to the paradoxes of Africanisation. Some local bishops, for example, resisted replacing deep-pocketed missionaries with unpredictable and less wealthy African personnel.

For European missionaries, in contrast, the creation of the Region of Cameroon came with the fear of 'the unknown', especially regarding having their first African superior. Appeasing these missionaries would lead to the creation of a dual leadership in Cameroon which eventually undermined Hebga's authority. In the capital city, Yaoundé, a *de facto* dual leadership was installed in the new region from the start. Philip Durand-Viel, former provincial of Paris, was appointed superior of Yaoundé and personal delegate of the current provincial of Paris in Cameroon, where Hebga had just been appointed regional superior.

Durand-Viel's prominence was another form of emboldened missionary Christianity in the context of a postcolonial mature Church. As the direct representative of the provincial of Paris in Cameroon, the provincial discussed major issues with Durand-Viel, including the missioning of the members of a region that already had a Cameroonian major superior. He was the one who, alongside the provincial, decided that the official date of the creation of the region be 9 September 1968.[4]

Paris's decision to appoint Durand-Viel might also reflect a certain lack of confidence in Hebga's abilities on Arrupe's part. From Paris's perspective, the dual leadership was necessary in order to groom Hebga, who was perceived by Paris as inexperienced. Informing Archbishop Zoa about the new statutory dispositions in Yaoundé, Lesage confirmed Durand-Viel, 'until further notice', as his 'Ordinary Delegate for the Fathers of Cameroon'.[5] He also reminded the bishop that Hebga was still 'green'. It was only after he had taken all these dispositions with Durand-Viel that Lesage informed the rest of the members of the new region.[6]

Dual leadership in Cameroon made it very difficult for Hebga, the African superior, to lead. Ultimately, while he succeeded in rooting the region into the local Church of Cameroon, his tenure did not pass without pain. Hebga had to deal with miscommunication and distrust in and from missionaries and his European superiors. Meanwhile, a group of first Cameroonian Jesuits with strong characters, who tended to disobey Jesuit

---

[4] P. Lesage, 'Lettre au P. Durand-Viel, le 19 juillet 1968'.
[5] Ibid.
[6] Jacques Lesage, provincial, 'Lettre aux Pères et Frères du Cameroun, 20 juillet 1968'.

authorities, consumed much of Hebga's attention during his five-year term (1968–73). By the end of his term, a European had replaced him as the first provincial of the VPAO. There would not be another African heading the province until 1996.

The creation of the Cameroon Region came at a time when missionaries were emboldened, with a well-qualified Cameroonian major superior. The Region was intended to be experimental and, despite its achievements in favour of Africanisation, was ultimately dissolved within a broader Jesuit jurisdiction that included all French former colonies and territories in Central and West Africa, and which had a Frenchman as a major superior.

Instead of simply transitioning from missionary to African Christianity, Cameroon – where Engelbert Mveng joined the Society before there was any Jesuit presence there (in 1951) – went from being a mission of Paris (1957) to having greater autonomy as a dependent Region of Paris with a Cameroonian major superior (1968), and finally settled in a less autonomous situation, reduced to one country among many others within the VPAO with a French missionary as major superior. Vandame, the superior, had been the superior of the Chad Mission since 1968. He replaced Hebga in Douala in 1973, and with this the Chadian Western-centred approach seemed to prevail over the Afro-Cameroonian approach. As Chapter 9 will show, a clash between the two competing visions was inevitable.

The Roman Catholic Church in Cameroon was more mature than in Chad. The first Catholic missionaries had settled in Cameroon in 1890 with the arrival of the Pallottines led by Heinrich Vieter (1853–1914). They had their first mass in Douala on 25 October 1890, before settling in Marienberg on 8 December the same year. The Pallottines expanded rapidly by creating missions at Edea in 1891, Engelbert in 1894, Douala in 1897, Grand Batanga in 1900, Eisiedeln (present day Buea) in 1907, and Victoria (Limbe) in 1908, the latter stations being part of what is present-day Anglophone Cameroon.[7]

The mission station of Minlaba (birthplace of Engelbert Mveng, the first Cameroonian Jesuit) was founded in 1912, the same year as that of Kumbo in the north-west.[8] This German-led missionary expansion was interrupted by the beginning of the First World War, after which the Pallottines were replaced by the Holy Ghost Fathers (from 1922) following a successful interlude by Cameroonian catechists (1916–21).

---

[7] Nicolas Ossama, *L'Eglise du Cameroun: Schéma historique (1890–2000)* (Yaoundé: PUCAC, 2011); Engelbert Mveng, *L'Eglise Catholique au Cameroun: 100 ans d'évangélisation 1890–1990* (Italy: Presso Grafiche Dehoniane, 1990).

[8] Ibid.

The arrival of the Pallottines in Cameroon took place forty years before the arrival of the first Catholic missions in Chad, and fifty years before the official recognition of the Chad Mission. By the time of the official recognition of the Chad Mission, there was already an active indigenous clergy and hierarchy in Cameroon.

The difference between the development of the Church in Chad and Cameroon was already perceptible in the context and the characters of those involved. Lyon was the founding province of the Chad Mission, while the Paris Province was in charge of Cameroon and Côte d'Ivoire.[9] The mission in Chad started at the initiative of one individual French Jesuit, while the official arrival of the Jesuits in Cameroon followed several invitations addressed to the French Jesuits by Cameroonian bishops. The bishop of Douala, Thomas Mongo (1914–88), was the first who received a positive answer from Paris.[10] The first Cameroonian became a Jesuit in 1951, joining the novitiate of Central Africa in Djuma, at a time when Cameroon was not on any Jesuit map. By the time French missionaries settled in Douala in 1957, there were already about ten Cameroonians in different stages of Jesuit training. And by the time the Region of Cameroon was suppressed in 1973, there was still not a single Chadian scholastic. Chad was still, thirteen years after independence and almost fifty years after the arrival of the first Jesuit, an all-European missionary enclave.

Despite these differences in the historical context of both countries, the destinies of Jesuit missions in Chad and Cameroon were linked from the beginning. For example, putting the Jesuits in charge of the entire territory of Chad in 1946 led the Oblates, who had been missioning in the western region of Chad, to move to northern Cameroon.[11] Additionally, some missionaries expelled from China and India after the Second World War chose to go to Cameroon, while the province of Lyon considered sending

---

[9] France had four provinces at the time: Champagne, Lyon, Paris, and Toulouse. In 1967, they all became part of the French assistancy, with the provincial of France promoting interprovincial collaboration, and coordinating France's relationships with Rome and some overseas missions. The provincials of the four provinces were part of the consult (advisory board) of France, with the provincial of France as chairman.

[10] Thomas Mongo (1914–88) was the first Cameroonian bishop of Douala. He was appointed auxiliary bishop of Douala in 1955 and became titular in 1957, succeeding Bishop Pierre Bonneau (r. 1955–57). He participated in the Second Vatican Council, and resigned from his seat in 1973.

[11] AJ-Fr M-Ly. Box 149: 'Consult minutes, Lyon, January 13, 1947'.

some of the expelled Jesuits to Chad.[12] Cameroon was also a necessary passage for Jesuit missionaries travelling to Chad.[13]

It was from the Cameroonian city of Douala that Charles Margot wrote in February 1947 to inform the Jesuit consultors of Lyon about the negative reaction of the Oblates after their 'eviction' from Chad. In this letter, Margot also warned his religious superiors about the interference of the French government in drawing missionary and ecclesiastical boundaries in Chad.[14] Finally, as discussed in Chapter 3 (footnotes 13–15), the first Africans who postulated becoming Jesuits in Chad were Cameroonians. They never joined the Society of Jesus, in part because the French apostolic vicar of Yaoundé (Cameroon) opposed their admission.[15] Despite the flux of religious personnel coming from its neighbours, the Chad Mission never opened up its leadership to Africans.

The Ossama Report and the Committee for the Creation of the Cameroon Region

The distinctive trajectory of Cameroon led to its creation as a Jesuit Region in 1968. The decisive act that preceded the creation of the Jesuit Region of Cameroon was the creation of a committee for that purpose. Presided over by Durand-Viel, the committee included three additional French missionaries: Roger Cuzon, Jean Geli, and Éric de Rosny. Hebga, Mveng, and Nicolas Ossama were its Cameroonian members.

According to Lesage, the context of the creation of the Region was 'the spirit of the Second Vatican Council and of our General Congregation [31st]'.[16] Both events called for 'openness and adaptation of our apostolic commitments, in an enlightened and progressive search for adaptation of the Society to its task in Cameroon'.[17] The immediate task of the committee was to study the present situation of Jesuit houses in Cameroon and to foresee their evolution in the years to come.[18] In that particular context, 'the

---

12 In Lyon, several consultors' meetings debated the situation of these missionaries, especially between April and September 1947.
13 Cf. M-Ly. Box 149: Correspondence of the provincial of Lyon on the Chad Mission, 1947–58.
14 M-Ly. Box 149: Charles Margot, 'Letter to the Consult, February 21, 1947'.
15 From Letters of J. du Bouchet to the provincial, 10 and 24 November 1948.
16 A-Fr 401: Jacques Lesage, 'Establishment of a Special Commission to Study a Regionalisation of Cameroon, January 10, 1968'.
17 Ibid.
18 Lesage, 'Création d'une commission spéciale chargée d'étudier une

Cameroonian Fathers would take the lead in a very broad regionalisation grouping of our efforts in Chad, Cameroon, Côte d'Ivoire and Nigeria'.[19]

This letter was the first to propose a broader map for the jurisdiction about to be created. It is worth noting that Lesage included all the territories in West Africa, regardless of their language or colonial heritage, where there was a Jesuit presence. The map included not only French colonies where such a presence existed, but also Cameroon and the former English colony of Nigeria. Cameroon, it should be recalled, was a trusteeship territory under the jurisdiction of the United Nations and was divided between England (1/5 of the territory) and France (4/5 of the territory).

This first proposal, therefore, did not follow colonial or linguistic lines. It aimed at coordinating Jesuit ministries in West Africa independently of their colonial past. As such, it was a progressive proposal, a decolonising one.

In March 1968, a report from the Committee written by its secretary, Ossama, stressed a single point: it was an 'absolutely indispensable condition for the success of the new institution' that the superior of the region be an African. This report, according to its author, was a revised version of a 9 February draft which had been rejected by the committee.[20] At the heart of the criticisms directed against this first draft,

> members felt that I [Ossama] should have stressed more the expression 'irreplaceable contribution of an African superior': rooted in his people, intimately aware of its needs, embodying the 'Africanity' of the Society, etc. The French members of the Committee, however, were concerned that expressions such as 'absolutely indispensable' might offend you [the Provincial]. All members, however, have asked that this wording be sent to you as it is: this is the Committee's view.[21]

The lines of discussion were clearly drawn. Just as in Chad, Cameroonian Jesuits wanted a superior of their own. But unlike Chad, where this superior was to be chosen from among the missionaries working in Chad (all Europeans), Cameroonians were open to having an African from another province – but absolutely an African, nevertheless.

"régionalisation du Cameroun, le 10 janvier 1968"'.

[19] Jacques Lesage, 'Au P. Mertens sur la régionalisation du Cameroun, 11 mars 1968'.

[20] There is rather a document containing a report dated 24 February, and not 9 February, which was the date of the meeting of the committee at Libermann. That meeting was presided over by Durand-Viel.

[21] Nicolas Ossama, 'Rapport de la Commission sur la régionalisation du Cameroun, le 24 février 1968'.

The first part of the report

The first part of Ossama's report gave a short chronology of the Jesuit presence in Cameroon. French Jesuits from Fernando Po, the report said, tried an implantation in the territory in 1883. Their efforts never came to fruition because of the opposition of German Chancellor Otto von Bismarck. It remains unclear how Bismarck would have impeded the arrival of a religious group in Cameroon in 1883. In fact, Germany would have no official role in Cameroon until the German-Douala treaty of 12 July 1884. Clear and direct evidence is still lacking on the Jesuit presence in Fernando Po during the same period (the mid-1880s), especially since the Spanish Jesuits had been expelled from the island, then a Spanish possession, in 1872.[22]

These initial attempts were followed by two unsuccessful invitations by Bishop René Graffin of Yaoundé in 1932 and 1948. In his first attempt, Graffin requested the Jesuits for the foundation of a seminary. In the second, he wanted them to open a school in his diocese.[23] Bishop Bonneau of Douala made similar requests: first a failed one in 1953, then a successful one, which resulted in the arrival of the Jesuits in Libermann in 1957.

Meanwhile, the first Cameroonians had joined the Jesuits. Starting with Mveng in 1951, there were eight by 1957, and five of them had made it their private profession.[24] New members followed. Among them were Siméon Mbarga, Philippe Azeufack, François Nzagpé, Eboussi Boulaga, Nicolas Ossama, and Meinrad-Pierre Hebga. By 1967, when the idea of a Cameroon Region was first mentioned, there had been sixteen vocations from Cameroon. Five other young men had joined from surrounding countries, including Chad, Côte d'Ivoire, and Guinea, but none of these had persevered.[25] Ernest Kombo had joined from Congo Brazzaville, was ordained in 1973, and remained a Jesuit until he was appointed bishop of Owando (r. 1990–2008) in his home country.

---

[22] On that Jesuit mission in Fernando Po, see my contribution: Jean Luc Enyegue, 'The Jesuits in Fernando Po, 1858–1872: An Incomplete Mission', in *Jesuits' Survival and Restoration: A Global History, 1773–1900*, ed. Robert Maryks (Leiden: Brill, 2015), 466–86.

[23] I found no evidence of this: neither in the Jesuit archives in Douala, nor in Graffin's correspondence in the archives of the archdiocese of Yaoundé.

[24] Nicolas Ossama, 'Rapport de la Commission sur la régionalisation du Cameroun, le 24 février 1968'.

[25] Nicolas Ossama, 'Rapport de la Commission sur la régionalisation du Cameroun, le 24 février 1968'.

In Africa overall, the catalogue of 1968 counted 928 Jesuit priests, 210 scholastics, and 266 Brothers, giving a total of 1,404.[26] In West Africa in particular, there were 9 Jesuits from Paris in Côte d'Ivoire. Nigeria counted 16 from the province of New York. Cameroon had 31 Jesuits from the province of Paris, and Chad had 77, mainly from Lyon, with a few from Milan-Venice and fewer from Spain.

The second part of the report

The second part of Ossama's report addressed the intended objectives of the region. All the members of the Committee admitted that the main purpose of the new institution was the implantation of the Society in a truly incarnated way. In a sense, they agreed with their provincial and acknowledged that the Society itself, 'according to its traditions, must adapt to the apostolic necessities of the countries where it is rooted'.[27] Yet, two competing understandings of the goal of the region emerged.

For the Africans, the new Cameroon Region meant 'the implantation of the Society in Cameroon in a major form, in a church that has reached its maturity, and therefore in its African form'.[28] The specific contribution of the Society to the work of the Church in the country would cover all fields, but especially the field of research and teaching on African Studies. The field of African Studies included ethnology, sociology, philosophy, pastoral theology, liturgy, pedagogy, and linguistics. This intellectual apostolate would 'help the Cameroonian people to develop their human potentialities, and the African church to give itself an original face within the universal church'.[29] Cameroonian Jesuits, unlike what we have seen from Chad, embraced a different aspect of Jesuit tradition: an elitist intellectual apostolate.

For French Jesuit missionaries working in Cameroon, on the other hand, the regionalisation of Cameroon was part of the broader context of the implementation of Vatican II in the African Church. However, as part of this 'localised' approach to Christianity, they also believed that the specific form of religious life, that of the Jesuits, ought to be preserved, alongside other forms of religious life. That there should not be a difference between the Society in Paris and the Society in Cameroon. That there was only one universal Society of Jesus. Instead of major reforms, what was really needed was some improvement in fraternal relationships. In

---

[26] Ibid.
[27] They were referring to the provincial's letter of 10 January 1968.
[28] Ibid.
[29] Ibid.

Cameroon, French missionaries defended the Catholicity of the Church from a perspective that insisted on the strict observance of traditional Jesuit identity, its universality, and unity. Jesuit distinctiveness ought to be emphasised not from the perspective of regional particularities (African vs European Jesuitism), but as compared to other Western congregations operating on African soil.

The third part of the report

The third part of Ossama's report covered the 'geographical extension of the Region'. A 'true incarnation of the Society' – that is to say its definitive implantation – meant bringing African vocations to the Society. African vocations to the Society imposed a geographical definition beyond the limits of Cameroon. These would stretch beyond the borders of Cameroon to almost all of West and Equatorial Africa.[30] The committee strongly insisted on the need for the Society 'to present itself immediately as a unifying force, a ferment of unity beyond the arbitrary and ill-digested limits of European colonial states in Africa!'[31] Jesuit ministries in West and Equatorial Africa (Côte d'Ivoire, Nigeria, Cameroon) should be treated the same in practice; Chad would be dealt with separately.

For all these reasons, the committee proposed several steps towards the regionalisation of Cameroon and beyond. A first step would bring together all the present and future African Jesuit vocations of West and Equatorial Africa, with the exception of Chad.[32] Additionally, all the houses founded in the Region by the province of Paris, as well as the non-African Jesuits already working there (Western missionaries), would come together. The second stage would include all the foundations of the Society 'in this part of Africa', whatever their origin, including those of Nigeria and Chad.[33] The committee expressed a wish that the new region be positively oriented towards a future unification of the Society in the entire African continent, in accordance with the wishes of the 31st GC, and the wishes Father General had expressed on several occasions.[34]

---

[30] Nicolas Ossama, 'Rapport de la Commission sur la régionalisation du Cameroun, le 24 février 1968'.
[31] Ibid.
[32] This detail is important. It means that in this early stage, Chad could be part of, but was not central to, the West African strategy.
[33] This time, the 'foundations' of Chad seemed important, but no mention was made of the all-French Jesuit personnel working there.
[34] The Committee is referring here to two of Pedro Arrupe's interventions.

In a sense, the committee, while explicitly setting the foundations for the creation of a 'Region of Cameroon', already had its gaze fixed on a broader project. The Region of Cameroon, even before its creation, had already projected its African ambitions. Upon reading the works of the leading Cameroonians of that committee, it is hard not to see in this projection their strong nationalism and Pan-Africanism. Mveng, for example, believed Cameroon to be 'Africa in miniature', and that the unity of the entire African continent would have its foundations on the feet of Mount Cameroon. Because of this Cameroonian nationalism and its African projection, the creation of the Region of Cameroon and that of the assistancy of Africa seemed to overlap.

The fourth part of the report

The final part of the report addressed the juridical status of the region, especially that of its superior. In other words:

> The Regional Superior of our future Region was to enjoy powers as important as the Father General's text on the Vietnam-Thailand Region, to which the Provincial explicitly refers. These powers correspond, practically, to the powers of a Vice-Provincial Dependent, and adapted to local circumstances [...] He must, logically, be an African.[35]

The text was not clear in its juridical wording. It talked about 'the Regional Superior', which, according to constitutions of the Society of Jesus, is the proper title of the major superior of a 'Region', be that region-dependent or independent. Then it equates his 'powers' to those of a 'Vice-Provincial Dependent', which would mean that instead of a region, Cameroon was being created as a vice-province dependent on another province, Paris in this case. The reader is left with no clear idea about what kind of jurisdiction the Committee wanted: would it be a region or a vice-province? Would it be dependent or independent? Finally, the report insisted that the major superior 'be adapted' to local circumstances. This final point makes sense only when associated with the explicit request that the ethnicity of this superior be 'African'.

It would not be an overstatement to affirm that the high esteem in which the Committee held its own abilities might have blinded it to seeing that it was already interfering with the attributions of the superior general of the

---

The first on 'Missionary Service, September 29, 1966', and the second on 'Interprovincial Collaboration, October 14, 1966'.

[35] Nicolas Ossama, 'Rapport de la Commission sur la régionalisation du Cameroun, le 24 février 1968'.

Figure 14 Revd Mveng's artwork for the mosaic above the altar at the Cathedral of Notre-Dame-des-Victoires de Yaoundé, used for the book cover of *Faith, Power and Family: Christianity and Social Change in French Cameroon* by Charlotte Walker-Said (James Currey, 2018).

order. He alone had the absolute power to nominate anyone he wanted as major superior. Using expressions such as 'absolutely indispensable' was to face some resistance from existing religious and juridical boundaries. The language of the document already contained the seeds of dissent.

In a sense, the Committee wanted to make Cameroon an autonomous jurisdiction, but only to have it quickly become the centre of a broader West African jurisdiction. Not only did Cameroon already have three important foundations, it also had the largest number of Jesuits of African origin in West Africa. It was agreed from the beginning of the process that financial ties with Paris would remain intact. However, there was also an explicit desire to deepen institutional links with the province of France, which was created in 1967, and so to move beyond the current exclusive relationship with Paris. Such an approach was more in tune with the development of the Society in France and would facilitate, in due course, the integration of other territories, such as Chad, into the region.[36]

Meinrad-Pierre Hebga: Regional Superior of Cameroon, 1968–73

Hebga seemed to be a superior under the supervision of Durand-Viel. When he put forward Hebga's name to the provincial for the position of regional superior, Durand-Viel also insisted Hebga be assisted by 'a strong French superior to avoid the risks related to the unknown that can be envisioned by appointing a Cameroonian'.[37] Following that request, the residence of Yaoundé, which up to this point had been dependent on the Community of Libermann Secondary School, had to become independent immediately. The envisioned 'strong French superior' was to be appointed superior of the Yaoundé community, while Hebga would remain in Douala. In practice, Hebga's term as regional superior was reduced to its simplest form. He was basically the superior of Libermann.

By appointing Durand-Viel superior of Yaoundé, Lesage, as already said, established a *de facto* dual leadership in Cameroon. This dual leadership revealed two competing visions of Jesuitism on African soil: one that believed in the universality and unity of the Society of Jesus and acted regardless of local contexts, and another that believed in the universality and unity of the Society of Jesus but paid attention to the circumstances of places, people, and time. To plant the universal Society locally would be the main preoccupation of the former, and to Africanise the Church, and with it the Society in Africa, would be the main objective of the latter.

Hebga's youth and religious training

Meinrad-Pierre Hebga was born in Edea, Cameroon, on 31 March 1928. His father, Marc Hebga, belonged to the first generation of Cameroonian catechists trained by the Pallottines in the 1910s.[38] Marc sent his son to the minor seminary in Edea and Akono, and from there Meinrad joined the major seminary of Yaoundé. He was ordained priest on 22 December

---

[36] Ibid.
[37] Lesage, 'Proposition du Père Durand-Viel comme Supérieur de Yaoundé, le 22 mai 1968'.
[38] Éric de Rosny, 'Homélie lors des obsèques de Hebga, mars 2008', *NPAO* 218 (May 2008).

1951 in Rome, following his theological studies at the Pontifical Gregorian University. He was parish priest for the archdiocese of Douala, under Bishop Mongo, from 1952 to 1957. During that period, Meinrad Hebga was among the authors of a book of African theology that made history, expressing African priests' concerns on the eve of the Second Vatican Council.[39]

Hebga joined the Society in 1957. Following two years of novitiate in Aix-en-Provence, he joined La Sorbonne University (Paris) for Licentiates in Theology and Social Sciences (1960–64). In his doctoral dissertation, Hebga sought to prove the rationality of paranormal phenomena in African traditions.[40] He joined Libermann Secondary School in 1965 as a teacher. Then he became director of the same school, rising to eventually become regional superior of the Jesuits in Cameroon from 1968 to 1973.[41]

At the end of his term in Libermann and his time as regional superior, Hebga spent a sabbatical year at John Carroll University, Cleveland (Ohio), in 1973.[42] There he received the baptism of the Holy Spirit. Following that religious experience, Hebga returned home and became the founder of the Catholic Charismatic movement in Cameroon.[43] In 1974, he joined the Faculty of Arts and Sciences of the Federal University of Cameroon, where he taught philosophy. He was visiting professor at the Catholic Institute of West Africa (1971–84) and the Pontifical Gregorian University of Rome (1977–78).

The nomination of Hebga as regional superior was a national event. All the religious and political elite of Douala attended the ceremony that inaugurated his term. Describing the event, Lesage wrote:

---

[39] A. Abble, ed., *Des prêtres noirs s'interrogent*, 2nd ed. (Paris: Cerf, 1957).
[40] Published under the title *La Rationalité d'un discours africain sur les phénomènes paranormaux* (Paris: L'Harmattan, 1998).
[41] Details about Hebga's training are taken from this special edition of the newsletter of the West African province: 'Obsèques du P. Meinrad Pierre Hebga', *Nouvelles de la PAO* (May 2008).
[42] Most biographers state that his time in Ohio was in 1972, which was not possible, since at that time Hebga was regional superior. In fact, it was around April 1973, as he was discussing what his mission would be after his term as regional superior, and asked to go to either an Anglophone country in Africa or the United States.
[43] On Hebga's contribution to the Catholic Charismatic movement in Cameroon, see: Ludovic Lado, *Catholic Pentecostalism and the Paradoxes of Africanization* (Leiden: Brill, 2009).

The Jesuit Region of Cameroon is now established. On September 9, 1968, Father Meinrad Hebga assumed his duties as Regional Superior and Rector of the Libermann High School, after having issued his solemn profession in the hands of Father Lesage, Provincial of Paris, in the presence of Bishop Mongo, bishop of Douala and Bishop Ndongmo [Albert], of Nkongsamba, who both enthusiastically welcomed the event as a deeper integration of the Society in Cameroon. The Federal Inspector of Coastal and Territorial Administration, Mr Sabbal Leco, also attended the ceremony.[44]

The presence of these African leaders in Hebga's inauguration was an indication of how important it was to have a Cameroonian running one of the elite schools in the country. A bloody civil war was still ravaging parts of the dioceses of Douala and Nkongsamba, which bishops Mongo and Ndongmo led respectively.[45] Hebga's role as a religious superior also made him part of the Cameroonian elite that was building an independent Cameroon.

Very quickly, though, Hebga was thrown into the midst of the debate about the reorganisation of the Jesuit presence in Africa. He seemed to understand his function as extending beyond the borders of Cameroon, and saw himself as a representative of African voices eager to shape the organisation of the Church in Africa. Less than two years into his term as regional superior, Hebga received a letter from Jean-Yves Calvez, provincial of France. Calvez informed him about a project to create a new Jesuit assistancy for Africa.[46] It was expected that Victor Mertens, former Belgian missionary in Zaïre and provincial of Central Africa, would be appointed regional assistant. In response to Calvez, Hebga expressed some concerns about having Mertens as Arrupe's assistant for Africa. He believed Mertens could be, despite his best intentions and an excellent knowledge of Africa, overwhelmed by the shifting dynamics in the continent. He also wondered what role Africans, still a minority in the Society, would play in that new jurisdiction. Would they not be drowned, he asked, in a wave of foreign missionaries?

For Hebga, these questions needed an urgent answer. Not only because they had become a central concern among African Jesuits, but also because African Jesuits were witnessing with distress the convenient silence of their White colleagues of Zimbabwe and South Africa in the face of

---

[44] Lesage, 'Lettre au P. Hebga, Régional, le 02 juin 1969'.
[45] Because of his 'contacts' with the UPC rebellion, Bishop Ndongmo was tried by Ahmadou Ahidjo (the first president of Cameroon), imprisoned, and forced into exile.
[46] A-Fr 410/3: Jean-Yves Calves, 'Lettre à Hebga, le 12 janvier 1970'.

Apartheid.⁴⁷ The rise of African leadership in the Church coincided with both a sense of nationalism and an increased loss of patience with the Apartheid regime.

Hebga's priorities as regional superior

For most of his term as regional superior, Hebga worked on negotiating a new convention with the bishops for the work of the Jesuits in the seminary of Otélé. He also spent countless hours on the *cura personalis* of the Cameroonian members of his region. From 1972, he led community discernment with other members of the region about the creation of the VPAO.

Hebga as superior was usually methodical in his governance style. He was concerned about 'the integrity' of religious life. As most of his Cameroonian colleagues were working with the administration of independent Cameroon, Hebga made sure their big salaries did not violate the spirit of their religious vows. He believed that the Society should not tolerate certain liberties, especially the religious vow of poverty:

> If by an excessive indulgence the Society leaves some of its men to trample religious life for years, to make money for themselves and their families, and not to depend on anyone, so we should all go, for each of us would be able to do the same.⁴⁸

Making money 'for oneself' and 'not depending on anyone' were signs that Hebga's concerns were not limited to the vow of poverty alone. On one occasion, a Jesuit accepted a position in the government's administration without his permission. Reacting to that violation of the religious vow of obedience, Hebga saw only one option: he had to dismiss this man for the sake of the integrity of religious life and that of the Society of Jesus.⁴⁹ Hebga asserted himself as a defender of 'authentic' religious life against the laxity of some of his Cameroonian colleagues. He seemed unwavering in confronting Jesuits who did not abide by their vows. This firmness also brought him challenges in his role as superior.

---

47   A-Fr 410/3: Hebga, 'Réponse à Calvez, le 5 mars 1970'. An exception can be made for the case of Roland Pichon. He claimed to have opposed Apartheid and been expelled from Zimbabwe. See: Roland Pichon, *Un Jésuite persona non grata* (Paris: Harmattan, 2008), 69–89.

48   A-Fr 410/4: Hebga, 'Lettre au R. P. Dujardin, Vice-Provincial, 26 Septembre 1972'.

49   Ibid.

Hebga's challenges as major superior

At the same time as he was trying to keep his fellow Cameroonians in line, Hebga had another challenge from European missionaries. In 1970, Hebga was surprised with a request from the provincial of Paris. The provincial asked him to step down as director of the school, and be replaced by Jean Géli or another French missionary.[50] He repeated that request the following year. In reaction to that petition, Hebga sarcastically expressed his frustration to have 'his very breath filtered by the "French consulates"' in Cameroon and Paris.[51] He could not but observe that, before he was appointed, French missionaries older than himself, Durand-Viel and Boumard, had held both positions of director of the school and superior of Cameroon. Now that an African was superior, the scope of his influence was being cut down.

Appalled by the provincial's proposal, Hebga offered to remain director of the school rather than regional superior. He believed times were changing in Cameroon, and Paris seemed not to understand the signs:

> The knowledge I have of the things of my country, Hebga said, does not allow me to believe that after 12 years of having French directors in a Cameroonian school, it is right and prudent to remove the first indigenous director before the end of his term to replace him by a Frenchman. And this, at a time when all Cameroonian scholastics would have left the school: our compatriots would not understand it. I am ready to do what you would decide, but I would render more concrete services as a director of the school than as a Regional Superior.[52]

In his reaction, Hebga gave indications that he had the best interests of the Society in his heart. Yet, perceptions mattered. Appointing a French missionary to replace him, in the 1970s, was simply a huge mistake. The political and ecclesial environment in Cameroon could not allow it.[53]

Hebga's letter went even further. He was known for his rhetorical use of irony and sarcasm. He used it to remind Paris of how 'easy' the provincial had made his task as regional superior. Had not the provincial surrounded him with Boumard in Douala and Durand-Viel in Yaoundé? Durand-Viel, Hebga recalled, had spent the last quarter-century in the Society as superior.

---

[50] Hebga, 'Lettre au Provincial Lesage, 17 avril 1970'.
[51] He is not using the Jesuit term 'consult', but the diplomatic representation, 'consulate'.
[52] Hebga, 'Lettre au Provincial Lesage, 17 avril 1970'.
[53] A major superior in the Society of Jesus has authority to suspend the mission of a Jesuit, including before the end of his term.

One might think he was ready to retire. Yet, he had broader authority in Yaoundé than Hebga did. Hebga made his thoughts more explicit. Since most French missionaries living in Cameroon were blessed by an annual visit from the Parisian provincial, these missionaries had no need to offer their manifestation of conscience to the regional superior of Cameroon.[54]

In substance, the basic functions of a Jesuit major superior were still in the hands of French Jesuits. Cameroonians, Hebga added, never had problems with racism. That was not, he believed, the case of most French missionaries. He narrated the story of one Jesuit who told him in Paris: 'they [the missionaries] would be panic-stricken if they did not see a superior of their race and nationality every year'.[55]

Therefore, Hebga concluded, the help the provincial generously offered through these appointments and his regular visits in Cameroon left Hebga spending only a total of two months a year as regional superior.[56] Expressing, again, the gap between Paris and Cameroon, he asked: 'What exactly was wrong about letting Cameroonians shape for a few years the spirit and the minds of their fellow compatriots?'[57]

The demand for Hebga to resign as director of the school came after he asked Paris to recall French lay volunteers who were working in the school. He requested that they be replaced immediately by Cameroonians.[58] Paris found that decision too hasty, yet, facing Hebga's strong insistence, they backed down.[59] Despite his limited knowledge of Africa, Lesage also understood that any growing tension between both men could be bad for the government of the order. He then reassured Hebga that he did not intend to limit Hebga's free exercise of his leadership as regional superior. Hebga

---

[54] The manifestation of conscience is an important tool for the government of the Jesuit order. Each year, every Jesuit receives a visit from his major superior, with whom he shares details of his religious experience and his mission. That conversation is important, as it allows the superior to get to know the individual Jesuit and show support to him, and give him what he considers the best orientation for the mission.

[55] Hebga, 'Lettre au Provincial Lesage, 17 avril 1970'.

[56] Ibid.

[57] Ibid.

[58] A-Fr 410/4: Hebga, 'Lettre à Jean-Yves Calvez, le 6 janvier 1971'; 'Réponse de Lesage, le 18 janvier 1971'. Lesage asked Hebga to find a compromise with the volunteers and not send them back to France. Two weeks later, on 6 February 1971, he suggested Hebga should step down as director of the school and appoint a French missionary.

[59] Lesage, 'Lettre à Hebga, 6 février 1971, sur la résidence du Régional et le remplacement de Hebga comme Recteur'.

could make his own decisions as major superior; Durand-Viel could not. As regional superior, Lesage continued, Hebga could also decide to keep his position as director of Libermann Secondary School, which was part of his region. As for the racist comments Hebga heard in Paris, he should not worry about them. In the future, Lesage would receive the manifestation of conscience from French missionaries only if Hebga judged it appropriate and necessary.[60]

Libermann Secondary School: A Laboratory for Africanisation, 1956-68

It is in the outreach work of the mission that the effectiveness of the jurisdictional change of the Society in Cameroon is more visible. By 1968, the three Jesuit apostolates in Cameroon were Libermann, the regional (international) major seminary of Otélé, and the Catholic chaplaincy. Twenty-one Jesuits worked in Libermann. Six of them were Cameroonians. The school had two journals: *Etapes* and *Cahiers Libermanniens*. It had a budget of 16,000,000 francs, including 12,076,370 from tuition fees, and 3,500,000 from state subsidies.[61]

A major factor that contributed to the creation of the Cameroon Region in 1968 was the Jesuits' willingness to assume the direction of Libermann School at an early stage. Opened by the Holy Ghost Fathers in 1950, the school came under Jesuit jurisdiction in 1957. In continuity with Mveng's major concern of Africanisation, the fact that almost all the first Cameroonian Jesuits worked in Libermann contributed to making the school a laboratory for Africanisation. Libermann, in fact, served several purposes. It helped them to practise their leadership skills, to launch their intellectual careers, and to test new curricula promoting African Studies.

On 11 June 1956, the consult of the provincial of Lyon had discussed the invitation extended to them by the bishop of Douala, Pierre Bonneau (1903-57). Bonneau wanted the Jesuits to take over Libermann, which he had created in 1950.[62] Six months later, in December 1956, the provincial visited Douala for what he called 'L'affaire Libermann' (The Libermann Affair).[63] His consultors rejected any involvement in Douala. They believed priority should be given to the Chad Mission.

[60] A-Pa. 151: Lesage, 'Lettre au P. Hebga, le 3 Mai 1970'.
[61] Ibid.
[62] Consult meeting, Lyon, 11 June 1956.
[63] From 1967 to 1976, France had one provincial coordinating the work of the four provincials in preparation for the unification of the four provinces into

The Jesuits in Chad were considering opening another high school in Fort-Archambault,[64] and since the Chad Mission was already overwhelming for Lyon, the consultors had no desire to extend that mission further. In 1957, Revd Jean-Baptiste Janssens, superior general of the Jesuits, recommended that the Paris Province, instead of Lyon, be in charge of Cameroon. In accepting that mission, Paris was also exempted from any involvement in Chad.[65] The first French Jesuits, from Paris, arrived in Douala in September 1957.[66] By that time, the country was in its last stretch towards independence.

Cameroon was not the most peaceful place to live in when the Jesuits arrived. From 1955, the nationalist party, the Union of the Populations of Cameroon (UPC) was formally prohibited. The UPC went underground, and the country quickly became immersed in a bloody civil war.[67] Ideologically, the UPC rejected the Union Française (French Union or French Commonwealth) and the 'Wider France'. It saw both projects as ways of perpetuating French colonialism. The party aimed, instead, at the immediate independence of Francophone Cameroon (also known as Eastern Cameroon), and its reunification with Anglophone Cameroon (Western Cameroon).

Douala, where Libermann was located, and its surrounding areas represented the UPC's strongholds. To be French in Cameroon in that particular context, especially in Douala, was risky even for missionaries. The *historia domus* of the Jesuit community of Libermann pointed to that terrifying context in 1960:

---

one. The creation of the West African province was taking place in this broader context of the reorganisation of the Society in France.

[64] Consult meeting, Lyon, 17 December 1956.
[65] Consult meeting, Lyon, 4 December 1957.
[66] The group of the first Jesuits who arrived in Cameroon included Luc-Antoine Boumard (1957) as director of Libermann and Philippe Durand-Viel (1963, former provincial of France). The latter was later appointed director of the school and 'superior of the Jesuits in Cameroon until 1968'. Cameroonian native Meinrad-Pierre Hebga succeeded him as director from 1968 to 1976, also taking on the role of superior of Cameroon from 1968 to 1973. Also present were Vincent Foutchantsé (1976–81) and Guy de Billy (from 1981). See: Engelbert Mveng, 'Camerún', *Diccionario Histórico de la Compañía de Jesús* (Madrid/Roma: IHSI/UPComillas, 2001), 613.
[67] Richard A. Joseph, 'Ruben Um Nyobè and the "Kamerun" Rebellion', *African Affairs* 73, no. 293 (October 1974): 428–48 – here, p. 431. Its leader, Ruben Um Nyobè, was ambushed and killed by the French military on 13 September 1958. That civil war went on until ten years after independence.

The terrorism that prevailed in the city the previous year now diminishes. Although the fear of the attacks still reigns during the night in Douala, the district in which the school is located is calm. The great event of the year was the independence of the Republic of Cameroon, which was proclaimed in a general jubilation on January 1st, 1960. Unfortunately, the terrorist attacks that had taken place the previous day did not allow the pupils from our school to go to the solemn mass at midnight that [the indigenous bishop] Thomas Mongo celebrated at the cathedral. On January 2, however, there were more joyful celebrations, thanks to the parade of Cameroonian youth. The passage of the pupils of Libermann was particularly applauded.[68]

The Jesuit missionaries were afraid of the 'attacks' on Europeans, but they also joined their students, the Cameroonian faculty, and the Cameroonian Church to celebrate the independence of Cameroon. In mentioning the word 'terrorism' more than once to describe the situation in Douala, the Jesuits were not only referring to the acts of violence the city had suffered years before independence – some of these directed towards Europeans; they were also embracing language used by French officials to describe nationalist movements in eastern Cameroon.[69] In this particular case, the UPC was the terrorist movement.

The students and Cameroonian faculty experienced this historical moment quite differently. They celebrated it more than they feared it. The 1960s were, above all, a period of independence and freedom from European domination; at least, that was what these Cameroonians believed.

Libermann Secondary School had to adjust to the new political environment. It quickly became a laboratory for Africanisation, although its leadership initially remained in the hands of French missionaries. In 1957, Luc-Antoine Boumard had been appointed director of the school. Three years later, Durand-Viel replaced Boumard. Durand-Viel combined

---

[68] Historia Domus, Dualensi collegi, 1959–60.
[69] Allied to the French Communist Party, the UPC was suppressed in 1955. It went underground and turned violent, causing 'the assassination of two non-UPC candidates in the elections, Dr Delangué and Mr Samuel Mpouma, as well as the burning of houses belonging to UPC opponents'. It also had churches burned in the western part of the country. The opposition of the Roman Catholic Church to Communism in these years found an echo chamber in large sectors of the Church in independent Cameroon. Bishops sympathetic to the movement, like Albert Ndongmo, were imprisoned, tortured, and forced into exile. It is not clear whether or not the Jesuits took into consideration this increase in violence when they began discussing the regionalisation of Cameroon. See: Joseph, 'Ruben Um Nyobè and the "Kamerun" Rebellion', 439.

the direction of the school with his role as the 'Ordinary Delegate of the Provincial of Paris for Cameroon'. In that position, he also 'coordinated' with the Jesuit houses of Yaoundé and Abidjan (Côte d'Ivoire).[70]

In the following years, though, young Cameroonians shaped the curriculum of the school. Most of them were Jesuits. The *historia domus* of the school reveals the names of this Cameroonian religious elite:

> On Monday, May 1st, [1960], Francois Nzagpe, first Jesuit ordained from Cameroon, took his final vows as a Jesuit [...] A few weeks later on 27 May it was the ordination of Father Fabien Eboussi. Paul Etoga, bishop of Mbalmayo, who was Eboussi's former pastor in Yangben, was kind enough to ordain him. Bishop Albert Ndongmo of Nkongsamba, Loucheur, Apostolic Prefect of Bafia, Father Laurent Provincial of Paris, and many fathers surrounded him.[71]

This list clearly shows the rise of an African Jesuit clergy, alongside young Cameroonian bishops with whom some of them had had common past experiences, often from the time when they were young seminarians. The fact that there are two 'firsts' in that list – Etoga was the first Cameroonian to become bishop, and Nzagpe was the first Cameroonian to be ordained priest in the Society of Jesus – also points to another reality. Consequently, one might ask whether this particular Church was simply too young for self-determination.

Independently of the youth of the African leadership, evidence shows that the impact was immediate for the Africanisation of the school curriculum. Africans led this process:

> Let us note again this year the creation of courses of African languages in classes of 6th and 5th grades. One hour a week, the pupils learn four languages, including the Bamileke, and the Bafang [...] Rev. Abega teaches linguistics; Mveng African art; and Barthelemy Nyom, professor at the major seminary, teaches some aspects of African anthropology. In this way we would like to set up a program of African culture adapted to the different classes.[72]

---

[70] 'Coordinated' put Durand-Viel on an equal footing with the superior of the community of INADES in Abidjan. That community enjoyed a special status: Jesuits working in Abidjan for INADES belonged to the Paris Province, but kept their independence from other Jesuits from the same province working in Cameroon. That autonomy ended with the creation of the West African vice-province in 1973.

[71] A-Fr 401–06: Historia Domus, Dualensi collegi, 1966–67.

[72] A-Fr 401–06: Historia Domus, Dualensi collegi, 1966–67.

Moreover:

> Under the impetus of Father Hebga, and of Father Ossama, African studies are developing in the school. The vernacular languages continue to be taught in the first cycle. Mr. André Ngangue will make a series of courses on the 'mythical history' of the Douala, and their relations with the neighboring ethnic groups. Fr Benoit Atangana gives a series of lectures on economic development and the African mentality.[73]

The first Cameroonian Jesuits working in Libermann came from the largest ethnic groups that were representative of the Christian south in Cameroon. Hebga and diocesan priest Nyom were Bassa; Mveng, Atangana, Azombo, and Ossama were Beti. Ngangue was Douala. The Bamileke language was taught, especially when Vincent Foutchantsé joined the faculty in the early 1960s.[74] Minor and major Catholic seminaries also taught the languages of Ewondo, Basa, and Douala.

By 1960, Libermann had its first graduates. These graduates received scholarships allowing them to pursue their education in France, Germany, the United States, and Switzerland. According to Richard Joseph, by not creating universities on African soil, the French planned to maintain their influence over their former African colonies. This forced most of their most talented students to go to France, where a system was put in place to influence them in favour of French interests.[75] Neocolonialism was in the making. After their education, most of them joined the new administration, and the private sector in Cameroon.[76] They became important members of the new administration and business class. They were loyal to France and built monuments after its generals in the streets of Yaoundé and Douala. They were also loyal to themselves, and eventually to Cameroon.

---

[73] A-Fr 401–06: Historia Domus, Dualensi collegi, 1967–68.
[74] From Jesuit catalogues of the Paris Province (from 1951 to 1983), information can be gathered about the first Cameroonian Jesuits. Here is a short chronology of the entrance of the first twelve, up to 1963: E. Mveng (1951), Simon Mbarga (1952), Nicolas Ossama (1953), Eboussi Boulaga (1955), Joseph Koutchoumow (1956), François Nzagpé (1956), M.-P. Hebga (1957), Soter Azombo (1957), Benoît Atangana (1959), Philippe Azeufack (1961), Vincent Foutchantsé (1962), and Théodore Nkoa (1963).
[75] See: Richard A. Joseph, *Gaullist Africa: Cameroon under Ahmadu Ahidjo* (Enugu, Nigeria: Fourth Dimension Publishers, 1978), 10.
[76] 'Enseignement secondaire au Cameroun, Collège Libermann', *Jésuites* 2 (1961): 29–35 – here, p. 35.

Otélé: An International Major Seminary in Cameroon

Founded in 1927 by Bishop François-Xavier Vogt, then vicar apostolic of Cameroon, the major seminary of Otélé was first entrusted to the care of the Holy Ghost Fathers. Six years later, the Benedictine fathers of the Engelbert Abbey (Switzerland) assumed its charge.[77] Archives of the archdiocese of Yaoundé reveal a challenging time for the seminary in the early 1960s. Cameroon had just gained political independence from France (1960) and England (1961) and achieved its reunification.

In this context, the French archbishop of Yaoundé, René Graffin, was forced to resign and a Cameroonian, Jean Zoa, was appointed as his successor. Zoa's appointment angered some members of the clergy. He had to stay in Rome for almost a year before taking office.[78] The void of leadership left the seminary in the hands of European leaders, who had lost faith in some of the same seminarians they had approved for the sacred orders the previous year. A strong reaction against the Europeans followed among seminarians.[79] They believed that their Western religious leaders were plotting on the back of the first Cameroonian bishop, and trying to weaken his position before he even took office.[80]

The resolution of the crisis in the seminary became the priority of Archbishop Zoa as he assumed his function in Yaoundé. Along with other members of the Cameroonian episcopate, Zoa called the Jesuits for help. The Jesuit superior general agreed that the Society should take charge of the seminary for five years, from 1963 to 1968. By the end of that term, the Jesuits would hand it over to an indigenous diocesan priest.

Located at Otélé, some eighty kilometres from Yaoundé, the mission of the seminary was to train the clergy of the eight existing dioceses of Cameroon and beyond.[81] Otélé welcomed seminarians from Cameroon, Chad, Central African Republic, Congo, and Gabon. A few seminarians from Equatorial Guinea joined it later. Bishop emeritus of Antananarivo, Victor Sartre, was its first director. In these early years, he spent his time between the Second Vatican Council and Cameroon. Roger Cuzon ran the

---

[77] 'Séminaire de Yaoundé', *JAF* 3 (1963): 45.
[78] A-CDO. B. 35: 'Otélé, 1962–1968. Constructions du Grand Séminaire de Nkol-Bisson'.
[79] Ibid.
[80] Ibid.
[81] 'Séminaire de Yaoundé', *JAF* 3 (1963): 45. These included Yaoundé, Nkongsamba, Douala, Garoua, Doumé, Mbalmayo, Sangmélima, and Buea in western Cameroon.

seminary in the absence of the director. Albert Cartier, Pierre Maurel, Jean Guerber, Charles Jacquet, and Jean-Noël Crespel were among the first faculty. Barthélémy Nyom, a diocesan Cameroonian priest, joined them. He later became the first African director of the seminary.

At the time, in the 1960s, there were several minor seminaries across Cameroon. However, only a dozen of the seminarians per year pursued their training for priesthood in the major seminary, leading to a shortage of ordained priests.[82] With the support of André Fouda, the local mayor of Yaoundé, in 1966 a new site was offered to build a seminary in Nkol-Bisson, closer to the centre of Cameroon's capital.[83]

By 1967, 9 French Jesuits and 1 Cameroonian priest of the diocese of Yaoundé were training a total of 74 seminarians. Three of these students were from Chad, 14 from the Central African Republic, and 2 from Gabon. The seminary had a budget of 10,000,000 francs. Sixty-two per cent of that budget came from Propaganda Fide, and 30 per cent from the bishops. The bishops financially supported all the Jesuits working in the seminary. Each of them received about 10,000 francs per year. Both the land and the buildings of the seminary belonged entirely to the dioceses.

The Jesuits who arrived in the seminary were supposed to train an indigenous clergy. Their curriculum, however, offered nothing on African cultures and peoples. Father Nyom and the first Cameroonian Jesuit who joined the seminary, Eboussi Boulaga, tried to fill that gap. Six years after the arrival of the Jesuits, in 1968, they had already reformed the curriculum of the seminary, which was returned to a diocesan leadership, with a Cameroonian as its director. A few Jesuits stayed in the faculty until 1978.

A meeting of the leadership of the seminary on 28 March 1968 recognised the positive transformation of the seminary since the arrival of the Jesuits in 1963.[84] There was a new infrastructure and a new spirit, all beneficial for an imminent takeover by a qualified Cameroonian indigenous clergy. Barthélémy Nyom, appointed director in 1968, became the face of this 'Africanisation' of the seminary. However, seminarians were still worried that the overwhelming presence of French missionaries among the faculty impeded the promotion of African cultures.[85]

There was a pressing need to increase the number of Cameroonians in the faculty. Some steps were taken in the organisation of community life

---

[82] Ibid.
[83] 'Grand séminaire d'Otélé', *JAF* 3 (1966): 42.
[84] A-Pa. 151: 'Bref rapport de l'équipe directoriale en vue de la préparation de la Conférence Episcopale du Cameroun, 28 mars 1968'.
[85] Ibid.

to allow seminarians to assume some responsibilities and have their opinions heard. As head of the studies in the seminary, Eboussi reformed the curriculum. Seminarians had one year studying classical letters, then two years of philosophy and three of theology. For three years, at least, enough time was given to seminarians who desired to learn practical skills like mechanics, masonry, agronomy, etc. But the bishop cut off this practical learning programme after three years.

Alongside the seminary, François-Xavier was the main Jesuit community in Yaoundé. Members of this community worked primarily in the federal university's chaplaincy. With the exception of Durand-Viel and Éric de Rosny, they were all Cameroonians,[86] while those who lived in the community of Otélé (the major seminary) were mostly foreign missionaries. The chaplaincy, also called the Catholic Institute of Yaoundé, had five Jesuits working full time, including three Cameroonians. Some of them worked as university professors as well as in government. Mveng had a museum and a workshop of African art. Ossama, Azombo, and Mveng were involved in the chaplaincy, which had a budget of 3,500,000 francs. Of this money, 1,250,000 francs were from Propaganda Fide. The total of all salaries from the government and bishops was 1,520,000 francs. Additionally, the Jesuits received about 500,000 for masses, 100,000 for other ministries, and 500,000 in donations from friends.[87] These salaries were enough to finally make the community of Yaoundé financially self-sufficient.

Hebga Held Responsible for 'The Cameroon Problem'

Victor Mertens represented a new reality in Jesuit governance in Rome. He was a Western missionary who had spent most of his adult life in Africa and, because of that, was elevated to represent Africa in Rome at a time when African Jesuits were pushing for Africanisation. The universalising vision was reinforced against a contextual vision of the Society. Once in Rome, Mertens complained that Hebga was not firm enough with the Cameroonian Jesuits who were causing trouble. On the other hand, Mertens suggested that Hebga's strong character and uncompromising attitude was making the Region ungovernable.[88]

---

[86] One missionary, Claude Huvé, also spent one year in this community. But for most of the time, the community seemed to consist of one French man leading a group of highly respected African Jesuits, while other missionaries living in Yaoundé resided in the seminary.
[87] Ossama Report, March 1968.
[88] A-Fr 410/4: Mertens, 'Lettre au P. Costes, le 24 Octobre 1972'.

In the first case, Mertens might be referring to Hebga's management of the Mveng case. Hebga protected Mveng from being dismissed from the Society. He might also have been referring to Hebga's 'uncompromising' dealing with Paris concerning his function as regional superior and director of the school. It is also possible that Mertens' harsh criticism of Hebga had to do with Hebga's reluctance to approve Mertens' appointment as Arrupe's Assistant for Africa. When consulted about this appointment, Hebga expressed concerns about the risk of a Congolese monopoly on the African assistancy. In doing so, he indirectly questioned the impartiality of Mertens, who was the first vice-provincial and then provincial of the Central African province.[89]

More than a clash between two characters, what we have here is primarily a clash between two agendas. Hebga opposed the appointment of Mertens as regional assistant for Africa, not on the basis of Mertens' personality or incompetence, but based on the fact that appointing a European missionary for such a position did not correspond to the 'signs of the times'. Hebga was afraid that Mertens would 'congolise or belgicise' the assistancy – that is, use his particular experience of Zaïre as a universal framework for the whole of Africa. To have a Belgian missionary holding the highest office related to Africa in the organisation of the Jesuit order was contrary to Hebga's understanding of Africanisation. Hebga's fear of Congolisation of the assistancy also conflicted with what Ossama's report revealed earlier about the Cameroonians' own agenda for 'Cameroonisation' of the region, and eventually of the assistancy. The appointment of Mertens, and that of Durand-Viel in Cameroon, made Hebga feel 'sous-tutelle' – that is, under colonial and missionary tutelage.[90]

---

[89] 'Father General is proposing Father Mertens as first Assistant of Africa. And at the same time, he requests names of African candidates for the Roman secretariat, eventually to replace one day the first holder. Obviously, for the moment, Father Mertens is the most appropriate man, but I have drawn the attention of Fr General to the apprehensions of the Jesuits of Southern Africa or Cameroon about the real danger of concentration [of power] around Congo: we cannot accept that the Province of Central Africa [Congo] monopolises the services of the Assistancy and congolises or belgicises us': Hebga, 'Lettre à Jean-Yves Calvez, le 6 janvier 1971'.

[90] This point will be raised again later when I discuss the Cameroonian reception of the creation of the West African vice-province in 1973. In fact, three years after that creation, Hebga published his *Emancipation d'Eglises sous-tutelle: Essai sur l'ère post-missionnaire* (Paris: Présence Africaine, 1976).

Lastly, while he was not directly responsible for Mveng's 'bad' character, Hebga, however, seemed to tolerate it extensively for the sake of his own understanding of Africanisation. Hebga knew that Mveng was needed in the Africanisation agenda. Yet, on 11 June 1973 – that is, a month before the creation of the VPAO, Archbishop Jean Zoa, with the permission of Arrupe[91] and the provincial of Paris,[92] agreed to receive two Cameroonians into his diocese.[93] These were Azombo and Mveng.[94]

Zoa wanted the Jesuits not only to train the local clergy and the chaplaincy, but also to create a theology department in the federal university. In addition to Mveng's tenure in the history department, Azombo also taught linguistics and African religions in the same university. The involvement of both in the university was part of their effort to transform the Church and society and move them towards greater Africanisation.[95] This presence of the Jesuits in a public university fulfilled Zoa's desire to have the Jesuits supporting young professionals (what he called 'apostolat des cadres'). By keeping Mveng, Hebga seemed committed to the Africanisation of the Church in Cameroon and to nation-building.

To evaluate Hebga's tenure as superior is to consider the difficult balance he had to find between different factions of the membership of the Society in Cameroon. Following his death in 2008, religious and political authorities in Cameroon and Africa unanimously praised 'a great man'. For Paul Biya, president of the Republic of Cameroon, a grateful nation mourned the death of the 'Former Regional Superior of the Jesuits of Cameroon, instigator and animator of the Charismatic Renewal and eminent researcher, [who] has marked the hearts and minds of many generations of men and women, in Cameroon and abroad, thanks to his exceptional faith, his humanism, and his erudition'.[96] Hebga's Jesuit colleague, missionary and historian Louis de Vaucelles, described Hebga's 'strong personality, full of character, endowed with a solid humour and a tempered character (sometimes explosive)'.[97] Many other friends, religious leaders, and people

---

[91] A-Fr 410/4: O. de Varine, 'Lettre au P. Hebga, le 3 juin 1973'.
[92] O. de Varine, 'Rapport [au P. G.] après la visite de la Région du Cameroun du 24 mars au 4 avril 1973', dated 18 April 1973. Ten pages.
[93] A-Fr 410/4: Hebga, 'Lettre à Jean Zoa, le 11 Juin 1973'.
[94] O. de Varine, 'Rapport [au P. G.] après la visite de la Région du Cameroun du 24 mars au 4 avril 1973', dated 18 April 1973.
[95] Ibid.
[96] Paul Biya, 'Au R.P. Jean-Roger Ndombi, 18 mars 2008'. B1911/CAB/PR.
[97] Louis de Vaucelles, 'Témoignage lors des obsèques du P. Hebga, Eglise Saint-Ignace, Paris, 14 mars 2008', *Nouvelles PAO* 218 (May 2008).

of every condition expressed their admiration for a man of science, a man of God, and a man who loved and cared for the poor.

It is possible that the conflicts in Yaoundé had a transformative impact on Hebga. Visiting Yaoundé in the context of the deliberations leading to the creation of the vice-province, O. de Varine, provincial of Paris, found 'a man totally different'. O. de Varine, however, attributed this change to a change of character by Hebga:

> I found Father Hebga deeply changed from what I was told of him. It is also the opinion of all the Fathers of Cameroon. The difficulties he met in governance have certainly made him more mature. And it seemed to me that he has become more flexible as a superior [...] It seemed to me very symptomatic that he did not think at all to be the future Provincial. He does not even want it. On the other hand, he would like to invest in the future in an ethnological research group created by Fr de Rosny.[98]

From my research, there is no evidence from internal deliberations, minutes of consultors' meetings, or other minutes of community meetings or *historia domus* that Hebga lacked the discernment, the knowledge, or the skills and competence to be a superior. On the contrary, these sources present him always explaining the perspective of his French and Roman superiors to members of his Region, and always abiding by the constitutions and norms of the Society. He acted decisively when he thought a Jesuit needed to be reprimanded, and with compassion when needed.[99]

In fact, O. de Varine was not the first provincial to express his satisfaction with Hebga's performance as superior. Before him, Lesage had recognised that Arrupe's intended goal in appointing Hebga as regional superior had been achieved. This appointment aimed at helping Hebga understand the weight of the responsibilities which are incumbent on a major superior. He concluded that the goal was clearly achieved.

Moreover, according to Lesage, the Society under Hebga's leadership was strongly founded and rooted in a dynamic local Church.[100] Even the crisis in the Cameroonian broader Church, especially with the political trial of Bishop Ndongmo, did not have a negative impact on the work of the

---

[98] O. de Varine, 'Rapport [au P. G.] après la visite de la Région du Cameroun du 24 mars au 4 avril 1973', dated 18 April 1973.

[99] Hebga pushed Azombo out of the Society, resisted calls to have Mveng leave the Society, and pushed back against Mveng when he did not show respect to Ossama, then his local superior.

[100] Jacques Lesage, 'Rapport [au P. General] après la visite de la Région du Cameroun, 6 au 14 avril 1971, datant du 1er mai 1971'. Seven pages.

Society or the solidarity among its Cameroonian members.[101] Concluding a visit, Lesage wrote:

> I leave [Cameroon] with a positive impression. After two years, Father Hebga deeply cares for the religious life of the Fathers. Even if some Fathers find it difficult to accept community prayer or no longer celebrate the daily Mass. He may be a bit strict with the Fathers, but Hebga also shows flexibilities where it should be. He is sometimes a bit isolated when he makes decisions.[102]

Coming from Lesage, this assessment of Hebga's tenure is likely to be credible. His report was not addressed to Hebga. And his relationship with Hebga had never been warm, as Lesage preferred to deal with Cameroon through Durand-Viel rather than Hebga. During Hebga's term, the communications between him and Paris were not always very good. Acknowledging that situation, Lesage had suggested that Hebga and Vandame – the superior of Chad at that time – try to reconcile. He believed such a *rapprochement* to be particularly necessary because of the advent of the vice-province that was about to be created.[103]

Conclusion

As the Jesuits in Yaoundé, Africans and Europeans alike, deliberated about the creation of the VPAO, they almost unanimously made two important proposals to Paris and Rome. First, it was imperative that the provincial be an African. Likewise, African Jesuits should play a bigger role in decision making. This was the condition to make the Society of Jesus in Africa truly African. Second, the new jurisdiction should include Cameroon, Chad, and Côte d'Ivoire, but also Nigeria and Senegal.

In the context of these deliberations, Fabien Eboussi warned against 'the ideologies of universalism' and 'internationalism'. The only places where these ideas were valued, he argued, were in dominated countries. The only values that were universal were those of powerful nations, including the Church and the Society. Therefore, the creation of a new vice-province could not overlook the fact that, in Africa, 'the Society [was] in a dominant-dominated global relationship'.[104]

---

[101] Ibid.
[102] Ibid.
[103] Lesage, 'Lettre à Hebga, le 16 janvier 1972'.
[104] A-Fr 401/3: 'Réunion des Pères de la Région sur le projet de vice-Province'.

Nobody, at the time, seemed to pay attention to Eboussi's criticism of the Jesuit missionary model in Africa. It was only once the vice-province was created that Eboussi expressed this opinion in a journal article, and the alarm was set off.[105] Dissent by Cameroonians had become public. At stake was the very nature of Roman Catholicism in Africa and globally after the Second Vatican Council and the 31st GC that elected Pedro Arrupe as superior general of the Jesuits.

---

[105] The next section on the reception of the creation of the vice-province will address Eboussi's interpretation of the post-missionary era in a more comprehensive way.

CHAPTER 9

Era of Dissent: Cameroonian Jesuits and Global Catholicism, 1974–78

The rebirth of missionary Christianity addressed in the previous chapters existed even in a place like Cameroon, when Cameroonians were leaders of Africanisation in the entire continent, but were still ruled or controlled by White missionaries. These Cameroonians fought to have churches adapted to their specific context and needs. Ossama's report of 1968 on the creation of the Cameroon Jesuit Region made it an 'absolute necessity' that the major superior of the region be African.[1] So, when the VPAO was created in 1973, with a map that reconstructed colonial boundaries and a White man as superior, African Jesuits dissented.

The case of Emmanuel Teguem discusses this dissent and broadens the debate beyond governance to the more profound roots of racial and class inequalities. These challenges are significant, and the effectiveness of Christianity transforming Africa is contingent on the ability to tackle them. African dissent, this chapter argues, cannot be comprehended fully unless one situates Africa and its people in the global divide that characterised the world and the Church in the 1970s, as well as the racial and social inequalities that prevailed.

In a world broken by injustice and inequalities, African Jesuits believed that to make the Church truly African meant something beyond cultural or liturgical adaptation. Africanising the Church also meant liberating Africans from the yoke of injustice, feeding the hungry, healing the sick, and caring for the poor. Christianity, to be credible in Africa, had to transform African lives and societies.

The focus on social transformation, however, exposed a divide among the Jesuits, and within Christianity globally. Some Jesuits believed that priestly ministries excluded social work and social activism. These Jesuits

---

[1] Nicolas Ossama, 'Rapport de la Commission sur la régionalisation du Cameroun, le 24 février 1968'.

were joined by critiques of development Christianity. In a few cases, these critiques equated the social gospel of the 1970s with Marxism. Others simply accused the Catholic Church of becoming a global non-governmental organisation (NGO) at the expense of true evangelism. For the first African Jesuits and for the 31st and 32nd GC of their order, social work was essential to the Jesuit mission and identity. Evangelism was primarily witnessing the gospel, which included social transformation and the possibility of giving one's life for the sake of justice.

The Farewell of Emmanuel Teguem: A Working-Class Jesuit Brother

Emmanuel Teguem was a Jesuit Brother who left the Society in 1969. He was 'working class', a young Cameroonian who worked with his hands and repaired bicycles before he joined the Jesuits on 12 October 1964. Teguem was in the Jesuit juniorate of Djuma (in the present-day Democratic Republic of Congo [DRC]). He might even have received a blessing directly from Arrupe during a visit after his election as superior general in 1965. Only five years after he joined, he was asked to leave the Society of Jesus. In two correspondences with Arrupe in 1969, Teguem described the reasons why he was leaving and what his new calling would be.

Writing first on 12 September 1969, Teguem introduced himself to Arrupe. He highlighted his strong working-class background. He detailed the life he had spent in the Jesuit juniorate of Djuma, where most of the first African Jesuits, including Engelbert Mveng, Boka di Mpasi of the Democratic Republic of Congo, and Chrisologue Mahame of Rwanda, did their novitiate. This was, for Teguem, a time of serious Jesuit training for which he was grateful. It was a time of suffering too. Now that he was back in Cameroon, he believed the Lord was calling him for another mission: to liberate African people.

In vowing to liberate his people, Teguem decried the absence of 'a Christian church adapted' to the realities of the African people and their culture. His study of the history of Western churches taught him that Christianity, while spiritual in essence, also worked for the development and transformation of societies. Why not, then, do the same in Africa, he asked? The Lord, the Brother said, convinced him that it was possible to bring water to the most remote villages and grow crops and cattle; that it was possible to build roads where the state was failing; and that it was possible to imagine a community life in which true love and fellowship would reign between parents and their children. This was not simply a call for Teguem alone; the Society of Jesus worldwide was to commit herself too:

I tell you this, Father General, because I am certain that the Lord, in calling me to undertake this long journey with my poor brothers, is also calling you. I will need you, need your moral and material support, and your prayers. Because feeding men is what this is all about, quenching their thirst, clothing them, curing them from diseases, bringing about a kingdom of justice and love, and it is up to you and I to do it with our prayers and material goods.[2]

In a second letter of 20 September 1969, Teguem recognised that the second half of the century had brought great changes in the self-consciousness of Africans. Suddenly, African Christians were awakening. They realised they were dominated and still colonised, 'étouffés' (muzzled). As Black people everywhere became aware of their potential, they wanted Africa to be transformed. Unfortunately, this change was also meeting resistance from Western missionaries, who were making it impossible for Africans to shine. They were framing the Africans' quest for authenticity as an 'anti-White men' religion. Any of the actions Africans took were scrutinised and contested.[3]

The issue of the so-called 'anti-White men' religion, according to Teguem, was simply a question of adaptation and teaching methods, not of religion as such. The real wish of Africans was to 'comprehend [comprendre] Christianity' for themselves. And how would anyone succeed in such an enterprise if there was no basic recognition of 'our africanity', if the way Africans think and 'comprehend' reality was not recognised? The African Christian elite did not need an 'anti-White men' religion; Africans wanted an 'African church', which White missionaries failed to build.[4]

For Teguem, those who accused African priests of kicking out White missionaries were simply acting out of pure jealousy. White missionaries coming to Africa saw Africans primarily as 'monkeys'. They were therefore shocked, horrified, when they saw Africans think by themselves, and when they saw them become leaders in charge of their own destiny. There were capable Africans who could be in charge of their own churches and help the Church grow. Those who accused these Africans of trying to kick out White missionaries were simply incapable individuals, jealous cowards who were weary of the rise of proud Africans.

[2] AFSI-CB 231: Emmanuel Teguem, 'Lettre au P. Général, 12 Sept. 1969'.
[3] AFSI-CB 231: Emmanuel Teguem, 'Lettre au P. Général, 20 Sept. 1969'.
[4] Ibid.

In Congo (Zaïre) like in Cameroon, Teguem warned, the spirit of Saint Ignatius was not being followed. Racism was a crude reality. In the professional school of Kikwit, a few days after the General's visit there,

> I saw white Jesuits asking Congolese Brothers to leave the dining room so that some white women and their kids can eat. The Brothers were allowed to come later and contend themselves with the leftovers. I witness the same spirit here in Cameroon. I made myself clear to the missionaries that I would not tolerate subversion and discrimination among us.[5]

If Teguem was now asking to leave the Society, or if he was being dismissed, it was because he printed some documents he was not supposed to. He was leaving without any bitterness. What he would not tolerate, however, was having Cameroonians divided among themselves. Moreover, God had prepared him, 'a proud African, Cameroonian, Bamiléké', to reform religious life. But God wanted him to enter the Society of Jesus first, to learn from her. This goal was achieved because God had helped him further realise that the same spirit that inspired and guided Saint Ignatius to create the Society could also inspire and guide a Black Cameroonian to reform all religious life and transform society. Teguem ended his letter asking the General and 'all religious, especially those in the Society', to pray for him. The love of God, he concluded, made him 'crazy' the day he joined the Society, and he was leaving the Society with the same love.[6]

Following his election as superior general in 1966, Arrupe made several visits to Africa. In speeches and meetings, he shared Pope Paul VI's belief that Africans should become their own missionaries.[7] Yet, as he implemented his vision, it became clear to some African Jesuits that he had kept Jesuit provinces within colonial boundaries. By also appointing missionaries as provincials, Arrupe's bold and clear vision[8] seemed to them like pouring 'new wine into old wineskins'.[9] The early African reaction to the implementation of Arrupe's vision was led by a Jesuit

---

[5] Ibid.
[6] Ibid.
[7] Pope Paul VI, 'Africae Terrarum', *AAS* 69 (Rome: 29 October 1967): 1073–102.
[8] Festo Mkenda, 'Pedro Arrupe and Africa: Clear Visions and Bold Steps in a Moment of Unsettling Transitions', *Archivum Historicum Societatis Iesu* 88, fasc. 176 (II 2019): 385–416.
[9] Jean Luc Enyegue, 'New Wine into Old Wineskins? African Reactions to Arrupe's Governing Vision (1965–1978)', *Archivum Historicum Societatis Iesu* 88, fasc. 176 (II 2019): 385–420.

intellectual elite, namely Eboussi, Hebga, and Mveng. Teguem shows that recent discussion of African reactions to Arrupe's vision was broader among Africans in the 1970s than initially thought. It was not limited to a handful of power-hungry intellectuals in the Cameroonian Jesuit elite. It was a broader African response to the challenges presented to them by the new world, which both the Second Vatican Council and the 31st GC of the Jesuits had not comprehensively addressed.

For these Cameroonian Jesuits, Africa had become independent, yet it was also becoming poorer, while new forms of White domination, neocolonialism, and an emboldened missionary Christianity were on the rise. Teguem was speaking a year after the creation of the Jesuit Region of Cameroon. He could speak to the struggle its Cameroonian major superior, Hebga, faced as he found himself under European and African pressure.

Teguem's voice is unique because, unlike Eboussi, Ossama, Hebga, and Mveng, who were university professors and priests, he was a working-class Jesuit and a Brother. That the Brothers were not eating with the Fathers, but on a second table, or even a third, in case of an unexpected visit by a European family, was, by itself, sufficiently indicative of the asymmetrical relationships that existed among the Jesuits themselves. Teguem drew attention to the issue of poverty and the need for the Society to address it. If Christianity had worked in the past for the development and transformation of countries, it ought to do the same in Africa. Christianity had to help transform African societies if it was to remain relevant.

Poverty vs Stipends: Priestly Ministries and the Call for Development Christianity

The 31st GC of the Jesuits that elected Arrupe in 1965–66 had addressed the question of poverty. However, it did so primarily as a spiritual issue. Delegates to this Congregation asked whether or not fully professed Jesuits should observe the purity of their religious vows to make poverty stricter and abrogate an 1824 dispensation that allowed Jesuits to receive stipends for their work.[10] In discussions about religious life and the Jesuit apostolates, some delegates, backed by postulates from provinces across the globe, pushed the Society to focus strictly on its 'priestly' ministries. Those included 'preaching the word of God and administering the

---

[10] John W. Padberg, *Together as a Companionship. A History of the Thirty-First, Thirty-Second, and Thirty-Third General Congregations of the Society of Jesus* (Saint Louis, MO: The Institute of Jesuit Sources, 1994), 15.

sacraments'.[11] The Society, they believed, should stop its involvements in temporal matters belonging to the realm of lay persons rather than priests. In response, the Congregation reaffirmed that 'works such as scholarly research, education, social ministries' were legitimate Jesuit ministries for the care of the souls.[12] The Congregation also went further, recognising art, poetry, music, theatre, and architecture as pathways to the human heart in which Jesuits should achieve greatness.[13]

As discussed in this Congregation, the issues of poverty and the nature of priestly ministries were, though indirectly, at the core of the divide about the very nature of the Society of Jesus after Vatican II and the 31st GC. The poorest of all continents, Africa could not escape the ramifications of this divide between rich and poor. The life of Teguem also suggests the existence of another gap between a Western working-class Christianity and an African working-class Christianity, which Teguem symbolised. The protest or the dissent of African Jesuits is to be situated in the context of this global debate that was taking place in the aula of the 31st GC.[14]

For instance, responding to an unidentified delegate who argued that the 1824 dispensation be abrogated, another delegate told him to then 'stop relying on the help they received from other provinces, stop asking their scholastics be educated gratis in other provinces, and stop suggesting that a central common fund should be set up, because the money needed would come from forbidden fruit, that is, the revenues of the work done by members of other provinces'.[15] The plural 'they' portrayed a competing reality between one group of Jesuits that was wealthy and pragmatic and another that, though poor, seemed to demand 'purity' in religious observance.

Behind the discussion on poverty and stipends, there seemed to be an issue of inequality and dependency within the Jesuit order itself. The gap between the rich and the poor seen on the global stage was shaking the foundations of the Society in its constitutions that defined the gratuity of ministries. This gap seemed to be hurting the unity among the membership of the order. African Jesuits might work as hard as Jesuits in Europe or the United States, but the stipends they received from their work were not enough to even train younger Jesuits or educate or feed their people.

---

[11] Ibid., 17.
[12] Ibid.
[13] Ibid., 20.
[14] Philip Kiley and John W. Padberg, *Jesuit Life & Mission Today: The Decrees of the 31st–35th General Congregations of the Society of Jesus*, vol. 1 (Saint Louis, MO: Institute of Jesuit Sources, 2009).
[15] Ibid., 15.

It was also a time when, across Africa, voices from Protestant Churches were influencing Catholic discourse on dependency. Those voices pushed for a moratorium on Western missionaries in order to achieve self-sustenance among African Churches.[16] Although the Vatican had condemned the three-self theory, promoted by Henry Venn and Rufus Anderson,[17] as contrary to Catholic doctrine,[18] African Jesuits like Mveng, Eboussi, and Teguem understood that doing God's work in a poor continent had a transformative and developing component. It meant being able to feed the hungry, heal the sick, grow crops, and even build bridges where there were none.

Proponents of 'strictly priestly' ministries in the Congregation might not have seen such apostolates as being proper to the Jesuits. Yet, these African Jesuits had, for their defence, the gospel and the history of Roman Catholicism. Not surprisingly, Teguem's call for development Christianity could be heard in Mveng as well as in Eboussi. It was an African calling amid growing pessimism and rising neocolonialism.

Mveng's Anthropological Pauperisation and Development Christianity

Following Eboussi's 'Dé-mission' (1974) and Hebga's *Émancipation des églises sous-tutelles* (1976), Mveng published 'De la sous-mission à la succession' (1978). The article was, in fact, a manifesto against the poverty of African churches. Europeans framed African churches as 'Young churches, minor churches, trusteed churches, even underdeveloped churches.'[19]

[16] Robert Reese, 'John Gatu and the Moratorium on Missionaries', *Missiology: An International Review* 42, no. 3 (2014): 245–56; John G. Gatu, *Joyfully Christian and Truly African* (Nairobi: Acton Publishers, 2006); John G. Gatu, *Fan into Flame. Rev. Dr John G. Gatu, an Autobiography* (Nairobi: Moran Publishers, 2016); Fabien Eboussi Boulaga, 'La dé-mission', *Spiritus* 56 (May–August 1974): 276–87.

[17] Max Warren, ed., *To Apply the Gospel: Selections from the Writings of Henry Venn* (Grand Rapids, MI: Eerdmans, 1971); J. F. A. Ajayi, 'Henry Venn and the Policy of Development', *Journal of the Historical Society of Nigeria* 1, no. 4 (December 1959): 331–42; Wilbert R. Shenk, 'The Missionary and Politics: Henry Venn's Guidelines', *Journal of Church and State* 24, no. 3 (1982): 525–34; Gerald H. Anderson, 'A Moratorium on Missionaries?' *Christian Century* 91, no. 2 (1974): 43–45.

[18] Pope Pius XII, 'Encyclical Letter "Ad apostolorum principis"', *AAS* 50 (1958): 601–14.

[19] Engelbert Mveng, 'De la sous-mission à la succession', in *Civilisation Noire et Eglise Catholique* (Paris: Présence Africaine, 1978), 267–76 – here, p. 267.

Mveng was so concerned with poverty that he elaborated a theology of liberation based on the concept of anthropological poverty. The essential condition of the African person, he argued, was anthropological poverty. This poverty was cultivated by centuries of slavery, colonialism, and racial opprobrium. Accidental in its causes, poverty had become the very definition of the African person. It was ontological.[20]

Before there was even a debate about poetry and art in the 31st GC, Mveng had already created, and published on, religious art and religious poetry as effective pathways for an authentic African Christianity.[21] For Mveng, there was a direct connection between art and poverty. He focused on artistic work and poetry as part of his effort to inculturate Christianity in Africa. Because African traditional religions (ATR) were pragmatic and both spiritual and materialistic in nature, symbolism and rhythm were inseparable in the inculturation of the Christian message in Africa. As explained by Rosalind I. J. Hackett, Mveng's work 'was concerned not just to promote African art and its expression of African thought and identity, but also to see how African theology and symbolism might become a basis for liturgy of the (Roman Catholic) church'.[22]

Mveng's artistic productions were not simply about fostering a new theology and liturgy with African symbols. He meant to address the materiality of African religiosity and to refocus on Christianity as an incarnate and transformative religion.[23] Religious art portrays lived religion, embodied in scarifications, hairstyles, or body adornment. Some of the African embodied arts are initiation marks, which are also symbols of power relations in society. For example, scarifications among the Sara

---

[20] Engelbert Mveng, *Théologie, libération et cultures africaines: Dialogue sur l'anthropologie négro-africaine* (Yaoundé and Paris: Clé, 1996); Thomas Banchoff and José Casanova, 'Introduction: The Jesuits and Globalization', in *The Jesuits and Globalization. Historical Legacies and Contemporary Challenges* (Washington, DC: Georgetown University Press, 2016), 1–26 – here, p. 18.

[21] Engelbert Mveng, *L'art d'Afrique Noire: Liturgie cosmique et langage religieux* (Tours: Mame, 1964); Engelbert Mveng, *Art nègre art chrétien?* (Rome: Les amis italiens de Présence Africaine, 1969); Rosalind I. J. Hackett, 'Art and Religion in Africa: Some Observations and Reflections', *Journal of Religion in Africa* 24 (November 1994): 294–308 – here, pp. 303–04.

[22] Hackett, 'Art and Religion in Africa', 303–04.

[23] Engelbert Mveng, 'A la recherche d'un nouveau dialogue entre le Christianisme, le génie culturel et les religions africaines actuelles', *Présence Africaine* 96 (1975): 443–66.

people of Chad are connected to social status. Royal thrones in western Cameroon are special, and transferred from generation to generation. So are masks.

For Mveng, therefore, African art, even religious art, was always political. This art was to contribute to the transformation of human beings and their social environment. Traditionally, art protected from the evil spirits that threatened stability and peace in society. The *njoo* and similar characters among the Bamiléké protected the hunter who gave food to the kingdom, and the baby who was its future.[24] It gave identity to individuals and marked particular spaces as sacred. Having a specific tattoo would say whether you were good or bad: prisoners were tattooed, as were the most beautiful women in central Cameroon.

Mveng followed up this 'poetry' by arguing in favour of transforming religion. Like Teguem, he believed that the effectiveness of a religious order like the Jesuits in Africa would be measured not only on its ability to address the spiritual needs of the people, but also, and maybe more importantly, on its commitment to transform societies and give education, water, food, clothes, and medicine to the needy. As he was leaving the Jesuits, Teguem reminded Arrupe that joining the Society deprived him from earning an income and producing riches. He was, in fact, challenging a vow of poverty that did not train African Jesuits to be productive for both their self-sustenance and their mission among their people, when these people were living in extreme poverty and misery.

Pushing a similar argument even further, Mveng believed that systemic racism that encouraged slavery and remained silent in the face of Apartheid or racial segregation could not be addressed with preaching alone. It had created a situation of systemic anthropological pauperisation which, if left unchecked, could lead to the human annihilation of Africans. Because this level of poverty was dehumanising, it was a Christian duty to address it at its roots and challenge the socioeconomic system enabling it.

According to Mveng, the importance of 'succession' in the aforementioned article could not be reduced to the religious realm. In the past, Francis of Assisi, Ignatius of Loyola, and the Benedictine reform had all helped to transform Western societies.[25] Likewise, he argued, Africans' succession to missionary religion should move the Church on three fronts: educational and economic reforms that would lift up the African societies;

---

[24] Ronald K. Engard, 'Myth and Political Economy in Bafut (Cameroon): The Structural History of an African Kingdom', *Paideuma* 34 (1988): 49–89 – here, p. 60.

[25] Mveng, 'De la sous-mission à la succession', 272.

the reform of religious life itself, especially its approach to religious vows; and an institutional reform that would make the Church more efficient in its organisation and apostolic planning.[26] In fact, Mveng called for the organisation of an African council that would solve African problems.[27]

Eboussi shared the same vision when, in his 'Dé-mission', he argued that African should reach economic independence, and that not doing so would leave real power and authority in the hands of those with money.[28] The perspective of these Cameroonian Jesuits could lead people to ask legitimate questions about the 'Jesuitness' of this 'development Christianity'. The secularising trend attached to it was what the Jesuits feared in Chad, and what those Jesuits in the 31st GC who wanted the Society focused on purely 'priestly' ministries wanted to avoid. Was this shift towards development Christianity not the root of all that had gone wrong with Roman Catholicism in the second half of the century? Had development Christianity not missed the point of an 'enchanted African imagination'?

Race and the Challenge of Development Christianity

It is possible to believe that the reaction of these Africans was isolated, reduced to a small elite of intellectuals more interested in power than in the actual work of evangelism. For Paul Gifford, the very fact that the Vatican paid little attention to Hebga's work to address an African 'enchanted imagination' was due to his intellectual credentials and fame.[29] Unlike Emmanuel Milingo of Zambia, Gifford argues, Hebga was not an ecclesiastic.[30] He was not, therefore, the centre of the Vatican's attention.

Hebga, the previous chapter showed, was a Jesuit major superior in Cameroon and known as such nationally and internationally. Through his ministry, he actually healed the sick and expelled demons through exorcism. The ordinary Cameroonian remembers him more as an exorcist than anything else. And if his work was not particularly targeted by the Vatican, as Gifford suggests, Ludovic Lado believes that it was because Hebga also followed 'authorizing processes' within Roman Catholicism.[31] Gifford's

---

[26] Ibid.
[27] Engelbert Mveng, 'Le Synode Africain, prolégomènes pour un Concile Africain?' *Concilium* 239 (1992): 149–69.
[28] Eboussi Boulaga, 'La dé-mission', 283.
[29] Paul Gifford, *Christianity, Development and Modernity in Africa* (Oxford: Oxford University Press, 2016), 124.
[30] Ibid., 107.
[31] Ludovic Lado, *Catholic Pentecostalism and the Paradoxes of Africanization*

interpretation of Hebga serves the purpose of his larger argument: that Roman Catholicism has become more of a global NGO than a movement committed to grassroots evangelism.

The question of development Christianity vs evangelism could well cover broader discussions among Christian denominations, mainline churches, Evangelicals or Pentecostals. However, as already evidenced in the Jesuit 31st GC, this issue, raised by Teguem, was being contemporaneously debated within global Catholicism and the Jesuit organisation itself. Some Jesuits tried to shift the work of the Jesuits away from this-worldly-oriented apostolates. Instead, they urged the Society to focus more on spiritual ministries, or on evangelism. For other Catholics and Jesuits, the question was rather whether the Church could turn its back on the cries of the poor and the oppressed and still remain faithful to itself.

By the time the Congregation concluded in 1966, Arrupe seemed to have made up his mind. A series of letters describe the new direction that he wanted the Jesuits to follow. Writing to the US Jesuits in 1967, he acknowledged that while race and poverty were not necessarily two aspects of the same problem in every case, it was an urgent matter for the Jesuits in the United States to 'eradicate racial injustice and grinding poverty'. Further, he confessed the reality of racism within the Jesuit order itself:

> It is chastening to recall that, before the Civil War, some American Jesuit houses owned Negro slaves. It is humbling to remember that, until recently, a number of Jesuit institutions did not admit qualified Negroes, even in areas where civil restrictions against integrated schools did not prevail, and this even in the case of Catholic Negroes. Even up to the present, some Jesuit institutions have effected what seems to be little more than token integration of the Negro.[32]

It has been said that, in the past, missionary Christianity often shared scientific racism.[33] Dana L. Robert has argued that the repudiation of paternalism was a precondition for the expansion of 'indigenous' initiatives.[34]

(Leiden: Brill, 2009), 197. Lado seems to be Gifford's main source on Hebga.

[32] Pedro Arrupe, 'Interracial Apostolate', in *Justice with Faith Today: Selected Letters and Addresses*, ed. Jerome Aixala (Saint Louis, MO: The Institute of Jesuit Sources, 1980), 18.

[33] Ogbu Kalu, *African Christianity: An African Story* (Trenton, NJ: Africa World Press, 2007), 14.

[34] Dana L. Robert, 'Shifting Southward: Global Christianity Since 1945', *International Bulletin of Missionary Research* 24, no. 2 (April 2000): 53.

And Joseph C. McKenna linked African resentment against racism and colonial rule to the European political left.[35]

A survey among the thirteen religious congregations operating in Abidjan in 1973 revealed that division among races was a major handicap for the Africanisation of the Church.[36] As the demographics of global Christianity moves southwards, this debate on race and social inequality is likely to continue.[37] Arrupe's letter was therefore highly significant. It was the most comprehensive document ever written by a Jesuit superior general on race, a topic which, with some very rare exceptions, had remained in the margins of Jesuit historiography until the 1930s. This was the decade when the Jesuits in the United States condemned racial discrimination and saw it as a major impediment for the Catholicisation of Black people.[38]

To argue that a Jesuit superior general was late in condemning racism might seem paradoxical, given the prominent role played by the American Jesuit John LaFarge in the crafting of Pope Pius XI's condemnation of Communism, as recently elaborated by Charles R. Gallagher,[39] and of Nazism.[40] Stephen J. Ochs also shows that LaFarge was equally decisive in shaping the policy of the US Conference of Catholic Bishops against racial discrimination.[41] Across the Atlantic, during the same decade, Belgian missiologist and Jesuit Pierre Charles worked to disentangle mission from both colonialism and racism.[42]

Arrupe's condemnation, however, had the weight of his office, and the force to direct American Jesuits towards a broader inclusive agenda. Still, his address to the American Jesuits focused on an issue which African

---

[35] Joseph C. McKenna, *Finding a Social Voice. The Church and Marxism in Africa* (New York: Fordham University Press, 1997), 40.

[36] CETA, 'Au sein des communautés non-catholiques: Conscientisation et Africanisation', *Telema* 1, no. 75 (April 1975), 81.

[37] Philip Jenkins, *The Next Christendom: The Coming of Global Christianity* (Oxford: Oxford University Press, 2002), 14.

[38] Editorial, 'Our Indians and Negroes', *Jesuit Missions* 11, no. 4 (April 1937): 87.

[39] Charles R. Gallagher, 'Decentering American Jesuit Anti-Communism: John LaFarge's United Front Strategy, 1934–39', *Journal of Jesuit Studies* 5 (2018): 97–121.

[40] Peter Eisner, *The Pope's Last Crusade: How an American Jesuit Helped Pope Pius XI's Campaign to Stop Hitler* (New York: William Morrow, 2013).

[41] Stephen J. Ochs, *Desegregating the Altar: The Josephites and the Struggle for Black Priests, 1871–1960* (Baton Rouge, LA: Louisiana State University Press, 1990), 429.

[42] Pierre Charles, *Racisme et catholicisme* (Tournai: Casterman, 1939).

Americans and African Jesuits shared as victims. By condemning the so-called 'anti-White men' religion, Teguem was addressing a difficult issue. The tension beneath the concept of 'anti-White men' religion in the 1970s focused on race, not religion as such. Arrupe understood this in his address to the Jesuits in the United States in 1967.[43] Within the broader context, however, Arrupe's intervention seemed isolated when compared to issues that dominated Roman Catholicism in Europe during the same period. Catholics in Europe and in the United States were concerned about birth control and the ideal family size in 1968.[44] Africans and Black people, in contrast, were paying closer attention to the assassination of a Black Protestant pastor with whose voice they could identify: Martin Luther King Jr.

Those Jesuits working in Africa were surprised that the ongoing Apartheid in South Africa was met with a certain amount of indifference from Western Catholics. It seemed more likely to them that a working-class African Catholic like Teguem could find a friend and a brother in a Black Protestant pastor in America than in an American working-class Catholic whose vote was very unpredictable – and indeed remains so, even in the twenty-first century – regarding Black people and minorities.

At the time Teguem was writing to Arrupe, African dissent had not reached the level of a 'missionary go home movement'.[45] The moratorium was ongoing among Protestants, and Eboussi's 'Dé-mission' came five years later. However, the accusation of 'anti-White men' religion, which Teguem denounced, was used against Africans who dared to challenge the predominance of White power in African political and religious affairs.

In 1965, five years after Cameroon's independence, Ossama denounced the willing blindness of Western and missionary Christianity in a conference at LaLouvesc, France. His paper drew the ire of his French audience, and he was branded 'anti-Catholic' and 'anti-Latin'.[46] Christian racism was also a major concern for Eboussi, which he addressed in his crusade against colonialism. He called the form of Christianity that allied itself with colonialism and the forces of oppression 'bourgeois Christianity' that was

---

[43] Arrupe, 'Interracial Apostolate'.

[44] Raymond H. Potvin and Thomas K. Burch, 'Fertility, Ideal Family-Size and Religious Orientation among U.S. Catholics', *Sociological Analysis* 29, no. 1 (1968): 28–34.

[45] Marcel Boivin, 'Missionaries Go Home?' *New Blackfriars* 53, no. 630 (November 1972): 494–502.

[46] A-Pa 162: Nicolas Ossama, '50 ans de l'Eglise au Cameroun. Session Missionnaire' (La Louvesc, 6–10 September 1965).

violent in nature, with 'something Luciferian about it'.[47] Coincidently, the Christian right was supporting oppressive regimes in Latin America. Some of those regimes were responsible for the murder of ecclesiastics who dared to defend the poor, including Oscar Romero, or Jesuits such as Rutilio Grande and Ignacio Ellacuría. These martyred ecclesiastics were called communists and Marxists.

Eboussi also worried that the history of the Society of Jesus in Africa revealed a blind spot on Black people in its apparent collusion with neocolonialism. Discussing the relationship between Africans and missionaries in 1973, Eboussi insisted that the only countries where Jesuit 'internationalism' and universal principles applied were in 'dominated countries'. The Society, he continued, should be aware that she was immersed in a global network that sustained the dialectic of 'dominant-dominé'.[48] It was imperative, he warned, for the Society to remain mindful of that historical fact. Eboussi said these words, the report concluded, 'with a calm and friendly voice, with no resentment'.[49]

Mveng, in contrast, was less composed while expressing his opinions. He was almost dismissed from the Society because of his anger, which, according to the missionaries, was caused by the economic situation of postcolonial Africa. Mveng, they said, believed neocolonialism was on the rise; and newly appointed African bishops were too dependent on White missionaries.[50] They insisted that he blamed the missionaries for all of Africa's problems.[51] Jean-Yves Calvez, who had become Arrupe's assistant for Western Europe, defended Mveng, arguing that he was better able to understand the economic situation of his continent than the Western missionaries.[52] Yet, Mveng's bad reputation followed him until he was murdered in 1995.

The conflict with Mveng, the missionaries admitted, was caused by Mveng's bad character and racial biases. Having 'bad character' was quasi-synonymous with what Teguem called 'crazy' in his letter to Arrupe.

---

[47] Cf. Fabien Eboussi Boulaga, *Christianity Without Fetishes. An African Critique and Recapture of Christianity*, trans. Robert R. Barr (Maryknoll, NY: Orbis Books, 1984), 30–32.

[48] O. de Varine, 'Rapport [au P. G.] après la visite de la Région du Cameroun du 24 mars au 4 avril 1973', dated 18 April 1973. Ten pages.

[49] Ibid.

[50] A-Pa. 162: Jacques Lesage, 'Rapport global sur la Régionalisation en cours au Cameroun, Paris, May 7, 1968'.

[51] Ibid.

[52] Ibid.

Figure 15 Charles Vandame celebrating mass in the Novitiate, Bafoussam in 2018 (Archives JHIA, Nairobi).

But, this tension was also reflective of the ideological struggles between conservative and progressive Jesuits and the orientation the order was supposed to take after the Second Vatican Council. Rather than focusing on the anger of individual Jesuits, which might lead to their dismissal, the issue, as framed by Arrupe himself, was about how 'angry' the Jesuits could effectively be in the face of perceived injustices and crushing suffering, and how much they could do about it.

Jesuits' Preferred Option for the Poor

The majority of the poor in the world at the time, as now, were non-White. After his interracial apostolate letter in 1967, Arrupe sent several letters calling for healing of the world from the violence that resulted from social injustice. In 1968, he wrote from Río, calling for radical change among the Jesuits. He urged them to commit the totality of their apostolic work to addressing the social injustice and violence that were dislocating Latin American societies.[53] That same year, he was in Medellín, encouraging the Jesuits to fully embrace the social apostolate.[54] Out of this new ori-

---

[53] Gianni La Bella, *Los Jesuitas. Del Vaticano II al Papa Francisco* (Bilbao: Mensajero, 2019), 100–01.
[54] Ibid., 102.

entation, new grassroots theologies emerged across the globe, including, in the Philippines, 'the Theology of the Community, the Worshipping Community, and the Community of Service'.[55]

In 1971, another letter from the General to the whole Society decried the 'slow, inconsistent, and organic reaction' Arrupe observed among the Jesuits in enacting change. Among the many causes of this 'lack of reaction' were 'fixed habits, attitudes and mentalities' as well as 'rigidity in works and structures'.[56] Change was needed among individuals, but also at a systemic level. That same year, in his speech during the Ordinary Synod of Bishops in Rome he argued that for the Church to be credible in this world, its members and leaders ought to be witnesses of justice.[57]

These debates were taking place in the period between 1969 and 1974 – that is, in the context leading up to the 32nd GC of the Jesuits (1974). The issue of social poverty, as already discussed, was not dealt with in depth by the 31st GC (1965–66). This congregation was the first ever attended by an African-born Jesuit: Daniel Pasu Pasu, with only twelve years as a Jesuit and one with less Jesuit experience, was among the delegates. By the time the 32nd GC convened in 1974, the African delegation was more diverse, with Hebga himself among the delegates. Arrupe had written his letter from Río (1967), and the Medellín Conference (1968) had also taken place with Arrupe's active participation.[58] For him and the Latin American Jesuits at least, the poor had become central to their apostolic concerns.

A major resolution taken by the 32nd GC was the preferential option for the poor. As he led the whole Society to embrace this apostolic orientation, Arrupe warned them about the dangers to come, 'despite our prudence and fidelity to our priesthood and religious charism [...] we would find friends or Jesuit relatives who would accuse us of Marxism or subversion, and will withdraw their friendship from us, consequently, their previous trust and financial support'.[59] He asked the congregation if it was ready 'to

---

[55] Pedro Arrupe, 'Dialogue with Filipino Coworkers', in *Justice with Faith Today: Selected Letters and Addresses*, ed. Jerome Aixala (Saint Louis, MO: The Institute of Jesuit Sources, 1980), 69–76.

[56] Pedro Arrupe, 'The Social Commitment of the Society of Jesus (1971)' in *Justice with Faith Today: Selected Letters and Addresses*, 29–59.

[57] Pedro Arrupe, 'Witnessing to Justice in the World (1972)', in *Justice with Faith Today: Selected Letters and Addresses*, 79–120.

[58] Cf. La Bella, *Los Jesuitas. Del Vaticano II al Papa Francisco*, 100–03.

[59] Padberg, *Together as a Companionship. A History of the Thirty-First, Thirty-Second, and Thirty-Third General Congregations of the Society of Jesus*, 50.

enter on the sterner way of the cross, that which will bring us misunderstanding from civil and ecclesiastical authorities and our best friends'.[60]

As the 32nd GC gathered in Rome in 1974, Arrupe's commitment to social justice had become even more decisive. Discussing the mission of the Society in the modern world, Decree Four of the Congregation acknowledged an 'increasingly interdependent world divided by injustice: injustice not only personal but institutionalised: built into economic, social, and political structures that dominate the life of nations and the international community'.[61] This injustice had a human face. For 'there are millions of men and women in our world, specific people with names and faces, who are suffering from poverty and hunger, from the unjust distribution of wealth and resources and from the consequences of racial, social, and political discrimination'.[62]

This institutionalised injustice 'leads to the enslavement not only of the oppressed, but of the oppressor as well – and to death'.[63] It did not take long. In March 1977, Rutilio Grande was assassinated in El Salvador. He was the fifth Jesuit murdered around the world in less than a year. Writing to the whole Society about 'Our Martyrs', Arrupe reconciled their work in defence of the poor and their evangelism:

> The five were men of average human gifts, leading obscure lives, more or less unrecognized, dwelling in small villages and totally dedicated to the daily service of the poor and suffering. These were sons of the Society who never took part in broad national controversies and who never made headlines in the news media. Their style of life was simple, austere, evangelical: it was a life that used them up slowly, day-by-day, in the service of 'the little ones'.[64]

Martyrdom meant witness. And witness meant living the gospel with one's own life. It was true evangelism, lived evangelism. In a world shattered by division and injustice, there seemed, for Arrupe, to be no greater love than giving one's life for the people one loves (John 15:13). Arrupe believed that 'If we follow Christ, persecution will come, as we have discovered

---

[60] Ibid.
[61] John W. Padberg, ed., *Documents of the Thirty First and Thirty Second General Congregations of the Society of Jesus* (Saint Louis, MO: The Institute of Jesuit Sources, 1977), 413.
[62] Ibid., 417.
[63] Ibid., 422.
[64] Pedro Arrupe, 'Our Recent Martyrs (1977)', in *Justice with Faith Today: Selected Letters and Addresses*, 205.

through experience in so many countries when we try to serve faith and promote justice'.[65] Therefore,

> To be able to carry out this vocation of ours, the Society today must count on men and on communities imbued with the 'mind of Christ', who serve Christ without limit or reservation, who joyfully live lives of evangelical simplicity and continuing self-sacrifice, thus offering to modern man an ideal for living and to the generous youth of our day a model and way of life.[66]

The adoption of the decree was difficult in the aula of the Congregation. Different tendencies struggled to reconcile their positions. Arrupe, at the conclusion of the Congregation, anticipated the even bigger struggle to come. The justice of the Gospel, he warned, can only be preached 'through and from the cross'. To work for justice will bring bitter consequences and pain, which will come sometimes from ecclesiastical authorities and even our best friends.[67]

Alongside the debate on faith and justice, the Congregation also adopted the inculturation of the Gospel as a priority, especially for the churches in Africa, Asia, and some countries of Latin America.[68] This inculturation supposed 'a unifying vision of salvation history'. This unifying vision also meant moving beyond old frontiers, including the concepts of 'mission, West/East, Third world, etc'. For the whole world was and is a single family 'whose members are beset by the same varied problems'.[69]

The unifying vision of Jesuit work in a world shattered by division and injustice helps explain the Jesuit approach to development Christianity. Not only has Catholicism always engaged in politics and culture, but development is the natural evolution of any incarnate religion. As inculturation emerged as a central mission for the Jesuits and the Church in Africa after the Second Vatican Council, it was important to revisit the essential materiality and pragmatism of the ATR.

Africans traditionally did not separate the call arising from their spiritual needs from the one that sprang from lacking basic human rights and goods. According to Eloi Messi Metogo, it was precisely because some

---

[65] Ibid., 207.
[66] Ibid., 208.
[67] Pedro Arrupe, 'On Justice with Faith (1974)', in *Justice with Faith Today: Selected Letters and Addresses*, 319.
[68] Padberg, *Documents of the Thirty First and Thirty Second General Congregations of the Society of Jesus*, 439.
[69] Pedro Arrupe, 'On Inculturation', *AR* XVII, fasc. 78 (May 1978): 256–81 – here, p. 257.

forms of Christianity created a dichotomy between the spiritual and the material that there were greater risks of religious indifference and materialistic atheism in Africa.[70]

This combination of the spiritual and material worlds was central to Hebga's healing and exorcising ministries. Not only did he theorise the rationality of paranormal phenomena like witchcraft,[71] he also created a charismatic movement where he preached on a regular basis, listened to and helped the sick and needy, and performed healing ministries and exorcisms. But, as Lado acknowledged, Hebga was not any kind of charismatic leader. He was a Catholic priest who founded and led a charismatic movement. As such, hierarchy and unity were of paramount importance to him; so was Catholic orthodoxy.[72]

Moreover, the material component was key for the very survival of the Church and the Society itself. African Jesuits like Mveng, Eboussi, Ossama, and Hebga, and especially Cameroon's larger Fang-Beti and Bamiléké groups,[73] all believed that a certain materialism was an important component of their traditional religiosity.[74] This materialism affected their perception of the missionaries and the Christian message they were preaching.[75] For Christianity to last, these African Jesuits argued, the Society in Africa could not ignore the suffering and poverty of African peoples, out of which it was drawing its African vocations. As sociologist of religion Patricia Wittberg argued, the demobilisation of membership in religious orders like the Jesuits could occur, among many reasons, because of the deprivation of material resources that would make their presence in the world and their mission irrelevant.[76] Likewise, Peter McDonough

---

[70] See: Eloi Messi Metogo, *Dieu peut-il mourir en Afrique? Essai sur l'indifférence religieuse en Afrique* (Paris: Karthala, 1997).

[71] Meinrad-P. Hebga, *La Rationalité d'un discours africain sur les phénomènes paranormaux* (Paris: L'Harmattan, 1998).

[72] Lado, *Catholic Pentecostalism and the Paradoxes of Africanization*, 10.

[73] Philippe Laburthe-Tolra, *Les Seigneurs de la forêt: Essai sur le passé historique, l'organisation sociale et les normes éthiques des anciens Beti du Cameroun*, 2nd ed. (Paris: L'Harmattan, 2009).

[74] Alexandre Nana, *Anthropologie Beti et sens chrétien de l'homme* (Paris: L'Harmattan, 2010).

[75] Philippe Laburthe-Tolra, 'Intentions missionnaires et perception africaine: Quelques données camerounaise', *Civilisations* 41, nos 1–2 (1993): 239–55.

[76] Patricia Wittberg, 'Declining Institutional Sponsorship and Religious Orders: A Study of Reverse Impacts', *Sociology of Religion* 61, no. 3 (2000): 315–24.

argues that 'organizations such as the Society of Jesus must provide emotional support for their members'.[77]

African Jesuits like Teguem were simply making the case that if Christianity ought to remain relevant in a continent considered by Collier and Gifford 'the bottom billion',[78] it could not fail to address poverty as what it is: systemic and global. For the Jesuits, keeping that tension between the global and the local, evangelism and action, was not simply a matter of provisional commitment. It was at the very core of their identity and spirituality. Jesuits work for the defence of the Christian faith and the promotion of justice, while remaining contemplatives in action and always trying to find God in everything.

Reform and the Dangers of a Jesuit Schism

By the time Teguem was writing to Arrupe in 1969, a group of Spanish Jesuits were already in full revolt against Arrupe. They, like Teguem, but for different reasons, believed that the 'spirit of Saint Ignatius was not being followed'. While Teguem discussed the matter because of racial segregation in his community and region and called for the reform of the Society that would pay attention to the poor and commit itself to developing means and producing resources to help them, the Spanish 'Vera Society' also called for reform, but of another kind. They believed the Jesuits should return to the strict observance of their religious vows the way Ignatius allegedly understood them, and move away from Arrupe's so-called 'Marxisising' tendencies.[79] Forty out of seventy-eight Spanish bishops approved this movement, and the Vatican had taken notice.[80]

Teguem proposed a reform of religious life that would make Christianity more 'comprehensible' for Africans. However, as discussed during a conference in the University of Notre Dame, the question African Jesuits were raising was about what it meant, in the 1970s, to be a Catholic and African. The answer was to be found in the dialectic of whether to Africanise Christianity or Catholicise Africanity. When one emphasises the former, it

---

[77] Peter McDonough, *Men Astutely Trained. A History of the Jesuits in the American Century* (New York: The Free Press, 1992), 8–9.
[78] Gifford, *Christianity, Development and Modernity in Africa*, 8.
[79] A detailed account of this movement can be found in: Urbano Valero, *Pablo VI y Los Jesuitas. Una Relación Intensa y Complicada, 1963–1978* (Bilbao: Mensajero, 2019), 90–118.
[80] La Bella, *Los Jesuitas. Del Vaticano II al Papa Francisco*, 109–23.

was then argued, there was the potential of schism; when one emphasises the latter, we have cultural Africanisation or inculturation.[81]

Arrupe and the Vatican ultimately opted for inculturation. By the beginning of the 1970s, the fear the Vatican had had at the beginning of the century that the collapse of colonialism might endanger the Church had vanished. The Vatican was concerned that the emphasis on particularisms might endanger the universality of the Catholic Church and its unity. Confronted with this dilemma, Cameroonian Jesuits had to answer to the question of whether the Church and the Society could Africanise without the two breaking apart, as was already happening among conservatives like Marcel Lefèbvre or in Spain with the Vera Society.

The consciousness of the African Jesuits from the mid 1970s and early 1980s reveals a dual approach. Hebga, for example, created a charismatic movement, *Ephphatha*, aimed at addressing the needs of Africa's sick, possessed, and enchanted children. The movement was a major success, and a form of Pentecostalisation of Roman Catholicism.[82] Alongside Cameroonian Sister Thérèse-Michelle Essomba Akamse, Mveng instead created the *Béatitudes*, an African religious congregation, on 20 September 1980.

Essomba Akamse had been a member of the international congregation of the Sisters of Saint Paul. When she left or was expelled from that congregation, she expressed a desire to create a secular African institute for African women. Her encounter with Mveng helped to transform that desire into reality, and she became the spiritual mentor of young religious women who joined the institute, as well as the administrator of all its activities. Alongside Essomba Akamse, Mveng, despite his many travels, was in charge of the men's novitiate. He was also the spiritual director of young men who joined the institute, gave classes, and raised money for the organisation.[83]

The *Béatitudes* aimed at creating a religious institute for the 'inculturation of religious life in Africa'. According to its rules, that institute would be 'born on African soil, designed, and realised by Africans, and for Africans'.[84] The success of the new religious organisation was rapid. With the support of bishops across Africa, young men and women left international religious congregations and diocesan seminaries to join

---

[81] Enyegue, 'Africanize Christianity or Christianize Africanity? The Cameroonian Reaction to Global Catholicism in the 1970's', presented at the conference 'Global History and Roman Catholicism' 22 (Notre Dame, IN: 2019).
[82] Lado, *Catholic Pentecostalism and the Paradoxes of Africanization*.
[83] A-CDO. B.108: 'N.D. Béatitudes. Rapport Mambu'.
[84] A-CDO. B. 28, 'Jésuites, 1997–2000'. And CDO. B.14: 'N.D. Béatitudes'.

the *Béatitudes* and its famous founder. Yet, only seven years into the experiment,[85] a conflict broke out between its two leaders. This ended four years later in 1992 with the suppression of the *Béatitudes*.

The sudden fall of the *Béatitudes* reveals challenges in moving Africanisation from an idealistic discourse to reality. It also brings back the issue of financial resources as a necessity for fostering an authentic African Christianity. The conflict broke out because Father Mveng and Sister Essomba quarrelled about material resources for the congregation, and who the true founder of the congregation actually was. Jean-Paul Messina discusses the roots of this conflict at length in his book *Engelbert Mveng*.[86]

Several of Messina's assertions became matters in the public domain after Mveng was murdered. According to Jean-François Channon of the newspaper *Le Messager*, Mveng also suspected the Sister of using the money that was raised for the congregation for her own profit. As a result, Mveng decided to expel the co-founder of the *Béatitudes* from the congregation, and took her to court, triggering a canonical review from the diocese. Briefly detained and released, she later became the main suspect during Mveng's murder in April 1995.[87]

Mveng had long been accused by his European peers of being a disobedient Jesuit.[88] He had an explanation for this 'so-called disobedience'. He defended his attitude as a calculated resistance against the transfer of the vestiges of the colonial and missionary society to the African modern society and Church. His struggle was against the neocolonisation of the Church:

> We have often been told about the crisis of authority that characterises churches and religious institutions under indigenous jurisdiction. And it has been repeated that African bishops and African superiors do not know how to be obeyed. The truth is, it is unacceptable to transfer to the indigenous hierarchy the kind of obedience practiced under foreign authority. In this latter form, there was no obedience at all, in the African sense of the

---

[85] The congregation was approved *ad experimentum*.
[86] Messina, *Engelbert Mveng: La plume et le pinceau: Un message pour l'Afrique du IIIème Millénaire, 1930–1995*, 114–24.
[87] Jean-François Channon, 'Quel avenir pour les Béatitudes', *Le Messager* 406 (11 April 1996).
[88] A-Fr 410/4: Hebga, 'Lettre au P. Mertens, le 25 Octobre 1971'. At one point, Ossama threatened to resign as superior. Ossama replaced Durand-Viel as superior of Yaoundé in 1971.

word. It was often an institutionalised terrorism. If Africans could suffer this terrorism in the hands of the foreign power, it becomes intolerable in the hands of its own brothers.[89]

Mveng was making a point that could shine some light on how he perceived the new African leadership of the Church and the Society in postcolonial Africa. He saw it as what historian Ogbu Kalu calls the continuous 'villagization' of postcolonial Africa – that is, the transfer of mental and social structures of traditional societies to the modern state.[90] In this particular case, it was the traditional colonial and missionary system that was being transferred into the postcolonial and post-missionary era. The nature of this transfer made it synonymous with neocolonialism. Such a transfer attested to the strength of missionary Christianity in postcolonial French Africa and the defensive position in which proponents of Africanisation leadership found themselves in. In that sense, even Hebga's strong defence of an 'authentic religious life' seemed, in Mveng's view, a continuation of the missionary and, therefore, Western perception of what religious life ought to be.

Not only was Mveng a 'problem theologian', suspected by Paris and Rome for pushing for an African council, the model of Africanisation he put in place in the *Béatitudes* also betrayed some of his own ideals. Mveng claimed, for example, that the necessary condition for true Africanisation was to make African churches financially autonomous.[91] Yet, records of the *Béatitudes* show that the congregation depended on foreign aid. One might argue that the failure of this project ultimately proved that Mveng was right. A Church, and a congregation, that depended on foreign aid could not but fail. In fact, Mveng spent so much time fundraising and travelling (mainly for conferences) that he ended up disengaging from the management of his organisation and the training of its members.

However, the early success of the *Béatitudes* testified not only to the fame of its founder, but also to the aspirations young Africans had for religious life. Those who were members of that congregation kept up a regular life of prayer and meditation. This religious experiment ultimately failed because of the human flaws of its leaders. In the context of African

---

[89] Engelbert Mveng, 'De la sous-mission à la succession', in *Civilisation Noire et Eglise Catholique* (Paris: Présence Africaine, 1978), 275.

[90] Ogbu Kalu, *African Christianity: An African Story* (Trenton, NJ: Africa World Press, 2007), 4.

[91] Engelbert Mveng, *L'Afrique dans l'Eglise: Paroles d'un croyant* (Paris: L'Harmattan, 1986), 70.

liberation and that of the women's decade,⁹² Mveng provided a mixed record as far as women's liberation was concerned. Moreover, the failure of the *Béatitudes* suggests a gender divide regarding what Africanisation was meant to be. African religious men did not necessarily have the same concerns or the same approach to power as African Christian women.

Reform rather than schism, therefore, seemed to have been a preferred way for this first group of African Jesuits to make the Society and the Church more responsive to the African context. The second approach was Eboussi's dismissal from the Society. He had reached the conclusion that he could not reconcile Catholic orthodoxy with his personal convictions. He ultimately left the Society, having concluded that he could not be, in good conscience, Catholic and African.

Eboussi, like his other African colleagues, did not use the term 'schism'. However, unless their use of Africanisation was a negotiating stance, taking their approach literally could have led to a Catholic and Jesuit schism in Africa. In *Christianity without Fetishes,* Eboussi understood African resistance to Western Christianity in an appraisal of African independent churches. According to Eboussi,

> The independent and dissident churches are the expression of the contemptuous rejection of this association, this caricature of Philadelphia which calls forth such sarcasm and 'ridicule by the infidel' [...] The dissident churches have sought to be places where a human being 'feels at home', where one has a face and a name no matter who one is.⁹³

Eboussi's criticism of the concept of universality as well as his call for ending the sending of Western missionary personnel was, at the time, irreconcilable with Arrupe's insistence on universality, a distinctive feature of the Jesuit order and the very meaning of 'Catholicity'. A similar

---

[92] John Baur, *2000 Years of Christianity in Africa: An African Church History* (Nairobi: Paulines, 1998).

[93] Eboussi Boulaga, *Christianity Without Fetishes*, 69. The use of 'feels at home' recalls one of the reasons why African independent churches were so well received in Africa. Cf. Frederick Burkewood Welbourn, *A Place to Feel at Home: A Study of Two Independent Churches in Western Kenya* (London, Nairobi: Oxford University Press, 1966). Martinus L. Daneel explains the rise of African independent churches as a 'quest for belonging': *Quest for Belonging: Introduction to a Study of African Independent Churches* (Gweru, Zimbabwe: Mambo Press, 1987). Eboussi, however, insisted that these words were not an endorsement of 'the opinion expressed by some that true Christianity is to be found today in African religious movements': ibid.

Figure 16 Éric de Rosny at a pan-African Assembly cultural event, Bonamoussadi Spiritual Center, Douala, 17 November 2011 (Archives JHIA, Nairobi).

concern shows just how the Vatican had become restless about the idea of Africanisation. Hebga recalled two historical events. During the Roman Synod of 1974, Augusto Fermo Azzolini (1908–92), the Italian Bishop of Makeni, Sierra Leone, accused defenders of Africanisation of creating confusion among the faithful. Instead of promoting an Africanisation that would be 'authentically Christian', they were instead promoting an ideology that was 'anti-Latin' and 'anti-Rome'.[94]

The second story was a Roman confirmation of Bishop Azzolini's fears. In 1976, the very influential Cardinal Giovanni Benelli (1921–82), then working for the Vatican State Department, attended the opening of the Catholic University of West Africa in Côte d'Ivoire. Benelli said, 'It is absurd to want to talk about an African faith, any more than we can talk about an African Christ although some episodes of the life of the Lord relate to Africa [...] But we cannot say that he is African, any more than Roman, French, or American, or Jew'.[95] These Catholic officials represented a conservative reinterpretation of the decrees of Vatican II. Conservative Catholics had become fearful that a particularising

[94] Meinrad-Pierre Hebga, *Dépassements* (Paris: Présence Africaine, 1978), 58.
[95] Ibid., 63.

interpretation of some of the Council's texts would break the unity of the Catholic Church itself.[96]

As for Arrupe, he had turned his focus towards liberation theology and eventually lost sight of the distinctive African issue of the time: the Africanisation of the Society. The All Africa Conference of Churches' report of 1974 used Africanisation as synonymous with liberation. It thus overshadowed, as historian Léon de Saint Moulin noted, a distinctive theme of African Christianity in the 1970s.[97] Moreover, in becoming the face of liberation theology and progressive Roman Catholicism, Arrupe also weakened his position with the conservative wing of the Vatican. Not only did he see his relationship with Pope Paul VI and the Vatican Curia grow tense,[98] he also had serious concerns about the unity of the Society, especially in his home country, Spain.

The 'Vera Societas' (True Society) was roaring in Spain, leading to the resignation of seven Spanish provincials on 18 March 1970. As the decade wore on, the movement was contained – though not totally suppressed – thanks to the intervention of the Archbishop of Toledo, Vincente Enrique y Tarancón (1907–94), and Pope John Paul II.[99] It remains unclear whether these European concerns influenced the actions Arrupe took in his restructuring of the work and jurisdictions of the Jesuits in Africa. The issue of a schism, however, was already hovering over the 1970s. Some conservative cardinals in Spain and Rome seemed more sympathetic to the ideas of Lefèbvre than of leaders like Arrupe. For these conservatives, Arrupe was institutionalising Marxism.[100]

A similar mood is said to have existed during the preparation of the Jesuit GC of 1974. Asked whether or not a GC should be convened, a delegate to the Congregation from the Mediterranean province (France) responded with a 'no'! Later, he expressed a real fear of a schism within the Jesuit Order.[101] This delegate detailed his opinion, arguing that 'Since

[96] The only schism that came out of Vatican II was that of Marcel Lefèbvre, then the French Archbishop of Dakar (Senegal).
[97] Saint Moulin, *Histoire des Jésuites en Afrique: Du XVIe siècle à nos jours* (Namur: Éd. Jésuites, 2016), 126–28.
[98] Jean Lacouture, *Jésuites: Les Revenants*, vol. 2 (Paris: Seuil, 1992), 450.
[99] Cf. Pedro Miguel Lamet, *Arrupe: testigo del siglo XX, profeta del XXI*, 1st ed. Biografías/Temas de hoy (Madrid: Temas de hoy, 2007), 334–36.
[100] Lacouture, *Jésuites: Les Revenants*, vol. 2, 462.
[101] A-Fr 70: 'Avis de la Congrégation de la Province de Méditerranée concernant l'obligation de convoquer la Congrégation Générale, 31 mars–3 avril 1970'. Fifty-four pages.

the structures of the Society are sometimes artificial and inadequate', the Society was called to task to develop 'other forms of consultation' that would foster greater participation. More concretely, he asked the Congregation 'to satisfy the desires of the representatives of the Third World to see the Society define its mission in terms no longer Western, but universal'.[102] The rest of this text expressed concerns about how the new restructuring would affect the unity of the Order and its adaptability to the new world political order.[103]

Conclusion

If traditional Christian countries like Spain or France were facing schismatic tendencies, then the debate around Africanisation became more worrisome, especially for some Roman officials who were openly pushing back against local particularisms. In that sense, the Africanisation championed by the first Cameroonian Jesuits was in a collision course with the Christianisation agenda promoted by the Vatican in the 1970s. The African side lost this initial battle. Teguem was dismissed from the Society. Eboussi left the Jesuits and priesthood in 1980. Mveng was murdered in 1995, in a house within an indigenous congregation he had cofounded. And Hebga spent the three final decades of his life focused on healing ministries and the charismatic movement he had created. Ossama has remained a Jesuit. These Jesuits, especially Mveng, Eboussi, and Hebga, remain major figures of discussion in Catholic intellectual circles in French Africa. Younger generations of African Catholics continue to draw on their thoughts and ideas for a twenty-first-century African Church that would address the actual needs of the African people.

Moreover, the story of Emmanuel Teguem is part of the Jesuits' new orientation in favour of the poor since the 31st GC, an orientation that was more strongly confirmed by the 32nd. What Teguem voiced was a new perspective that confirmed what other Cameroonian Jesuits had argued about: the need to build an Africanised Church that responded to the actual cultural, spiritual, and material needs of their people. These churches were built in support of newly independent African states.

However, unlike Ossama, Eboussi, Hebga, and Mveng, who spoke as priests and intellectuals, Teguem was a Brother with a working-class background. The vocation of this working-class Jesuit is therefore a

---

[102] Ibid.
[103] Ibid.

confirmation that a structural 'malaise' affected all the first Cameroonian Jesuits from the bottom up. It also attests to the urgency of changing course. The question of succession, as later addressed by Mveng, was therefore more than a religious matter. It was about creating a Church that would transform and improve the social conditions of all Africans. It was a project of a *mission civilisatrice* which, unlike the Frenchified previous one, would focus on the actual needs of African people and the betterment of their government.

Conclusion

The Chad Mission and the Failure of Africanisation

The contemporary Jesuit mission in West and Central Africa began in Chad in 1935. Although initially conceived by a single individual, it was associated with the vagaries of the colonial system. From the time the mission was officially approved in 1946, the first Jesuits collaborated with the colonial administration in their deployment and in the organisation of the mission. They considered themselves to represent the cultural and spiritual arm of the French colonial project of civilisation in Africa, and were intimately connected to this. The ideological battles of France were the spiritual battles of the missionaries on the Chadian terrain. For instance, in the context of the Cold War, France opposed the Marxist–communist Eastern Bloc, and in Chad, the fight against the communist 'invasion' and the secularism of the Chadian elites was one of the objectives of the mission. The French empire was threatened by a double political crisis in Vietnam (threatened by Communism) and in Algeria (where the nationalists embraced Pan-Arabism); on the ground in Chad, the Jesuit mission intended to stop the progression of this Islam towards the south. In France, the working class turned its back on Christianity and scholars believe that France was on the way to becoming a mission country itself. In Chad, as everywhere in French-speaking Africa, the culprit of this reversal of the working classes was Communism. It was to be countered in Chad by a mass evangelisation, often anti-elite.

While this triple crisis created confusion among the French, in search of the recovery of France's prestige, the mission was built as a civilising mission, a form of 'Frenchification'. This Frenchification presupposed the exclusivity of French missionary personnel, the isolation of Chadian Islam from the great international *umma*, the conversion of less radical Islam to Christianity, and an anti-Americanism that explained the initial distant relations with the Protestant churches.

Moreover, as the book has shown, Chad had a predominantly rural population, with low levels of literacy and little knowledge of the Christian faith. The Jesuit mission therefore took a populist turn and embraced mass evangelisation. Churches were built and baptisms were carried out en masse with the help of Jesuit Brothers. The Bible and catechism were translated into Chadian languages. The mission benefitted from the support of young French scholastics and lay volunteers and, above all, Chadian catechists trained by the Jesuits themselves. These catechists were married couples and children. If the Jesuits seemed to enjoy this populism because of their open anti-elitism, this evangelisation of the masses also failed to produce candidates for the priesthood and religious life. As the book has argued, the absence of local vocations, and strategic choices that closed the door to sub-regional vocations, also put the Jesuits at odds with the Vatican's priority: the constitution of an African clergy as the basis for the Africanisation of the Church.

With decolonisation and the country's march towards political independence, Jesuit missionaries in Chad consolidated their control of the mission. The ordination of missionary bishops accelerated from 1958 to 1962, to the surprise of regional observers whose churches had embraced the Vatican's agenda of Africanisation. The situation was so worrisome that in 1969, Charles Vandame, the head of the mission, concluded that the Chad Mission remained colonial in its personnel, structures, methods, and liturgy. The Second Vatican Council and its *aggiornamento* came and went. Chad's Cultural Revolution, pushed by President François Tombalbaye, claimed to return to Chad's traditional values in what was perceived as a religious war against Christendom and its foreign agents. Yet, both the Council and the Cultural Revolution left the organisation of the mission in Chad mostly unchanged. On the contrary, with the election of Arrupe as superior general of the order and his vision of an African Church run by Africans, the missionaries in Chad considered a juridical evolution to make their mission a vice-province or a province. They finally gave up on this project, realising that by creating such a jurisdiction, they would create a White ghetto in the heart of an African continent irresistibly moving towards its ecclesial Africanisation following the political one of the 1960s.

The debate on this jurisdictional evolution of Chad took place at the time when Arrupe decided to reorganise the Jesuit missions in Africa. In the absence of a vice-province or province, Chad tried to reconcile with Cameroon. At least in Cameroon there was already a strong Africanised

Church and a Society of Jesus that, although still predominantly missionary, counted some of the Cameroonian intellectual elite among its leaders.

The link between Chad with Cameroon was thus made official with the creation of the VPAO in 1973. Against all odds for the Cameroonians, who believed in the vision of Pope Paul VI and Pedro Arrupe, the Chadian model emerged victorious from this restructuring. The superior was a French missionary from Chad. The map was faithful to colonial lines. And the Cameroonian dependent region was suppressed, its Cameroonian leadership sidelined. It was thus on Cameroonian soil that the last debate on Africanisation took place, in the 1970s – that is, ten years after independence. As already mentioned in the Introduction, Cameroon was the ground of the historical event that served as the starting point of this book. It is also the ground for its Conclusion.

De Rosny and Mveng

On 7 March 2012, the Church of Saint Ignatius in Paris was packed with people from different social and racial backgrounds. The Cameroonian ambassador in Paris represented his government. Reverend Jean-Roger Pascal Ndombi, Regional Assistant for Africa in the Jesuit Curia in Rome, presided over the Eucharist. Wearing their traditional uniforms, representatives of *Beyum ba Bato*, the *Ngondo* – the supreme council of the Sawa – also came to bid farewell to one of their most illustrious members: Jesuit Father Eric Dibounjé.

As the mass concluded, Georges Dibounjé, in Douala language, greeted the attendants on behalf of the *Ngondo*: 'The Sawa people are speechless', Georges said. 'The news is terrible! The Baobab has fallen! Dibounje has gone to find Cain Dibounje, his "African ancestor".'[1] Georges wished his 'brother' Eric had died in Douala, 'alongside his brothers'. Yet, he bowed to God's will: 'Go! Go! Dibounje go', he concluded. 'The Sawa people, your people accompany you on your journey to Tete Cain Dibounje Tukuru; the Bambambe will welcome you with the respect you deserve.'[2]

Other masses celebrated the memory of Eric Dibounjé in Cameroon. Jean Toto Moukouo, a representative of the alumni of Libermann Secondary School, remembered the departed Jesuit with great emotion. He sang a melody allegedly composed by Engelbert Mveng, the first Cameroonian

---

[1] Cyrille Younkam, 'Compte rendu de la messe de requiem du P. de Rosny', *Nouvelles PAO* 244 (2012): 5–7 – here, p. 5.

[2] A-PAO: Pierre Maurel, 'Notice nécrologique du P. Eric de Rosny', *Nouvelles de la PAO* 244 (2012): 2–4.

Jesuit.[3] In the Catholic centre of the University of Yaoundé I, anthropologist Ludovic Lado noted the significance of the moment: Dibounje, Lado said, 'had opened the eyes of the Christian faith to Africans; and Africans had opened his eyes to African cultures'.[4]

Eric Dibounjé's name at birth in 1930 was Éric de Rosny. A member of the French nobility of Boulogne (France), as we have heard, he joined the Jesuits at the age of nineteen, was part of the Committee for the Creation of the Jesuit Region of Cameroon in 1968, and played a fundamental role in the creation of the VPAO (1972–73). When the VPAO was renamed the Jesuit Province of West Africa (PAO) in 1983, de Rosny was appointed its first provincial (r. 1984–90).

De Rosny's experience with secondary school students at Libermann had awakened his desire to immerse himself in the Douala culture. By the time the debates over the creation of the VPAO were taking place in the 1970s, he was learning the Douala language.[5] He was also initiated into the *ndimsi*, the Douala secret world of hidden realities where the fate of individuals is decided. At completion of his initiation, from 1970–75, he became an *nganga*.[6]

[3] From a report by Thédore Noudjitoloum, then a Jesuit novice from Chad: *Nouvelles de la PAO* 244, p. 12.
[4] From Stéphane Mbogue's report, ibid., 11.
[5] From 1969 onwards, de Rosny had been in a personal crisis, wondering whether or not he should return to Africa: Éric de Rosny, *Les yeux de ma chèvre: Sur les pas des maîtres de la nuit en pays Douala* (Paris: Pocket, 1996), 35–37; 'Mission terminée?', *Etudes* (May 1970): 737–46. The title of his article was taken from a novel: Mongo Beti, *Mission terminée* (Paris: Corrêa, 1957).
[6] In the process of transformation of European Christianity into African Christianity, John K. Thornton has demonstrated that the *nganga*, the traditional 'magical and medicinal practitioners' also known as 'fetishers', were often in competition with European Jesuits, who considered their work to be sinful (John K. Thornton, 'The Development of an African Catholic Church in the Kingdom of Kongo, 1491–1750', *Journal of African History* 25 [1984]: 147–67 – here, p. 157). In de Rosny's case, the meaning of *nganga* remained the same. An *nganga* is a traditional healer, and is often synonymous with 'witch doctor' (Éric de Rosny, *Les yeux de ma chèvre*, 48). According to de Rosny, the Jesuits arrived in Cameroon in a context of crisis, when missionaries had serious concerns about their future in a mature Africanised Christianity. Instead of withdrawing like some of his European colleagues, he decided to embrace African cultures and received initiation to become an *nganga* himself. Rosny, *L'Afrique des guérisons*, 14 and 19.

Like Roberto de Nobili and Matteo Ricci before him, de Rosny adopted a traditional Jesuit approach to accommodation.[7] Yet unlike the Chinese or the Malabar rites controversies that followed their accommodation in China and India, controversies that led the Vatican to delay the indigenisation that started with the creation of Propaganda Fide in 1622, de Rosny was universally accepted and praised. In 1984, he, a French missionary belonging to an elite Cameroonian initiatory and cultic society[8] – an *nganga* – became the Jesuit provincial of French West Africa.[9]

This book has traced the Africanisation of the Jesuit mission in Cameroon and Chad. The fact that an Africanised French missionary effectively became Jesuit provincial of Cameroon is confirmation that twentieth-century Jesuit globalism was not totally antithetical to Africanisation. As we have seen, however, decades after independence, it was still too risky to implement Africanisation under the African leadership that existed in the Society of Jesus. European missionaries, not wanting to be ruled by the first African Jesuits, also feared the emphasis of the latter on 'Africanisation' rather than 'Christianisation'. This prioritisation of Africanisation seemed radical for them as well as for proponents of a more moderate form of inculturation.

The missionaries were not the only ones concerned by a rising African leadership in the Church. Government officials in Cameroon and Chad used the African ecclesiastical elite to build their nations, yet they did not encourage the way in which African ecclesiastics were becoming national heroes to the point of overshadowing their own often-contested political leadership.

[7] In the African context, Jesuit accommodation corresponds to what John Thornton calls 'inclusive conversion'. According to Thornton, 'The inclusive concept means that all aspects of the culture of the target country that are not directly contrary to the fundamental doctrine of the Church are considered acceptable. Indeed, the ultimate result is that virtually the only behavior necessary to be a Christian is self-identification and recognition of the Catholic Church as the only Church and the Pope as its head': Thornton, 'The Development of an African Catholic Church', 152.

[8] Ralph A. Austen, 'Tradition, Invention and History: The Case of the Ngondo (Cameroon)', *Cahiers d'Etudes Africaines* 32, no. 126 (1992): 285–309 – here, p. 301.

[9] According to Pierre Maurel, when de Rosny became the provincial assistant in 1982, he 'was afraid that his ministry as nganga had marginalised him from the life of the Society', as if Africanisation was synonymous with marginalisation in the Society of Jesus. Pierre Maurel, 'Notice nécrologique du P. Eric de Rosny', *NPAO* 244 (2012): 3.

Figure 17 Mveng shown in a wall painting at the Jesuit Community, Hekima University College, Nairobi (Simu 2009).

The Cameroon government's approval of of a French ecclesiastic like de Rosny also served as a diplomatic tool to signal the government's Francophilia as opposed to a form of nationalism which, traditionally, had seemed Francophobic. In 2012, for example, the government of Cameroon recognised de Rosny's exemplary model as a missionary and his academic achievements.[10] By the time of this public recognition, however, de Rosny's mission had effectively been terminated. He died in March 2012.

[10] AJ-Fr 'Une rue Père Eric de Rosny à Douala' [not classified]. Also reported on the site of the archives of the Jesuit Province of Francophone Western

For many observers of the history of Cameroon, if there is one Jesuit who deserves public acclaim, it is Engelbert Mveng. This first Cameroonian Jesuit, more than any other Jesuit, actively worked to build the nation-state of independent Cameroon. Ironically, his publications on the history and culture of the country are more significant than de Rosny's. Yet he has failed to receive equal recognition because he never managed to gain wider, global support, and was met with suspicion among the political and ecclesiastical elite at home.

Memories of both de Rosny and Mveng connect them to one Cameroonian novelist. Mongo Beti, as seen in the Introduction, inspired de Rosny in one novel.[11] He also gave a fictionalised account of Mveng's death in another. In 1999, the same author published another novel whose title does not lack a Cameroonian theatrical humour: *Trop de soleil tue l'amour* (Too much sun kills love)! This work is a *Roman à clef* on the tragic death of Mveng, one of the leaders of the African resistance against the whitening of the Church in postcolonial Africa.[12]

The main character of *Trop de soleil tue l'amour*, Zamakwé (Zam), is an alcoholic and sex-addicted political reporter. He lives in an African capital. His collection of jazz CDs has been stolen, and the body of a murdered individual has been found inside his home. Zam links the two events and his own fate to the routine of an African capital. 'At home,' he says, 'death squads operate with impunity; a great scholar, a future Nobel Prize winner perhaps, is murdered almost in indifference, after many other victims, including peaceful ecclesiastics abroad.'[13]

The name of the murdered intellectual is Father Maurice Mzilikazi. The criminal investigation into Zamakwé over the murder of the priest suspects a woman is involved. To highlight some proximity between the murdered priest and the government, Beti writes, Mzilikazi 'was not really a true dissident'. While Mzilikazi, he continues, had sometimes, though 'elegantly', supported the oppressive regime by calling the adversaries of the regime 'troublemakers', he had also received grants from politicians and fallen into the trap of a common technique the government used to silence the intelligentsia of the country. The nationalism of the priest ultimately clashes with the anti-nationalism (and pro-French agenda) of the government he has helped to build.

Europe: <http://www.jesuites.com/une-rue-pere-eric-de-rosny-a-douala/> [accessed 12 February 2018].

[11] Beti, *Mission terminée*; de Rosny, 'Mission Terminée?'
[12] Mongo Beti, *Trop de soleil tue l'amour* (Paris: Julliard, 1999).
[13] Ibid., 9.

As the first police report is made public, Zam, like the rest of the country, is petrified. The murder of the priest and scholar, the police report, looks like a sacrificial ritual: Mzilikazi is naked, and has been tortured and strangled. A large amount of money has been left on his table, and a sinister rumour circulates that the brain of the priest has been taken.[14]

Father Mzilikazi is a fictional character. Yet, one can hardly miss the parallel with Mveng's death and speculation about motives for his murder. Mveng was an intellectual priest who had received international awards and was a friend of the Senegalese President (and member of the Académie Française) Léopold-Sédar Senghor. He too was strangled and tortured before being killed. The intruders to his house that night left money beside his bed untouched. A year after the murder, Thomas Atenga of *Le Messager* newspaper expressed concerns about the 'laxity of the prosecution'. He also decried the confusion 'about the exact circumstances, the true motives of the crime'.[15] Atenga voiced his frustration as Cameroonians continued 'to guess, on the basis of presumptions, the mystic, esoteric, and political' motives of Mveng's death.[16] A woman, Atenga's colleague Jean-François Channon argued, Thérèse-Michelle Essomba Akamse, co-founder, with Mveng, of the *Béatitudes,* was widely presumed guilty of the attack.[17]

Thérèse-Michelle Akamse and her alleged accomplice, Dominique Omballa, were arrested and questioned. They were later released under the orders of the Minister of Justice,[18] himself a former student of Libermann Secondary School. Given the strangulation of so many clergy in Cameroon over the years, Sister Essomba could not have murdered all, if any, of them. Yet what remains true is that the government never thoroughly investigated cases of suspected murders of clergy. In *Trop de soleil tue l'amour*, Zamakwe explains this lack of resolve by the government to investigate those crimes: the government was behind the murder of the ecclesiastics who opposed its corruption.

Engelbert Mveng, this book has shown, was the first Cameroonian Jesuit, and one among his Jesuit colleagues who fought for the Africanisation of the leadership in the Church. He also contributed significantly to the building of independent Cameroon as a nation-state. Mveng's

---

[14] Ibid., 23–24.
[15] A-CDO. B. 28: Thomas Atenga, 'Mort sans sépulture', *Le Messager* 406 (6 April 1996).
[16] Ibid.
[17] Ibid.
[18] A-CDO. B. 28: Jean-François Channon, 'Quel avenir pour les Béatitudes?' *Le Messager* 406 (6 April 1996).

Histoire du Cameroun shaped the national consciousness of generations of Cameroonians.[19] A version of this book became a handbook of the history of Cameroon. He published it with Beling-Nkoumba Ndoumbé, and the book was used in secondary schools for decades. His artistic works became prominent in churches across the continent. A monument he helped design became the symbol of the reunification of Anglophone and Francophone Cameroons in 1972.[20]

Yet, when the Cameroonian government named a street after a Jesuit in Douala in 2012, it did not give it Mveng's name or that of any other Cameroonian. Instead, it named the street after Éric de Rosny, a French missionary who fought with France during the Algerian War of Independence.[21] De Rosny had only became a Cameroonian by adoption after he completed his initiation among the Sawa people. He was also a member of the council of the *Ngondo*. Sometimes considered politically subversive by the colonial administration, the *Ngondo* was often under surveillance. The colonial administration also co-opted it and manipulated its leaders to advance both the political interests of the leaders of the *Ngondo* and those of France.[22] De Rosny's initiation had, in fact, prompted suspicion among the Douala people that he might have sacrificed his master of initiation.[23] His initiation experience later shaped his ethnographic research on the Sawa and their traditional medicinal practices. Like Hebga, he used his knowledge as an *nganga* to heal the sick.

The rise of de Rosny in the Society of Jesus, and his public recognition through having a street named after him by a Francophile and, for some historians, overtly anti-nationalist, government[24] coincided with the increased ostracism of Mveng within the Jesuit order and within the local Church of Cameroon. It also led to the progressive popularisation

---

[19] Engelbert Mveng and Beling-Nkoumba. *Manuel d'histoire du Cameroun* (Yaoundé: CEPER, 1969).

[20] The Reunification Monument is an important symbol of modern Cameroon, though a contested one. See Joseph Lon Nfi, 'The Powerlessness of Cameroon's Reunification Monuments', *East West Journal of Humanities* 4, no. 1 (2013): 127.

[21] Éric de Rosny, *Les yeux de ma chèvre*, 24.

[22] Cf. Austen, 'Tradition, Invention and History'.

[23] Éric de Rosny, *Healers in the Night*, trans. Robert R. Barr (Maryknoll, NY: Orbis Books, 1985), 251ff.

[24] Wang Sonnè, 'Cameroon: Why are the Names of Great Historical Figures from the 1950s Taboo in the Mouth Of President Paul Biya?' *Africa Development* 22, no. 2 (January 1997): 131–49.

and fictionalisation of his memory in Cameroon. This contrast between the memorialisation and reputations of the two Jesuits that were the most significant in the Africanisation of Jesuit Cameroon is vividly expressed in the creation of the VPAO explored in this book. In the 1970s, a European version of Africanisation, be it in the form of vernacularisation, jurisdictional mapping, or leadership, was approved by Rome, Paris, and ultimately by an African government friendly to France. In contrast, the African-led, nationalist, and postcolonial version of Africanisation was marginalised. This sealed the survival of missionary Christianity beyond African independence and the rise of an African-led Christianity.

The book has argued that radical thinkers like Mveng were ostracised because of their nationalistic inclinations. They were unacceptable to the Church which, although it encouraged different forms of indigenisation in the twentieth century, consistently opposed nationalism. Mveng was sidelined, then praised after his death, by global Jesuits who had feared that an extreme emphasis on African particularism could threaten the Jesuits' claim for universality. Mveng was ultimately rejected by a postcolonial government of Cameroon that was overtly anti-nationalist and Francophile; the masses even suspected the government of having murdered him. In a sense, once it has been established that the missionaries were not willing to be ruled by Africans, it becomes clear that a cross-cultural mission effectively undermined the local Church. There existed an asymmetrical power dynamic between Mveng and de Rosny. The majority of mission personnel were still French, holding all levels of power, and were supported by powerful allies in Paris and Rome. Concerns that a powerful missionary Church was undermining the local one were already raised by missiologists like Henry Venn and Rufus Anderson. In their three-self theory, which influenced the thought of African radical thinkers like John Gatu, Eboussi Boulaga, Hebga, and Mveng, they argued for the euthanasia of the mission as a precondition for the emergence of an authentic local Church in which missionaries with cross-cultural experience would not play leading roles.

Competing Catholicisms in Postcolonial Chad and Cameroon

The fates of de Rosny and Mveng help us to analyse and reflect upon the winners and losers of competing Catholicities in French Africa in the twentieth century. In 1965, only five years after the independence of most African countries, Kenneth Latourette asked whether or not the Church would survive 'the erasure of colonialism to which it had been associated' and the anti-Christian attacks from communists.[25] Recent shifts in global Christianity show that the Church prospered more than at any time in history as it Africanised.[26] The creation of the VPAO further demonstrates that, alongside this booming Africanised Christian Church,[27] the missionary Church survived as well.

As missionaries like de Rosny often led large organisations, they also self-Africanised and contributed to the growing Church in the context of what has been often wrongly considered the post-missionary era. The new Jesuit global ethos homogenised Jesuit works in West Francophone Africa by mingling and suppressing local differences in Chad and Cameroon. It thus contributed to the survival of colonial-like missionary structures and leaderships. The Chad Mission survived Chad's nationalism by adopting a bottom-up vernacularisation under the leadership of Western missionaries. By expanding Chad's influence within the VPAO, the autonomous Jesuit Region of Cameroon was suppressed and realigned to the new Jesuit global vision. The creation of the VPAO led to negative reactions from the first Cameroonian Jesuits. Most of these Cameroonians were, like Mveng, renowned Africanisers and defenders of African particularism within global Christianity.

The African resistance to the creation of the VPAO in its structure and leadership was caused by disagreements on Church governance. It also arose from the position the first Cameroonian Jesuits held within the building of independent Cameroon as a nation-state. Inside the Church, their approach to Africanisation was unique insofar as it transcended broadly accepted liturgical adaptation, paradigmatic liberation theology, and vernacularisation. Cameroonian Jesuits used Africanisation to address Church governance and its structures in light of the politics of postcolonial Africa. If the missionary Church were associated with colonialism in its making, they argued, having the Church dominated by White missionaries after independence was a form of neocolonialism.

The creation of the VPAO also demonstrated the existence of different, even competing modes of localisation within Jesuit globalism. This

---

[25] In: Kenneth Scott Latourette, 'Colonialism and Missions: Progressive Separation', *Journal of Church and State* 7, no. 3 (Autumn 1965): 341.

[26] David B. Barrett, ed., *World Christian Encyclopedia: A Comparative Survey of Churches and Religions in the Modern World, AD 1900–2000* (Nairobi: Oxford University Press, 1982), 4.

[27] Todd M. Johnson and Peter F. Crossing, 'Christianity 2014: Independent Christianity and Slum Dwellers', *International Bulletin of Missionary Research* 38, no. 1 (January 2014): 28–29.

'glocalisation' was effective even within the limits of a single Jesuit jurisdiction such as the VPAO. Pedro Arrupe decided to restructure and harmonise the work of Jesuit missions in Africa. This process of harmonisation was made possible only after separate historical processes had been discontinued and merged into one through:

1 Creating the VPAO, which interrupted the institutional evolution of Cameroon as an autonomous jurisdiction.

2 Breaking the triangle of France–New France–Senegal, which was the centre of French colonialism in West Africa.

3 The all-French community of The African Institute for Economic and Social Development (INADES) (Côte d'Ivoire) for the first time considering having an African from Cameroon as its superior; and

4 Missionaries leaving Chad for the first time and going to Cameroon, Congo Brazzaville, Burkina Faso, and elsewhere.

Weakened during this process, the Jesuit Mission in West Africa came to see the missions as a form of neocolonialism, and as a setback to Africanisation. The creation of the VPAO, from their perspective, was a historical anachronism in the context of increased African personnel and the promotion of an African leadership in the Church and in national politics. This historical anachronism contradicted a policy the Vatican had openly championed.

The first Cameroonian Jesuits focused their fight on the Jesuit failure to nurture Africanisation of the mission's leadership, but they became increasingly ostracised not only inside the Church but also inside the nation-state of Cameroon, which they had helped to build. The rise of Éric de Rosny represented, within the VPAO, an institutional co-optation – and softening – of Africanisation as the first Cameroonian Jesuits understood it. De Rosny's initiation to the *Ngondo* and teaching of Cameroonian anthropology at the university resulted in his appointment as leader of the Jesuits in West Africa, adding another dimension to what it meant to be 'African'. A White man could be African. Not to admit this would have reduced the Cameroonian claim for an African leadership to race in the same way as they themselves accused some missionaries of practising racism. De Rosny's elevation by the state and acceptance by the Vatican plainly show the complexity of competing Christianities in Africa in the 1970s.

The outcome of the competition in Cameroon and Chad was a win for the Vatican. From the start, its Africanisation agenda was based on fear that the collapse of the colonial empires might lead to the collapse of the

Church unless it Africanised. As the debate was taking place in Cameroon in the 1970s, Chad's Catholicism had survived Chad's political nationalism despite an entirely European mission personnel. In Cameroon, the Church had also survived the struggles of a violent nationalist movement, and ten years after independence, the Vatican had strong allies among the Cameroonian bishops it had carefully selected. For the Vatican, the Africanisation of the missions in Chad and Cameroon added another dimension to complex issues of faith and universal social justice. The very existence of the Vatican is to affirm that the Church is universal and has shared beliefs and practices across cultures and nations. Any localisation of the Church cannot jeopardise those shared beliefs. Extreme nationalism thus threatens directly what the Vatican represents. It contains the risk of schism. On the other hand, the Vatican had to cope with the rising Church of the poor and its emphasis on social justice and liberation. As the Jesuits under Arrupe's leadership embraced the concept of the preferential option for the poor, they were faced with strong criticisms from the Vatican and among certain corners of the Jesuit order in Europe. Arrupe was accused of Marxism for his support of liberation theology and dissenting Jesuits. As his influence diminished, he could not embrace the nationalism and inclinations towards liberation of the first Cameroonian Jesuits without consequences for the order itself, especially in its young African implantation.

De Rosny's elevation further represented a unique challenge for the Church in the context of public recuperation or suppression of colonial and nationalist memories. The postcolonial state built monuments to General Leclerc, named streets after General de Gaulle, and elevated de Rosny, a missionary and veteran of the Algerian War of Independence,[28] yet it signally failed to raise monuments for Cameroonian nationalists who died during the war. The state also proved itself unable to solve – or even pursue thoroughly – the assassination of several ecclesiastics, including Mveng. The Cameroonian government's recognition of de Rosny thus ran – and runs – the risk of further aligning the missionary Church that survived Cameroonian nationalism with a political regime considered neocolonial and oppressive, with its conflicting and wounding memories.

With the rise of De Rosny, the roles in the Jesuit debate over Africanisation were effectively reversed. The Cameroonian political elite recognised as exemplary models for the Church and the state those same missionaries who had resisted the Africanisation of the leadership pushed by the first Cameroonian Jesuits. While de Rosny was being elevated in the Society

---

[28] de Rosny, *Les yeux de ma chèvre*, 24.

and by the Cameroonian government, the survival of Mveng's memories was taking place in crowded classrooms of students reading his history of their country. Churches used his paintings; popular fiction reproduced his stories of those times. This reversal might reinforce the perception of neocolonialism in the Church, and the Jesuits' unintended contribution to its making. Yet, in this competition, the popularisation of Mveng's memory also democratises it. It makes his impact more lasting among the populace, and places him on the winning side of competing Catholicisms.

Basis for Change

Memory, French philosopher Paul Ricœur once said, 'ensures temporal continuity, by allowing us to move along the axis of time; it allows us to recognize ourselves and to say I, my'.[29] The role of history, in its turn, is to 'defatalise the past', and to rescue an unkept promise. According to Ricœur,

> People of the past had hopes and projects, many of which were unfulfilled; a good number of our utopias would be empty if we could not fill them with promises of people of the past that were undelivered, thwarted, and destroyed. Basically, every period is surrounded by an aura of hopes that were not fulfilled; it is this aura that permits renewals in the future, and perhaps this is how utopia could be cured of its congenital illness.[30]

The Constitutions of the Society of Jesus have never completely closed. As an institution, the Jesuit order was meant to remain a promise in the Church and in the world. It is always open to the reinterpretation of its identity and mission as a necessary condition for its self-renewal over time. As the Jesuit order adjusts to new realities, it contributes to transforming the Church *ad intra* and society *ad extra*.

African historians may look back at the 1970s and see the seeds of neocolonialism in the ideas of some Jesuits studied in this book. Others might see the exact opposite, and consider the ideas of Ossama, Eboussi, Hebga, Mveng, and Teguem as antithetical to colonialism, missionary Christianity, and even Jesuit globalism. For some of those critics, the first African Jesuits might well join the side of 'anti-Jesuitism'.[31] In this book,

---

[29] Paul Ricœur, *Critique and Conviction: Conversations with François Azouvi and Marc de Launay* (Cambridge, UK: Polity Press in association with Blackwell Publishers, 1998), 124.

[30] Ibid., 125.

[31] Talking about 'Jesuit Anti-Jesuitism', Sabina Pavone attributes it to 'ex-Jesuits alienated from the Society or from those within the Society who were

however, I have argued that the efforts of these early Jesuits in Africa should be recognised not only for what they actually did achieve but for the hopes and unfulfilled promises they embodied. They articulated a vision of complete Africanisation of the Church, albeit one that remains unrealised. Their most important hope, in the 1970s, was the creation and reform of religious structures and institutions in Africa where Africans could feel at home.[32] Fulfilling those hopes is to continue part of the work the missionaries started. It is also a commitment to perfect this work and to transform the Church and society in a way that meets the ultimate goal of both evangelism and development: the lifting up of the human and care for God's creation.

The discordance between Arrupe's vision of Africanisation and its implementation reflects the gap between what Maurice Blondel calls la 'volonté voulante et la volonté voulue' (The willing will and the willed will). This gap is shown in the limitations of history writing, a discipline that sometimes prioritises the achievements of individual agency over institutional processes, the wider mission, and determination for change.[33] Nevertheless, this book has, I hope, shown that a respected superior general of the Jesuits like Arrupe did not lack the will or the power to implement his ideas.[34] He was checked by the complexities of the institution he

---

unable to advance'. Jesuit anti-Jesuitism was also 'one marker of internal tensions and even dissension within the Society over time [...] A common theme in critical Jesuit writings was that the order was in danger of breaking with the ideals of Ignatius and of descending into factions and political maneuvering [...] Their aim seems to have been to initiate a debate on the future of the order, criticizing the behavior of the superiors who, the texts alleged, were driving a substantial number of adherents to abandon the Society': Sabina Pavone, 'The History of Anti-Jesuitism: National and Global Dimensions', in *The Jesuits and Globalization. Historical Legacies and Contemporary Challenges* (Washington, DC: Georgetown University Press, 2016), 111–30 – here, pp. 119–20.

[32] Frederick Burkewood Welbourn, *A Place to Feel at Home: A Study of Two Independent Churches in Western Kenya* (Oxford, Nairobi: Oxford University Press, 1966).

[33] De Certeau, *The Writing of History*, 100. Fernand Braudel, for example, was 'concerned to place individuals and events in context, in their milieu, but he makes them intelligible at the price of revealing their fundamental unimportance' as compared to geography (Peter Burke, *The French Historical Revolution: The Annales School, 1929–89, Key Contemporary Thinkers* [Stanford, CA: Stanford University Press, 1990], 39).

[34] In fact, the power of the superior general of the Jesuit, as Luke Clossey

Figure 18 Pedro Arrupe shown in a wall painting at the Jesuit Community, Hekima University College, Nairobi (Simu 2009).

was leading, an institution steeped in – and to some extent curtailed by – its own 400-year heritage. Yet, despite its revered traditions, the Jesuit order, like many Catholic institutions in the 1970s, was during this period also in search of its true identity and mission in an ever-evolving world. In this book, embracing competition in this quest is perceived as an asset and not a hindrance to universality, unity, and creative fidelity.

This book also contributes to a renewed interest in and re-evaluation of the merits of institutional history. The creation of the VPAO presents a

---

reminds us, is 'constitutionally extra-constitutional, for the Constitutions authorized a general to ignore any of its provisions': Luke Clossey, *Salvation and Globalization in the Early Jesuit Missions* (New York: Cambridge University Press, 2008), 23.

case in which a strong institution served as a check to both a charismatic leadership and radical thinkers among its members. The strength of the institution becomes the antidote to the will of power of the strongman's rule and to the anarchy that threatens all revolutions.[35] What was at stake in the final chapters of this book was not the charisma of a single Jesuit as such, yet this book shows how the will of individual agents can produce change. At a time when historians from the margins are returning to conversations about race and inequality, this book has, I hope, shown the importance of revisiting institutional history in the context of the paradigm of social history, as well as the emphasis of the latter on individual agency. This methodological approach is ever more important at a time when strongmen rise to power by appealing to the fears local citizens have of a global world without frontiers. The impact of the institution cannot, as we have seen, be dismissed.

The Vatican and the Jesuits in their respective and competing Africanisation agendas were part of a historical struggle not only between Christian progressivism and Christian conservatism, Africans and Western missionaries, Lyon and Paris, African Jesuits and African bishops, colonialism and postcolonialism, but also over who would call the agenda of the Jesuit order in Africa. What was and what could be the role of the Society of Jesus in Cameroon and Chad in a postcolonial world? So Africans, among whom one might find bishops more Roman than the Romans, alongside some radicals whose ideas were perceived as standing on the limits of what Catholicism would allow, fought for control of their religion in their own countries.

In the 1970s, as we have seen, the concept of *missio ad gentes* – that is, taking the message of Christ to those who had not yet embraced it in foreign lands, was brought to an end for Jesuit missionaries working in an increasingly Africanised Church and facing de-Christianisation in Europe. Vatican II eliminated the foreignness of the fixed boundaries of mission. *Missio ad gentes* was replaced by new frontiers identified by global ideologies, the expansion of discourse on human rights, sexual revolution, the abundance of wealth, and the embracing of all sorts of freedoms. Amid this confusion, the Jesuits in Cameroon and Chad, as elsewhere, struggled to find a new direction for themselves. The 31st and 32nd GCs helped the

---

[35] As Michel-Rolph Trouillot says, 'history is power' even if that power is sometimes invisible. Even the purest historical narratives 'would demonstrate to us that retrieval and recollection proceed unequally' in Michel-Rolph Trouillot, *Silencing the Past: Power and the Production of History* (Boston: Beacon Press, 1995), 53.

Jesuits to confront the challenges presented by this new world of political and economic interdependence, highlighting the issues of wealth inequality and fundamentalism associated with them.

At the same time that the Jesuits were facing complex issues that threatened their identity and mission, postcolonialism in the making brought further disruption. The *Competing Catholicisms* outlined in this book foreshadowed the longer struggle for social justice and the meaning of the preferential option for the poor that would be the focus of this postcolonial Christianity. At times, their implementation of the new Order in Africa, even in Arrupe's own judgement, seemed grindingly slow, but what was happening with Catholicities in Chad and Cameroon was no less than the reformulation and reshaping of an age-old institution. The Jesuit mission was inseparable from the identity of the Jesuits and at times it appeared intractable. Yet, as one mission was terminated, a new one did begin. An older Society of Jesus gave birth to a new one. In Africa, the Jesuits learned that postcolonialism was born with its own paradoxes and inevitable competitions. The Vatican, the Jesuits, and Africanisation are, therefore, a work in progress.

Bibliography

Archival Collections

Archives de la Province d'Afrique Centrale (ACE), Collection 'L'Archiviste de la Province d'Afrique Centrale 1' [ACE 5.AA1].
Collection 'Ancienne Province de France' [Former Jesuit Province of France]. A-Fr 410–16, F-Afc, and F-Afc 2/11. Jesuit archives, Vanves, France.
Collection 'Ancienne Province de Lyon' [Former Jesuit Province of Lyon]. Correspondence M-Ly. 102–49. Registre des Consultes M-Ly. 174–7. Litterae Annuae 1949–81. M-Ly. 234–36. Jesuit archives, Vanves, France. Frédéric de Bélinay. 'Dossier Personnel'. M-Ly. Boxes 1457–59. Jesuit archives, Vanves, France.
Collection 'Ancienne Province de Paris' [Former Jesuit Province of Paris]. A-Pa. 124–62; 186–229. Jesuit archives, Vanves, France.
Collection A-PAO. TCH 19–20. Jesuit Archive of the West Africa Province, Douala, Cameroon. 'TCH', in this collection, stands for Chad.
Collection 'Documents du Tchad'. A-CEFOD'. B 254. Bibliothèque CEFOD [CEFOD Library], N'Djamena, Chad.
'Journal Collection Telema'. JHIA, 158. Jesuit Historical Institute in Africa, Nairobi, Kenya.

Interviews and Personal Correspondence

Galli, Agide (written and email): Italian missionary. Former provincial of the VPAO (1979–83), former Regional Assistant for Africa (1984–95).
Vandame, Charles (written): French missionary, former superior of the Chad Mission (1968–73); first provincial of the VPAO (1973–79); archbishop emeritus of N'Djamena.

Books, Book Chapters, and Articles

Abble, A. ed. *Des prêtres noirs s'interrogent*. 2nd ed. Paris: Cerf, 1957.
Abeille, Guy. 'Les Protestants et nous'. *JAF* 2 (1962): 45–46.
Abwa, Daniel. *Commissaires et Haut-Commissaires de la France au Cameroun (1916–1930)*. Yaoundé: Presses Universitaires de Yaoundé, 1998.
Agence France-Press. 'Tchad: Tombalbaye assimile la coopération avec la France à "une nouvelle forme de colonialisme"'. *Le Monde*, 13 December 1973, 2.
Agonga, Aquinata N. 'Hoping Against All Hope: The Survival of the Jesuits in Southern Africa (1875–1900)'. In *Jesuits' Survival and Restoration: A Global History, 1773–1900*, ed. Robert Maryks. Leiden: Brill, 2015.
Ajayi, J. F. A. *Christian Missions in Nigeria 1841–1891: The Making of a New Elite*. Ibadan: University of Ibadan Press, 1965.
—— 'Henry Venn and the Policy of Development'. *Journal of the Historical Society of Nigeria* 1, no. 4 (December 1959): 331–42.
Alima, Jos-Blaise. 'Tchad: Le deuxième front'. *JA* 605 (12 August 1972): 22–23.
Anderson, Gerald H. 'A Moratorium on Missionaries?' *Christian Century* 91, no. 2 (1974): 43–45.
Arditi, Claude. 'Le Tchad et le monde arabe: Essai d'analyse des relations commerciales de la période précoloniale à aujourd'hui'. *Afrique Contemporaine* 3, no. 207 (2003): 185–98.
Arrupe, Pedro. 'Allocutio R.P. Petri Arrupe, Praesidis Unionis Superiorum Generalium, Ad Conferentias Episcopales Africae et Madecassensem in Urbe Abidjan'. *AR* 15 (22 August 1970): 680–84.
—— 'Apostolatus S. I. in Africa'. *AR* 15 (March 1972): 859–78.
—— 'Dialogue with Filipino Coworkers'. In *Justice with Faith Today: Selected Letters and Addresses,* ed. Jerome Aixala, 69–76. Saint Louis, MO: The Institute of Jesuit Sources, 1980.
—— 'Interracial Apostolate'. In *Justice with Faith Today: Selected Letters and Addresses*, ed. Jerome Aixala, 13–27. Saint Louis, MO: The Institute of Jesuit Sources, 1980.
—— 'On Inculturation'. *AR* XVII, fasc. 78 (May 1978): 256–81.
—— 'On Justice with Faith (1974)'. In *Justice with Faith Today: Selected Letters and Addresses*, 2nd ed., 317–20. Saint Louis, MO: The Institute of Jesuit Sources, 1980.
—— 'Our Recent Martyrs (1977)'. In *Justice with Faith Today: Selected Letters and Addresses*, 2nd ed., 205–08. Saint Louis, MO: The Institute of Jesuit Sources, 1980.

—— 'The Social Commitment of the Society of Jesus (1971)'. In *Justice with Faith Today: Selected Letters and Addresses*, ed. Jerome Aixala, 29–59. Saint Louis, MO: The Institute of Jesuit Sources, 1980.

—— 'Witnessing to Justice in the World (1972)'. In *Justice with Faith Today: Selected Letters and Addresses*, ed. Jerome Aixala, 79–120. Saint Louis, MO: The Institute of Jesuit Sources, 1980.

Artidi, Claude. 'Le Tchad et le monde arabe: essai d'analyse des relations commerciales de la période précoloniale à aujourd'hui'. *Afrique Contemporaine* 3, no. 207 (2003): 185–98.

Atenga, Thomas. 'Mort sans sépulture'. *Le Messager* 406 (6 April 1996).

Austen, Ralph A. 'Tradition, Invention and History: The Case of the Ngondo (Cameroon)'. *Cahiers d'Etudes Africaines* 32, no. 126 (1992): 285–309.

Azevedo, Mario Joaquim. *Cameroon and Chad in Historical and Contemporary Perspectives*. Lewiston, NY: E. Mellen Press, 1988.

—— *Chad: A Nation in Search of Its Future*. Boulder, CO: Westview Press, 1998.

—— *The Roots of Violence: A History of War in Chad*. London: Routledge, 2005.

Baba Kake, Ibrahima, and Elikia M'Bokolo. *Histoire Générale de l'Afrique, Des Missionnaires Aux Explorateurs*. 12 vols. Tournai: Casterman SA, 1978.

Banchoff, Thomas, and José Casanova, eds 'Introduction: The Jesuits and Globalization'. In *The Jesuits and Globalization. Historical Legacies and Contemporary Challenges*, 1–26. Washington, DC: Georgetown University Press, 2016.

Baratier, General. *Souvenirs de La Mission Marchand*. Paris: Grasset, 1941.

Barrett, David B., *Schism and Renewal in Africa: An Analysis of Six Thousand Contemporary Religious Movements*. London: Oxford University Press, 1968.

—— ed. *World Christian Encyclopedia: A Comparative Survey of Churches and Religions in the Modern World, AD 1900–2000*. Nairobi: Oxford University Press, 1982.

Barth, Heinrich. *Travels and Discoveries in North and Central Africa. From the Journal of an Expedition Undertaken under the Auspices of H.B.M's Government, in the Years 1849–1855*. Philadelphia, PA: J. W. Bradley, 1859.

Baur, John. *2000 Years of Christianity in Africa: An African Church History*. Nairobi: Paulines, 1998.

Beaver, R. Pierce. 'Missions and the New Nationalism'. *Journal of Church and State* 3, no. 2 (November 1961): 149–71.

—— 'Nationalism and Missions'. *Church History* 26, no. 1 (March 1957): 22–42.

Belcher, Wendy L. 'Sisters Debating the Jesuits: The Role of African Women in Defeating Portuguese Proto-Colonialism in Seventeenth-Century Abyssinia'. *Northeast African Studies* 13, no. 1 (2013): 121–66.
Belmonte, Granito di, and Fumasoni-Biondi. 'Erigitur Nova Praefectura Apostolica Arcis Lamy (in Tchad) et Societatis (Prov. Lugdunensi) Committitur'. *AAS* 11 (1947): 216–17.
Benedict XV, Pope. 'Maximum Illud. De Fide Catholica per Orbem Terrarum Propaganda'. *AAS* 11 (30 November 1919): 440–55.
Bernard, Giroux. 'L'action Catholique à l'ombre de La Grande Guerre. L'exemple de Quelques Aumôniers de La Jeunesse Étudiante Chrétienne'. *Revue d'Histoire de l'Eglise de France* 99, no. 1 (January 2013): 95–114.
Beti, Mongo. *Mission terminée*. 1st ed. Paris: Corrêa, 1957.
—— *Mission terminée*. Paris: Buchet-Chastel, 1975.
—— *Trop de soleil tue l'amour*. Paris: Julliard, 1999.
Blanchard, Pascal, and Gilles Boëtsch. 'La France de Pétain et l'Afrique: Images et propagandes coloniales'. *Canadian Journal of African Studies* 28, no. 1 (1994): 1–31.
Bloch, Marc. *The Historian's Craft*. 1st American ed. New York: Knopf, 1953.
Boavida, Isabel, Hervé Pennec, and Manuel J Ramos, eds *Pedro Paez's History of Ethiopia, 1622*. 2 vols. London: Ashgate, 2011.
Bodin, Michel. 'La géographie du recrutement des soldats africains (1944–1954)'. *Guerres Mondiales et Conflits Contemporains* 189 (1998): 123–34.
Boer, J. H. *Missionary Messengers of Liberation in a Colonial Context. A Case Study of the Sudan United Mission*. 2 vols. Amsterdam, 1979.
Boisson, Jacques. *L'histoire du Tchad et de Fort Archambault*. Besançon: Editions du Scorpion, 1966.
Boivin, Marcel. 'Missionaries Go Home?' *New Blackfriars* 53, no. 630 (November 1972): 494–502.
Bouquet, Christian. 'Genèse et Évolution de l'habitat Rural Dans Le Bas-Chari Tchadien'. *Etudes Rurales* 70 (June 1978): 52.
—— *Tchad: genèse d'un conflit*. Paris: Harmattan, 1982.
Brachet, Julien, and Judith Scheele. 'Les années écroulées: Vestiges, développement et autonomie à Faya-Largeau, Tchad'. *L'Homme* 215/16 (December 2015): 279–305.
Buck, Raymond. 'Consultation in the Chad'. In *BMM-Martyrs* (Foreign Secretary, 1974).
Burke, Peter. *The French Historical Revolution: The Annales School, 1929–89. Key Contemporary Thinkers*. Stanford, CA: Stanford University Press, 1990.
Cabot, Jean. 'La mise en valeur des régions du Moyen-Logone'. *Annales de Géographie* 341 (February 1955): 35–46.

Cador, Grégoire. *L'héritage de Simon Mpeke: Prêtre de Jésus et frère universel*. Paris: Lethielleux: Desclée de Brouwer, 2009.
Caraman, Philip. *The Lost Empire: The Story of the Jesuits in Ethiopia*. Notre Dame, IN: University of Notre Dame Press, 1985.
Cardoso, Mattheus. *Le Catéchisme Kikongo de 1624*, trans. François Bontick. Brussells: Académie Royale des Sciences d'Outre-Mer, 1978.
Certeau, Michel de. *The Writing of History: European Perspectives*. New York: Columbia University Press, 1988.
CETA 'Au sein des communautés non-Catholiques: Conscientisation et Africanisation'. *Telema* 1, no. 75, April 1975.
Chabert, Revd. 'Le Père Chabert au Tchad'. *JAF* 45 (February 1971): 26–27.
Chamedes, Giuliana. 'The Catholic Origins of Economic Development after World War II'. *French Politics, Culture & Society* 33, no. 2 (Summer 2015): 55–75.
Charles, Pierre. 'Colonisation'. *Revue Missionnaire des Jésuites Belges* XI (March 1936): 101–12.
—— 'La missiologie'. *Revue Congo* 1 (1929): 658–63.
—— *Principes et méthodes de l'activite missionnaire en dehors du catholicisme*. Louvain: AUCAM, 1932.
—— *Racisme et catholicisme*. Tournai: Casterman, 1939.
—— *Robe sans couture: Essai sur le Luthéranisme Catholique*. Bruges: Charles Beyaert, 1923.
Clossey, Luke. *Salvation and Globalization in the Early Jesuit Missions*. New York: Cambridge University Press, 2008.
Comaroff, Jean, and John Comaroff. *Of Revelation and Revolution: The Dialectics of Modernity on a South African Frontier*. Vol. 2, 2 vols. Chicago, IL: University of Chicago Press, 1997.
'Compte-rendu de la Consulte et de la réunion des supérieurs de maison suite à la consultation demandée par la Père Costes'. *Nouvelles SJ Tchad* 16 (29 May 1973).
Congar, Yves. *La crise dans l'église et Mgr Lefèbvre*. Paris: Cerf, 1976.
Conklin, Alice L. *A Mission to Civilize: The Republican Idea of Empire in France and West Africa, 1895–1930*. Stanford, CA: Stanford University Press, 1997.
Cooper, Barbara M. *Evangelical Christians in the Muslim Sahel*. Bloomington, IN: Indiana University Press, 2006.
Coquery-Vidrovitch, Catherine. 'Colonisation ou impérialisme: La politique africaine de la France entre les deux guerres'. *Le Mouvement Social* 107 (1979): 51–76.
Coudray, Henri. 'Langue, religion, identité, pouvoir: le contentieux linguistique franco-arabe au Tchad'. *Centre Al-Mouna* 1 (1998): 19–69.

Cuchet, Guillaume. 'Nouvelles perspectives historiographiques sur les prêtres-ouvriers (1943–1954)'. *Vingtième Siècle. Revue d'histoire* 87 (July 2005): 177–87.

Dalmais, Paul. 'La mission du Tchad et les chrétiens de Fort-Lamy'. *Mitte Me* 11 (1966): 26–27.

—— 'L'avenir religieux du Tchad'. *Etudes* (January 1956): 39–51.

—— 'Le Tchad, mission stratégique'. *Vivante Afrique* 203 (June–July 1959): 3–6.

—— 'Un monde qui naît: La mission du Tchad'. *Jésuites* 3 (1959): 31–37.

Daneel, Martinus L. *Quest for Belonging: Introduction to a Study of African Independent Churches*. Gweru: Mambo Press, 1987.

'Décès du P. Louis Forobert'. *Nouvelles de la PAO* 222 (21 February 2009): 9–13.

DeNapoli Morris, Alanna Catherine. 'Female Missionaries in The Jesuit Relations: A Study of the Creators of the Ursulines Seminary in Quebec'. A Thesis Submitted in Partial Fulfilment of the Requirements for the Masters of Theological Studies, Weston Jesuit School of Theology, 2005.

Dévost, Godefroy Clovis. *Les Capucins canadiens au Tchad*. Montréal: Éditions de l'Écho, 2003.

Dingammadji, Arnaud. *Ngarta Tombalbaye: Parcours et rôle dans la vie politique du Tchad (1959–1975)*. Paris: Harmattan, 2007.

Diop, Majhemout, David Birmingham, Ivan Hrbek, Alfredo Margarido, and Djibril Tamsir Niane. 'Tropical and Equatorial Africa under French, Portuguese and Spanish Domination, 1935–45'. In *Histoire Générale de l'Afrique*. Vol. 8, 8 vols, 58–75. Paris: UNESCO, 1999.

Do Coucto, Antonio. *Gentilis Angollae in Fidei Mysteriis Eruditus: Opusculum Reginae Fidelissimae Mariae I Jussu Denuo Excussum*. Lisboa: Olisipone, 1784.

Dossier. 'Vers la fin du schisme? Levée de l'excommunication des évêques lefebvristes. Textes et réactions'. *Documentation Catholique* 2419 (1 March 2009): 235–55.

Dramé, Papa, and Saul Samir. 'Le projet d'Eurafrique en France (1946–1960): quête de puissance ou atavisme colonial?' *Guerres Mondiales et Conflits Contemporains* 4 (2004): 95–114.

Duval, Armand. 'Jalons pour une réflexion sur l'adaptation'. *Revue du Clergé Africain* 27 (November 1972): 605–24.

Eboussi Boulaga, Fabien. *Christianity without Fetishes. An African Critique and Recapture of Christianity.* Translated by Robert R. Barr. Maryknoll, NY: Orbis Books, 1984.

—— 'La dé-mission'. *Spiritus* 56 (May–August 1974): 276–87.

Eglise de Pala. '70 ans de l'arrivée du premier missionnaire à Kou, l'Eglise du Tchad passe de 5 à 7 diocèses'. *Bulletin Diocésain de Pala* 115 (January 1999): 7–8.

Eisner, Peter. *The Pope's Last Crusade: How an American Jesuit Helped Pope Pius XI's Campaign to Stop Hitler*. New York: William Morrow, 2013.

Ela, Jean-Marc. *Le cri de l'homme Africain: questions aux chrétiens et aux églises d'Afrique*. Paris: L'Harmattan, 1980.

―― *Ma foi d'Africain*. Paris: Karthala, 1985.

―― ed. *Voici le temps des héritiers. Eglises d'Afrique et voie nouvelle*. Paris: Karthala, 1981.

Engard, Ronald K. 'Myth and Political Economy in Bafut (Cameroon): The Structural History of an African Kingdom'. *Paideuma* 34 (1988): 49–89.

Enyegue, Jean Luc. 'Africanize Christianity or Christianize Africanity? The Cameroonian Reaction to Global Catholicism in the 1970s'. Presented at the conference 'Global History and Roman Catholicism' 22. Notre Dame, IN, 2019.

―― 'New Wine into Old Wineskins? African Reactions to Arrupe's Governing Vision (1965–1978)'. *Archivum Historicum Societatis Iesu* 88, fasc. 176 (II 2019): 385–420.

―― 'The Adulteresses Were Reformers: The Perception and Position of Women in the Religious Fight of Fernando Poo, 1843–1900'. In *Encounters between Jesuits and Protestants in Africa,* eds Robert Maryks and Festo Mkenda. Boston: Brill, 2017.

―― 'The Jesuits in Fernando Po, 1858–1872: An Incomplete Mission'. In *Jesuits' Survival and Restoration: A Global History, 1773–1900*, 466–86. Leiden: Brill, 2015.

Faure, Pierre. *Monseigneur Paul Dalmais dans la guerre du Tchad: Document pour l'histoire*. Paris [publisher not known], 2003.

Fedry, Jacques, and P. Djiraingue. *Prières traditionnelles du Pays Sara*. Sarh: CEL, 1977.

Finke, Roger, and Rodney Stark. 'Religious Economies and Sacred Canopies: Religious Mobilization in American Cities, 1906'. *American Sociological Review* 53, no. 1 (February 1988): 41–49.

Fortier, Joseph. 'Chad'. In *Diccionario Histórico de la Compañía de Jesús*, 1:745–51. Madrid/Rome: IHSI/UPComillas, 2001.

―― *Frédéric de Bélinay: Pionnier des missions du Tchad*. Vols 1–2. 2 vols. Tchad, 1988.

―― *Les débuts de l'évangélisation au Moyen Chari, Diocèse de Sarh (Les Pionniers) 1946–1966*. 2 vols. Sarh: n.p., 1991.

Foster, Elizabeth. *African Catholic: Decolonization and the Transformation of the Church*. Cambridge, MA: Harvard University Press, 2019.

—— 'A Mission in Transition: Monsignor Joseph Faye and the Decolonization of the Catholic Church in Senegal'. In *In God's Empire: French Missionaries and the Modern World*, eds O. White and J. P. Daughton, 257–77. New York: Oxford University Press, 2012.

—— 'Entirely Christian and Entirely African: Catholic African Students in France in the Era of Independence'. *The Journal of African History* 56, no. 2 (2015): 239–59.

—— *Faith in Empire: Religion, Politics, and Colonial Rule in French Senegal, 1880–1940*. Stanford, CA: Stanford University Press, 2013.

Foster, Elizabeth, and Giuliana Chamedes. 'Introduction: Decolonization and Religion in Modern French History'. *French Politics, Culture & Society* 33, no. 2 (2015): 1–10.

Foucault, Michel. *The Archaeology of Knowledge: And the Discourse on Language*. New York: Vintage Books, 2010.

—— *The Order of Things: An Archaeology of the Human Sciences*. New York: Vintage Books, 1994.

Foureau, Ferdinand. *Documents Scientifiques de la Mission Saharienne: Mission Foureau-Lamy.* Paris: Masson et Cie, 1903.

Fox, Jonathan, and Ephraim Tabory. 'Contemporary Evidence Regarding the Impact of State Regulation of Religion on Religious Participation and Belief'. *Sociology of Religion* 69, no. 3 (Fall 2008): 245–71.

Franc, P. 'Fort-Archambault, Samuel Noir'. *JAF* 2 (1964): 48.

Friedlander, María-José, and Bob Friedlander. *Hidden Treasures of Ethiopia. A Guide to the Remote Churches of an Ancient Land*. New York: I. B. Tauris, 2015.

Fuchs, Peter. *La religion des Hadjeray.* Paris: L'Harmattan, 1997.

Fuglestad, Finn. 'Les révoltes des Touaregs du Niger (1916–1917)'. *Cahiers d'Études Africaines* 13, no. 49 (1973): 82–120.

Gallagher, Charles R. 'Decentering American Jesuit Anti-Communism: John LaFarge's United Front Strategy, 1934–39'. *Journal of Jesuit Studies* 5 (2018): 97–121.

Gamble, Harry. 'La crise de l'enseignement en Afrique Occidentale Française (1944–1950)'. *Histoire de l'Éducation* 128 (2010): 129–62.

Gatu, John G. *Fan into Flame. Rev. Dr John G. Gatu, an Autobiography.* Nairobi: Moran Publishers, 2016.

—— *Joyfully Christian and Truly African*. Nairobi: Acton Publishers, 2006.

Gebrekidan, Fikru Negash. 'Ethiopia and Congo: A Tale of Two Medieval Kingdoms'. *Callaloo* 33, no. 1 (2010): 223–38.

Géli, Jean. 'La consécration de Mgr. Dalmais, premier évêque du Tchad'. *Jésuites* 3 (1958): 35–38.

—— 'Ordination de Mgr Paul Dalmais'. *JAF* 3 (1958): 35.

Genova, James E. 'Constructing Identity in Post-War France: Citizenship, Nationality, and the Lamine Guèye Law, 1946–1953'. *The International History Review* 26, no. 1 (2004): 56–79.
Gerebern, Pater. *Pioniers 25 Jaar in de Ubangimissie Der Belgische Capucijnen*. Antwerpen: Franciscaansche Standaard, 1935.
Gide, André. *Voyage au Congo: Suivi du retour du Tchad*. Paris, 1929.
Gifford, Paul. *Christianity, Development and Modernity in Africa*. Oxford: Oxford University Press, 2016.
Ginio, Ruth. 'Marshal Pétain Spoke to Schoolchildren: Vichy Propaganda in French West Africa, 1940–1943'. *The International Journal of African Historical Studies* 33, no. 2 (2000): 291–312.
——— 'Vichy Rule in French West Africa: Prelude to Decolonization?' *French Colonial History* 4 (2003): 205–26.
Girardet, Raoul. 'L'apothéose de la "Plus Grande France": L'idée coloniale devant l'opinion française, 1930–1935'. *Revue Française de Science Politique* 18, no. 6 (December 1968): 1085–114.
Girling, Kristian. 'Jesuit Contributions to the Iraqi Education System in the 1930s and Later'. *International Studies in Catholic Education* 8, no. 2 (2016): 179–92.
Go, Julian. *Postcolonial Thought and Social Theory*. New York: Oxford University Press, 2016.
Gonçalves, Nuno da Silva, and Philip Kiley donor. *Os Jesuitas e a Missão de Cabo Verde (1604–1642)*. Lisboa: Brotéria, 1996.
Goodwin, Doris Kearns. *Team of Rivals: The Political Genius of Abraham Lincoln*. London: Penguin, 2009.
Gouraud, Henri Joseph Eugène. *Zinder-Tchad: Souvenirs d'un Africain* (Paris: Plon, 1944).
'Grand séminaire d'Otélé'. *JAF* 3 (1966): 42.
Gray, Richard. 'Christian Traces and a Franciscan Mission in Central Sudan'. *Journal of African Studies* 7 (1967): 392–93.
Grendler, Paul F. 'The Culture of the Jesuit Teacher 1548–1773'. *Journal of Jesuit Studies* 3 (2016): 17–41.
Guerivière, Jean de la. 'Tchad: Subversion contre l'initiation'. *Le Monde*, 11 December 1973, 8.
Gutting, Gary. *Foucault: A Very Short Introduction*. Oxford: Oxford University Press, 2005.
Hackett, Rosalind I. J. 'Art and Religion in Africa: Some Observations and Reflections'. *Journal of Religion in Africa* 24 (November 1994): 294–308.
Hair, P. E. H. 'Jesuit Documents on the Guinea of Cape Verde and the Cape Verde Islands, 1585–1617 in English Translation'. *History in Africa* 16 (1989): 375–81.

Hallaire, Jacques. *Au confluent des traditions de la savane et de la forêt. Étude thématique des contes Sar (Moyen-Chari, Tchad)*. N'Djamena: CEFOD, 1987.
—— 'Drame de conscience au pays Sara'. *JAF* 3 (1966): 41.
—— 'Evangile et coutumes'. *JAF* 1 (1963): 44.
—— '[Introduction de la] culture attelée au Tchad'. *JAF* 3 (1962): 47–48.
—— 'L'évangile sara: difficulté d'une traduction'. *JAF* 1 (1962): 46.
Hallaire, A., and J. Fedry. *Naissance d'une église africaine: Lettres et chroniques du Pays Sarh*. Paris: Karthala, 1998.
Hastings, Adrian (ed.). *A World History of Christianity*. Grand Rapids, MI: Eerdmans, 1999.
Hebga, Meinrad-P. 'Acculturation et chances d'un humanisme africain moderne'. *Présence Africaine* 68 (1968): 164–74.
—— *Afrique de La Raison, Afrique de La Foi*. Paris: Karthala, 1995.
—— 'Christianisme et négritude'. In *Des prêtres noirs s'interrogent*, 189–203. Rencontres 47. Paris: Présence Africaine, 1956.
—— *Dépassements*. Paris: Présence Africaine, 1978.
—— *Emancipation d'églises sous-tutelle: Essai sur l'ère post-missionnaire*. Paris: Présence Africaine, 1976.
—— *La Rationalité d'un discours africain sur les phénomènes paranormaux*. Paris: L'Harmattan, 1998.
—— 'L'homme vit aussi de fierté: vers la perte de l'identité africaine?' *Présence Africaine* 99–100 (1976): 19–40.
—— *Personnalité africaine et Catholicisme*. Paris: Présence Africaine, 1963.
Hefner, Robert W. 'Introduction: The Unexpected Modern-Gender, Piety, and Politics in the Global Pentecostal Surge'. In *Global Pentecostalism in the 21st Century*, eds Robert W. Hefner and Peter L. Berger. Bloomington, IN: Indiana University Press, 2013.
Hielscher, Hans. 'Les Blancs en Afrique noire: Du colonialisme au néocolonialisme'. Republished in *JA* 590 (29 April 1972): 18–22.
Hunt, Lynn. *Writing History in the Global Era*. 1st ed. New York: W.W. Norton & Company, 2014.
Ignatius of Loyola. 'Al P. Nunes Barreto, Roma, 24 Febrero 1555'. In *Obras Completas de Ignacio de Loyola*, 965–66. Madrid: BAC, 1982.
—— *The Spiritual Exercises of St Ignatius of Loyola*. Trans. George E. Ganss. New York: Vintage, 2000.
Ilboudo, Jean. *Vía Crucis Africae: Way of the Cross, Way to Resurrection*. Nairobi, JESAM, 2006.
Irísarri, José. *Misión de Fernando Poo, 1859*. Barcelona: Ceibas, 1998.
Jaulin, Robert. *La Mort Sara. L'ordre de la Vie ou la Pensée de la Mort au Tchad*. Paris: Plon, 1966.

Jenkins, Philip. *The Next Christendom: The Coming of Global Christianity*. Oxford: Oxford University Press, 2002.

John XXIII, Pope. 'Encyclical Letter "Princeps Pastorum"'. *AAS* 51 (1959): 833–64.

Johnson, Todd M., and Peter F. Crossing. 'Christianity 2014: Independent Christianity and Slum Dwellers'. *International Bulletin of Missionary Research* 38, no. 1 (January 2014): 28–29.

Joseph, Richard A. *Gaullist Africa: Cameroon under Ahmadu Ahidjo*. Enugu: Fourth Dimension Publishers, 1978.

—— 'Ruben Um Nyobè and the "Kamerun" Rebellion'. *African Affairs* 73, no. 293 (October 1974): 428–48.

Kalu, Ogbu. *African Christianity: An African Story*. Trenton, NJ: Africa World Press, 2007.

Kane, Ousmane. *Beyond Timbuktu: An Intellectual History of Muslim West Africa*. Cambridge, MA: Harvard University Press, 2016.

—— L'"islamisme" d'hier et d'aujourd'hui: Quelques enseignements de l'Afrique de l'Ouest'. *Cahiers d'Études Africaines* 52, no. 206/207. L'islam au-delà des categories (2012): 545–74.

Kanya-Forstner, A. S. 'French Missions to the Central Sudan in the 1890s: The Role of Algerian Agents and Interpreters'. *Paideuma* 40 (1994): 15–35.

Kaplan, Steven. 'The Africanization of Missionary Christianity: History and Typology'. *Journal of Religion in Africa* 16, no. 3 (1986): 166–86.

Kennedy, Thomas Frank. 'Jesuits and Music: The European Tradition, 1547–1622'. PhD Musicology, University of California Santa Clara, 1982.

—— *Music and the Jesuit Mission in the New World*. Saint Louis, MO: Seminar on Jesuit Spirituality, 2007.

Kiley, Philip, and John W. Padberg. *Jesuit Life & Mission Today: The Decrees of the 31st-35th General Congregations of the Society of Jesus*. Vol. 1. Saint Louis, MO: Institute of Jesuit Sources, 2009.

Kirby, Erika L., et al. 'The Jesuit Difference(?): Narratives of Negotiating Spiritual Values and Secular Practices'. *Communication Studies* 57, no. 1 (2006): 87–105.

Kitson, Simon. 'From Enthusiasm to Disenchantment: The French Police and the Vichy Regime, 1940–1944'. *Contemporary European History* 11, no. 3 (August 2002): 371–90.

Kollman, Paul. 'At the Origins of Mission and Missiology: A Study in the Dynamics of Religious Language'. *Journal of the American Academy of Religion* 79, no. 2 (June 2011): 425–58.

La Bella, Gianni. *Los Jesuitas. Del Vaticano II al Papa Francisco*. Bilbao: Mensajero, 2019.

Labrador, Carmen. *El sistema educativo de la Compania de Jesus. Continuidad e innovacion. Ante el cuarto centenario de la Ratio Studiorum*. Madrid: UPComillas, 1987.

Laburthe-Tolra, Philippe. 'Intentions missionnaires et perception africaine: Quelques données camerounaise'. *Civilisations* 41, nos 1–2 (1993): 239–55.

—— *Les Seigneurs de la forêt: Essai sur le passé historique, l'organisation sociale et les normes éthiques des anciens Beti du Cameroun*. 2nd ed. Paris: L'Harmattan, 2009.

Lacouture, Jean. *Jésuites: Les Revenants*. 2 vols. Paris: Seuil, 1992.

—— *Jesuits: A Multibiography*. Washington, DC: Counterpoint, 1995.

Lado, Ludovic. *Catholic Pentecostalism and the Paradoxes of Africanization*. Leiden: Brill, 2009.

Lamet, Pedro Miguel. *Arrupe: testigo del siglo XX, profeta del XXI*. 1st ed. Madrid: Temas de hoy, 2007.

Lamy, François Joseph. *Le Commandant Lamy d'après sa correspondance et ses souvenirs de Campagne (1858–1900)*. Paris: Hachette, 1903.

Lanoue, Éric. '"Le temps des missionnaires n'est plus!": Le devenir postcolonial de l'enseignement catholique en Côte d'Ivoire (1958–2000). *Cahiers d'Études Africaines* 43 (2003): 99–120.

Laqua-O'Donnell, Simone. *Women and the Counter-Reformation in Early Modern Münster*. Oxford: Oxford University Press, 2014.

Latourette, Kenneth Scott. 'Colonialism and Missions: Progressive Separation'. *Journal of Church and State* 7, no. 3 (Autumn 1965): 330–49.

Lecoq, P. 'Eglise en dur'. *JAF* 4 (1965): 45–46.

Leonard, Lori. 'Women Who Changed into Men: A Gendered History of Precarity in "Useful Chad"'. *Africa* 89, no. 3 (2019): 521–40.

Lesmes, Frias. *Historia de la Compañía de Jesús en su Asistencia moderna de España*. Madrid: Razón y Fe, 1923.

'Lien entre le but dernier des missions et la création du clergé indigène exposé dans l'encyclique "Evangelii Praecones"'. *Revue du Clergé Africain* (1948): 345–47.

Lomazzi, Luis. 'Aide pour la mission'. *JAF* 4 (1962): 38.

Lovie, Jacques. *La Savoie dans la vie française de 1860 à 1875*. Paris: Presses Universitaires de France, 1963.

Magni, Alexius A. 'R.P. Norbertus de Boynes a R.P. Alexio A. Mgni Ut Vicarii Generalis Partes Ad Tempus Agat Constituitur'. ARSI (11 April 1944).

Malaxecheverria, José. *La Compania de Jesus por la instruccion del Pueblo Vasco en los siglos XVII y XVIII*. San Sebastian: Gariby, 1926.

Malloum, General. 'Le 13 Avril 1975, Pour un Tchad nouveau'. *Tchad et Culture* 86 (May 1975): 2–3.

Mann, Gregory. *From Empires to NGOs in the West African Sahel. The Road to Nongovernmentality*. New York: Cambridge University Press, 2015.

—— 'Immigrants and Arguments in France and West Africa'. *Comparative Studies in Society and History* 45, no. 2 (April 2003): 362–85.

Margot, Charles. 'Mes chers noirs'. *Lettres du Tchad* 4 (February 1948): 1–10.

—— 'Nos Noirs'. *Missi* 10 (October 1948): 238.

Martel, André. 'L'Afrique Française Libre: Support d'effort de guerre française et Allié, 1940–1942'. In *Le Général Leclerc et l'Afrique Française Libre, 1940–1942*, 87–105. Paris: Fondation Maréchal Leclerc, 1987.

Martin, André. 'Kabalay, croissance chrétienne'. *JAF* 1 (1963): 40.

Martin, Thomas. 'Albert Sarraut, French Colonial Development, and the Communist Threat, 1919–1930'. *The Journal of Modern History* 77, no. 4 (December 2005): 917–55.

Maryks, Robert, ed. *Jesuits' Survival and Restoration: A Global History, 1773–1900*. Leiden: Brill, 2015.

Mathieu, Augustin. 'Renforts pour la Mission des Hadjeray'. *Lettres du Tchad* (October 1959): 4.

Maurel, Pierre. 'Notice nécrologique du P. Éric de Rosny'. *NPAO* 244 (2012): 2–4.

Mbairougol, Maioulam. 'Implantation et impact des missions protestantes dans le Logone Occidental au Sud du Tchad: 1926–1997'. MA thesis in History, University of Ngaoundéré, 2009.

Mbembe, Achille. *On the Post-Colony*. Berkeley: University of California Press, 2001.

McDonough, Peter. *Men Astutely Trained. A History of the Jesuits in the American Century*. New York: The Free Press, 1992.

McEwan, Dorothea. *A Catholic Sudan: Dream, Mission, Reality*. Roma: Stabilimento Tipografico Julia, 1987.

McGreevy, John T. *American Jesuits and the World: How an Embattled Religious Order Made Modern Catholicism Global*. Princeton, NJ: Princeton University Press, 2016.

—— 'Restored Jesuits: Notes towards a Global History'. In *The Jesuits and Globalization. Historical Legacies and Contemporary Challenges*, 131–46. Washington, DC: Georgetown University Press, 2016.

McKenna, Joseph C. *Finding a Social Voice. The Church and Marxism in Africa*. New York: Fordham University Press, 1997.

Méjan, François. *Le Vatican contre la France d'Outre-Mer?* Paris: Librairie Fischbacher, 1957.

Mertens, Victor. 'La place et l'attitude des missionnaires étrangers aujourd'hui en Afrique'. *Chine–Madagascar* 145 (December 1973): 5–11.

Messi Metogo, Eloi. *Dieu peut-il mourir en Afrique? Essai sur l'indifférence religieuse en Afrique.* Paris: Karthala, 1997.
Messina, Jean-Paul. *Engelbert Mveng: La plume et le pinceau: Un message pour l'Afrique du IIIème millénaire, 1930–1995.* Yaoundé: PUCAC, 2003.
—— *Jean Zoa, Prêtre, Archevêque de Yaoundé: 1922–1998.* Paris: Karthala, 2000.
Meyer, Birgit. 'Christianity in Africa: From African Independent to Pentecostal-Charismatic Churches'. *Annual Review of Anthropology* 33, no. 1 (2004): 448.
Meynier, André. 'Formation de catéchistes à Kyabe'. *JAF* 4 (1962): 43–44.
—— 'Kyabé, travaux quotidiens'. *JAF* 1 (1963): 41–42.
Miege, Jean-Louis. 'La Libye et le commerce transsaharien au XIXe siècle'. *Revue de l'Occident Musulman et de La Méditerranée* 19 (1975): 136.
Ministère de la France d'Outre-Mer, *Le Tchad.* Paris: Agence de la France d'Outre-Mer, 1950.
Mkenda, Festo. *A Mission for Everyone: A Story of the Jesuits in Eastern Africa (1555–2012).* Nairobi: Saint Paul, 2013.
Murray, Alison. 'Framing Greater France: Images of Africa in French Documentary Film, 1920–1940'. ed. Roland Simon. PhD dissertation, University of Virginia, 1998.
Mveng, Engelbert. 'A la recherche d'un nouveau dialogue entre le Christianisme, le génie culturel et les religions africaines actuelles'. *Présence Africaine* 96 (1975): 443–66.
—— *Art nègre art chrétien?* Rome: Les amis italiens de Présence Africaine, 1969.
—— 'Camerún'. In *Diccionario Histórico de La Compañía de Jesús*, 612–15. Madrid/Rome: IHSI/UPComillas, 2001.
—— 'De la sous-mission à la succession'. In *Civilisation Noire et Eglise Catholique*, 267–76. Paris: Présence Africaine, 1978.
—— *Histoire du Cameroun.* 1st ed. Paris: Présence Africaine, 1963.
—— *L'Afrique dans l'Eglise: Paroles d'un croyant.* Paris: L'Harmattan, 1986.
—— *L'art d'Afrique Noire: Liturgie cosmique et langage religieux.* Tours: Mame, 1964.
—— *L'Eglise Catholique au Cameroun: 100 ans d'évangélisation 1890–1990.* Rome: Presso Grafiche Dehoniane, 1990.
—— 'Le Synode Africain, prolégomènes pour un Concile Africain?' *Concilium* 239 (1992): 149–69.
—— *Théologie, libération et cultures africaines: Dialogue sur l'anthropologie négro-africaine.* Yaoundé, Cameroon, and Paris: Clé, 1996.

Mveng, Engelbert, and Beling-Nkoumba. *Manuel d'histoire du Cameroun*. Yaoundé: CEPER, 1969.
Nana, Alexandre. *Anthropologie Beti et sens chrétien de l'homme*. Paris: L'Harmattan, 2010.
Nelson, Samuel, and Philip S. Gorski. 'Conditions of Religious Belonging: Confessionalization, De-Parochialization, and the Euro-American Divergence'. *International Sociology* 29, no. 1 (2014): 3–21.
Nfi, Joseph Lon. 'The Powerlessness of Cameroon's Reunification Monuments'. *East West Journal of Humanities* 4 (2013): 125–34.
Ngothe Gatta, Gali. *Tchad, La Grande Guerre pour le pouvoir, 1979–1980*. N'Djamena: Centre Al-Mouna, 2007.
Noudjalbaye, Ngaryanan. 'L'Eglise Baptiste dans la tempête Au Tchad (1973–1975)'. Direction de la Documentation de la Présidence de la République, 1976. CEFOD. A-CEFOD. Box: CF.B. 01285 CF.
Noudjitoloum, Théodore. *Nouvelles de la PAO* 244: 12.
Ochs, Stephen J. *Desegregating the Altar: The Josephites and the Struggle for Black Priests, 1871–1960*. Baton Rouge: Louisiana State University Press, 1990.
O'Malley, John W. *Four Cultures of the West*. Cambridge, MA: Belknap Press of Harvard University Press, 2004.
O'Malley, John W., Gauvin A. Bailey, and Steven J. Harris. *The Jesuits II: Cultures, Sciences, and the Arts, 1540–1773*. Toronto: University of Toronto Press, 2006.
Onomo Etaba, Roger. 'Maximum Illud, de Benoît XV, et l'oeuvre missionnaire au Cameroun (1890–1935): Entre anticipations, applications et contradictions'. *Présence Africaine* 172 (2005): 125–45.
Orosz, Kenneth J. 'The "Catechist War" in Interwar French Cameroon'. In *In God's Empire. French Missionaries and the Modern World* (Oxford: Oxford University Press, 2012.
Ossama, Nicolas. '50 ans de l'Eglise au Cameroun. Session Missionnaire' (La Louvesc, 6–10 September 1965).
—— *L'Eglise du Cameroun: Schéma historique (1890–2000)*. Yaoundé: PUCAC, 2011.
Owono-Kouma, Auguste. 'La riposte des leaders de l'UPC aux vicaires apostoliques du Cameroun. Analyse historico-littéraire de la réaction des nationalistes camerounais à la Lettre Commune d'avril 1955'. *Histoire et Missions Chrétiennes* 10 (June 2009): 119–39.
Padberg, John W., ed. *Documents of the Thirty First and Thirty Second General Congregations of the Society of Jesus*. Saint Louis, MO: The Institute of Jesuit Sources, 1977.

—— *Together as a Companionship. A History of the Thirty-First, Thirty-Second, and Thirty-Third General Congregations of the Society of Jesus.* Saint Louis, MO: The Institute of Jesuit Sources, 1994.

Pakenham, Thomas. *The Scramble for Africa. The White Man's Conquest of the Dark Continent from 1876 to 1912* (New York: Random House, 1991), 359–61.

Palayer, P. *Dictionnaire Kenga (Tchad)*. Louvain: Peeters, 2004.

—— *Eléments de grammaire Sar (Tchad)*. Pol, 1970.

—— *Grammaire du Dadjo d'Eref*. Paris: Peeters, 2011.

—— *Lexique de plantes du pays Sar, plantes spontanées et cultivées.* n.p., 1977.

Pastells, Pablo. *Misión de la Compañía de Jesús de Filipinas en el siglo XIX.* Vol. 1. Barcelona: Tip. y Lib., 1916.

Paul VI, Pope. 'Africae Terrarum'. *AAS* 69 (Rome: 29 October 1967): 1073–102.

—— 'Excellentissimis Viris et Legatorum Coetu in Ugandensis Republica'. *AAS* 11 (1 August 1969): 580–86.

—— 'Homilia in sollemni canonizatione Beatorum: Caroli Lwanga, Matthiae Mulumba Kalemba et viginti sociorum Martyrum Ugandensium'. *AAS* 56 (18 October 1964): 907–08.

Pavone, Sabina. 'The History of Anti-Jesuitism: National and Global Dimensions'. In *The Jesuits and Globalization. Historical Legacies and Contemporary Challenges*, 111–30. Washington, DC: Georgetown University Press, 2016.

Pellissier, Pierre. *Fachoda et La Mission Marchand, 1896–1899*. Paris: Perrin, 2011.

Pennell, C. R. 'Ideology and Practical Politics: A Case Study of the Rif War in Morocco, 1921–1926'. *International Journal of Middle East Studies* 14, no. 1 (February 1982): 19–33.

Phipps, William E. 'The Influence of Christian Missions on the Rise of Nationalism in Central Africa'. *International Review of Mission* 57, no. 226 (April 1968): 229–32.

Pichon, Roland. 'Bediondo, le salut sur les murs'. *JAF* 1 (1964): 41.

—— *Un Jésuite persona non grata*. Paris: Harmattan, 2008.

Pierret, François. *Les Débuts de la Bonne Nouvelle Au Tchad, 1920–1951.* Archives of the Jesuit Historical Institute in Africa. Nairobi: n.p., 1971.

Pius XI, Pope. 'Rerum Ecclesiae'. *AAS* 72 (28 February 1926): 65–83.

Pius XII, Pope. 'Encyclical Letter "Ad apostolorum principis"'. *AAS* 50 (1958): 601–14.

—— 'Exhortation de Pie XII au clergé indigène (28 Juin 1948)'. *Revue du Clergé Africain* (1948): 372–79.

—— 'L'encyclique "Fidei Donum" (21 Avril 1957) sur la situation des missions notamment en Afrique'. *Revue du Clergé Africain* (1957): 321–37.
—— 'Lettre Encyclique ad Sinarum gentem'. *AAS* 47 (1955): 5–14.
Pledge, Robert. 'Chad: France's African War'. *Africa Report* (1 June 1970): 16–19.
Plumey, Yves. *Mission Tchad-Cameroun, l'annonce de l'évangile au Nord-Cameroun et au Mayo-Kébbi*. Italie: Editions Oblates, 1990.
Pommerol, Julien de. *Dictionnaire Arabe Tchadien-Français*. Paris: Karthala, 1999.
—— *Grammaire pratique de l'arabe Tchadien*. Paris: Karthala, 1999.
—— *J'apprends l'arabe Tchadien*. Paris: Karthala, 1999.
—— *L'arabe Tchadien. Emergence d'une langue véhiculaire*. Paris: Karthala, 1997.
Potvin, Raymond H., and Thomas K. Burch. 'Fertility, Ideal Family-Size and Religious Orientation among U.S. Catholics'. *Sociological Analysis* 29, no. 1 (1968): 28–34.
Raisson, Pierre. 'Le Père Joseph du Bouchet, 1890–1970'. *Jésuites* (1971): 177–79.
Reeck, Matt. 'The Paradoxes of Description in André Gide's *Voyage au Congo and Le Retour du Tchad*'. *South Central Review* 36, no. 1 (Spring 2019), 82–103.
Reese, Robert. 'John Gatu and the Moratorium on Missionaries'. *Missiology: An International Review* 42, no. 3 (2014): 245–56.
Reese, Scott S. 'Islam in Africa/Africans and Islam'. *The Journal of African History* 55, no. 1 (2014): 17–26.
Remy, Adrien. *Les Spiritains face à l'indépendance du Cameroun*. Yaoundé: PUCAC, 2012.
Ricœur, Paul. *Critique and Conviction: Conversations with François Azouvi and Marc de Launay*. Cambridge, UK: Polity Press in association with Blackwell Publishers, 1998.
—— *Memory, History, Forgetting*. Chicago, IL: University of Chicago Press, 2004.
Robert, Dana L. *Christian Mission: How Christianity Became a World Religion*. Malden, MA: Blackwell, 2009.
—— 'Shifting Southward: Global Christianity Since 1945'. *International Bulletin of Missionary Research* 24, no. 2 (April 2000): 50–58.
—— 'The First Globalization: The Internationalization of the Protestant Missionary Movement Between the World Wars'. *International Bulletin of Missionary Research* 26, no. 2 (2002): 50.
Rosny, Éric de. *Healers in the Night*. Translated by Robert R. Barr. Maryknoll, NY: Orbis Books, 1985.

—— *L'Afrique des guérisons*. Collection Les Afriques. Paris: Karthala, 1992.
—— *Les yeux de ma chèvre: Sur les pas des maîtres de la nuit en pays Douala*. Paris: Pocket, 1996.
—— 'Mission terminée?' *Etudes* (May 1970), 737–46.
Sabatier, Peggy R. 'Charles Béart, "Bon Père" or "Le Colonialisme Incarné?": Colonial School Director and the Ambiguities of Paternalism'. *Proceedings of the Meeting of the French Colonial Historical Society* 4 (1979): 141–56.
—— '"Elite" Education in French West Africa: The Era of Limits, 1903–1945'. *The International Journal of African Historical Studies* 11, no. 2 (1978): 247–66.
Saint Moulin, Léon de. *Histoire des Jésuites en Afrique: Du XVIe siècle à nos jours*. Namur: Éd. Jésuites, 2016.
—— *Translating the Message: The Missionary Impact on Culture*. Maryknoll, NY: Orbis Books, 1989.
Salameh, Franck. 'A Man for Others: The Life and Times of Lebanese Jesuit Henri Lammens, 1862–1937'. *The Journal of the Middle East and Africa* 9, no. 2 (2018): 213–36.
Salamone, Frank A. 'Mixed Messages at the Mission'. *Anthropos* 86, nos 4–6 (1991): 488.
Samson, Fabienne. 'Les classifications en Islam'. *Cahiers d'Études Africaines* 52, nos 206/07 (2012): 335–36.
Sanneh, Lamin O. *Abolitionists Abroad. American Blacks and the Making of Modern West Africa*. Cambridge, MA: Harvard University Press, 1999.
Scaglione, Aldo. *The Liberal Arts and the Jesuit College System*. Amsterdam: John Benjamins, 1986.
Scheele, Judith. 'Ravens Reconsidered: Raiding and Theft among Tubu-Speakers in Northern Chad'. *African Studies Review* 34 (2018): 135–55.
Schmid, Dorothée. 'La Turquie et l'Union pour la Méditerranée: un partenariat calculé'. *Politique Étrangère* 1 (2008): 65–76.
'Séminaire de Yaoundé'. *JAF* 3 (1963): 45.
Sesboüé, Bernard, and Florian Michel. *De Mgr Lefèbvre à Mgr Williamson. Anatomie d'un schisme*. Paris: Lethielleux/DDB, 2009.
Shenk, Wilbert R. 'The Missionary and Politics: Henry Venn's Guidelines'. *Journal of Church and State* 24, no. 3 (1982): 525–34.
Sileck, Assaïd Gamar. 'Bilinguisme: les véritables enjeux'. *N'Djamena-Hebdo* 76 (25 February 1993): 8.
Soares, Benjamin F. '"Being as Good Muslims as Frenchmen": On Islam and Colonial Modernity in West Africa'. *Journal of Religion in Africa* 39, no. 1 (2009): 91–120.
Sonnè, Wang. 'Cameroon: Why Are the Names of Great Historical Figures from the 1950s Taboo in the Mouth of President Paul Biya?' *Africa Development* 22, no. 2 (January 1997): 131–49.

Soria, José Luis Ferrer. *Naissance et épanouissement d'une jeune communauté chrétienne au Tchad* (Paris: Éd. Centres Sèvres, 1976).
Souza, Isidore de. 'Pouvons-nous rester Africains tout en étant membre d'une religion importée?' *Telema* 4 (April 1974): 23–33.
Spaulding, Jay, and Lidwien Kapteijns, 'Land Tenure and the State in the Precolonial Sudan'. *Northeast African Studies* 9, no. 1 (2002): 33–66.
Stark, Rodney, and James C. McCann. 'Market Forces and Catholic Commitment: Exploring the New Paradigm'. *Journal for the Scientific Study of Religion* 32, no. 2 (June 1993): 111–24.
Thornton, John K. 'Conquest and Theology. The Jesuits in Angola, 1548–1650'. *Journal of Jesuit Studies* 1 (2014): 245–59.
—— 'The Development of an African Catholic Church in the Kingdom of Kongo, 1491–1750'. *Journal of African History* 25 (1984): 147–67.
Tissier de Mallerais, Bernard. *The Biography: Marcel Lefebvre*. Kansas City, MO: Angelus Press, 2002.
Tombalbaye, N'Garta. 'Les principes de l'initiation au Yondo ainsi que ceux du Christianisme et de l'islam s'accordent'. *Agence Tchadienne Presse* 3054 (30 April 1974): 1–5.
—— 'Nous avons agi conformément à notre Révolution Culturelle'. *Agence Tchadienne de Presse* 3036 (8 April 1974).
Triaud, Jean-Louis. 'Les "trous de Mémoire" dans l'histoire africaine. La Sanûsiyya au Tchad: Le cas du Ouaddaï'. *Revue Française d'Histoire d'Outre-Mer* 83, no. 311 (1996): 5.
Trouillot, Michel-Rolph. *Silencing the Past: Power and the Production of History*. Boston: Beacon Press, 1995.
Unknown. 'La Compagnie en Afrique et Madagascar'. *La Compagnie en Afrique et Madagascar* 41 (October 1970): 147.
—— 'Le malaise du monde'. *Revue Politique et Parlementaire* 559 (September 1946): 176–77.
Usera y Alarcón, Jerónimo M. *Memoria de la isla de Fernando Poo* (Madrid: T. Aguado, 1848).
Valero, Urbano. *Pablo VI y los Jesuitas. Una relación intensa y complicada, 1963–1978*. Bilbao: Mensajero, 2019.
Vallet, Maurice. 'Le laïcisme dans l'enseignement actuel'. *Etudes Religieuses* 189 (5 November 1926): 257–81.
Vandame, Charles. 'Anniversaire national'. *JAF* 2 (1964): 46–47.
—— *Cinquante ans de la vie de l'Eglise Catholique au Tchad*. Paris: L'Harmattan, 2012.
Vandame, Charles, and Benjamin Bamani. *La joie de servir*. Paris: Sarment-jubilé, 2009.
Vansina, Jan. 'The Doom of Early African History?' *History in Africa* 24 (1997): 337–43.

Venet, Henri. 'Problèmes du séminaire'. *JAF* 3 (1964): 44–45.
Venn, Henry. *To Apply the Gospel: Selections from the Writings of Henry Venn*. Grand Rapids, MI: Eerdmans, 1971.
Verschave, François-Xavier. *La Françafrique: Le plus long scandale de la République* (Paris: Stock, 2006)
Vikor, Knut S. 'An Episode of Saharan Rivalry: The French Occupation of Kawar, 1906'. *The International Journal of African Historical Studies* 18, no. 4 (1985): 708–13.
Wake, Eleanor. *Framing the Sacred: The Indian Churches of Early Colonial Mexico*. Norman, OK: University of Oklahoma Press, 2010.
Walker-Said, Charlotte. 'Christian Social Movements in Cameroon at the End of Empire: Transnational Solidarities and the Communion of the World Church'. In *Relocating World Christianity: Interdisciplinary Studies in Universal and Local Expressions of Christianity*, 189–212. Leiden: Brill, 2017.
—— *Faith, Power and Family: Christianity and Social Change in French Cameroon*. Religion in Transforming Africa. Woodbridge, UK: James Currey, 2018.
Walls, Andrew F. *The Cross-Cultural Process in Christian History*. Maryknoll, NY: Orbis Books, 2002.
—— *The Missionary Movement in Christian History: Studies in the Transmission of Faith*. Maryknoll, NY: Orbis Books, 1996.
Ward, Haruko Nawata. 'Naitō Julia and Women Catechists in the Jesuit Mission in Japan and the Philippines'. In *Putting Names with Faces: Women's Impact in Mission History* (Nashville, TN: Abingdon Press, 2012), 249.
Wariboko, Nimi. *Nigerian Pentecostalism*. Rochester, NY: University of Rochester Press, 2014.
Waton, P. 'Auteurs préférés des jeunes'. *JAF* 1 (1964): 45.
Wauthier, C. 'Les sectes messianiques et les églises séparatistes en Afrique'. *JA* 605 (12 August 1972): 52–53.
Welbourn, Frederick Burkewood. *A Place to Feel at Home: A Study of Two Independent Churches in Western Kenya*. London and Nairobi: Oxford University Press, 1966.
Williams, Kim-Eric. 'Cameroon'. In *Dictionary of Lutheran and the Lutheran Traditions*. Grand Rapids, MI: Baker Academic, 2017.
Wittberg, Patricia. 'Declining Institutional Sponsorship and Religious Orders: A Study of Reverse Impacts'. *Sociology of Religion* 61, no. 3 (2000): 315–24.
Woodberry, Robert D. 'Missionary Roots of Liberal Democracy'. *American Political Science Review* 106, no. 2 (May 2012): 244–74.
Worbe, André. 'School for Muslims'. *JAF* 1 (1963): 45–46.

Worcester, Thomas. 'A Restored Society or a New Society of Jesus?' In *Jesuits' Survival and Restoration*, 13–33. Leiden: Brill, 2015.
Wynands, Marie-Pierre. '(Re)Christianizing the Popular Classes. The Catholic Church and Faith Training, 1921–1939'. *Revue Française de Science Politique* 66, no. 2 (2017): 43–61.
Yang, Fenggang. 'The Red, Black, and Gray Markets of Religion in China'. *The Sociological Quarterly* 47, no. 1 (Winter 2006): 93–122.
Younkam, Cyrille. 'Compte rendu de la messe de requiem du P. de Rosny'. *Nouvelles PAO* 244 (2012): 5–7.
Zarandona, Antonio. 'Proyecto de una Misión a las Islas Españolas del Golfo de Guinea. Presentado en la Dirección de Ultramar Por A-Z, El 4 de Mayo de 1857'. n.d., AHA. C 458, n. 8570009.

Journals

Acta Apostolicae Sedis (AAS), from 1908.
Acta Romana Societatis Iesu (AR), from 1906.
Courrier du Tchad, Nov. 1947–Jan. 1952, printed.
Courriers Province de Lyon, 1933–60.
Compagnie, 1945–52; 507. *Compagnie (Courrier des Provinces de France),* 1966–67.
Information, then *Documentation – Office de Presse SJ de Rome,* from 1971–85.
Jésuites de l'Assistance de France (JAF), 1953–55; 502 (1956–58), 503 (1959–61), 503 (1962–64), 504 (1962–64), 505 (1965–66), 506 (1967–68).
Jésuites de France, 1969–74. 531–532b (1987–91).
Jésuites en Afrique, Lettres de la VPAO, 1976–82.
Lettres du Tchad, from 1946–56, handout; then printed.
Lettres du Tchad, from 1957–66, printed.
Lettres du Tchad, from 1967–68, printed.
Lettres du Tchad, from 1969–72, printed.
Nouvelles d'Afrique et d'Asie, Oct. 1955–Jan. 1965.
Nouvelles VPAO, from 1976–82; then 1983–87, handout.

Reports

Adam Matthew Publications, 'SUM in Nigeria, the Cameroons, Chad, Sudan, and other African territories'. Annual Report 1973, published on 3 February 1974.

Newspapers and Periodicals

Canard Déchaîné, 'A cause du succès spectaculaire du Yondo, LA TARTUFFERIE RELIGIEUSE AUX ABOIS'. N'Garta Tombalbaye. 0046 (11 November 1974): 1 and 6.

—— 'Ça y est! Du pétrole au Tchad'. 0044 (24 October 1974).

—— 'Conférence de presse du Président Tombalbaye a Paris'. N'Garta Tombalbaye. 0047 (23 November 1974): 3.

—— 'Ils ne sont pas morts'. Illiya Romba. 0052 (5 February 1975).

—— 'L'affaire des missionnaires d'Andoum'. Pasteur Burgera. 0053 (18 February 1975).

—— 'Mme Thevenet affirme: Tous nos prédicateurs sont revenus sains et saufs de l'initiation'. 0052 (5 February 1975): 6.

—— 'Ne trahissons pas le Yondo'. Needi Brahim Seid. 0048 (7 December 1974): 6.

—— 'Retour du Yondo'. 0043 (12 October 1974).

—— 'Témoignage d'une vraie Chrétienne'. 0052 (5 February 1975): 1–2.

—— 'Tombalbaye à Paris le 20 Novembre 1974'. N'Garta Tombalbaye. 0045 (3 November 1974): 1 and 6.

Jésuites, 'Au bout du Tchad'. Claude Pairault. 3 (1960): 46.

—— 'Au Tchad'. 2 (1960): 36–40.

—— 'Enseignement secondaire au Cameroun, Collège Libermann'. 2 (1961): 29–35.

—— 'Le R. P. Véniat nous parle du Tchad'. Henri Véniat. 1 (1960): 42.

—— 'Missionnaires de l'Assistance de France: Tchad'. 4 (1960): 36–38.

—— 'Tchad, Damandji, un missionnaire révise ses méthodes'. P. Robinne. 4 (1961): 40–41.

Jesuit Missions, 'Our Indians and Negroes'. 11, no. 4 (April 1937): 87.

New York Times, 'Africans Ask Pontiff for Married Priests'. 4 July 1970, 13.

Index

Accommodation
  Au yondo 17, 95, 123
  Chinese 124, 150, 259
Accommodating 68, 111, 123, 151
African Christianity 1, 12, 21, 180, 195, 198, 233, 247, 251
African Traditional Religions,
  Religionists 7, 233, 19
Africanism
  Pan 7
  Catholic 8, 205
Africanity 185, 195, 201, 228, 245
Africanisation
  Discourse on 4
  Dynamics of 3, 4
  Ecclesiastical (clerical) 3, 4, 5, 9, 10, 11, 37, 38, 39, 40, 44, 45, 50, 57, 63, 64, 74, 79, 84, 90, 95, 96, 97, 99, 104, 125, 175, 177, 189, 195, 219, 237, 250, 256, 265, 266
  Leaders of 11, 13, 76, 88, 91, 140, 142, 146, 196, 248, 250, 259, 262, 266, 267
  Movement 6, 7, 18, 20, 151, 168, 175, 180, 213, 215, 216, 222, 226, 246, 247, 248, 250, 251, 252, 257, 259, 264, 265, 267, 269, 271, 272
Akamse (T. M.) 246, 262
Animists 111, 116, 172
Arrupe (P.) 5, 7, 9, 10, 12, 13, 14, 20, 36, 58, 115, 143, 160, 169, 192, 194, 225, 227, 229, 234, 236, 238, 239, 240, 241, 242, 243, 245, 246, 251, 256, 257, 266, 267, 269, 270
Azombo (S.) 217, 220, 222, 223

Bible 90, 96, 137, 138, 155, 183

Birba 80
Bloch, Marc 33
Boynes (N.) 36, 59, 60
Brazzaville 5, 43, 49, 51, 107, 117, 141, 190, 202, 266
Burkina Faso 80, 117, 190, 266

Calvez (J. Y.) 190, 191, 209, 239
Cameroon Region 198, 200, 202, 203, 213
  Cameroonians 4, 13, 76, 80, 81, 176, 179, 181, 182, 193, 199, 200, 201, 202, 205, 211, 212, 213, 215, 219, 220, 221, 222, 225, 226, 229, 257, 262, 263, 265
Catechism, Catechists 38, 45, 64, 74, 77, 89, 100, 116, 124, 125, 130, 133, 134, 136, 138, 140, 145, 147, 148, 151, 157, 179, 183, 184, 189, 207, 256
Catholicism, Catholicisms 8, 9, 10, 12, 19, 20, 25, 28, 29, 31, 32, 35, 36, 37, 38, 46, 56, 60, 77, 78, 83, 90, 96, 98, 99, 100, 102, 111, 116, 124, 145, 175, 176, 178, 185, 225, 232, 235, 236, 238, 243, 246, 251, 265, 267, 268, 271, 272
Catholicity 8, 13, 19, 46, 56, 140, 146, 195, 204, 249
Chad Mission 8, 11, 13, 14, 32, 36, 44, 46, 53, 56, 58, 60, 62, 64, 67, 68, 71, 73, 74, 75, 76, 77, 79, 82, 84, 86, 87, 88, 91, 95, 109, 111, 136, 141, 148, 149, 168, 178, 186, 188, 190, 191, 192, 199, 200, 213, 214, 255, 256, 265
Christianities 1, 3, 4, 8, 22, 173, 360, 379
Christianisation 138, 140, 151, 252, 259, 271

Churches 13, 17, 20, 52, 62, 109, 129, 132, 140, 146,152, 154, 155, 159, 162, 164, 167, 168, 200, 203, 214, 216, 234
Civility, Civilising, Civilisation 20, 25, 28, 29, 30, 31, 35, 36, 37, 41, 45, 52, 55, 56, 60, 72, 105, 105, 107, 117, 155, 156, 161, 162, 175, 181, 255
Colonialism, Colonies 4, 7, 9, 10, 19, 25, 32, 33, 34, 37, 39, 40, 41, 42, 43, 44, 45, 48, 51, 53, 54, 58, 59, 65, 71, 96, 106, 108, 121, 154, 155, 161, 171, 198, 201, 214, 217, 233, 237, 238, 246, 264, 265, 271
Communism, Communists 7, 8, 26, 28, 31, 32, 34, 36, 37, 38, 44, 47, 49, 56, 57, 59, 70, 71, 74, 103, 106, 107, 108, 111, 124, 125, 128, 146, 160, 237, 255
Competing, Competition 6, 7, 8, 9, 14, 15, 16, 17, 20, 26, 27, 29, 34, 36, 38, 43, 45, 79, 84, 95, 119, 128, 154, 165, 175, 178, 180, 183, 198, 203, 207, 231, 264, 265, 266, 268, 270, 271, 272
Conflict 11, 15, 65, 118, 150, 159, 172, 239, 247
Congar 36
Construction 47, 53, 75, 77, 85, 86, 87, 88, 92, 125, 132, 135
Controversy 142, 150, 172
Costes (André) 190, 191
Creation 156, 159, 178, 186, 191, 193, 195, 197, 198, 200, 205, 210, 213, 222, 223, 224, 226, 230, 257, 258, 259, 264, 265, 266, 269, 270
Crisis 1, 28, 35, 37, 56, 97, 157, 159, 171, 218, 223, 247, 255
Crusade 64, 143, 146, 238

Dalmais (P.) 14, 19, 69, 71, 73, 74, 84, 92, 97, 128, 129, 137, 139, 141, 142, 143, 144, 145, 145, 146, 147, 148, 149, 150, 152, 153, 154, 156, 157, 158, 159, 160, 166, 167, 168, 169, 170, 172, 178, 179, 180, 181, 183, 192
Daniel (Yvan) 35
de Bélinay (F.) 5, 6, 14, 25, 29, 30, 31, 32, 44, 47, 50, 51, 52, 53, 54, 55, 56, 57, 58, 60, 61, 62, 65, 66, 67, 68, 69, 70, 71, 72, 73, 74, 76, 77, 84, 90, 91, 95, 129, 160, 178, 179
de Gaulle 34, 36, 38, 39, 41, 42, 43, 49, 53, 55, 67, 68, 91, 106, 143, 267
de Rosny 1, 2, 3, 4, 5, 11, 14, 20, 200, 220, 223, 250, 257, 258, 259, 260, 261, 263, 264, 265, 266, 267
de Varine (O.) 191, 223
du Bouchet (J.) 14, 36, 57, 58, 60, 61, 73, 74, 75, 76, 77, 78, 79, 80, 81, 82, 84, 85, 86, 90, 91, 92, 95, 98, 112, 132, 152, 179, 182

Eboué (F.) 41, 130
Eboussi Boulaga (F.) 193, 196, 202, 216, 217, 219, 220, 224, 225, 230, 232, 235, 238, 239, 244, 249, 252, 264, 268
Education 6, 45, 47, 48, 49, 53, 64, 83, 89, 95, 96, 98, 99, 101, 103, 104, 105, 106, 107, 110, 111, 112, 113, 114, 115, 116, 117, 119, 120, 121, 122, 124, 125, 126, 127, 128, 129, 130, 131, 132, 133, 135, 137, 138, 139, 140, 184, 185, 217, 231, 234
Elite 8, 26, 32, 33, 37, 39, 48, 49, 56, 63, 64, 65, 71, 75, 84, 95, 96, 98, 99, 103, 104, 105, 106, 112, 113, 115, 121, 125, 128, 129, 138, 142, 143, 146, 147, 160, 172, 175, 178, 208, 209, 216, 228, 230, 235, 255, 257, 259, 261, 267
Empire 42, 43, 44, 45, 56, 60, 67, 71, 99, 105, 106, 108, 118, 120, 121, 127, 148, 168, 255
Evangelism, Evangelisation 7, 8, 11, 12, 15, 25, 27, 28, 29, 30, 31, 32, 40, 41, 44, 49, 50, 51, 55, 56, 57, 62, 65, 68, 77, 85, 86, 87, 88, 89, 95, 96, 98, 99, 100, 103, 104, 112, 121, 122, 123, 125, 132, 133, 135, 137, 138, 140, 154, 156, 163, 164, 172, 175, 176, 183, 186, 227, 235, 236, 242, 243, 245, 255, 256, 269

Evolué 31, 48, 71, 105, 125, 128, 129, 147, 160

France 31, 32, 33, 34, 35, 36, 37, 38, 39, 40, 41, 42, 43, 44, 48, 49, 51, 52, 53, 55, 56, 58, 59, 60, 63, 65, 68, 70, 71, 72, 73, 74, 77, 78, 79, 82, 87, 90, 91, 95, 96, 104, 105, 106, 107, 109, 110, 119, 120, 126, 131, 132, 139, 145, 148, 153, 154, 159, 163, 170, 171, 178, 186, 188, 189, 191, 195, 199, 201, 207, 212, 213, 214, 217, 218, 238, 253, 255, 263, 264, 266
 Wider France 32, 41, 55, 65, 90, 96, 105, 106, 107, 109, 131, 132, 214
French West Africa 5, 7, 8, 10, 20, 32, 33, 38, 42, 45, 259
Frenchification 25, 28, 31, 37, 39, 40, 42, 48, 56, 90, 92, 95, 96, 98, 105, 106, 131, 255

Gallicanism 7, 8, 46, 56, 98, 103, 124
Garteri (M.) 151
Gatu 232, 264
Global 7, 8, 9, 12, 14, 15, 16, 17, 19, 20, 21, 25, 32, 35, 38, 42, 46, 49, 50, 52, 53, 54, 58, 59, 60, 62, 83, 92, 95, 109, 118, 119, 172, 185, 224, 226, 227, 231, 236, 237, 239, 245, 246, 261, 264, 265, 269, 271
Godin 35

Hebga (M. P.) 1, 2, 4, 14, 19, 20, 165, 186, 188, 193, 194, 196, 197, 198, 200, 202, 207, 208, 209, 210, 211, 212, 213, 214, 217, 220, 221, 222, 223, 224, 225, 230, 235, 236, 241, 244, 246, 247, 250, 252, 263, 264, 268
Hierarchy 38, 44, 45, 46, 194, 199, 244, 247

Ideology 26, 33, 35, 41, 43, 46, 47, 54, 56, 59, 60, 68, 70, 71, 74, 79, 95, 98, 104, 105, 119, 122, 128, 132, 146, 156, 167, 186, 190, 224, 240, 250, 255, 271
Ignatius (Loyola) 3, 4, 65, 66, 89, 99, 138, 138, 141, 229, 234, 245, 257, 269

Ilboudo (J.) 80
Inculturation 95, 178, 233, 243, 246, 259
Independence 1, 2, 3, 4, 8, 11, 13, 20, 27, 32, 39, 43, 45, 63, 64, 71, 74, 84, 90, 95, 96, 99, 104, 108, 112, 113, 114, 115, 118, 122, 126, 127, 132, 133, 134, 135, 140, 141, 142, 150, 165, 170, 171, 175, 176, 177, 180, 181, 182, 188, 189, 190, 191, 192, 193, 194, 199, 205, 207, 209, 210, 214, 215, 216, 218, 230, 235, 238, 249, 252, 256, 257, 259, 261, 262, 263, 264, 265, 267
Indigenous, Indigenisation 32, 34, 42, 43, 44, 46, 47, 48, 49, 55, 74, 79, 82, 88, 90, 98, 105, 106, 107, 129, 148, 160, 161, 169, 178, 181, 183, 187, 188, 190, 195, 199, 211, 215, 218, 219, 236, 247, 252, 259, 264
Institute, Institution 11, 12, 14, 15, 16, 17, 20, 66, 74, 86, 87, 188, 190, 192, 194, 195, 201, 203, 207, 208, 220, 235, 236, 246, 247, 266, 268, 269, 270, 271, 272
Islam 8, 20, 25, 27, 28, 31, 32, 36, 37, 38, 40, 47, 50, 51, 52, 53, 54, 55, 56, 57, 64, 83, 84, 99, 107, 111, 113, 114, 115, 116, 117, 118, 119, 120, 121, 126, 128, 146, 147, 149, 161, 162, 171, 181, 255

Janssens (J. B.) 2, 69, 82, 214
Jesuitism 11, 35, 58, 175, 204, 207, 268, 269
Jesuits 1, 2, 3, 4, 5, 6, 7, 8, 9, 10, 11, 12, 13, 14, 17, 18, 19, 20, 21, 25, 29, 30, 32, 36, 37, 44, 46, 47, 50, 55, 56, 58, 59, 60, 62, 65, 66, 69, 71, 72, 73, 79, 80, 81, 82, 83, 84, 86, 87, 88, 89, 90, 91, 92, 95, 96, 98, 99, 100, 101, 104, 105, 107, 109, 110, 112, 114, 115, 116, 117, 120, 121,124, 125, 128, 130, 131, 132, 133, 135, 137, 138, 139, 140, 141, 142, 143, 144, 147, 150, 151, 152, 153, 160, 164, 175, 176, 178, 183, 184, 185, 188, 190, 192, 195, 198, 199, 200, 202, 203, 204, 209, 212, 213, 214, 216, 219, 220, 222, 225, 226, 227, 230, 231, 236, 237, 239,

241, 242, 245, 249, 251, 255, 256, 257, 258, 259, 263, 264, 265, 266, 268, 269, 271, 272

Leadership   7, 8, 10, 11, 16, 17, 20, 26, 30, 32, 36, 39, 40, 44, 45, 50, 56, 76, 77, 84, 88, 91, 92, 95, 96, 97, 135, 138, 142, 146, 157, 168, 176, 178, 179, 180, 182, 183, 192, 195, 196, 200, 207, 210, 212, 213, 215, 216, 218, 219, 223, 248, 257, 259, 262, 264, 265, 266, 267, 271
Leclerc (P.)   36, 41, 47, 67, 75, 267
Ledechowski (V.)   85, 110
Lefèbvre (M.)   11, 34, 35, 36, 56, 57, 59, 67, 72, 77, 81, 91, 136, 145, 246, 251
Lesage (J.)   194, 196, 197, 200, 201, 207, 208, 209, 211, 212, 213, 223, 224, 239
Libermann   194, 195, 197, 201, 202, 207, 208, 209, 213, 214, 215, 217, 257, 258, 262

Martyr   66, 70, 73, 87, 154, 158, 184, 185, 239, 242
Mertens (V.)   192, 201, 209, 221
Military   3, 27, 32, 32, 37, 40, 43, 47, 51, 52, 60, 65, 67, 69, 74, 75, 76, 121, 158, 170, 177, 186, 214
Mission
  civilisatrice   32, 37, 41, 45, 56, 78, 90, 91, 96, 103, 105, 139, 253
  terminée   1, 4, 20, 258, 261
Missionary Christianity   175, 177, 178, 180, 182, 197, 226, 230, 236, 238, 248, 264, 268
Muslim(s)   7, 15, 25, 27, 30, 38, 40, 48, 51, 52, 53, 54, 62, 64, 71, 72, 86, 95, 98, 99, 104, 107, 109, 110, 111, 112, 113, 114, 115, 117, 118, 119, 120, 121, 122, 125, 126, 127, 128, 137, 153, 154, 157, 167, 171, 181
Mveng (E.)   4, 14, 19, 20, 111, 198, 200, 202, 205, 214, 216, 217, 220, 221, 222, 223, 227, 230, 232, 233, 234, 235, 239, 244, 246, 248, 249, 252, 253, 257, 260, 261, 262, 263, 264, 265, 268

Nationalism   3, 26, 32, 34, 38, 42, 43, 46, 47, 56, 63, 64, 70, 71, 75, 96, 99, 103, 104, 113, 114, 119, 121, 122, 129, 138, 156, 160, 168, 170, 177, 182, 205, 210, 214, 215, 260, 261, 263, 264, 265, 267
Neocolonialism   8, 10, 20, 142, 154, 162, 165, 178, 217, 230, 232, 239, 248, 265, 266, 268
Ngaïbi (F.)   3, 178, 181
Nzagpé (F.)   178, 180, 202, 216, 217

Ossama (N.)   187, 198, 200, 201, 202, 204, 217, 220, 226, 230, 238, 244, 247, 252, 268
Otélé   195, 210, 213, 218, 220

Pasu Pasu (Daniel)   241
Persecution   142, 143, 153, 154, 159, 163, 164, 165, 166, 168, 172, 242
Pétain   26, 33, 34, 42
Pope   3, 4, 7, 9, 40, 44, 45, 64, 66, 83, 111, 146, 168, 169, 175, 185, 229
Populace   1, 15, 35, 38, 47, 56, 64, 67, 79, 89, 99, 117, 118, 122, 130, 138, 150, 151, 268
Postcolonialism   8, 11, 13, 19, 99, 104, 170, 173, 177, 190, 195, 199, 239, 248, 261, 264, 265, 266, 271, 272
Protestant   7, 8, 26, 36, 37, 38, 44, 50, 54, 55, 62, 63, 64, 72, 84, 96, 97, 101, 104, 108, 109, 112, 125, 126, 127, 128, 132, 139, 142, 147, 148, 150, 153, 156, 157, 158, 160, 161, 162, 163, 164, 165, 166, 174, 175, 183, 232, 238, 256

Revolution   14, 15, 20, 33, 59, 68, 70, 95, 96, 103, 123, 129, 132, 134, 141, 142, 147, 150, 152, 153, 154, 155, 157, 158, 159, 161, 162, 164, 165, 167, 170, 171, 172, 256
Rite   9, 46, 123, 134, 142, 150, 158, 169, 172, 259

Sacredness   26, 46, 63, 72, 87, 120, 156, 218, 234

Secularism   25, 32, 35, 37, 38, 49, 56, 99, 110, 129, 140, 181, 235, 256, 106, 115, 118, 140, 246
Senegal   38, 39, 40, 117, 142, 224, 251, 266
Society of Jesus   3, 4, 36, 58, 59, 64, 66, 79, 80, 88, 110, 115, 137, 169, 176, 195, 196, 200, 203, 205, 207, 210, 211, 216, 224, 227, 229, 230, 231, 239, 242, 243, 245, 257, 259, 263, 268, 271, 272
Sudan   15, 26, 27, 40, 49, 50, 54, 63, 109, 110, 114, 153, 154, 164, 183
Survival   8, 29, 32, 38, 40, 44, 58, 100, 101, 122, 142, 190, 202, 243, 264, 265, 268

Teguem (E.)   4, 14, 226, 227, 228, 229, 230, 231, 232, 234, 235, 236, 238, 239, 245, 252, 268
Tombalbaye (F.)   14, 63, 96, 125, 127, 128, 129, 134, 142, 143, 152, 153, 154, 155, 156, 157, 159, 160, 161, 162, 163, 165, 166, 167, 170, 171, 178, 195, 256
Transition from missionary to African Christianity   1, 9, 19, 32, 38, 39, 56, 59, 104, 195
Translation(s)   35, 74, 77, 78, 82, 89, 96, 100, 121, 134, 183, 256

Ubangi   26, 40, 62, 95
Universality   13, 19, 46, 64, 109, 176, 179, 203, 204, 207, 221, 224, 238, 239, 246, 249, 252, 264, 267, 271

Vala (A.)   86, 185

Vandame (C.)   69, 69, 115, 130, 141, 144, 152, 153, 158, 165, 177, 182, 187, 188, 189, 190, 191, 192, 193, 198, 224, 240, 256
Vatican   13, 20, 28, 32, 34, 35, 36, 38, 39, 40, 4447, 55, 56, 58, 64, 70, 71, 72, 73, 76, 77, 79, 81, 82, 83, 84, 85, 86, 88, 91, 110, 111, 114, 115, 118, 123, 124, 136, 140, 145, 146, 151, 166, 168, 169, 170, 175, 176, 177, 180, 182, 185, 195, 199, 200, 203, 208, 218, 225, 230, 231, 232, 235, 240, 243, 245, 246, 250, 251, 252, 256, 259, 266, 267, 271, 272
Véniat (H.)   14, 20, 86, 135, 169, 175, 177, 178, 179, 180, 181, 182, 183, 187, 192, 193
Vernacularisation   77, 85, 88, 124, 151, 183, 185, 186, 264, 265
VPAO   3, 5, 11, 12, 13, 17, 18, 21, 120, 121, 178, 191, 192, 198, 210, 222, 224, 226, 257, 258, 264, 265, 266, 270

War   3, 8, 9, 25, 26, 28, 31, 32, 34, 35, 36, 38, 39, 40, 41, 42, 43, 44, 46, 47, 48, 49, 50, 51, 52, 54, 58, 59, 60, 65, 67, 70, 71, 75, 78, 90, 105, 108, 116, 118, 121, 122, 125, 126, 133, 135, 146, 148, 150, 153, 154, 157, 167, 170, 178, 198, 199, 209, 214, 236, 255, 256, 263, 267

Yondo   97, 123, 129, 134, 135, 150, 151, 152, 153, 155, 156, 157, 159, 161, 162, 163, 165, 172

Zoa (J.)   14, 45, 111, 175, 179, 180, 193, 197, 218, 221, 222

Previously published titles in the series

Violent Conversion: Brazilian Pentecostalism and Urban Women in Mozambique, Linda Van de Kamp (2016)

Beyond Religious Tolerance: Muslim, Christian & Traditionalist Encounters in an African Town, edited by Insa Nolte, Olukoya Ogen and Rebecca Jones (2017)

Faith, Power and Family: Christianity and Social Change in French Cameroon, Charlotte Walker-Said (2018)

Contesting Catholics: Benedicto Kiwanuka and the Birth of Postcolonial Uganda, Jonathon L. Earle and J. J. Carney (2021)

Islamic Scholarship in Africa: New Directions and Global Contexts, edited by Ousmane Oumar Kane (2021)

From Rebels to Rulers: Writing Legitimacy in the Early Sokoto State, Paul Naylor (2021)

Sacred Queer Stories: Ugandan LGBTQ+ Refugee Lives and the Bible, Adriaan Van Klinken and Johanna Stiebert, with Sebyala Brian and Fredrick Hudson (2021)

Labour & Christianity in the Mission: African Workers in Tanganyika and Zanzibar, 1864–1926, Michelle Liebst (2021)

The Genocide against the Tutsi, and the Rwandan Churches: Between Grief and Denial, Philippe Denis (2022)

Competing Catholicisms: The Jesuits, the Vatican & the Making of Postcolonial French Africa, Jean Luc Enyegue, SJ (2022)

Islam in Uganda: The Muslim Minority, Nationalism & Political Power, Joseph Kasule (2022)

Spiritual Contestations: The Violence of Peace in South Sudan, Naomi Ruth Pendle (2023)

Mystical Power and Politics on the Swahili Coast, Nathalie Arnold Koenings (2024)

Religious Plurality in Africa: Coexistence, Conviviality, Conflict, edited by Marloes Janson, Kai Kresse, Benedikt Pontzen, and Hassan Mwakimako (2024)

www.ingramcontent.com/pod-product-compliance
Lightning Source LLC
Chambersburg PA
CBHW051600230426
43668CB00013B/1923